REFRAMING QUALITATIVE RESEARCH ETHICS

ADVANCES IN RESEARCH ETHICS AND INTEGRITY

Series Editor: Dr Ron Iphofen, *FAcSS, Independent Consultant, UK*

Recent volumes:

Volume 1: Finding Common Ground: Consensus in Research Ethics Across the Social Sciences, Edited by *Ron Iphofen*

Volume 2: The Ethics of Online Research, Edited by *Kandy Woodfield*

Volume 3: Virtue Ethics in the Conduct and Governance of Social Science Research, Edited by *Nathan Emmerich*

Volume 4: Ethics and Integrity in Health and Life Sciences Research, Edited by *Zvonimir Koporc*

Volume 5: Ethics and Integrity in Visual Research Methods, Edited by *Savannah Dodd*

Volume 6: Indigenous Research Ethics: Claiming Research Sovereignty Beyond Deficit and the Colonial Legacy, Edited by *Lily George, Juan Tauri and Lindsey Te Ata o Tu MacDonald*

Volume 7: Ethics and Integrity in Research with Children and Young People, Edited by *Grace Spencer*

Volume 8: Ethical Issues in Covert, Security and Surveillance Research, Edited by *Ron Iphofen and Dónal O'Mathúna*

Volume 9: Ethics and Integrity in Research with Older People and Service Users: Moving Beyond the Rhetoric, Edited by *Roger O'Sullivan*

Volume 10: Ethical AI Surveillance in the Workplace, By *Mihalis Kritikos* and Edited by *Ron Iphofen*

Volume 11: Advances in Disability Research Ethics, Edited by *Anne Good, Iris Elliott and Sharon Mallon*

EDITORIAL ADVISORY GROUP

ADVANCES IN RESEARCH ETHICS AND INTEGRITY VOLUME 12

REFRAMING QUALITATIVE RESEARCH ETHICS

EDITED BY

HELEN BUSBY

Independent Research Ethics Consultant, UK

emerald PUBLISHING

United Kingdom – North America – Japan
India – Malaysia – China

Emerald Publishing Limited
Emerald Publishing, Floor 5, Northspring, 21-23 Wellington Street, Leeds LS1 4DL.

First edition 2025

British Library Cataloguing in Publication Data
A catalogue record for this book is available from the British Library

ISBN: 978-1-83608-313-9 (Print)
ISBN: 978-1-83608-312-2 (Online)
ISBN: 978-1-83608-314-6 (Epub)

ISSN: 2398-6018 (Series)

Printed and bound by CPI Group (UK) Ltd, Croydon, CR0 4YY

INVESTOR IN PEOPLE

CONTENTS

ABOUT THE EDITOR

Helen Busby is an independent research ethics consultant, advising on the management of complex ethical issues in research involving fieldwork in multiple countries.

After studying Medical Anthropology and Sociology at the Universities of Brunel and Nottingham (UK) and holding Postdoc Fellowships at the latter, she led multidisciplinary research at the Universities of Nottingham and Leicester. Having particular interests in qualitative approaches, and building on her earlier involvement in research on public health and primary care, she was a Principal Investigator for research projects about blood donation, stem cell banking, and social frameworks of altruism. She was a member of two local National Health Service research ethics committees during this time.

These interests led to an involvement in research ethics at an international level: since 2010, she has acted as an ethics reviewer for European Union research agencies and as an ethics advisor for several research consortia. Between 2017 and 2023, she was a Consultant to the global health ethics unit of the World Health Organization (WHO), working with the Secretariat to the Research Ethics Review Committee at WHO headquarters in Geneva.

Her research is published in *Sociology of Health and Illness*, *Clinical Ethics*, *Health: An Interdisciplinary Journal for the Social Study of Health Illness and Medicine*, *European Law Review*, and other journals in these fields. She has also contributed chapters to edited books – engaging with fellow researchers, writers, and practitioners along the way. Her most recent book chapter is: 'Modes of Influence: What Can We Learn from International Codes of Ethics for Health-Related Research?' In R. Iphofen and D. O'Mathúna (Eds.), 2022, *Ethical Evidence and Policymaking: Interdisciplinary and International Research* (Policy Press).

ABOUT THE CONTRIBUTORS

Bree Akesson is the Canada Research Chair (Tier II) in Global Adversity and Wellbeing, Associate Director of the Centre for Research on Security Practices, and Associate Professor of Social Work at Wilfrid Laurier University in Canada. She has worked for nearly 25 years with children and families impacted by war and displacement in settings such as Chechnya, Northern Uganda, Palestine, Lebanon, Afghanistan, and Bangladesh. Her programme of research ranges from micro-level understandings of the experiences of war-affected populations to macro-level initiatives to strengthen global social support systems. Her ongoing research projects include the perinatal experiences of Rohingya refugee families in Bangladesh, the impact of climate change on refugee families displaced by war, and integrated service access for temporary and precarious status migrants in Canada.

Nienke Boesveldt is a principal researcher of (partly peer-led) longitudinal research on homelessness and mental health from both service user and professional perspective at the Sociology Department of the University of Amsterdam, the Netherlands. She has published numerous academic reports and receives broad recognition for organising regularly, and for different target groups, workshops, lectures, and seminars, and for building a bridge between scientific knowledge and policy practice. With the partly peer-led data, she has published articles, including 'Mixed Methods on Adverse Childhood Experiences predicting Transitional and Recurrent Homelessness' (*Journal of Community Psychology*, 2024) with Willemijn van Dungen and Bram Orobio de Castro, 'Governing the Homeless in the Netherlands: Incremental Change Towards Providing Housing First' (*The Routledge Handbook of Global Perspectives on Homelessness, Law & Policy*, Bevan, C. (Ed.), 2023), and 'Housing the Homeless: Shifting Sites of Managing the Poor in the Netherlands' (*Urban Studies*, 2023) with Dolly Loomans.

Nicole Brown is a social researcher and author, whose expertise lies with social research practice. She works at University College London and Social Research & Practice and Education Ltd. She conceptualises her work as sitting on the cusp of practice/teaching/research, thereby emphasising that through thinking-doing-being each area of expertise intersects with and impacts on another. In that sense, her practices as a fiction writer, poet, and educator as well as her activist work in response to, on the back of and as research, represent an extension of her conceptualisation of research practice. Her publications include *Making the Most of Your Research Journal*, *Embodied Inquiry: Research Methods*, *Photovoice Reimagined*, and *Creativity in Education: International Perspectives*. She shares her work at https://www.nicole-brown.co.uk, and her social media handles are @ncjbrown and @AbleismAcademia.

Neda Deneva (SYNYO) holds a PhD in Sociology and Social Anthropology from the Central European University. She has worked on the topic of transnational migration to and from Bulgaria and Romania with a focus on labour and citizenship regimes within the European Union, care work, and processes of the transnationalisation of the family. During her postdoctoral work, she has explored the mutually dependent modalities of labour and citizenship and the way they transform and are simultaneously conditioned by care and social reproduction, especially in the context of recent post-socialist reindustrialisation and migration.

Anke Erdmann is professor for Chronic Illness and Long-Term Care at Kiel University of Applied Sciences. She is also affiliated to the Medical Ethics Working Group, Kiel University, Germany. She studied sociology, philosophy, nursing science, and social work and received her doctorate in 2015 with a qualitative evaluation study on integrative validation therapy, a particularly appreciative form of communication and care for people with dementia. During her postdoc, she focussed on ethical issues related to chronic illness: end-of-life-decision-making in amyotrophic lateral sclerosis (ALS), collecting lifestyle data with mobile health technologies from people with inflammatory bowel diseases (IBD), body image, disclosure of illness, stigma and self-perception in chronic inflammatory diseases, and deception in dementia care. She works predominantly with qualitative methods, and research ethics issues are a further focus of her work.

Karen Frensch has worked in research project management for over 20 years as the Project manager for the Partnerships for Children and Families Project and the Global Adversity and Wellbeing Research Group in the Faculty of Social Work at Wilfrid Laurier University in Canada. Specialising in qualitative research methods, her collaborations with scholars and professionals in children's mental health, child welfare, and family studies have focussed on social service system improvements to better meet the needs of children and families. She has co-authored two books *Creating Positive Systems of Child and Family Welfare: Congruence With the Everyday Lives of Children and Parents* by Cameron, Fine, Maiter, Frensch, and Freymond (University of Toronto Press) and *Necessary But Not Sufficient: Improving Community Living for Youth After Residential Mental Health Programs* by Cameron, Frensch, Smit-Quosai, Pancer, and Preyde (University of Toronto Press).

Joyla Furlano (PhD) is a Postdoctoral Fellow in the Department of Family Medicine at Queen's University (Canada), as well as an instructor in the School of Nursing and a Research Associate in the Department of Pathology and Laboratory Medicine at Western University. Her research is rooted in community-based approaches – promoting health equity in hospital settings and developing culturally relevant health resources for Indigenous communities in Canada. With a strong passion for brain health, she is an active member of the Canadian Consortium on Neurodegeneration in Aging, where she collaborates with researchers nationwide to address dementia care challenges faced by Indigenous peoples. In 2023, she completed a postgraduate certificate in Equity in Brain Health at the Global Brain Health Institute (Trinity College, Dublin), where she worked with a global team of researchers, healthcare professionals, and artists to address brain health inequities worldwide.

Michael Herzfeld is Ernest E. Monrad Professor of the Social Sciences Emeritus in the Department of Anthropology at Harvard University, where he taught from 1991 through the end of 2018. He is also IIAS Professor of Critical Heritage Studies Emeritus, Leiden University; a member of the Collegio del Dottorato di Ricerca in Beni Culturali, Formazione e Territorio, Università di Roma 'Tor Vergata'; and Senior Advisor, Critical Heritage Studies Initiative, International Institute of Asian Studies, Leiden. He is the author of 13 books, 2 films, and numerous articles and reviews. His research has included extensive ethnographic fieldwork in Greece, Italy, and Thailand. In addition to a DPhil from Oxford University (1976) and a DLitt from the University of Birmingham (1989), he holds honorary doctorates from the Université Libre de Bruxelles (2005), the University of Macedonia, Thessaloniki (2011), the University of Crete (2013), and the University of St Andrews (2023). In 2021, he was made an honorary citizen of Greece.

Mark Israel is a Director of Australasian Human Research Ethics Consultancy Services (AHRECS) and Adjunct Professor at Curtin University and University of Western Australia. He provides advice on research ethics and integrity to higher education institutions, research agencies, and government and non-government organisations in Australia as well as in various parts of Asia and Europe. He has a degree in law and postgraduate qualifications in sociology, criminology, and education from Oxford, Cambridge, and Flinders Universities and over 100 publications in the areas of higher education policy and practice, research ethics and integrity, and criminology and socio-legal studies. He is a Principal Fellow of the Higher Education Academy and Fellow of the Academy of Social Sciences. He has received the Prime Minister's Award for Australian University Teacher of the Year and grants and consultancies from the European Commission, the Australian Research Council, the Criminology Research Council, and the Australian Government Office for Learning and Teaching.

Alana Kehoe (MA) is a dedicated professional in emergency preparedness and disaster management with a strong focus on working with Indigenous communities. Holding a Master's degree in Anthropology from the University of Western Ontario, she has conducted significant research on the impact of colonialism on Indigenous peoples' experiences with wildfire. Her expertise extends to developing tailored emergency preparedness programmes and delivering training that addresses the unique needs of Indigenous audiences. Her previous research role on Dr Lloy Wylie's Health Equity Action Research team involved researching health equity for Indigenous populations in Canada. Her work is characterised by her commitment to enhancing community resilience and advancing cultural safety in emergency response.

Kaya Klaver (MA Social Work, University of Antwerp) is a social worker and researcher at the University of Antwerp. As a youth worker, she has experience in youth care. In a previous project funded by the Flemish government, she conducted in-depth interviews with people on religious (de)conversion in the Flemish context. Currently, she is working as a Junior Researcher on the European-funded project ReIncluGen. During this project, she did extensive ethnographic fieldwork, conducted photo-eliciting interviews with migrantised women and staff members of civil society organisations. Her research interests include topics such as migration, religion and gender, as well as their intersections.

Fride Haram Klykken is a Postdoctoral Research Fellow at Center for the Science of Learning and Technology (SLATE), University of Bergen, Norway, where she currently works with digital inclusion and critical data literacy on the EduTrust AI project. Her research interests include the practices of teaching and learning, education and technology, ethics and trust, and research ethics. She has a PhD in Education, and her doctoral research engaged video-ethnography to investigate the material relationality of everyday classroom practice.

Amal Miri (University of Antwerp, Belgium) holds a PhD in Gender and Diversity from Ghent University. In her ethnographic doctoral research at the intersection of marriage migration, motherhood, and integration, she conducted participatory research with Moroccan women in Flanders. In the past, she worked as a project researcher at ELLA, a non-profit organisation promoting the empowerment of minoritised women in Brussels and Flanders. Starting from 2023, she co-supervised and coordinated the Horizon Europe ReIncluGen project on gender empowerment and inclusion at the University of Antwerp. Additionally, she is chair of EMPACT, a Flemish socio-cultural umbrella organisation supporting and strengthening minoritised civil society organisations.

Hildah L. Mokgolodi (PhD), Department of Educational Foundation, Faculty of Education, University of Botswana. She is a Professional Counsellor and Counsellor Educator for graduate and undergraduate levels at the University of Botswana. Other than several additional counselling courses, she offers a course in Ethics and Legal Issues in Counselling and Research Projects in Counselling. Additionally, she offers both clinical and research supervision to students during their practicums and internships. Participating as a member of the institutional ethics review board enhanced her experience in ethical qualitative research. She has conducted qualitative research studies in counselling with interest in retired professionals, Indigenous issues, evaluation, and career development as her research interests.

Nina Peršak is Scientific Director and Senior Research Fellow of the Institute for Criminal-Law Ethics and Criminology in Ljubljana and Full Professor of Law (habilitation) of the University of Maribor, Slovenia. She holds a PhD in Law from University of Ljubljana, and a Master's in Law (LLM) and a Master's in Social and Developmental Psychology (MPhil), both, from the University of Cambridge. She is also Academic Consultant of Ghent University, Belgium, Co-Director of the Working Group 'Equity and Criminal Justice' of the Berkeley Center on Comparative Equality and Anti-Discrimination Law, UC Berkeley, and an Independent Ethics Expert, providing ethics advice, opinion, and trainings on research ethics to various bodies.

Sarah Potthoff is a Postdoctoral Researcher at the Institute for Medical Ethics, History, and Theories of Medicine, University of Münster, Germany. She studied sociology and literature at Bielefeld University and completed her PhD in sociology in 2016 with an ethnographic study on negotiation processes of gender justice and diversity before women's courts (Nari Adalats) in South India. During her postdoc, she worked as a Lecturer in Qualitative Methods and as a Research Assistant at the Ruhr University Bochum and at Kiel University. She coordinated and led several qualitative empirical research projects focussing on advanced psychiatric directives, psychological pressure and coercion in psychiatry, research ethics, and ethical review practices in qualitative health research. Methodologically, she specialises in grounded theory methodology, ethnography, and qualitative content analysis. Since September 2024, she has been working at the University of Münster conducting qualitative research on social dimensions of chronic pain.

Rhonda M. Shaw is an Associate Professor of Sociology at Te Herenga Waka—Victoria University of Wellington, Aotearoa New Zealand. Since 2002, Rhonda's research has involved empirical study on donating and receiving human biological materials and services, with specific reference to organ donation and transplantation, assisted human reproduction and family building, and human milk sharing. Rhonda's teaching expertise includes gender and sexuality studies and social science research ethics. Her research has been published in journals including *Sociology of Health & Illness*, *Body & Society*, *Medical Humanities*, *Health: An Interdisciplinary Journal for the Social Study of Health Illness and Medicine*, *Culture, Health & Sexuality*, *Social Science & Medicine*, *Qualitative Health Research*, *Journal of Gender Studies*, *Sociological Research Online* and *Sociology*. Rhonda is editor of *Bioethics Beyond Altruism: Donating and Transforming Human Biological Materials* (Palgrave Macmillan, 2017) and *Reproductive Citizenship: Technologies, Rights and Relationships* (Palgrave Macmillan, 2022).

Margaret Sleeboom-Faulkner is Professor of Social and Medical Anthropology at the University of Sussex, UK, with a regional focus of China and Japan. For nearly two decades, her research has engaged with developments in the life sciences and biotechnologies in Asian societies, as well as their role in the global dynamics of research collaborations and regulation. The concerns discussed in her chapter – clashes of formalised research ethics and with ethics as experience in daily lives – emerged in her long-term field research, some of which is published in *Global Morality and Life Science Practices in Asia: Assemblages of Life* (Palgrave MacMillan, 2014) and *Regulatory Violence: The Global Dynamics of Regulatory Experimentation in Biomedicine and Health* (CUP, 2025). The formative impact of formalised ethics on communication and conversations in field research has been a main theme in her engagement with ethics review in anthropology. An example of this is the EthNav.

Lore van Praag (Master, PhD Ghent University) is Assistant Professor at the Erasmus University of Rotterdam, where she works on climate change, gender, social inequalities, and diversity. Over the years, she has gained a lot of research expertise in participating in interdisciplinary research projects (Belspo Migradapt, H2020 MICADO, H2020 PERCEPTIONS, H2020 COVINFORM, Erasmus+ ACCORD) and coordinating research projects, such as the Validiv project on multilingualism in primary schools in Flanders (SBO project), the RESL.Eu on Early School Leavers in Europe (FP7), the ReIncluGen project (Horizon Europe), and ROCLIMI (Resilient Delta Initiative). Currently, her research interests are mainly focussed on environmental migration, migrant perspectives on climate adaptation, education, gender empowerment, and diversity. She has published international and national articles in peer-reviewed journals and books (https://orcid.org/0000-0003-2861-7523).

Helena Webb is an Assistant Professor in the School of Computer Science at the University of Nottingham. She is an experienced socio-technical researcher, working on projects that explore the connections between computing and society. She specialises in the use of qualitative methods and has a particular interest in understanding how people interact with and through technology, as well as in research to foster innovation for social good. She publishes her work in social science, computer science, and interdisciplinary venues and has written several articles on ethics and good practice in research on the Internet and social media.

Lloy Wylie (PhD) is an interdisciplinary specialist in implementing equity, diversity, and inclusion in health professional education, policy, and practice. She is an advisor on accreditation standards in medical education for Indigenous health in Canada and internationally. She provides expert advice on ethics for health and medical research with underserved populations. Her main areas of research are in health systems and health services, with a focus on equity and improvement of health services and access through community-based participatory research. As the lead of the Health Equity Action Research Team, her research focusses on Indigenous, immigrant, and refugee health, drawing on cultural safety as a framework for health system improvements to advance equity in health care. She is an Associate Professor in the Schulich Interfaculty Programme in Public Health at Western University in Canada. As an award-winning educator, she develops innovative programmes in community-engaged learning in public health.

ABOUT THE SERIES EDITOR

Ron Iphofen, FAcSS, is Executive Editor of the Emerald book series *Advances in Research Ethics and Integrity* and edited Volume 1 in the series, *Finding Common Ground: Consensus in Research Ethics Across the Social Sciences* (2017). He is an Independent Research Consultant, a Fellow of the UK Academy of Social Sciences, the Higher Education Academy, and the Royal Society of Medicine. Since retiring as Director of Postgraduate Studies in the School of Healthcare Sciences, Bangor University, his major activity has been as an Adviser to the European Commission (EC) and its agencies, the European Research Council (ERC), and the Research Executive Agency (REA) from the Seventh Framework Programme (FP7) to the current Horizon Europe. His consultancy work has covered a range of research agencies (in government and independent) globally. He was Vice Chair of the UK Social Research Association, updated their Ethics Guidelines and now convenes the SRA's Research Ethics Forum. He was scientific consultant on the EC RESPECT project – establishing pan-European standards in the social sciences and chaired the Ethics and Societal Impact Advisory Group for another EC-funded European Demonstration Project on mass transit security (SECUR-ED). He has advised the UK Research Integrity Office; the National Disability Authority (NDA) of the Irish Ministry of Justice; the UK Parliamentary Office of Science and Technology; the Scottish Executive; UK Government Social Research; National Centre for Social Research; the Audit Commission; the Food Standards Agency; the Ministry of Justice; the BIG Lottery; a UK Local Authorities' Consortium; Skills Development Scotland; Agence Nationale de la Recherche (ANR the French Research Funding agency); the Social Sciences and Humanities Research Council (SSHRC) in Canada; and in Ireland the National Disability Authority (NDA) of the Ministry of Justice and the Institute of Public Health, among many others. He was Founding Executive Editor of the Emerald gerontology journal *Quality in Ageing and Older Adults*. He published *Ethical Decision Making in Social Research: A Practical Guide* (Palgrave Macmillan, 2009 and 2011), coedited with Martin Tolich *The SAGE Handbook of Qualitative Research Ethics* (Sage, 2018) and edited the SPRINGER Nature *Handbook of Scientific Research and Integrity* (2020). Between 2018 and 2021, he was Principal Investigator (PI) on a €2.8M European Commission-funded project (PRO-RES) aimed at promoting ethics and integrity in all non-medical research. He co-edited three open access publications for the PRO-RES Project: *Ethical Issues in Covert, Security and Surveillance Research*, Emerald Publishing (2022); *Ethical Evidence and Policymaking: Interdisciplinary and International Research*, Bristol University Press (2022); and *Ethics, Integrity and Policymaking: The Value of the Case Study*, Springer (2022) (https://roniphofen.com/).

SERIES PREFACE

Advances in Research Ethics and Integrity grew out of the foundational work of a group of Fellows of the UK Academy of Social Sciences (AcSS) who were all concerned to ensure that lessons learned from previous work in the research ethics field were built upon and improved. Unnecessary duplications of or ignorance of earlier work were seen as hindrances to progress. Individual researchers, research professions and society all suffer in having to pay the costs in time, energy and money of delayed progress and superfluous repetitions. There is little excuse for failure to build on existing knowledge and practice given modern search technologies. Our concern was to aid well-motivated researchers to quickly discover existing progress made in ethical research in terms of topic, method and/or discipline and to move on with their own work more productively.

Given the plethora of ethics codes and guidelines, it can be difficult for researchers to judge those most relevant to their proposed activity. Long-standing issues in the field are confronted afresh by novice researchers so that it is no wonder they can despair in their search for guidance. Even experienced researchers may be tempted by the 'checklist mentality' that can characterise the meeting of formalised ethics review requirements.

If risks of harm to the public and to researchers are to be kept to a minimum and if professional standards in the conduct of scientific research are to be maintained, the more that fundamental understandings of ethical behaviour in research are shared the better. If progress is made in one sphere, everyone gains from it being generally acknowledged and understood. If foundational work is conducted, everyone gains from being able to build on and develop further that work.

It should not be assumed that formal ethics review committees are able to resolve the dilemmas or meet the challenges involved. Enough has been written about such review bodies to make their limitations clear. They cannot follow researchers into the field to monitor what goes on, nor can they anticipate all emergent ethical dilemmas or dissemination risks. There is no adequate penalty for neglect through incompetence, or worse, for conscious omissions of evidence. We have to rely upon the virtues of the individual researcher alongside the skills of journal reviewers and funding agency evaluators. Scientific integrity must be constantly monitored at the corporate and at the individual levels.

New problems, issues and concerns and new ways of collecting data continue to emerge regularly. This should not be surprising as social, economic and technological change necessitate constant re-evaluation of research conduct. Standard approaches to research ethics such as valid informed consent, inclusion/exclusion criteria, vulnerable subjects and covert studies need to be reconsidered as developing social contexts and methodological innovation, interdisciplinary research and economic pressures pose new challenges to convention. Developments in social media blur the distinction between 'the public' and the 'private'.

This series proposed to address such new and continuing challenges for funders, research managers, research ethics committees and researchers in the field. The concerns and interests are well recognised globally but with varying commitments at both the procedural and the practical levels. This series is designed to suggest realistic solutions to these challenges, and this practical angle is the unique selling proposition for the series. Each volume will raise and address the key issues in the debates but also strive to suggest ways forward that maintain the key ethical concerns of respect for human rights and dignity, while sustaining pragmatic guidance for future research developments.

We seek to help researchers think through the potential harms and benefits of their work in the proposal stage and assist their reflection of the big ethical moments that they face in the field often when there may be no one to advise them in terms of their societal impact and acceptance. The series aims to adopt an approach that promotes good practice and sets principles, values and standards that serve as models to aid successful research outcomes. There is clear international appeal as commissioners and researchers alike share a vested interest in the global promotion of professional virtues that lead to the public acceptability of good research. In an increasingly global research world, there is little point in applying too localised a morality, nor one that implies a solely Western hegemony of values. If standards 'matter', it seems evident that they should 'matter' to and for all. Only then can the growth of interdisciplinary and multinational projects be accomplished effectively and with a shared concern for potential harms and benefits.

While the diversity of experience and unique local interests is acknowledged, there are existing, proven models of good practice which can help research practitioners in emergent nations build their policies and processes to suit their own circumstances. We need to see that consensus positions effectively guide the work of scientists across the globe and secure minimal participant harm and maximum societal benefit – and, additionally, that instances of fraudulence, corruption and dishonesty in science decrease as a consequence.

Truly independent formal ethics scrutiny can help maintain the integrity of research professions in an era of enhanced concerns over data security, privacy and human rights legislation. But it is essential to guard against rigid conformity to what can become administrative procedures and corporate protectionism. Consistency in 'proper behaviour' does not imply uniformity. Having principles does not lead inexorably to an adherence to principlism. Sincerely held principles can be in conflict in differing contexts. No one practice is necessarily the best approach in all circumstances. But if researchers are aware of the range of possible ways in which their work can be accomplished ethically and with integrity, they can be free to apply the approach that works or is necessary in their setting. Guides to 'good' ways of doing things should not be taken as the 'only' way of proceeding. A rigidity in outlook does no favours to methodological innovation, nor to the research subjects or participants that they are supposed to protect. If there were to be any principles that should be rigidly adhered to they should include flexibility, open-mindedness, the recognition of the range of challenging situations to be met in the field – principles that in essence amount to a sense of proportionality.

Such principles should apply equally to researchers and ethics reviewers alike. Reviewers need to think afresh about each new research proposal, to detach from pre-formed opinions and prejudices, while still learning from and applying the lessons of the past. Principles such as these must also apply to funding and commissioning agencies, to research institutions and to professional associations and their learned societies. Our integrity as researchers demands that we recognise that the rights of our funders and research participants and/or subjects are to be valued alongside our cherished research goals and seek to embody such principles in the research process from the outset. This series strives to seek just how that might be accomplished in the best interests of all.

Ron Iphofen, Series Editor

ACKNOWLEDGEMENTS

I would like to thank the AREI editorial advisory board for sharing their expertise with me. Particular mention must be made of Ron Iphofen, Series Editor, and Robert Dingwall, who offered important intellectual input and leads and helped in other important ways. I am grateful to all the peer reviewers who gave us their thoughts on the first drafts of the chapters. Mike Sandys was an enthusiastic supporter of this project. Finally, I was fortunate to have enthusiastic and timely support from the team at Emerald Publishing, including from Senior Commissioning Editor Katy Mathers, Lydia Cutmore (Content Development Editor) and Abinaya Chinnasamy (Book Project Editor).

Helen Busby, Editor

INTRODUCTION

CHAPTER 1

QUALITATIVE RESEARCH ETHICS: CHANGING CONTEXTS AND NEW METHODOLOGIES

Helen Busby

Independent Research Ethics Consultant, UK

ABSTRACT

Practitioners of social science research have long reflected on ethical and moral aspects of conducting research in this field, and mandatory research ethics review was introduced for social science research in some countries from the 1990s. Moving to qualitative research, recent years have seen the emergence of a range of innovative methodologies and approaches – including visual methods, novel technologies, autoethnography, involvement of peer researchers, and analysis of user-generated online data – which bring new ethical challenges. This chapter situates the emergence of research ethics review for social science research in a broad historical trajectory, considers the critiques of such processes by social scientists, and analyses the implications of changing contexts and new methodologies for qualitative research ethics. I argue that generic models of research ethics review are undermined by the complexity of qualitative research methodologies and draw on researchers' experience in these fields to rethink and reframe ethics oversight of qualitative research.

Keywords: Ethics in qualitative research; qualitative methodologies; research ethics; Declaration of Helsinki; innovative qualitative methodologies

Reframing Qualitative Research Ethics
Advances in Research Ethics and Integrity, Volume 12, 3–18

ISSN: 2398-6018/doi:10.1108/S2398-601820250000012001

INTRODUCTION

Questions of norms have been integral to social research since the advocates of anthropology, sociology, and social policy first began to articulate these disciplines and their methods.[1] Added to this, reflection on the moral aspects of conducting sociological and anthropological research – although not yet formulated in terms of research ethics – emerged in some of the pioneer university departments for these disciplines earlier than is generally recognised.[2] Discussions explicitly addressing ethical issues in the social sciences were published from the 1960s and 1970s onwards, after which time debates on researchers' responsibilities from an ethical perspective proliferated across diverse countries and regions, with codes of ethics being initiated, debated, expanded, and overhauled during the 1980s and 1990s (Fluehr-Lobban, 2002). Notwithstanding these emerging reflections on ethics within the academy, external pressures brought mandatory research ethics review to the table for social scientists in some countries from the 1990s, opening up a new and challenging phase in the relationship between social scientists and research ethics.

Over the intervening years, much has been written about research ethics in the social sciences, and new contexts have emerged that could hardly have been imagined just a few decades ago. These shifts have been brought about in part by the growth of qualitative research and by the influence of its practitioners, who have drawn on their own research to problematise tenacious assumptions about research ethics. We have now arrived at a point where qualitative researchers have extensive experience of ethics review of social science research, many have been members of research ethics committees (RECs) and institutional review boards (IRBs), and some have contributed to policies and guidance that influences research ethics oversight at local, national, and international levels. Given the experience of today's qualitative research practitioners, it is timely to explore the current state of play in this field. Just as Guillemin and Gillam (2004, p. 262) differentiated between 'ethics in practice' and 'procedural ethics', it is useful here to distinguish between the nuances of reflection on ethical issues during fieldwork and the formalities of institutional research ethics procedures: the brief for contributors to this volume was to draw on their own experience of fieldwork to inform suggestions for change and so to begin to reimagine how institutional support for qualitative research ethics should look.

In the first section of this chapter, I briefly situate the emergence of ethics review processes for social science research in a historical trajectory. In the second, I look to balance an acknowledgement of the scholarly literature that is critical of research ethics review in the social sciences with a counterchallenge: I argue that, notwithstanding the importance of these critiques and their significance in pointing to how things should be done differently, ethics review still has the potential to support innovative qualitative research in today's landscape.

RECs aim to provide guidance in an environment where new ideas and methodologies abound. In the third part of the chapter, I explore the significance of some of these changes: not only have qualitative methodologies evolved considerably, even since the turn of the century, there are also contemporary social phenomena that either did not exist then or were not recognised or articulated at that time. While a short introduction cannot comprehensively encompass all such changes, I will describe selected changes thematically, because this volume is as much about the authors grappling with their significance as it is about how procedural ethics can do justice to them.

RESEARCH ETHICS REVIEW AND QUALITATIVE RESEARCH: HISTORICAL PERSPECTIVES

Formal rules for international research ethics for clinical research were first codified in the years after the Second World War and set out in the Declaration of Helsinki in 1964.[3] Only later, during its first revision, was a recommendation added that clinical investigators should seek review of their protocol by an independent committee of peers prior to undertaking their research.[4] In this clause lies the origins of RECs and IRBs, as they subsequently became known.[5,6]

The story of how the remit of research ethics review for interventional clinical research changed from being advisory to mandatory in character, was then extended to broader health-related research and finally, in some jurisdictions, came to encompass research across other disciplines is deserving of its own in-depth historical account. That account would need to distinguish between the distinctive trajectory in some Anglophone countries in the Global North (including the United States, Canada, the United Kingdom, Ireland, Australia, and New Zealand), which have largely mandated research ethics review for social research, and the directions taken elsewhere.[7] To tell it succinctly, the expansion of research ethics review from health research into other fields had a great deal to do with the expansion of the state into funding and steering research and with the perceived need for control and accountability of research conducted in universities. In many cases, the initial steps towards the inclusion of the social sciences in research ethics review came via the expansion of the remit of RECs and IRBs in the health sector to include scrutiny of social research involving patients: the steady growth of qualitative research applied to health offered a significant opening for such bodies to become involved with qualitative methodologies. Later, qualitative research gained increasing recognition in the expanding field of multidisciplinary global health research, which has brought more of its practitioners into the ambit of RECs that are primarily clinically orientated (Liamputtong & Rice, 2020).

Turning to the question of ethics review of qualitative research per se, the situation is extremely diverse: just as not all ethics committees encompass social science research, so too 'presumed isomorphism' about ethics committees' approach to handling social science research is problematic (Hedgecoe, 2012, p. 79). While some countries require ethics review for all social science research, most do not (Tapscott & Machón, 2024, p. 5). However, other levers, notably the policies of major research funders – and later of academic journals – have resulted in a de facto requirement for research ethics review for sweeping parts of the research portfolio across many regions. Diverse kinds of institutions and organisations now have committees whose remit includes the review of social science research. As with the establishment of IRBs in research organisations in the United States from the 1990s, RECs became widespread in clinical research establishments in numerous other countries during this period. In a second phase of development, these committees gradually extended and consolidated their mandates from the early 2000s, although the chronology for these developments varies. University ethics committees, in particular, vary enormously, as does the way in which they handle social science research (Carniel et al., 2022; Dove & Douglas, 2023; Elfenbein & Hoffman, 2024). As non-governmental organisations became more involved in partnerships with researchers, some set up ethics committees to review research proposals within their organisations. Finally, international bodies including the World Health Organization and Médecins Sans Frontières established their own influential RECs (Schopper et al., 2009). Given their involvement in a wide range of fields, social scientists may interact with any of these types of ethics review bodies. Although this volume cannot document the range of policies and practices in research ethics review across different organisations and sectors, the following chapters raise some common themes which transcend the specificities of institutional contexts.

THE CRITIQUE FROM THE SOCIAL SCIENCES

There are multiple grounds for questioning the legitimacy of, and necessity for, research ethics reviews in the social sciences. At the heart of this challenge is a critique of the way that the nature of potential risks for participants tends to be blurred across the medical and social sciences: biomedical ethics frameworks have only limited applicability to the terrain of social science research, it is argued, and this gives further strength to concerns about the impact of ethics reviews on our research.

I begin with the objection to the appropriateness of predicating ethics review for social science research on a biomedical paradigm, which still appears to underpin some such reviews. Fundamental to this objection is the concern that ethics reviews of qualitative research draw on 'imaginations of risk' that are rooted in clinical research ethics (Bell & Wynn, 2023, p. 537). A central tenet in biomedical ethics is the avoidance of unnecessary harm, and consequently, committees in this tradition will typically expend considerable effort evaluating the physiological risks as well as other kinds of harm that may arise from a research intervention or, more precisely, with weighing up the possibility of harm against the potential benefits to participants. Although participating in social research does not usually entail physical hazards (Dingwall, 2008), other kinds of harm should be considered (Hammersley & Traianou, 2015). Perhaps the most well-recognised risk of social harm relates to the divulging of information considered to be confidential during research, in that negative consequences may follow if such information came to be known more widely. Beyond the consequences of wider disclosure, the processes of reflection and interpretation entailed in qualitative research may in themselves cause problems or challenges for participants, although this is not always predictable or calculable (Bringedal Houge, 2023; Kostovicova & Knott, 2022).

Related to this critique is a questioning of the relevance of the concept of vulnerability in relation to non-clinical research.[8] Van den Hoonaard (2018) sees in 'vulnerability' a concept that is, in general, wrongly applied to research ethics review in the field of social sciences. However, this argument tends to overlook the way that discussions about vulnerability have evolved in the clinical research ethics community, where there has been a move away from labelling groups or subpopulations as vulnerable (Council for International Organizations of Medical Sciences, 2016). For example, Luna conceives the concept of vulnerability 'via the notion of layers' considering that:

> We do not face 'a solid and unique vulnerability' that exhausts the category [...]. These layers may overlap: some may be related to problems with informed consent, others to violations of human rights, to social circumstances, or to the characteristics of the person involved. (Luna, 2019, p. 88)

This approach opens up nuanced ways of applying the concept of vulnerability that are arguably more relevant to qualitative research. The problem seems to be that the concept of vulnerability ossifies once incorporated into pre-review processes prior to ethics review, and once proposals reach a review committee, its members need to have a sophisticated understanding of the dimensions of vulnerability *and* the expertise to apply it if this concept is to be useful in this context.

Given that prospective ethics review inevitably involves providing an explanation of what is to be done in a research project, the tension between this anticipatory mode and the need for qualitative projects to maintain space to evolve has also preoccupied critics of RECs and IRBs. This dynamic has caused particular difficulties for anthropologists undertaking participant observation; when, as in anthropology, research questions are typically broadly defined, it may be both impracticable and epistemologically incorrect to closely anticipate the path that such fieldwork will take. In some institutions, RECs have come to expect detailed plans for such research, an expectation which arguably constrains, and may even prevent, the possibility of carrying out ethnographic fieldwork in future (Herzfeld, 2023).

At first glance, it may seem that interview-based studies are more predictable and so would fit better into a framework of anticipatory review: qualitative interview methods may appear to be similar to a questionnaire study, and RECs have become more accustomed to these approaches over time (Dingwall, 2016, p. 33). However, this perception of similarity masks important differences, given the extent to which qualitative interviewers may improvise questions for each interviewee and develop sensitising themes in the course of their research: if RECs work with an implicit model of a questionnaire-like study, qualitative researchers are obliged to present a definitive list of questions that will be asked in interviews, whereas from a methodological perspective it is good practice to keep open the possibility of changing these questions as a project develops. Hence, qualitative researchers may find themselves colluding with a REC's notion of fixed methods and predetermined ethical issues, despite knowing that it is by no means unusual for significant ethical dilemmas to arise once qualitative research is underway (Taquette & da Matta Souza, 2022).

The tendency for RECs to formulate risk in biomedical terms and to impose default requirements accordingly has been seen in terms of a kind of 'ethical imperialism' (Schrag, 2010), as international bioethics capacity-building initiatives have had a considerable influence on policies in the Global South (Israel, 2018). From this perspective, a twin dynamic of colonisation and colonialism is reflected in such initiatives, and it is argued that the unthinking adoption of procedures for clinical research into the governance of social science projects has resulted in ethically problematic procedures. A notable example is the expectation that informed consent processes for social science research should follow a template designed with clinical research in mind: researchers have testified to the inhibiting effect of asking people to sign informed consent forms (ICFs) prior to taking part in social research, questioned the morality and cultural appropriateness of asking people to do so, and traced the way that tenacious assumptions derived from biomedical research are embedded in ICFs for research in the humanities and social sciences.[9] The expectation of a detailed focus on risk management may be even more problematic when research funded elsewhere is to take place in a low- or middle-income country, as international ethics reviews are commonly freighted with additional precautions rooted in the aim of avoiding exploitation. Even in international health research, there is now a degree of acknowledgement that this dynamic has some negative consequences, and the way forward is actively debated (Wright et al., 2023).

The arguments levelled at anticipatory ethics reviews of social science research are substantial, but it does not necessarily follow that ethical issues arising from qualitative research should be managed by the responsible researchers alone. An alternative position is to argue that processes for a proportionate iterative review should be in place (Hickey et al., 2022). In a similar vein, Stevenson et al. (2015) make a useful distinction between research traditions where a predictive approach may be appropriate and those that follow a more reflexive approach where it will be less so, setting out different approaches for the ethics review process accordingly:

> The predictive nature of ethical problems means that the role of ethics boards in the first tradition is to evaluate the extent to which researchers have been able to effectively foresee ethical problems, and to design an ethically appropriate research protocol. In iterative approaches, because ethics are not 'pre-conceived' their role is facilitative, aiming to help researchers to think through possible problems. (pp. 5–6)

This, they continue, means that the role of an ethics committee member for such research should be framed in terms of being a 'critical reader' rather than a judge (Stevenson et al., 2015, p. 6). Working in the iterative mode, an ethics committee may be able to offer more appropriate advice and support to researchers, especially bearing in mind the challenges facing new researchers and the complexities entailed in working on large multidisciplinary projects.

A third key area of criticism of research ethics reviews for the social sciences centres on the social and economic costs of implementing them. It is suggested that mandating ethics committees to apply a conventional ethics rubric to social science research may impact on the kind of work that researchers choose to do. Indeed, some researchers have described how, based on their experiences of research ethics reviews, they came to avoid working with certain populations and using particular methodologies knowing that such research would be scrutinised more intensively (Bledsoe et al., 2007, p. 619). Some deem research ethics review to be disproportionate to the extent that they consider this form of scrutiny to be 'anti-democratic', in that it prevents social scientists from freely deciding their research priorities and so adversely impacts upon academic freedom (Dingwall, 2016, pp. 30–31). According to van den Hoonaard (2011), whose analysis focusses on RECs and IRBs in the United Kingdom, the United States, and Canada, there are substantial economic costs associated with research ethics reviews and associated infrastructures. Added to this, social costs arise from the barriers that ethics reviews pose to innovative research being freely conducted; furthermore, ethics review systems in some universities have come to embed a 'command and control' mechanism through which otherwise disorderly academic agendas are managed (Dingwall, 2016, pp. 31–32). A related concern is that RECs in effect act as a mechanism for reputation management and risk mitigation in this context. These critiques are as much to do with the wider shift to an audit culture in universities, where we have seen an expansion of other kinds of monitoring such as institutional 'pre-reviews', internal and external peer reviews and quality checks, as with ethics reviews specifically. Nonetheless, these analyses point to the possibility that research ethics review can be deployed, even weaponised, by powerful individuals and units in organisations, both within and beyond the university sector and, as researchers may be unwilling to speak about this, we do not necessarily know the full story.

Although the claim that research ethics review is anti-democratic is a serious one, taken to its logical conclusion it appears to dismiss the legitimacy of anyone other than the responsible investigators having a role in considering ethical issues entailed in their research. There seems to be an assumption at play in some of these critiques that social scientists are 'more ethical' than other researchers, which may not stand the test of evidence. Those of us who have been involved in ethics assessment and review panels have occasionally encountered proposals in the social science field that are characterised by a strong ethos of entitlement to undertake research that may be extremely intrusive, accompanied by a lack of due regard for its impact on participants. Do we really want to accept that the investigators responsible for such proposals are the only people who should consider whether some limits or modifications are advisable for such projects? Added to this, the claim that scrutiny by a REC or IRB will inevitably impede good social research and undermine innovation is contested. Some counter that requiring a discussion about ethics can be conducive for innovation, compared to encouraging individual researchers to make fully autonomous decisions about research. For example, Carniel et al. (2022) have described how in their own institution, research ethics reviews are informed by an in-depth understanding of, and dialogue about, specific methodologies. From this point of view, we are reminded that sharing proposals with colleagues for ethics review can be reciprocated with generous advice which, rather than hindering research activity, 'holds the capacity for enhancing understandings of the research process' (Carniel et al., 2022, p. 150).

To sum up, although each of the key critiques of ethics review for social science research referred to above is important, the extent to which they offset the case for research ethics review in this field is debatable. Many of the problems that have been identified lie not with research ethics review in principle but in the overlaying of such discussions with excessive bureaucracy and in expecting RECs and IRBs to act as regulators without giving them the tools and sophisticated remit expected of a modern regulator. It is paradoxical that for many researchers, 'ethics' has become synonymous with getting approval via institutional procedures, seen as simply another hurdle to be cleared. Far from entailing a process of moral reasoning that is intrinsically part of research, the lens through which ethical issues are viewed then becomes focussed on the tasks that must be undertaken prior to the review: following a series of questions and prompts associated with preparing a submission for ethics review may well result in a thinned-out account of such issues.

In this volume, the aim is to draw on qualitative traditions to give context and meaning to accounts of qualitative research ethics, which will in turn inform proposals for reframing how institutions can best support ethical qualitative research. Particularly relevant here is the concept of thick description, a term which became widely known through Geertz's (1973) writing and was then elaborated by Denzin, who noted that 'A thick description [...] presents detail, context, emotion, and the webs of social relationships that join persons to one another [and] inserts history into experience' (Denzin, 1989, p. 83, brackets added). This calls for narratives that are 'meaningful, interpretative, relational, authentic, contextualised, and linked' (Younas et al., 2023, p. 4). While this volume does not pretend to offer an in-depth ethnographic account of research ethics, the contributors take inspiration from this tradition.

QUALITATIVE RESEARCH ETHICS IN PRACTICE

The extent to which shifts in context have radically changed the nature of qualitative research has been elaborated in depth in a number of recent publications (Denzin et al., 2023; Thambinathan & Kinsella, 2021). Yet we can identify some core tenets that consistently buttress the wider qualitative project (Iphofen & Tolich, 2018). Notable among these is the importance of positionality: it is acknowledged that 'researchers have multiple identities that are fluid, context situated, and inform the positions from which they engage with and make meaning of the world' (Bayeck, 2022, p. 1). This means that, rather than seeking to eliminate or control for this aspect, the researcher's relationships are seen as a part and parcel of the research. For this reason, an explicit concern with the relational aspects of their research and elaboration of these is common to the narratives of research in this volume. This dynamic, different from fields of research which aim to eliminate the researcher's influence from the analysis – or at least to control for it – shapes how ethical issues are to be addressed. For example, reflection on the process of obtaining informed consent can become part of the research, which will then inform the approach taken to an issue all too often viewed in generic terms. As Fride Klykken explores in this volume, care about the ethics of undertaking research continues into the recruitment and informed consent processes: using examples from an ethnographic study of an upper secondary school classroom, she argues that this 'entails a continuous relational negotiation that needs attention throughout the research process'. Similarly, Hildah Mokgolodi's account of her experience of researching the perspectives of retired educators in Botswana skilfully deploys empathy to unpack the ethical issues she encountered, going beyond those anticipated by her REC. Increasingly, community engagement is seen as an important precursor to undertaking research, so that important conversations about aligning research priorities with those of communities can take place earlier. As Lloy Wylie et al. underline in their chapter, researchers may already have worked (or have lived) in their study communities for years and have highly relevant knowledge of them. Despite this experience, however, there can be a marked dissonance between an ethics committee's bird's eye view of what is ethical and an experienced, engaged researcher's view, as Metro (2014) has explored in a paper about her fieldwork with Burmese teachers in Thailand.

Even before considering the experience that participants may have of research, it is apt to begin with the question about whether a particular research project should be undertaken at all: if it involves collection of 'primary data' from participants, it is worthwhile carefully considering the reasons for doing so and whether this is likely to be acceptable to those participants, before the question of research ethics review arises. Hildah Mokgolodi's chapter elaborates a restraint that has led her to sometimes prefer using data that have already been collected, rather than initiating data collection anew herself: at a time when it is well documented that some participant groups face multiple demands from researchers, the question of whether to revisit groups or populations that are at risk of being over-researched is an important and under-explored issue in qualitative research.

Staying with the early stages of setting up a project, a raised awareness of ethical issues broadly conceived can be discerned in the recent development of deploying peer researchers to assist with engaging and recruiting participants. These approaches, although reminiscent of the tradition of using key informants in ethnography, embody a more contemporary aim of explicitly decentering the researcher–participant divide. Yet translating the principle of participation by people with lived experience into practice raises challenges which are deserving of further reflection. Nienke Boesveldt offers a granular account of how the involvement of peer researchers in her research subtly altered the kinds of questions that were asked in interviews and how participants responded: here, methodological and ethical issues are shown to be interpenetrated.

A notable shift in the way in which qualitative research is undertaken has been the move from a disciplinary to a 'transdisciplinary' landscape for many fields of study (Leavy, 2020). In more pragmatic terms, there has been an expansion of qualitative research embedded in multi-method projects. Qualitative researchers working in larger global health research projects, for example, have testified to the difficulties of raising their ethical concerns, especially those which involve questioning the policies of organisations that are gatekeepers, funders, and stakeholders: at times it seems that 'ethics' can become part of a defensive dynamic in this context, with objections to the asking of such questions being framed as an 'ethical discourse' (Parker & Allen, 2015, p. 36). At the same time, qualitative research in health settings has raised particular challenges, as Sarah Potthoff and Anke Erdmann acknowledge in their chapter, which includes proposals for more in-depth engagement between REC members, researchers, and participants in this context. They remind us that ethics committees should have appropriate qualitative expertise when reviewing such projects and go further to propose representation of patients and/or representatives of participant groups in the discussion to improve the contextual information available in these deliberations. One size does not fit all, however, in qualitative research, and therefore continuous ethical awareness and reflexivity are needed to address ethical issues on a case-by-case basis (Taquette & da Matta Souza, 2022). We have seen in multidisciplinary projects beyond the health field too that qualitative researchers have deployed technologies in novel ways, raising new questions that have not so far been well explored. Being interested in the experience of war-affected families, Bree Akesson and Karen Frensch describe how they deployed GPS data within their multi-method project, arguing that this can be used as an important tool within an overall qualitative approach, and exploring how the ethical concerns that arose from these uses of this technology were addressed, in part by enabling their participants to lead on its use.

The writings of autoethnographers, in which researchers narrate and draw directly on their own experience as data for analysis, have generated intense interest and some controversy in recent years (Tolich, 2010). Such accounts inevitably entangle others, and questions arise about the others' potential vulnerability and their rights to consent or decline to be involved and/or included. It is worth remembering that autobiographical elements have been included in ethnographic writing from over 100 years ago, even though the term 'autoethnography' did not come into use until more recently (Adams & Holman Jones, 2024). However, there is a sense in which autoethnography is between a rock and a hard place, as researchers proposing to write in this genre are criticised for not following ethical standards, yet they may find it difficult to obtain an ethics review. Nevertheless, there is an emerging body of work pointing to appropriate ethical practices for autoethnographic studies (Gibbs, 2018; Tolich, 2010). In this volume, Nicole Brown underscores the value of ethics reviews in providing iterative feedback and advice for university-based researchers who plan to undertake this kind of writing.

Historically, the handling of written texts – especially field notes and interview transcripts – has been central to the discussion of qualitative research ethics. Ethical concerns here go beyond the considerations of privacy and practices of anonymisation that dominate many a discussion, given that validity and ethics are interpenetrated in qualitative research. For Sanjek, writing before digitisation, field-note evidence is seen as one of the canons of validity for ethnography alongside theoretical candour about the choices made in fieldwork and the provision of a level of detailed description about 'the ethnographer's path' (Sanjek,

1990, p. 395). At that point, ethnographers relied primarily on detailed handwritten notes made in the field, and the extent to which people might be identifiable from these varied according to individual fieldworkers' ways of making them. Notes and recordings of qualitative investigations were seen as a valuable in-depth record of an encounter that belonged to the researcher, although they might sometimes be shared with the interviewee or informant. In recent years, as the digitisation of data has progressed apace, the relationship that researchers have with these kinds of data has become complicated by an expectation that others should be able to access these data in the future. Having had an early impetus as an activist movement, 'Open Science' has become associated with institutional requirements relating to access to data and research outputs. Even though evaluating data management was not traditionally considered to be within the remit of a REC or IRB, these committees increasingly find themselves expected to mediate institutional expectations for data archiving. In this volume, Margaret Sleeboom-Faulkner documents how in many universities archiving requirements have been redefined as ethical issues, and explores the consequences of this entangling of research ethics and data storage.

New questions about the social lives of data are not confined to the handling of written materials: dilemmas have also arisen about the handling of visual materials as their use has become more common in qualitative research, and user-generated data such as social media posts and blogs may also test the boundaries of research ethics policies. As we see in Helena Webb's account, researchers with experience of working with these modalities may be well-placed to offer input to REC policies addressing them and to wider discussions about what ethical practice should look like in this context.

CONCLUSION

As the contributions in this volume will show, qualitative research may entail several methodological innovations that intersect with each other, and these in turn shape the possibilities for respectful decisions about the use of data provided by participants. For instance, Lore Van Praag and her co-authors point to a more participatory approach to research ethics in which decisions about the use of visual images generated in their research are not seen as owned by researchers, nor by ethics committees but rather as something which participants may help to shape. This approach is consistent with a recognition of the moral reasoning that participants, patients, and other non-specialists engage in when making decisions about research, which has been eloquently advocated by Kleinman (1999).

Space precludes an extended discussion of the wider ethical implications of the developments discussed above, but it should be clear that the complexity of this terrain undermines the notion that fixed rules on how research must be conducted are credible in this landscape. Many RECs will be unfamiliar with methods such as autoethnography, involvement of peer researchers, fictionalising accounts, or analysing user-generated online content. Hence, pleas made some years ago for such committees to deploy humility when reviewing methodologies with which they are less familiar, adopt the role of the learner, and ask open questions remain relevant (Tolich & Fitzgerald, 2006).

It would be damaging to see a situation evolve where researchers cannot communicate effectively with their RECs or IRBs, as has been reported by some researchers who have devised 'escape routes', doing what they believe is right in contradiction to the expectations of their IRBs (Katz, 2006, p. 499). Beyond having an opportunity to explain their own proposals to ethics committees, it is important for researchers to be able to explore meaningful solutions to ethical challenges and to write freely about the implications of these. I hope that the following narratives by researchers of their experiences in the field, and their proposals for change, will be fruitful for a much-needed reframing of institutional research ethics to better serve the commitment of researchers in the social sciences and the interests of their participants.

NOTES

1. The interest in moral aspects is of course not exclusive to qualitative traditions: Durkheim's work on moral statistics (Durkheim & Simons, 1992 [1897]) and Titmuss' analyses of social statistics (Oakley & Ashton, 1997) are representative of the interest in social norms in quantitative sociology and social policy.

2. An early example can be found in Vivien Palmer's (1928) *Field Studies in Sociology*, which codified advice to students doing fieldwork in the Chicago school of sociology and addressed such issues as perceptions of researchers' competence and professionalism, the imperative to avoid overstepping into an informant's private thoughts, and noted that the informant 'must also be made to feel that any statements which he desires to have treated confidentially will be guarded, and he should be told what disposition is to be made of the data which he contributes. The current mores and situations in a group always dictate additional principles which must be observed' (p. 173). Studer and Chubin's (1977) paper also offers interesting reflections on sociologists' professional responsibilities which seem to anticipate the coming of ethics governance as we now know it. For authoritative analyses of the history of anthropology's engagements with ethics, see Mills (2003) and MacClancy and Fuentes (2015).

3. For valuable historical accounts of the development of research ethics in clinical research, see Schmidt et al. (2020) and Hazelgrove (2002).

4. Clause 2, Section 1 of the Declaration of Helsinki as revised in 1975 introduces for the first time the principle of a research protocol being considered by a committee of peers, who would offer advice to the responsible physician-researcher (World Medical Association, 1975).

5. I consider the terms 'research ethics committee', 'institutional review board', and 'ethics review board' to be interchangeable in the context of this discussion. Although each has its own distinct context and framework in different jurisdictions, they have broadly the same functions in terms of being mandated by policy or law to formally review research protocols for their ethical soundness. While there is considerable variation in the mandate, remit, and constitution of such committees/boards, our interests in this volume lie primarily with their *processes* of formal ethics review of qualitative research.

6. While the United States was one of the prime movers of the Declaration of Helsinki, disagreements over subsequent versions later led to a divergence between the Food and Drug Administration (FDA) and the World Medical Association (Moreno, 2020). It is clear that the regulatory frameworks in the United States had a significant impact on research ethics practices elsewhere – notably through their influence on National Institutes of Health (NIH)-funded research conducted in other countries – but it is beyond the scope of this chapter to analyse the shape and extent of this impact.

7. See, for example, Nortjé et al. (2017) and Davies (2020) for critical overviews of the development of RECs in low- and middle-income countries.

8. There is a parallel argument that in health research ethics too, the concept of vulnerability risks being deployed so broadly as to cloud rather than illuminate ethical judgement (Schroeder & Gefenas, 2009).

9. Comments on the imposition of inappropriate expectations for the informed consent process are so ubiquitous as to make it impracticable to provide an overview of the literature on this point here. However, see Halkias (2024) for a searing account of how institutional handling of informed consent requirements can, at worst, seriously compromise the integrity of research. For discussion of cultural competence as it applies to research ethics more broadly, see George et al. (2020).

ACKNOWLEDGEMENTS

I am grateful to Ron Iphofen and to the peer reviewer for their thoughtful comments on an earlier version of this chapter. I also want to acknowledge Robert Dingwall's generous help, in particular by drawing my attention to the salience of several sociological works published in the early and mid-20th century to contemporary ethical concerns.

REFERENCES

Adams, T., & Holman Jones, S. (2024). Autoethnography as becoming–with. In N. K. Denzin, Y. S. Lincoln, M. D. Giardina, & G. S. Cannella (Eds.), *The SAGE handbook of qualitative research* (6th ed., pp. 421–436). Sage Publications.

Bayeck, R. Y. (2022). Positionality: The interplay of space, context and identity. *International Journal of Qualitative Methods*, *21*, 1–9. https://doi.org/10.1177/16094069221114745

Bell, K., & Wynn, L. (2023). Research ethics committees, ethnographers and imaginations of risk. *Ethnography*, *24*(4), 537–558. https://doi.org/10.1177/1466138120983862

Bledsoe, C. H., Sherin, B., Gallinsky, A. G., Headley, N. M., Heimer, C. M., Kjeldgaard, E., Lindgren, J., Miller, J. D., Roloff, M. E., & Uttal, D. E. (2007). Regulating creativity: Research and survival in the IRB iron cage. *Northwestern University Law Review*, *101*(2), 593–641.

Bringedal Houge, A. (2023). Violent re-presentations: Reflections on the ethics of re-presentation in violence research. *Qualitative Research*, *23*(5), 1244–1260. https://doi.org/10.1177/14687941221079532

Carniel, J., Hickey, A., Southey, K., Brömdal, A., Crowley-Cyr, L., Eacersall, D., Farmer, W., Gehrmann, R., Machin, T., & Pillay, Y. (2022). The ethics review and the humanities and social sciences: Disciplinary distinctions in ethics review processes. *Research Ethics*, *19*(2), 139–156. https://doi.org/10.1177/17470161221147202

Council for International Organizations of Medical Sciences. (2016). *International ethical guidelines for health-related research involving humans* (4th ed.). CIOMS. https://doi.org/10.56759/rgxl7405

Davies, S. E. (2020). The introduction of research ethics review procedures at a university in South Africa: Review outcomes of a social science research ethics committee. *Research Ethics*, *16*(1–2), 1–26. https://doi.org/10.1177/1747016119898408

Denzin, N. K. (1989). *Interpretive interactionism*. Sage Publications.

Denzin, N. K., Lincoln, Y. S., Giardina, M. D., & Cannella, G. S. (Eds.). (2023). *The SAGE handbook of qualitative research* (6th ed.). Sage Publications.

Dingwall, R. (2008). The ethical case against ethical regulation in humanities and social science research. *Twenty-First Century Society*, *3*(1), 1–12. https://www.tandfonline.com/doi/abs/10.1080/17450140701749189

Dingwall, R. (2016). The social costs of ethics regulation. In W. van den Hoonaard & A. Hamilton (Eds.), *The ethics rupture: Exploring alternatives to formal research-ethics review* (pp. 25–42). University of Toronto Press. https://www.degruyter.com/document/doi/10.3138/9781442616653-004/html

Dove, E., & Douglas, C. (2023). Ethics governance in Scottish universities: How can we do better? A qualitative study. *Research Ethics*, *19*(2), 166–198. https://doi.org/10.1177/17470161221147801

Durkheim, E., & Simons, J. (Trans.) (1992). Suicide and fertility: A study of moral statistics. *European Journal of Population*, *8*, 175–197. https://doi.org/10.1007/BF01797209 (Original work published 1897).

Elfenbein, T. W., & Hoffman, A. S. (2024). Towards meaningful institutional change: Responsive bureaucracy and the governance of anthropological ethics. *Anthropology Today*, *40*, 4–7. https://doi.org/10.1111/1467-8322.12871

Fluehr-Lobban, C. (Ed.). (2002). *Ethics and the profession of anthropology: Dialogue for ethically conscious practice*. Alta Mira Press.

Geertz, C. (1973). *The interpretation of cultures: Selected essays*. Basic Books.

George, L., Tauri J., & Macdonald, L. (Eds.) (2020). Indigenous research ethics: Claiming research sovereignty beyond deficit and the colonial legacy. *Advances in research ethics and integrity* (Vol. 6). Emerald Publishing. https://www.emerald.com/insight/publication/doi/10.1108/S2398-6018202006

Gibbs, A. (2018). Ethical issues when undertaking autoethnographic research with families. In R. Iphofen & M. Tolich (Eds.), *The SAGE handbook of qualitative research ethics* (pp. 148–160). Sage Publications.

Guillemin, M., & Gillam, L. (2004). Ethics, reflexivity, and "ethically important moments" in research. *Qualitative Inquiry*, *10*(2), 261–280. https://doi.org/10.1177/1077800403262360

Halkias, A. (2024). Far from neutral: Research ethics committees, interdisciplinarity and fieldwork. *Anthropology Today*, *40*(2), 21–25. https://doi.org/10.1111/1467-8322.12876

Hammersley, M., & Traianou, A. (2015). *Ethics in qualitative research: Controversies and contexts*. Sage. https://doi.org/10.4135/9781473957619

Hazelgrove, J. (2002). The old faith and the new science: The Nuremberg Code and human experimentation ethics in Britain, 1946–73. *Social History of Medicine*, *15*(1), 109–135.

Hedgecoe, A. (2012). The problems of presumed isomorphism and the ethics review of social science: A response to Schrag. *Research Ethics*, *8*, 79–86.

Herzfeld, M. (2023). Ethnographic responsibility: Can the bureaucratization of research ethics be ethical? *Anthropology Today*, *39*(3), 3–6 https://doi.org/10.1111/1467-8322.12811.

Hickey, A., Davis, S., Farmer, W., Dawidowicz, J., Moloney, C., Lamont-Mills, A., Carniel, J., Pillay, Y., Akenson, D., Brömdal, A., Gehrmann, R., Mills, D., Kolbe-Alexander, T., Machin, T., Reich, S., Southey, K., Crowley-Cyr, L., Watanabe, T., Davenport, J., … Maxwell, J. (2022). Beyond criticism of ethics review boards: Strategies for engaging research communities and enhancing ethical review processes. *Journal of Academic Ethics*, *20*, 549–567. https://doi.org/10.1007/s10805-021-09430-4

Iphofen, R., & Tolich, M. (2018). Foundational issues in qualitative research ethics. In R. Iphofen & M. Tolich (Eds.), *The SAGE handbook of qualitative research ethics* (pp. 1–18). Sage.

Israel, M. (2018). Ethical imperialism? Exporting research ethics to the global south. In R. Iphofen & M. Tolich (Eds.), *The SAGE handbook of qualitative research ethics* (pp. 89–102). Sage Publications.

Katz, J. (2006). Ethical escape routes for underground ethnographers. *American Ethnologist*, *33*(4), 499–506. https://doi.org/10.1525/ae.2006.33.4.499

Kleinman, A. (1999). Moral experience and ethical reflection: Can ethnography reconcile them? A quandary for "the new bioethics". *Daedalus*, *128*(4), 69–97.

Kostovicova, D., & Knott, E. (2022). Harm, change and unpredictability: The ethics of interviews in conflict research. *Qualitative Research*, *22*(1), 56–73. https://doi.org/10.1177/1468794120975657

Leavy, P. (2020). A changing terrain: Qualitative research in the age of transdisciplinarity and public scholarship. In P. Leavy (Ed.), *The Oxford handbook of qualitative research* (2nd ed., pp. 1183–1195). Oxford Handbooks. https://doi.org/10.1093/oxfordhb/9780190847388.013.39

Liamputtong, P., & Rice, Z. S. (2020). Qualitative research in global health research. In R. Haring, I. Kickbusch, D. Ganten, & M. Moeti (Eds.), *Handbook of global health* (pp. 1–26). Springer. https://doi.org/10.1007/978-3-030-05325-3_10-1

Luna, F. (2019). Identifying and evaluating layers of vulnerability – A way forward. *Developing World Bioethics*, *19*, 86–95. https://doi.org/10.1111/dewb.12206

MacClancy, J., & Fuentes, A. (2015). The ethical fieldworker, and other problems. In J. MacClancy & A. Fuentes (Eds.), *Ethics in the field: Contemporary challenges* (pp. 1–23). Berghan.

Metro, R. (2014). From the form to the face to face: IRBs, ethnographic researchers, and human subjects translate consent. *Anthropology & Education Quarterly*, *45*(2), 167–184. https://doi.org/10.1111/aeq.12057

Mills, D. (2003). 'Like a horse in blinkers'? A political history of anthropology's research ethics. In P. Caplan (Ed.), *The ethics of anthropology: Debates and dilemmas* (pp. 35–53). Taylor and Francis. https://doi.org/10.4324/9780203633670

Moreno, D. (2020). The Declaration of Helsinki and the "American Stamp". In U. Schmidt, A. Frewer, & D. Sprumont (Eds.), *Ethical research: The Declaration of Helsinki, and the past, present, and future of human experimentation* (pp. 351–368). Oxford University Press.

Nortjé, N., Visagie, R., & Wessels, J. (Eds.). (2017). *Social science research ethics in Africa*. (Research Ethics Forum, Vol. 7). Springer. https://link.springer.com/book/10.1007/978-3-030-15402-8

Oakley, A., & Ashton, J. (Eds.). (1997). *Titmuss, R. M. The gift relationship: From human blood to social policy*. Original edition with new chapters. LSE Books.

Palmer, V. (1928). *Field studies in sociology*. University of Chicago Press.

Parker, M., & Allen, T. (2015). Questioning ethics in global health. In J. MacClancy & A. Fuentes (Eds.), *Ethics in the field: Contemporary challenges* (pp. 24–41). Berghahn.

Sanjek, R. (1990). On ethnographic validity. In R. Sanjek (Ed.), *Fieldnotes: The makings of anthropology* (pp. 385–418). Cornell University Press. https://doi.org/10.7591/9781501711954-017

Schmidt, U., Frewer, A., & Sprumont, D. (Eds.). (2020). *Ethical research: The Declaration of Helsinki, and the past, present, and future of human experimentation*. Oxford University Press.

Schopper, D., Upshur, R., Matthys, F., Singh, J. A., Bandewar, S. S., Ahmad, A., & van Dongen, E. (2009). Research ethics review in humanitarian contexts: The experience of the independent ethics review board of Médecins Sans Frontières. *PLoS Medicine*, *6*(7). https://doi.org/10.1371/journal.pmed.1000115

Schrag, Z. (2010). *Ethical imperialism: Institutional review boards and the social sciences, 1965-2009*. Johns Hopkins University Press. https://doi.org/10.1371/journal.pmed.1000115

Schroeder, D., & Gefenas, E. (2009). Vulnerability: Too vague and too broad? *Cambridge Quarterly Journal of Healthcare Ethics*, *18*(2), 113–121. 10.1017/S0963180109090203

Stevenson, F. A., Gibson, W., Pelletier, C., Chrysikou, V., & Park, S. (2015). Reconsidering 'ethics' and 'quality' in healthcare research: The case for an iterative ethical paradigm. *BMC Medical Ethics*, *16*(21), 1–9. https://doi.org/10.1186/s12910-015-0004-1

Studer, K. E., & Chubin, D. E. (1977). Ethics and the unintended consequences of social research: A perspective from the sociology of science. *Policy Science*, *8*, 111–124. https://doi.org/10.1007/BF01712288

Tapscott, R., & Machón, D. R. (2024). Procedural ethics for social science research: Introducing the research ethics governance dataset. *Journal of Peace Research*, 1–10. https://doi.org/10.1177/00223433241249352

Taquette, S. R., & da Matta Souza, L. M. B. (2022). Ethical dilemmas in qualitative research: A critical literature review. *International Journal of Qualitative Methods*, *21*. https://doi.org/10.1177/16094069221078731

Thambinathan, V., & Kinsella, E. A. (2021). Decolonizing methodologies in qualitative research: Creating spaces for transformative praxis. *International Journal of Qualitative Methods*, *20*. https://doi.org/10.1177/16094069211014766

Tolich, M. (2010). A critique of current practice: Ten foundational guidelines for autoethnographers. *Qualitative Health Research*, *20*(12), 1599–1610. https://journals.sagepub.com/doi/10.1177/1049732310376076

Tolich, M., & Fitzgerald M. H. (2006). If ethics committees were designed for ethnography. *Journal of Empirical Research on Human Research Ethics*, *1*(2), 71–78. https://journals.sagepub.com/doi/10.1525/jer.2006.1.2.71

van den Hoonaard, W. C. (2011). *Seduction of ethics: Transforming the social sciences*. University of Toronto Press.

van den Hoonaard, W. C. (2018). The vulnerability of vulnerability: Why social science researchers should abandon the doctrine of vulnerability. In R. Iphofen & M. Tolich (Eds.), *The SAGE handbook of qualitative research ethics* (pp. 305–321). Sage.

World Medical Association. (1975). *Declaration of Helsinki – Recommendations guiding medical doctors in biomedical research involving human subjects*. https://www.wma.net/policies-post/wma-declaration-of-helsinki-ethical-principles-for-medical-research-involving-human-subjects/

Wright, K., Aagaard, N., Amr Yusuf, A., Atuire, C., Campbell, K., Littler, K., Mandil, A., Mathur, R., Okeibunor, J., Reis, A., Ribeiro, M., Saenz, C., Sekhoacha, M., Shamsi Gooshki, E., Amir Singh, J., & Upshur, R. (2023). Preparing ethical review systems for emergencies: Next steps. *BMC Medical Ethics*, *24*, 92. https://doi.org/10.1186/s12910-023-00957-2

Younas, A., Fàbregues, S., Durante, A., Escalante, E. L., Inayat, S., & Ali, P. (2023). Proposing the "MIRACLE" narrative framework for providing thick description in qualitative research. *International Journal of Qualitative Methods*, *22*, 1–13. https://doi.org/10.1177/16094069221147162

REIMAGINING QUALITATIVE RESEARCH ETHICS: NARRATIVES AND CASE STUDIES

CHAPTER 2

ETHICS REVIEW AND YOUTUBE RESEARCH WITH FERTILITY PRESERVATION VLOGGERS

Rhonda M. Shaw

Te Herenga Waka—Victoria University of Wellington, Aotearoa New Zealand

ABSTRACT

This chapter draws on the author's experience of the ethics application process for a study based in Aotearoa New Zealand documenting the fertility preservation journeys of cisgender, transgender, and non-binary people who seek to freeze their gametes for health, career, and gender transition reasons. The study design entailed face-to-face interviews and focus group discussions. Due to the COVID-19 outbreak in Aotearoa in early 2020, followed by government-mandated lockdown periods, recruitment for the interviews and focus groups was postponed until the research team was able to talk to people in-person. The original focus of the study was adapted to accommodate data collection via YouTube, with its large database and accessibility to publicly available video blogs. While there is no consensus among social researchers and institutional ethics committees regarding research ethics around publicly available data online, our university ethics committee took the view that social media content produced by people who connect and interact with others constitutes 'human subject research', and therefore, ethics clearance was required for participant recruitment and selection and data collection. In this chapter, I reflect on the ethics review process relating to the study, the issues raised by the ethics committee at different stages of the project,

Reframing Qualitative Research Ethics
Advances in Research Ethics and Integrity, Volume 12, 21–35

Published under exclusive licence by Emerald Publishing Limited
ISSN: 2398-6018/doi:10.1108/S2398-601820250000012002

and the methodological approach the research team took to address the committee's concerns. I conclude with a discussion of the governance process of ethics review and of the importance of dialogue between researchers, ethics committees, and advisory support teams in understanding the dynamic and changing landscape of online social research.

Keywords: Aotearoa New Zealand; cisgender and transgender people; ethics of care; institutional ethics committees; vloggers

INTRODUCTION

Gamete cryopreservation (ovarian egg and sperm freezing) is regarded as a risk-management technology that provides the option to extend fertility later in life. First developed as a medical treatment to freeze and store sperm for cancer patients (Gosden, 2014), advanced cryopreservation techniques have extended egg freezing to cisgender women concerned about age-related fertility decline (van de Wiel, 2020; Waldby, 2015). More recently, gamete freezing has been used by transgender and non-binary (trans) people[1] interested in preserving their reproductive material prior to medically transitioning.[2]

Whether people are freezing their eggs or sperm in anticipation of future infertility or because they want to delay reproductive decision-making, gamete freezing maintains the possibility of having genetically related children sometime in the future. Unlike other forms of assisted human reproduction for people who are experiencing issues trying to conceive (e.g., in vitro fertilisation), gamete freezing treats infertility before it happens. Though access to fertility preservation is available to people in many jurisdictions globally (e.g., Aotearoa New Zealand, Australia, the United Kingdom), costs differ significantly for egg and sperm preservation and entitlements to publicly available or private funding. In addition to barriers to accessing services, a key issue for trans people is whether providers have covered gamete preservation as part of professional advice and counselling around gender-affirming healthcare; now a requirement by international guidelines (Coleman et al., 2022).

This chapter discusses the study design, data collection, and research ethics application process for a sociological project based in Aotearoa New Zealand (Aotearoa) entitled *Reproductive Futures: Views and Experiences of Fertility Preservation*. The study applied document analysis and qualitative research methods to investigate the fertility preservation journeys of trans and cisgender young adults involved in decision-making around gamete freezing for health, career, and gender transition reasons. The aim was to contribute empirical data about people's motivations and experiences of accessing and preserving reproductive materials to international literature and to better understand how diverse groups of young adults in Aotearoa negotiate and manage their relationships with service providers in relation to the prospect of family formation. Alongside the academic aims of the study, the research team sought to shed light on the challenges and difficulties young people have accessing fertility preservation and to assist policymakers seeking to improve healthcare services around equity of access.

In this chapter, I reflect on the ethics and epistemological framework underpinning the study, the issues raised by the institutional ethics committee[3] approving the research prior to commencing the project, and the shift in methodological approach adopted by the researchers to address the committee's ethics review concerns. I conclude with comments about the way forward for research ethics processes in view of the dynamic landscape of social media data and how these data should be treated and used in qualitative research. In doing so, I reiterate a position taken by the Association of Internet Researchers (Frankze et al., 2020, 2.3.4) on qualitative research involving social media that, 'the issues raised by Internet research are *ethical* problems precisely because they evoke more than one ethically defensible response to a specific dilemma or problem'.

METHODS

The *Reproductive Futures* study began in 2020. Along with focus group discussions, the author and lead investigator (Rhonda) and research assistant on the project (Alex) planned in-depth interviews with 18- to 30-year-old New Zealanders about their knowledge, decision-making, and reasons for seeking access to assisted reproductive technologies to preserve their fertility. As such, we set out to conduct up to 6 focus groups of 4–6 people (maximum 36 participants) and 10 (or potentially more) semi-structured face-to-face individual interviews. Concomitantly, we aimed to conduct a content analysis of video blogs (vlogs) by English-speaking cisgender and trans people who had discussed their fertility preservation journeys online (maximum 30 people).

The virtual ethnography was designed with YouTube videos in mind. YouTube offers a public platform for people to share their experiences, build virtual communities, and educate viewers. As discussed elsewhere (Ker & Shaw, 2022; Shaw & Ker, 2024), we felt this methodology would offer a valuable way of gaining insight into issues that affect people experiencing health-related issues, as well as providing understanding of trans and non-binary people's views of fertility preservation in relation to the desire for family and parenthood. The choice of methodology was based on preliminary observations regarding the dearth of public information on this topic in Aotearoa. Our website and document searches in the early phases of the project indicated a lack of diverse representation of people who did not fit the dominant narrative of assisted reproductive technologies aimed at heterosexual, Pākehā (non-Māori of European descent), cisgender individuals and couples. The analysis of secondary data from YouTube videos and video comments was designed to include a content analysis of up to 30 'talking head'-style videos made by individual video bloggers (vloggers), rather than by clinics or organisations, to analyse aspects of self-representation. Our focus was to understand the narratives told throughout the videos (how people make sense of fertility preservation options) and thereby highlight common themes across videos.

APPLYING FOR RESEARCH ETHICS APPROVAL

The ethics review process at our university requires researchers to explain any ethical issues their proposed study raises and how researchers intend to address these issues. To ensure our study was ethically responsible, I identified several areas of ongoing concern related to our proposed research methods. The first tension concerned the question of digital culture and the increasing trend since the turn of the 21st century towards greater self-disclosure in the form of first-person narratives about intimate experiences and emotion in public; a cultural transformation, Eva Illouz (2007, p. 4) argues, 'finds its most potent expression in the technology of the Internet'. A positive outcome of this development for sociologists working in the field of health research has been the championing of stories around illness narratives across a range of social media platforms, enabling users to share relatable illness experiences with others. While I felt reasonably confident about people becoming increasingly comfortable with telling stories about medical journeys, illness and health-related experiences in public and on the internet, a key concern for our study was how to determine the boundary between social media users' understandings of 'public' and 'private' in relation to their intended audiences in online spaces against technical definitions of 'publicly available data'. I expand on this below in the section on *Ethical considerations*.

A second ethical issue for us prior to embarking on the project was around researcher positionality and our expertise as a two-person team collaboratively engaging in research on a sensitive topic. While the ethics application form at our university at the time of writing did not provide a specific text field for researchers to insert details about the expertise and experience of the research team to undertake their proposed study, we were aware the committee had increasingly come to expect inclusion of these details in various places throughout the application.[4] This requirement is particularly the case for applicants seeking to do research with Māori (Indigenous inhabitants of Aotearoa), who must address their responsibilities to Te Tiriti (Treaty of Waitangi)[5] and show how their research protects the principles outlined in the university's Te Tiriti o Waitangi Statute (see Gibson et al., 2020), Pasifika populations, and participants from vulnerable, marginal, and minoritised groups.

Given our respective experience researching sensitive topics in the fields of health, gender, and sexuality research, Alex and I were accustomed to reflecting on our positionality and the potential for power imbalances when working with vulnerable groups as a researched population (Shaw et al., 2020). As a cisgender person and the lead investigator of the study, I had over two decades research experience conducting studies with people from diverse and marginal groups on previous projects relating to assisted human reproduction, fertility help-seeking, and family building. Alex, who identified as a transmasculine health researcher, had recently completed a dissertation collecting qualitative data exploring people's experiences of accessing gender-affirming hormone therapy in Aotearoa and had experience working on several national youth health and well-being surveys focusing on developing items around gender diversity and facilitating consultation processes with gender-diverse community members.

Our methodological approach for the *Reproductive Futures* project adopted a research ethic of care informed by feminist epistemology and qualitative and digital ethics (Costley & Gibbs, 2006; Dieterle, 2021; Doucet & Mauthner, 2008) that incorporated tenets of trans epistemology (Radi, 2019). This entailed what ethics of care researchers identify as epistemic responsibility grounded in relationships and accountability for data gathering, analysis, and reporting processes. Following Radi (2019), trans epistemology is a perspective that centres trans people's lived experience in producing knowledge about trans people. As a theoretical approach, this perspective accords credibility to the way trans people understand and articulate their health and illness experiences, rather than relying on the accepted language of medical discourse and health practitioners to assign epistemic authority to trans people's testimonies (Carel, 2016, p. 3).

In line with this approach, the focus of the study was to record trans participants' vlog narratives from their perspective as experiential experts (Akrich et al., 2008; Wehling et al., 2015). As we regarded the vloggers as experts of their experience, with intimate knowledge of their own bodies and identities in relation to fertility preservation, it was important to acknowledge their voice and opinions. In short, we wanted to know what the vloggers were saying, how they were saying it, who they were saying it to and why. This was important not only for conducting the interviews and relationship-building with research participants, led by Alex, the assistant investigator of the study, but for interpreting the vlogs. The study's epistemic approach therefore included research praxis agreement about our respective positionality and social location with respect to recruitment and data collection to assist trustworthiness in the study for the vlog documentation and participant interviews. For my part, it also entailed rethinking academic conventions around recognition of authorship in outputs documenting trans and non-binary people's perspectives (see Streed et al., 2023).

As we were researching sensitive issues around health, delayed and disrupted fertility, and gender transitioning, community safety was a paramount concern. Some of the trans individuals we sought to interview were vulnerable due to their experiences of social disadvantage and discrimination as marginalised members of groups in mainstream Aotearoa (Veale et al., 2019). We took it that individuals from mainstream groups may also be vulnerable, given the focus of the study on health and well-being issues around cancer treatment, chemotherapy, infertility, and challenges accessing fertility preservation technologies to build future families. We used socially and culturally appropriate frameworks to guide the study, based on prior research experience in this field, background consultation with fertility specialists, healthcare professionals, and LGBTQ+ advocacy groups from an adjunct study on *Experts' Views of Assisted Reproduction*,[6] and were cognisant of ethical issues around vulnerability and conducting qualitative research on sensitive topics with vulnerable and marginal individuals and groups (Shaw et al., 2020). In accord with intersectional analysis, we acknowledged that there would be aspects of participants' accounts we would be 'outsider researchers' to (Bourke, 2014). We were therefore mindful of potential biases that not only informed my positioning as a cisgender researcher but also Alex's interpretation of the data in relation to transfeminine and culturally specific experiences and decision-making around fertility preservation and how these differentials might shape our data analysis.

We assured the ethics committee that we would respond sensitively to study participants by maintaining privacy, confidentiality, and cultural safety and had developed protocols for responding empathically and ethically to participants should they become uncomfortable or upset. We also provided participants with a sheet including a list of services about helplines and organisations targeted to fertility issues. As the interviews and focus groups were designed to be participant directed, we did not anticipate unsettling participants unduly. To minimise the risks of deception and of identifying vloggers, we intended to report any findings in such a way that protected all vloggers' identities. In our ethics application, we stated that we would not include any visual data and would only use pseudonyms when reporting quotes or comments. We would remove any identifying markers such as locations or personal names from these quotes. Due to the intimate nature of fertility preservation, we decided not to include any data that described graphic or highly sensitive information about people's bodies. We supposed that due to the large numbers of videos on fertility preservation on YouTube, the risk of identification was low.

Based on our knowledge of the field and our view that taking data from unknowing subjects without offering anything in return is unethical, our relational ethic entailed reciprocation in the form of ongoing communication and a written report to the vloggers who consented to the use of their data. Outputs from the larger project were also disseminated in the media (Shaw, 2021) and shared with healthcare professionals and advocates working in the field of gender-affirming healthcare who participated in the *Experts' Views* study. Although we believed our research approach constituted low risk, we felt that sharing reports with participants would mitigate potential harm if they stumbled upon our outputs online and found the interpretation of data disagreeable or challenging.

COVID-19

We originally envisaged recruiting participants for face-to-face interviews and focus group discussions. However, due to the COVID-19 outbreak in Aotearoa in early 2020, we postponed recruitment for the interviews and focus groups until we were able to talk to people face-to-face and in-person. This was further affected by New Zealand government-mandated lockdown periods throughout 2020 and 2021 and difficulties getting people to talk in groups, due to the spread of COVID-19.[7] The initial focus of the study was subsequently adapted to accommodate the data collection via online social media as a first step, with interviews and focus groups to follow at a later stage. We successfully sought an ethics amendment to the original project to change the minimum age of vloggers from 18 to 16 years of age and to increase the number of vlogs observed from 30 to 60 to ensure thorough comparative analysis of the medical, career-related, and gender transition narratives. Two further amendments were approved to extend the data collection timeframe of the project.

YouTube was chosen as the data collection site due to its large database and accessibility to publicly available vlogs. We organised the data collection and analysis for the study around the three groups related to health, career, and gender transition. There were two searches for cisgender people's vlogs: in October 2020, we included 29 videos that met our inclusion criteria, uploaded to YouTube between April 2009 and September 2020, and then in July 2021, we added 10 further videos, uploaded to YouTube between February 2017 and March 2021. Videos were included if they involved self-filmed footage and personal commentary about the fertility preservation process through either a vlog style or if the video was produced and uploaded by an organisation and the video profiled individuals' experiences. We then added nine videos to the dataset from our study on trans people's vlogs on fertility preservation, uploaded to YouTube between June 2015 and October 2019. Two videos were then excluded from analysis; one video was subsequently made private by the vlogger, and one was a general documentary about egg freezing. In total, 46 videos from cisgender and trans vloggers were included in the study.

ETHICAL CONSIDERATIONS

There is considerable international debate among social researchers, as well as variation between different institutional ethics committee policies,[8] regarding specifics around exemptions or consent waivers for publicly available data on the internet and social media. Some university policies permit their research ethics committees (RECs) to treat material on websites, blogs, discussion boards, etc. as publicly available text produced for a general audience and, as such, do not require researchers to obtain consent from individuals to include quotations or reference their material. This is also a position taken by some international researchers regarding YouTube videos (Jacobs & Kelemi, 2020, Patterson, 2018). Harrington maintains, for example, that 'anonymization or asking for informed consent could be unethical' in the case of YouTube vlogs, stating: 'YouTube vlogs are public performances involving personal storytelling. [...] From both a legal and ethical standpoint these texts should be treated as publications that must be cited, rather than private conversations taking place in public' (Harrington, 2024, p. 10). Likewise, scholars such as Giles (2017) argue that research ethics clearance is not required because YouTube copyright agreements enable the public use of videos. Other researchers maintain that 'social media data is at least implicitly public' (Wilson, 2022, p. 147).

As a point of difference for our study, our university ethics committee distinguishes between data in the public domain and data that YouTube creators implicitly expect to be kept to the site they have posted to. Though social media data are to some extent 'already produced', as Halford (2018, p. 17) observes, the committee viewed the use of vlog data for research purposes as human subject research and not 'secondary textual analysis' (Roberts, 2015, p. 318). As a condition of ethics clearance, we were required to seek consent from the vloggers to use confidential quotations from their videos. The vlogs we sought to access were not deemed exempt from ethics review, in line with our university's Human Ethics Policy around risk mitigation. Section 4.3 of the Policy reads: 'Some kinds of human research are exempt from review, such as activities of negligible ethical risk, as outlined in the Human Ethics Guidelines' (Victoria University of Wellington, 2019, p. 2).

Given that the videos included sensitive personal information produced by potentially vulnerable persons, unlikely to be intended as 'position statements' (Ravn et al., 2019), it was determined that some vloggers may not consent to their narratives being used for academic analysis and could construe this as a 'breach of contextual privacy' (Hennell et al., 2020); a view also taken by Schuman et al. (2019) in their analysis of Veterans' vlogs about war trauma. The committee sent us a Revise and Resubmit letter asking for a recruitment email and new information sheet and consent form to send to the YouTube creators. They recommended that we contact vloggers, where possible, requesting permission for use to minimise their 'potential surprise' upon reading the article. The committee speculated that this 'is not inconceivable if this is an area of deep concern to them' (email communication, 30 January 2020).

The committee's starting point was that research involving social media content constitutes human research (i.e., research involving human participants, their data, or tissue).[9] Though it was not made explicit, a key perspective informing the committee's feedback was that social media content is not merely publicly available information in a technical sense but produced by people who emotionally and intellectually connect and interact with others they consider to be their intended audience. Sociologists Ravn et al. (2019) have referred to these imagined online audiences by drawing on Lauren Berlant's (2008) concept of an 'intimate public'. According to Berlant (2008, p. 5),

> An intimate public operates when a market opens up to a bloc of consumers, claiming to circulate texts and things that express those people's particular core interests and desires. When this kind of 'culture of circulation' takes hold, participants in the intimate public *feel* as though it expresses what is common among them, a subjective likeness that seems to emanate from their history and their ongoing attachments and actions.

The concept lends itself to analysing narratives on social media platforms because although strangers in an intimate public share an expressed repertoire of common feeling and are 'emotionally literate in each other's experience' (Berlant, 2008, p. 5), they are physically distant. Key to understanding Berlant's notion of intimate publics is the contention that scripts governing emotional alignment and belonging in personal life migrate from the public sphere to people's private worlds. These scripts legitimise the public storytelling of intimate experiences for the benefit of others, providing therapeutic tools to cope with suffering and how to live 'as a certain kind of being in the world' (Berlant, 2008, p. viii). While Berlant – and Illouz (2007) – critically theorise the public self-disclosure of intimate narratives as a new phase in capitalism and emotional culture, Ravn et al. (2019) frame the stories of intimate publics through a humanist lens. Rather than viewing digital content as data detached from persons, Ravn and colleagues argue for a reflexive approach to social media research ethics that accounts for what people posting and creating online understand as 'their' public.

A condition of ethics approval for our project, as stated above, was that we seek informed consent from the fertility preservation vloggers to use confidential quotations from their videos. The committee surmised that some vloggers may have an expectation of privacy, despite using a publicly accessible platform, and might not agree to their narratives being re-used for research purposes; a point noted by scholars in academic discussions of online methods of data collection (e.g., Halford, 2018; Roberts, 2015). Accordingly, we contacted vloggers who provided contact details on their YouTube channels to explain the study and ask for their permission to use their quotes.

For the trans vloggers' study, 15 vloggers were contacted, 6 responded and gave their written consent. When we double-checked their vlogs, we noticed that one vlogger had made their YouTube video private and unavailable. Contacting the cisgender vloggers for consent to use their narrative accounts was not as successful. On 23 July 2021, the lead investigator sent 14 invitations inviting the cisgender vloggers to consent to participate in the study. At the end of the week (31 July 2021), two people replied and said 'yes' and one person (a talent agency spokesperson acting on behalf of someone) said 'no'. There were no replies to a reminder invitation.

After receiving relatively few responses to emails requesting the cisgender vloggers' consent for us to use their narratives, I considered alternative ways of presenting the findings that minimised the risk of identifying vloggers. As the response rate from the cisgender vloggers was low, I sought inspiration from Willis's (2019) study with members of the UK Parliament and method of creating composite narratives from one-to-one elite interviews. In Willis's study, interview data were synthesised to construct stories based on participants' lived experiences, while not attributing events or details to particular people. We adapted this technique to present detailed accounts of people's fertility preservation journeys while keeping participants' identities confidential (see Burles & Bally, 2018; Willis, 2019). In creating these interpretive accounts, we were asking readers to 'put their faith in the researcher's judgement' (Willis, 2019, p. 474). Despite concerns about the 'fabrication' of data reducing its credibility, we took Annette Markham's (2012) view that 'all data are narrowed, altered, and abstracted through various filters before they are analysed' (p. 341). Following Markham's perspective, researchers reflect on and develop their own relationship to the data they generate, so all qualitative research involves an element of creativity, interpretation, and construction. As such, even data collected in naturalistic observational settings are to some extent rendered perspectival by the very nature of the researcher's point of view. Based on the ways in which composite narratives have been used across disciplines, we concluded that this method would provide a 'credible and concise' (Johnston et al., 2023, p. 2) way to present research findings (Shaw & Ker, 2024).

To create our composite narratives, Alex first listed each vloggers' demographic details and categorised them into five groups, creating a fictional person/profile and name for each narrative. From here, we added some of the details under each profile, such as the vlogger's reasons for making vlogs, the vlog format, and their reasons for undergoing fertility preservation. While most details are based on the vloggers' actual experiences, some details (such as a vlogger's country of residence) were altered to maintain their anonymity. Unlike Willis (2019), who presents verbatim quotes from interview data, we chose not to present direct quotes from the videos but instead created our own quotes, through synthesising similar quotes, which aimed to capture the 'emotional truth' of participants' experiences, rather than the 'narrative truth' (Orbach, 2000, cited in Willis, 2019, p. 472). We then mapped the representative quotes and experiences onto each profile and wrote up the narratives of gamete freezers from different demographic groups; those undergoing cancer treatment, cisgender women contemplating egg freezing for age-related reasons, and trans people concerned about infertility due to gender transition (Shaw & Ker, 2024). Although the low response rate to our call for study participation from the vloggers was disappointing, the decision to use composite data worked well and gave us an alternative way to present the issues the vloggers raised.

QUESTIONS FOR FUTURE ETHICS REVIEW

Staff and student researchers at universities in Aotearoa must comply with institutional policies and procedures for ethical review or risk-facing sanctions for research misconduct. From time to time, researchers raise objections to recommendations by institutional ethics committees regarding the use of electronic media as a source of data for research purposes.[10] This is no surprise given the lack of consensus among researchers across social media platforms about the definition of public data, differences between institutional policies about what does and does not require human ethics review, and long-standing resistance, 'cynicism and rumbles of dissatisfaction' (Bell & Wynn, 2023, p. 538) from researchers who regard ethics committees as overly vigilant (Brown et al., 2020).

We did not question the stance of our committee with respect to our study on the grounds that vloggers may have used YouTube to personally document and diarise their fertility preservation journeys and to communicate with a specific audience, rather than produce content to share with unknown others. Although our committee's advice was cautious, we accepted that using YouTube content without creators' informed consent, even when data are anonymised and all identifying detail removed, may be construed as covert observation and thereby risk harming the vloggers (Ker & Shaw, 2022, pp. 81–82).

It might be assumed that it would be difficult for us to gain consent from the trans vloggers due to the low trust within vulnerable and minoritised communities. Our modest recruitment success can be attributed to open and transparent dialogue with potential participants about the aims and intended outcomes of the study, disclosure about researcher positionality centring trans-led research and scholarship (Streed et al., 2023), and ongoing exchange with the vloggers beyond the project's end: an approach that we advocate in digital research ethics going forward.

We are deeply gratified that our study was successful and for ongoing opportunities to ensure the research findings are impactful. That said, lack of clarity remains about coverage of the term 'human subjects research' and its definition in ethics policies. The differences, for example, between face-to-face interviews with human participants that are interventions into people's lives which generate new data and the analysis of online observational data already produced by creators of YouTube vlogs need to be fleshed out and explicitly communicated to researchers (Wilson, 2022). Although we stand by our decision to use composite data for the cisgender vlogs as an effective response to the data gathering dilemma imposed by the committee's recommendation, we were not invited by the ethics administrator who contacted us with the committee's ruling to discuss the implications of their decision or to consider alternatives. With the benefit of hindsight, the option of an opt-out approach explaining the study to the vloggers could have sufficed as permission to use their quotes. By putting their vlogs on a public website, users have presumably agreed to the YouTube Terms of Service (YouTube, 2019) and have created video content with the knowledge that it is publicly accessible. As the Terms of Service do permit citation and referencing of YouTube videos, we could have sent the vloggers a return receipt email with information about the study and asked, 'Do you object to us using your vlog? If so, please reply to this message with the words "I opt out"', as a valid alternative to an opt-in situation that requires sending participants information and consent forms asking them to print, sign, scan, and return them. Likewise, where we received no response from the vloggers, our email message could have stated that quotes from people's video content would be included in our research without identifying information. As these options were not suggested by the reviewers of our application, nor by the research ethics team that advises the committee and researchers at the university, we felt obliged to comply with the opt-in requirement.

In addition to my researcher role at the university, I have long-term service experience as an ethics committee member, sub-committee, and central committee convenor. In the convenor role, I work in partnership with ethics administrators and support recommendations made by committee members reviewing applications to ensure research across the university proceeds ethically and in line with the Human Ethics Policy and Guidelines. The role of convenor and that of the committee also entails reflection and review of policy and guidelines. Ethics policy review requires conversations and consultation with researchers, teaching staff, and a range of stakeholders across the university and can be a slow process: a point well noted by Gibson et al. (2020) in their discussion of a key question in the university ethics application form relating to the Treaty of Waitangi.

Commenting on the ethics policy in their discussion, ex-committee member Ocean Mercier observed strong echoes of 'free, prior informed consent' in the committee's 'focus on how information is delivered to participants, and how consent is obtained' (Gibson et al., 2020, p. 98), remarking that this emphasis does not always accord with research guidelines developed by Māori researchers. Questioning informed consent protocol, albeit for different reasons, is also applicable to online digital research. In our study, we took an ethics of care approach based on relationship-building that acknowledged respect for individual participant autonomy. At the same time, we aimed to centre the views and experiences of people seeking access to fertility preservation as a matter of reproductive justice. Had we placed greater emphasis on the latter, we may have been disappointed, as the ethical requirements of the committee resulted in fewer voices being heard and included in the online study, potentially impacting desired research and policy-oriented outcomes: a tension Bell and Wynn (2023, p. 549) identify when ethics committees 'attempt to *wed* deontological and consequentialist principles in the process of ethics review'.

CONCLUSION

Institutional ethics committees and review boards citing Association of Internet Research guidelines advocate for situational case-based rather than rule-based approaches to digital research ethics, acknowledging the need for nuanced ethical treatment across various digital platforms. While one size does not fit all, the risk appetite of ethics committees, the extent to which they support researchers' reflexive judgement in the lead up to undertaking social media research, inconsistencies between review responses across studies, and the presence of dominant voices and differences of opinion between committee reviewers and administrative teams can significantly influence the review process and outcomes of applicants' projects. At a national level, it would be helpful to know how researchers from other universities in Aotearoa, and those internationally, where ethics policy around publicly available data and social media research may be less circumscribed, would have dealt with the review comments we received on our application. As Halford (2018, p. 17) suggests, it is only when researchers 'share experiences and explore the points of overlap and difference' in different disciplinary, institutional, and jurisdictional contexts that we 'develop our understanding of the ethical issues involved in using social media data' beyond outdated precedents and checklists. An additional step in this process is ongoing dialogue, communication, and relationship-building between administrators, ethics committees, and researchers.

DISCLOSURE STATEMENT

No conflict of interest was reported by the author. The author held the university's Human Ethics Committee Deputy Convenor role from May 2021 to May 2022 and the role of convenor from February 2022 to February 2025.

NOTES

1. While the term *trans* is used inclusively to include transgender and non-binary people who identify with a gender that is different than the sex they were assigned at birth, the author acknowledges that not all people use or relate to this term. The term 'cisgender' is used to refer to people who identify with the gender that corresponds to their sex assigned at birth.
2. Medical transition refers to accessing healthcare and medical treatment such as taking gender-affirming hormones or undergoing genital surgeries. These procedures may adversely affect fertility (Baram et al., 2019; Mattawanon et al., 2018).
3. Namely, the Human Ethics Committee of Te Herenga Waka–Victoria University of Wellington.

4. Our knowledge of this aspect of the ethics review process was based on our respective roles as applicants who had submitted many applications for research ethics approval. In the case of the lead investigator, this entailed ethics applications over the course of several decades and experience as a long-term member of the university ethics committee.

5. The original Te Tiriti o Waitangi (Treaty of Waitangi), signed in 1840, is Aotearoa New Zealand's founding document between Māori and the Crown.

6. This background study by the lead investigator began in 2018 and received university ethics clearance (application number: 0000024373). The study documents the views of fertility specialists, counsellors, legal scholars, bioethicists, and stakeholders about assisted reproduction, anticipatory technologies such as fertility preservation techniques, and perspectives on compensation and payment for reproductive materials and services.

7. In late 2021, when the lockdown periods were lifted, we returned to the interview study and talked with thirteen 18- to 30-year-old trans and non-binary individuals about their views and experiences of accessing fertility preservation in healthcare settings and their decision-making about future family formation (Ker & Shaw, 2024). The planned focus group discussions were abandoned, as we had reached the ethics approval end date for data collection and had begun work on other projects.

8. Unlike Australia and Canada, for example, human ethics policy review is set at the university level in Aotearoa New Zealand and while all institutional ethics committees must be accredited by the Health Research Council, there is no national ethics standard. Accordingly, the formats and organisational structure of ethics committees throughout Aotearoa New Zealand vary widely (Tolich et al., 2016).

9. The definition of human research used in our university policy is in line with the Australian *National Statement on Ethical Conduct in Human Research*, which says 'Human research is conducted with or about people, or their data or tissue' (National Health and Medical Research Council, 2023, p. 7).

10. The use of passive netnography (Kozinets, 2010) is a case in point.

ACKNOWLEDGEMENTS

Thank you to the FHSS Joint Research Committee at Te Herenga Waka–Victoria University of Wellington for funding the *Reproductive Futures* project (grant number: 224801).

REFERENCES

Akrich, M., Nunes, J., Paterson, F., & Rabeharisoa, V. (2008). *The dynamics of patient organizations in Europe* (pp. 13–82). Presses des Mines. https://books.openedition.org/pressesmines/1577?lang=en

Baram, S., Myers, S. A., Yee, S., & Librach, C. L. (2019). Fertility preservation for transgender adolescents and young adults: A systematic review. *Human Reproduction Update*, *25*(6), 694–716.

Bell, K., & Wynn, L. (2023). Research ethics committees, ethnographers and imaginations of risk. *Ethnography*, *24*(4), 537–558. https://doi.org/10.1177/1466138120983862

Berlant, L. (2008). *The female complaint: The unfinished business of sentimentality in American culture*. Duke University Press. https://www.dukeupress.edu/the-female-complaint

Bourke, B. (2014). Positionality: Reflecting on the researcher process. *The Qualitative Report*, *19*(33), 1–9. https://nsuworks.nova.edu/tqr/vol19/iss33/3/

Brown, C., Spiro, J., & Quinton, S. (2020). The role of research ethics committees: Friend or foe in educational research? An exploratory study. *British Educational Research Journal*, *46*(4), 747–769. https://bera-journals.onlinelibrary.wiley.com/doi/full/10.1002/berj.3654

Burles, M. C., & Bally, J. M. G. (2018). Ethical, practical, and methodological considerations for unobtrusive qualitative research about personal narratives shared on the internet. *International Journal of Qualitative Methods*, *17*(1), 1–9. https://journals.sagepub.com/doi/10.1177/1609406918788203

Carel, H. (2016). *Phenomenology of illness*. Oxford University Press.

Coleman, E., Radix, A. E., Bouman, W. P., Brown, G. R., De Vries, A. L. C., Deutsch, M. B., Ettner, R., Fraser, L., Goodman, M., Green, J., Hancock, A. B., Johnson, T. W., Karasic, D. H., Knudson,

G. A., Leibowitz, S. F., Meyer-Bahlburg, H. F. L., Monstrey, S. J., Motmans, J., Nahata, L., … & Arcelus, J. (2022). Standards of care for the health of transgender and gender diverse people, version 8. *International Journal of Transgender Health*, *23*(Suppl.), S1–S259. https://www.tandfonline.com/doi/full/10.1080/26895269.2022.2100644

Costley, C., & Gibbs, P. (2006). Researching others: Care as an ethic for practitioner researchers. *Studies in Higher Education*, *31*(1), 89–98. https://www.tandfonline.com/doi/abs/10.1080/03075070500392375

Dieterle, B. (2021). People as data? Developing an ethical framework for feminist digital research. *Computers and Composition*, *59*, 1–9.

Doucet, A., & Mauthner, N. (2008). Knowing responsibly: Linking ethics, research practice and epistemology. In M. Mauthner, M. Birch, J. Jessop, & T. Miller (Eds.), *Ethics in qualitative research* (pp. 123–145). Sage Publications.

Frankze, A. S., Bechmann, A., Zimmer, M., Ess, C., & the Association of Internet Researchers. (2020). *Internet research: Ethical guidelines 3.0*. https://aoir.org/reports/ethics3.pdf

Gibson, L., Mercier, O. R., & Kiddle, R. (2020). Engaging with 'that treaty question' on a university ethics committee in Aotearoa New Zealand. In L. George, J. Tauri, & L. Te Ata o Tu MacDonald (Eds.), *Indigenous research ethics: Claiming research sovereignty beyond deficit and the colonial legacy* (Vol. 6, pp. 95–108). Emerald Publishing.

Giles, D. (2017). Online discussion forums: A rich and vibrant source of data. In V. Braun, V. Clarke, & D. Gray (Eds.), *Collecting qualitative data: A practical guide to textual, media and virtual techniques* (pp. 189–210). Cambridge University Press.

Gosden, R. G. (2014). General principles of cryopreservation. In Z. Rosenwaks & P. M. Wassarman (Eds.), *Human fertility: Methods and protocols* (pp. 261–268). Springer.

Halford, S. (2018). The ethical disruptions of social media data: Tales from the field. In K. Woodfield (Ed.), *The ethics of online research* (Vol. 2) (pp. 13–25). Emerald Publishing.

Harrington, C. (2024). Making ethical judgement calls about qualitative social media research on sensitive issues. *International Journal of Social Research Methodology*, 1–10. https://doi.org/10.1080/13645579.2024.239376

Hennell, K., Limmer, M., & Piacentini, M. (2020). Ethical dilemmas using social media in qualitative social research: A case study of online participant observation. *Sociological Research Online*, *25*(3), 473–489. https://journals.sagepub.com/doi/10.1177/1360780419888933

Illouz, E. (2007). *Cold intimacies: The making of emotional capitalism*. Polity Press.

Jacobs, L., & Kelemi, A. (2020). Natural hair chronicles of black female vloggers: Influences on their psychological well-being. *Journal of Psychology in Africa*, *30*(4), 342–347. https://www.tandfonline.com/doi/full/10.1080/14330237.2020.1796046

Johnston, O., Wildy, H., & Shand, J. (2023). Student voices that resonate – Constructing composite narratives that represent students' classroom experiences. *Qualitative Research*, *23*(1), 108–124. https://journals.sagepub.com/doi/full/10.1177/14687941211016158

Ker, A., & Shaw, R. M. (2022). Exploring the experiential expertise of trans people's YouTube vlogs on fertility preservation. In R. M. Shaw (Ed.), *Reproductive citizenship: Technologies, rights and relationships* (pp. 75–100). Palgrave Macmillan.

Ker, A., & Shaw, R. M. (2024). Trans reproductive imaginaries: Access and barriers to fertility preservation and family creation. *LGBTQ+ Family: An Interdisciplinary Journal*, *20*(2), 140–155. https://www.tandfonline.com/doi/full/10.1080/27703371.2024.2304747

Kozinets, R. (2010). *Netnography: Doing ethnographic research online*. Sage.

Markham, A. (2012). Fabrication as ethical practice: Qualitative inquiry in ambiguous internet contexts. *Information, Communication and Society*, *15*(3), 334–353. https://www.tandfonline.com/doi/abs/10.1080/1369118X.2011.641993

Mattawanon, N., Spencer, J. B., Schirmer, D. A., & Tangpricha, V. (2018). Fertility preservation options in transgender people: A review. *Reviews in Endocrine and Metabolic Disorders*, *19*(3), 231–242.

National Health and Medical Research Council. (2023). *National statement on ethical conduct in human research*. National Health and Medical Research Council. https://www.nhmrc.gov.au/about-us/publications/national-statement-ethical-conduct-human-research-2023

Orbach, S. (2000). *The impossibility of sex*. Penguin.

Patterson, A. N. (2018). YouTube generated video clips as qualitative research data: One researcher's reflections on the process. *Qualitative Inquiry*, *24*(10), 759–767. https://journals.sagepub.com/doi/10.1177/1077800418788107

Radi, B. (2019). On trans epistemology: Critiques, contributions, and challenges. *Transgender Studies Quarterly*, *6*(1), 43–63.

Ravn, S., Barnwell, A., & Neves, B. N. (2019). What is "publicly available data"? Exploring blurred public-private boundaries and ethical practices through a case study on Instagram. *Journal of Empirical Research on Human Research Ethics*, *15*(1–2), 40–45. https://journals.sagepub.com/doi/full/10.1177/1556264619850736

Roberts, L. D. (2015). Ethical Issues in conducting qualitative research in online communities. *Qualitative Research in Psychology*, *12*, 314–325. https://www.tandfonline.com/doi/full/10.1080/14780887.2015.1008909

Schuman, D. L., Lawrence, K. A., & Pope, N. (2019). Broadcasting war trauma: An exploratory netnography of veterans' YouTube vlogs. *Qualitative Health Research*, *29*(3), 357–370. https://journals.sagepub.com/doi/abs/10.1177/1049732318797623?journalCode=qhra

Shaw, R. M. (2021, August 17). Egg freezing's equality problem. *Newsroom*. https://www.newsroom.co.nz/ideasroom/egg-freezings-equality-problem

Shaw, R. M., Howe, J., Beazer, J., & Carr, T. (2020). Ethics and positionality in qualitative research with vulnerable and marginal groups. *Qualitative Research*, *20*(3), 277–293. https://journals.sagepub.com/doi/abs/10.1177/1468794119841839?journalCode=qrja

Shaw, R. M., & Ker, A. (2024). Narratives of relationality and time in fertility preservation vlogs. *Feminist Media Studies*, *24*(3), 514–530. https://www.tandfonline.com/doi/full/10.1080/14680777.2023.2200591

Streed, C. G., Jr., Perlson, J. E., Abrams, M. P., & Lett, E. (2023). On, with, by – Advancing transgender health research and clinical practice. *Health Equity*, *7*(1), 162–165. https://doi.org/10.1089/heq.2022.0146

Tolich, M., Bathurst, R., Deckert, A., Flanagan, P., Gremillion, H., & Grimshaw, M. (2016). One size does not fit all: Organisational diversity in New Zealand tertiary sector ethics committees. *Kōtuitui: New Zealand Journal of Social Sciences Online*, *11*(1), 23–35. https://www.tandfonline.com/doi/full/10.1080/1177083X.2015.1035732

van de Wiel, L. (2020). *Freezing fertility: Oocyte cryopreservation and the gender politics of aging*. New York University Press.

Veale, J., Byrne, J., Tan, K., Guy, S., Yee, A., Nopera, T., & Bentham, R. (2019). *Counting ourselves: The health and wellbeing of trans and non-binary people in Aotearoa New Zealand*. Transgender Health Research Lab: University of Waikato. https://countingourselves.nz/2018-survey-report/

Victoria University of Wellington. (2019). *Human ethics policy*. https://www.wgtn.ac.nz/documents/policy/research-policy/human-ethics-policy.pdf

Waldby, C. (2015). "Banking time": Egg freezing and the negotiation of future fertility. *Culture, Health & Sexuality*, *17*(4), 470–482. https://www.tandfonline.com/doi/abs/10.1080/13691058.2014.951881

Wehling, P., Viehöver, W., & Koenen, S. (2015). Patient associations, health social movements and the public shaping of biomedical research: An introduction. In P. Wehling, W. Viehöver, & S. Koenen (Eds.), *The public shaping of medical research: Patient associations, health movements and biomedicine* (pp. 1–20). Routledge.

Willis, R. (2019). The use of composite narratives to present interview findings. *Qualitative Research*, *19*(4), 471–480. https://journals.sagepub.com/doi/10.1177/1468794118787711

Wilson, S. L. (2022). *Social media as social science data*. Cambridge University Press.

YouTube. (2019). *Terms of service*. https://www.youtube.com/t/terms?archive=20191210

CHAPTER 3

PEER RESEARCHERS IN QUALITATIVE RESEARCH ON HOMELESSNESS AND MENTAL HEALTH: A REFLEXIVE JOURNEY FROM DATA VALIDITY TO RELATIONS OF ETHICAL LABOUR

Nienke Boesveldt

University of Amsterdam, The Netherlands

ABSTRACT

Peer research, in which people with lived experience of the phenomenon under study participate as researchers, is growing in popularity, especially in the social and health sciences. While peer research is meant to democratise knowledge-making, enhance the validity of collected data, and help to gain access to hard-to-reach populations, its mainstreaming has introduced new challenges surrounding the co-optation of lived experience. This chapter reflects on an ongoing longitudinal research project on homelessness and mental health services in the Netherlands, in which pairs of academic and peer researchers have, to date, conducted 956 interviews with people with client experience of these services. A randomised subsample of 30 interviews was coded specifically to analyse peer research methodology and its impact on data validity as well as

Reframing Qualitative Research Ethics
Advances in Research Ethics and Integrity, Volume 12, 37–56

ISSN: 2398-6018/doi:10.1108/S2398-601820250000012003

the daily ethical dimensions of a research project involving vulnerable participants. This chapter analyses the interview strategies, including 'self-disclosure' and 'establishing common ground', of members of our research team as well as the benefits and challenges of doing peer research as they unfold in intersecting relations of ethical labour. Writing this prompted beneficial reflection on the extent to which striving for data validity is compatible with the aim of peer research to achieve social justice. While the team offers training, support, and feedback sessions to reflect on interviewing practice, is this enough? It is my hope that the additional value of peer research is evident in this chapter. Still, I wish to highlight that peer research requires additional institutional support and is not for 'free'.

Keywords: Expert by experience; homelessness; peer researcher; research ethics in practice; community-based research practice

INTRODUCTION

Peer research requires collaboration with people from different walks of life and reflection on one's positionality, responsibilities, and assumptions about what research entails. All came into play in the writing of this chapter: starting as an inquiry into the validity of data produced by peer research, it morphed into a more reflexive account of employing peer researchers in a longitudinal research project on homelessness and sheltered living as well as the possibilities and challenges presented by this methodology.

Involving Community Members and Peers in Research

The past two decades have witnessed growing recognition of the value of experiential knowledge in processes of recovery, in implementing social policy, and in social scientific and health research (Devotta et al., 2016; Fortuna et al., 2022; Voronka, 2019). The engagement of community members is the animating idea behind community-based (participatory) research (Israel et al., 1998), which generally aims to involve groups that have historically been excluded from 'knowledge-making'. Peer involvement in research – in short, 'peer research' – involves people with lived experience of the group or phenomenon being studied in various stages of the research process. By bringing lived experience into the research setting, peer research potentially challenges the role of the neutral researcher who objectively collects data and does not interfere in the lives of research participants as well as the underlying positivist paradigm that assumes an objective reality and knowledge about this reality (Israel et al., 1998).

Community-based research often has emancipatory goals. Committed to benefiting participants 'either through direct intervention or by using the results to inform action for change' (Israel et al., 1998, p. 175), it strives to democratise knowledge-making. Community-based peer research has also been lauded for offering capacity building and financial opportunities to people from marginalised communities. Since it is undertaken by, or together with, people with lived experience, the method can also improve research access to hard-to-reach populations (Elliott et al., 2002; Warr et al., 2011).

Peer researchers often play key roles in recruiting participants; they can also more easily handle sensitive issues that arise during qualitative research on subjects such as homelessness and mental health (Devotta et al., 2016; Elliott et al., 2002). Much has been written about the ethical dilemmas that accompany the raising of sensitive issues in interviews, especially among researchers who also have a counselling profession (cf. Johnson & Clarke, 2003). DeWalt and DeWalt (2002), for instance, emphasise the need to protect the scientific integrity of the interview by not offering help to research participants. While supportive of this view, Johnson and Clarke (2003) detail the many ethical dilemmas researchers struggle with when pursuing research among vulnerable participants.

Peer researchers commonly have three implicit tasks: the disclosure of personal experience and undertaking of emotional labour and (often) advocacy (Devotta et al., 2016; Edwards & Alexander, 2011). Their involvement in the research process spans the collection and analysis of data, especially the contextualisation of findings (Devotta et al., 2016). One article in which a group of peer researchers analysed data from a larger study focused on the 'messy text' that would have been overlooked in non-peer research (Voronka et al., 2014, p. 257); the discussion suggests that peer researchers, with appropriate and adequate resources, are often better placed to access and analyse data on sensitive or emotional topics that can be inaccessible to research teams that do not include experts by experience. Peer research thus interrogates the role of the researcher in qualitative research.

Several scholars have written about the ethical challenges of working with peer researchers (Banks et al., 2013; Devotta et al., 2016; Greene, 2013; Greene et al., 2009; Guta et al., 2013). Recurrent concerns include unequal power relations, the precarity of their labour, uneven financial compensation, and insufficient support from academic researchers and universities.

Mainstreaming Peer Work and Research

Peer work has become increasingly mainstream in mental health services as well as in policy-making and research. The recovery movement, which grew out of the 'patient' movement of the 1980s, advocated for involving people with experiential expertise in systems of care (Voronka, 2017). Although peer work grew out of this movement to challenge dominant practices in mental health and social services, Voronka, who identifies as a peer researcher, now argues that peer workers have become part of the system governing clients. She writes: 'the meaning and practice of recovery and peer support are significantly recalibrated when they move from "movements" into "models", and such models [...] are absorbed into dominant mental health practices' (Voronka, 2017, p. 334). As peer work becomes mainstream, it runs the risk of losing its emancipatory and transformative goals. Voronka even argues that peer work has become a way to manage madness and to make it marketable. There is a body of literature specifically dealing with the pros and cons of mainstreaming innovations. Here I find the concept of isomorphism (Di Maggio & Powel, 1983) helpful, since this literature deals with the phenomenon that 'once a set of organizations emerges as a field, a paradox arises: rational actors make their organizations increasingly similar as they try to change them' (p. 147). In this way, it also describes the upscaling of initiatives such as peer work well, noting that this may come with some good things, like the importance of acknowledgement or acquired income. It also accounts for risk, like the pressure of legal frameworks and professional norms from the for-profit private or public sectors being imposed. These tensions are clearly visible in the mainstreaming of peer work.

Similar considerations arise in peer research, where the goals of capacity building and empowering community-based researchers risk becoming instruments of governance. Like other peer workers, and peer researchers, being able to contribute through their lived experiences and relate to those of the respondents adds a specific value to the data collected and the expertise in the research team (Guta et al., 2013). Lived experiences of distress are thereby instrumentalised to enhance research. Training or capacity building is not always pursued in dialogue with peer researchers, which means it does not always align with their interests, thereby undermining the emancipatory aims of peer research (Greene et al., 2009; Guta et al., 2013).

A further challenge in working with peer researchers is the risk of essentialising or homogenising the diversity of experience (Devotta et al., 2016; Greene et al., 2009; Guta et al., 2013; Voronka, 2016). Peer researchers of course bring a wide range of experiences and positionalities to their work. Greene et al. (2009) note that the identity of the peer researcher is complex and that they are not always 'insiders' in the hard-to-reach populations, since this is influenced by a number of factors such as history of community involvement and experience of one's self; the boundary between 'insider' and 'outsider' – for both peer and academic researchers – is fluid. Maintaining the distinction between academic and peer researcher can also 'unintentionally strengthen the problematic "us" and "them" assumptions of biomedical psychiatry' (Tseris et al., 2022, p. 719), once again casting the peer researcher in the role of the 'other'. This point will appear highly relevant in this chapter, where I will show why the ostensible binary opposition of peer versus academic researcher may be ultimately unattainable.

We have seen above how involving community members and peers in research has become a more commonly used approach, improving research access to hard-to-reach populations and to some extent democratising knowledge-making. At the same time, peer research potentially challenges the role of the neutral researcher. We see mainstreaming peer work and research identifying a need for appropriate and adequate resources to support peer research. Scholars have also identified a risk of instrumentalisation of peer researchers and their lived experience in scientific research. This may interfere with the interests of peer researchers, for example, by homogenising the diversity of experience or explicitly casting the peer researcher in the role of the 'other'. In the above, it has been well illustrated how focusing solely on the outcome of research and not on the process of the research risks overlooking some of the strengths and weaknesses of peer research (Guta et al., 2014). In what follows, I will formulate answers to the question as to how exactly strategies deployed by peer researchers in interviews may affect the validity of the obtained data as well as the ethical process of conducting research. To better understand this question, I analyse data from a peer research project on homelessness and sheltered living in the Netherlands.

METHOD

Participatory Research in the Netherlands

Participatory research, in which community members including peers participate in research, is becoming more common in the Netherlands, although it primarily takes place outside of universities. Several projects involving peer researchers in the Netherlands are discussed in a recent PhD thesis on the ethics of participatory health research (Groot-Sluijsmans, 2021). While the Netherlands Institute for Health Services Research has made the participation of stakeholders, including those making use of health services, one of its criteria for relevance,[1] to date its website only mentions education and training, not research, as peer-to-peer activities. Community-based research in the Netherlands suffers from a lack of continuity and possibilities for tenure for peer researchers. Groot-Sluijsmans (2021) describes the development of peer research in the country, in partnership with health institutions and service-user organisations. She writes:

> [...] in The Netherlands, most academics are not educated in the practice of involving people with lived experiences in research. There are only a few workshops that train researchers how to involve people in this way, and these tend to focus on practical knowledge and tips and tricks. Rather than draw on an established methodology, most academics practice with an approach based on trial and error. (pp. 10–11)

Although universities are well-positioned to – and would benefit from – supporting peer research, this rarely happens. As a result, research in the Netherlands has yet to address the involvement of peer researchers in research settings.

A Longitudinal Project on Homelessness and Mental Health

Our longitudinal research project on homelessness and sheltered living in several Dutch regions was initiated and led by the author of this chapter. Between 2018 and 2022, a total of 956 semi-structured interviews[2] were conducted by pairs of academic and peer researchers.[3] Most of the academic researchers and one peer researcher were employed by the university, while others were interns.

Peer researchers have 'lived experience' of the issues or systems being studied. In our project, peer researchers have lived experience of homelessness, sheltered living, and/or use of mental health services. Some have been part of the project since 2018; some joined later while others have since left. At the time of writing, nine peer researchers are active in the project. Upon joining, they participate in a specially designed training programme covering the basic principles of research and interviewing as well as the ethical dilemmas often encountered over the course of research. The entire research team regularly participates in these training sessions as well as in intervision, which entails taking part in intercollegiate meetings led by an outside mediator and focused on personal dilemmas encountered at work. Individual peer researchers also take part in the university's executive programmes for professionals on 'Homelessness and Mental Health' as well as a second programme on 'Mental Health Innovations in the Social Domain'. The aim here is to transfer knowledge to team members and to create professional opportunities beyond their volunteer work as peer researchers.

The primary task of peer researchers in our project is to conduct interviews with people with experience of homelessness and/or sheltered living. Part of the protocol for interviewing is that peer researchers themselves decide on self-disclosure, which can also mean they only mention being an expert at the beginning of the interview. Additionally, peer researchers are involved, to varying degrees, in other stages of the research. While our project most closely aligns with what Roche et al. (2010) call the 'employment model' in which peer researchers participate in various stages of research, the peer researchers in our project (with a single exception) are not employed by the university but work as volunteers in the project. They have volunteer agreements with the university and receive allowances in line with Dutch law.[4]

Analysis

A simple randomised sample of 30 interviews was selected for the purpose of analysing the methodology of working with peer researchers. Inclusion criteria were a peer interviewer being present during the interview and the participant giving consent that their data be used for other research. The focus of this analysis was on the strategies of peer researchers, academic researchers, and participants. We also looked at the dynamic among these three groups to see exactly how the strategies used by peer researchers in interviews may affect the validity of the obtained data, as well as the ethical process of conducting research.

The transcripts of these interviews were coded using Atlas.ti version 22. A total of 8 main codes and 55 subcodes were developed inductively. After 15 interviews, we developed an initial outline of the most prominent codes, which we used for the remaining 15 interviews. As additional codes including self-disclosure, experiences with support services, recognition, and compliments still emerged, a second round of coding ensured that all interviews were coded using the same coding outline. Several academic researchers, including the author, were involved in this process to ensure intercoder reliability. When relevant, audio files of the interviews allowed us to include tone of voice and laughter in the analysis, although nonverbal cues such as body language remain absent. Analysis focused on the interactions between peer researchers and research participants and the strategies of peer researchers in the interviews to use their knowledge of the experience being researched – in this case, of homelessness.

Guta et al. (2013, p. 443) argue that the mainstreaming of community-based peer research, especially in public health, can be at odds with its emancipatory goals as community engagement and social justice often take a backseat to administrative and financial constraints. When this happens, 'lived experience' can become an administrative box to tick rather than a meaningful engagement with experiential knowledge. Reflexivity – better understanding how the researcher's presence and influence construct research and knowledge (Finlay, 2002) – is key to peer research (Devotta et al., 2016), while paying attention to its day-to-day ethical dilemmas strengthens this. To this end, I analysed the sampled interviews within the everyday reality of the research project. Here I relied on my own diary, the personal experiences of other team members, documents produced by the university's ethics review board and research team members, and an additional interview with one of our peer researchers participating in one of the university's executive programmes for professionals.

RESULTS

Analysis of the strategies and dynamics in 30 interviews found that peer researchers frequently relied on specific strategies of 'self-disclosure' and 'establishing common ground' to encourage research participants to share information, specifically on sensitive topics such as trauma, the impact of homelessness, and the difficulties of recovery. Also, some academic researchers were found to be disclosing their lived experiences, showcasing the porous boundaries between roles in the project. Still, another strategy was observed that blocked participants from sharing their stories, negotiating validation. This section elaborates on these strategies, their strengths, as well as weaknesses. I further situate these strategies in the context of the research project, the dilemmas encountered in peer research, and academic intervision.

Self-disclosure

Some form of explicit or implicit self-disclosure is expected of peer researchers (Ibáñez-Carrasco et al., 2019). Practices here vary greatly (Guta et al., 2013). Some regularly mention their personal experiences during interviews; others state that they are peer researchers in the introduction and rarely share personal experiences thereafter.

Self-disclosure commences with the introductions at the start of each interview. These introductions are not always included in the transcripts as they often occur before consent is given and recording begins. Peer researchers always disclose that they are present in the role of peer researcher, sometimes offering specifics about their experiences with mental health care or homelessness. Following the introduction, only in a few instances was there direct mention of the experiences or position of the peer researcher. One participant responded to the peer researcher's introduction: 'Yes, well, beautiful. Good that you want to help people. Wonderful'. Another participant also responded with praise: 'Wow, that's good, you turned it around well'. More often, interviews proceeded and participants began to introduce themselves.

In the introduction phase of the interview, academic researchers usually mention their qualifications to establish themselves as scientific researchers. This is in line with expectations in the literature and possibly with those of research participants (cf. DeWalt & DeWalt, 2002; Johnson & Clarke, 2003). But peer research challenges the role of the scientific researcher as a neutral observer. Our sample of interviews contained an instance of an academic researcher, after introducing the study, mentioning that she is visually impaired: 'So that's what I do and I also always tell people that I'm visually impaired, so that I work slightly differently from my colleagues'. The participant's response was very positive: 'Well, I think it's very clever what you're doing', 'you are a go-getter', 'and you're probably good at it too, what more could you want?' Both peer and academic researchers received praise for their work.

Peer researchers at times explicitly talked about their personal experiences. In one interview, peer researcher James interviewed Raymond together with an academic researcher; the academic researcher kept track of the topic list while James delved deeper into specific topics such as help with finances to encourage free-flowing conversation. At the time of the interview, Raymond was 'couch surfing' and was receiving support from a specialised care organisation to search for a home. Towards the end of the interview, James asks Raymond whether he thinks he will need support once he has a place of his own. Raymond responds that he will not, but that the Dutch system forces him to accept support to gain access to social services. James responds:

> This is why I asked, Raymond. I recognize much in the way you experience and look at things [...] The question I just asked you, whether you will need support when you have a house of your own; if I would have been asked that question at the time, I would have, with the knowledge I have about myself now, answered: I need to learn to structure my finances and household.

James continues by offering an example of how old patterns continue to reverberate in his current life. Raymond responds by saying that he understands what James means and returns to an earlier question about his social network. He also elaborates on his previous answer about not needing support, that he would prefer if possible to remain with his current social worker as he trusts her and she motivates him. James 'cashes in' on the rapport that has been building over the course of the interview and shares something personal, hoping it will resonate with Raymond and create transparency in the how and why of his questioning. Raymond responds to James' disclosure by deepening his answers.

Researchers sometimes mention their own experiences to support or empower the participant. In this example, James' decision to disclose a personal story can be seen as an effort to motivate Raymond to consider using support services once he is securely housed. Peer researchers are often motivated by a drive for social and political justice and by empathy for research participants, which may result in wanting to improve their lives (Greene et al., 2009, p. 370). Indeed, peer researchers sometimes struggle to *not* offer help or advice (Devotta et al., 2016).

Some peer researchers in our project are also peer workers in organisations where they directly support clients, while several academic researchers have a professional background in social work or mental health care. Both academic and peer researchers in the project thus regularly encounter questions of whether, when, and to what extent to offer support to participants. While academic researchers have generally had more training to reflect on their role as researchers, maintaining distance and refraining from interfering in their participants' lives, these themes are also covered in our training sessions for peer researchers. Indeed, most researchers struggle with these issues and bring them up in team meetings, training sessions, and intervision.

Porous Boundaries Between Roles in the Project

The role of academic researcher does not require the self-disclosure of personal experience. Nevertheless, the sampled interviews included two instances of academic researchers disclosing their lived experiences. Such self-disclosure by academic researchers suggests that the binary opposition of peer and academic researcher can be misleading. During interviews, academic researchers use the same strategies – self-disclosure, naming recognition, acknowledging participants' experiences, diverging from the interview guide – although in general they do so less frequently. Academic researchers are also motivated in their work by lived experience. While their experiences and how they affect interactions with research participants of course differs between individuals, neither peer nor academic researcher is a clear-cut identity and role. Although academic researchers may disclose their lived experiences to close colleagues during the training programme as well as during interviews, this is rare. When it happens during interviews, academic researchers do the work that comes with being a peer researcher. But more often, this role in the team is explicitly accorded to the peer researcher.

On several occasions, the academic members of our team were warned by their teachers or colleagues – including by scholars with experiential expertise – not to go public with their personal experiences, in large part to 'safeguard scientific objectivity'. At other times, the researchers in question were deemed academic oddities and risked being recognised in their careers for their experiential expertise alone, which they objected to. One team member, who is often supported by the university's communications department in interacting with outside media, asked for advice to the communications department on how they would see this member going public. The response from this department was: Where do you draw the line of the personal? How do you prevent it from only being about your background? and How do you safeguard scientific objectivity?

The ostensible duality of peer and academic researchers, that appeared to be less clear-cut, was both challenged and confirmed by the set-up of the research project. While the valuing of experiential knowledge motivated the team to involve peer researchers in the study, its institutional questioning (safeguarding scientific objectivity, risking being seen as an academic oddity, or attention only being about this background) has led our academic researchers with experiential knowledge to downplay the personal to safeguard their careers.

Establishing Common Ground

While the previous examples of self-disclosure were initiated by interviewers, establishing common ground is a form of self-disclosure that generally happens in response to something expressed by the participant. In what follows, I discuss an example of a peer researcher more directly responding to something mentioned by the participant. Peer researchers frequently express recognition about daily concerns, such as being bothered by a neighbour who plays a musical instrument, sharing a certain taste in music, having a past job in common, or having children and worrying about them. Although academic researchers sometimes also share such moments of recognition, in our sample of interviews, they did so less often than peer researchers. This again points to the different roles in the interviews, with peer researchers having greater liberty to diverge from the interview guide. Moreover, minimal self-disclosure is part of the peer researcher's job, meaning they will be required to share information about themselves, e.g. about being a peer researcher, to establish connection with participants based on shared experience.

In the following example, the peer interviewer sought to establish common ground with a participant to make him more comfortable and to deepen the conversation. Struggling to explain why he still needs therapy, the participant gradually falls into silence. The academic interviewer asks whether he is still all right. The peer researcher then intervenes, joking by asking about last night's dinner and that he'll check with the chef. All three begin laughing out loud, releasing some of the built-up tension. The peer interviewer then resumes the interview by recounting an experience of his own:

Peer researcher:	But I understand, when you've experienced psychosis somewhere and you don't feel comfortable there, I would … For instance, I once had an anxiety attack at Zeeman [a retail clothing store] and collapsed and sat there for one and a half hours. So I never go to Zeeman anymore. I can't go in there …
Participant:	Yes, that area is just …
Peer researcher:	Yes.
Participant:	And then something happens. It can be colours, I can be smells …
Peer researcher:	Yes, it can be smells, yes.

This passage is a callback to the participant's narrative on avoiding spaces where he had previously experienced crises. Throughout the interview, both the academic and peer researcher are sensitive to the participant's predicament, never expressing judgement. By sharing the experience of not wanting to re-enter a space that holds traumatic memory, the peer researcher validates the participant's experience and creates rapport between them. The participant continues to disclose feeling dissatisfied with himself and the need to recover, for his own good and that of his daughter. Devotta et al. (2016, p. 669) describe peer research as a challenging craft, which is fully on display in this interview: the peer researcher employs humour, personal experience, and sensitivity to help the participant feel safe enough to tell his story.

Participants' experiences with the social or (mental) health services and complaints about waiting lists for services and treatment were often met with recognition by peer researchers. For instance, participants and peer researchers often shared their experiences of staying in night shelters and the insecurity of such unstable living arrangements. Sharing such experiences and expressing recognition can build rapport, create a sense of safety in interviews, and offer validation to participants. In one interview, the participant talked about the constant changes in institutions, shelters, and available support. It is a difficult interview; the participant carries a lot of trauma and the peer researcher struggles to find common ground as their lives have unfolded in very different ways. At one point, the peer researcher states that he recognises the impact of constantly having to move: 'I really feel that, Mark. I had that for one and a half years. From crisis shelter to crisis shelter. One and a half years. In every place you could stay, six or three months, at most'. The participant responds by stating that these changes are not normal, that constantly encountering new people and places is draining. The academic researcher responds with 'While you desire a little stability', which the participant affirms, saying that he is now content to be in a place where he can stay for longer. In this case, the peer and academic researcher together are able to facilitate conversation on the impact of unstable housing by validating the participant's critique. Like the previous example, it shows interviewing to be a craft, with peer interviewers holding the difficult task of sensing when it is suitable to share personal experiences and when to further probe participants.

Peer researchers also risk becoming too directive through their comments about policy, society, or the public services. We see this in an interview with a lot of interaction between the peer researcher and participant. The participant repeatedly expresses recognition of the peer researcher and his lived experience; they find common ground throughout the interview. At one point, the participant is detailing his negative experiences in a certain shelter, of how things are organised there, to which the peer researcher repeatedly responds: 'It shouldn't be like that', which the participant acknowledges. The peer researcher's focus on how things should be – and how the participant's experiences contradict policy – while possibly experienced as validations, may have deterred the participant from sharing further details about his experience. At one point, the peer researcher asks: 'What was your name there? Number so many?', referring to the sense clients sometimes have of being treated like numbers rather than persons by the social or health services. The participant replies by stating that he was 'Victor'. This question by the peer researcher can be seen as leading the participant's narrative, blurring the nuance in his experience. These examples again illustrate the risk of assuming common ground or a shared interpretation of experience.

Negotiating Validation

In the interviews, peer as well as academic researchers often offer acknowledgement to participants, for instance, stating that they understand an experience must have been hard. Such acknowledgement can take the form of compliments, for instance, that they are impressed by how the participant has dealt with a situation. While acknowledgement and compliments can function as prompts for participants to keep talking as well as to help them feel safe enough to share their stories, there were a few occasions when compliments seemed to block participants from sharing their stories. This could entail an interviewer assuming how a participant experienced an event – instances that can be seen as undermining the interview's validity. In the passage below, the peer researcher compliments the participant on becoming the chair of a client council:

Peer researcher:	A beautiful step forwards.
Participant:	Yes, definitely.
Peer researcher:	A good step for yourself also. That must give you a good feeling, right?
Participant:	I want to deliver good work.
Peer researcher:	You apparently do so, because otherwise you wouldn't be chair, right?
Participant:	No, that's right.

In the above passage the peer researcher assumes what the participant must be feeling about his new position ('it must give a good feeling') and then checks this assumption with him. The participant replies that he wants to deliver good work, suggesting he may harbour insecurities about this topic or that his feelings about the new position are ambiguous. But rather than using this comment as a prompt for further inquiry, another compliment follows. The trail of compliments arguably hampers the conversation and leaves insufficient space for the participant to delve into his experience. Towards the end of the interview, the subject of work resurfaces. The participant states that while he receives compliments about his work as chair, he wants to do more and would prefer a paid job. The peer researcher assures him that his current work is worthwhile and that it must be a 'boost'. The participant keeps repeating that he wants something more, which the peer researcher acknowledges by expressing hope that he will find a job that suits him. In this interview, repeated reassurances and compliments by the peer researcher may have obscured the participant's negative or difficult feelings.

Space for Feedback and Learning

This last example emphasises the need for training and intervision on open, curiosity-driven research skills. During training sessions, researchers discuss interview transcripts to improve their skills; how to best ask open questions is a recurring theme. Besides regular training, intervision, and team meetings, academic and peer researcher debrief after interviews, discussing what they heard and experienced, what went well, and what could be improved. But it is not always easy to give feedback to fellow researchers, a process complicated by the dynamics between different roles in the project. Academic researchers were at times hesitant to offer critical feedback to peer researchers, which requires skills that not everybody is trained in. When an interviewing pair is newly established, they are still building trust and getting to know each other, which makes it more difficult to have open debriefing sessions. Academic researchers sometimes do not want to burden peer researchers with feedback, especially since they work in the project as volunteers.

Pointing to the positive dimensions in participants' stories, for instance, through compliments, is one way to deal with the emotional intensity of the interviews. Participants' stories can be tragic and hard to process for both peer and academic researchers. In such situations, debriefing is a much-needed opportunity to emotionally process what was said during the interview.

Intersecting Relations of Ethical Labour

We begin this section with a vignette from a conversation between one of our peer colleagues and a (former) team member:

> I just keep it concrete and say, 'I'm an expert by experience and I work for FACT', and that is enough. Very occasionally, they tell us something and then I think, okay, it would be functional to refer to my own experience. I then tell them and that builds a bridge. Very occasionally I get background stories from people in advance and if I see that someone has been in a women's shelter, I tell them that I have worked in such a shelter. If I see that someone has been addicted, I tell them that I have also been addicted.
>
> Usually, if you say you're an expert by experience, they already know that your role has changed, that you have gone through recovery, and that you've been where not everyone else has been, you know? That already creates a bond. Then you already have something reciprocal. That's what such a conversation should be: a kind of reciprocity. You show vulnerability and then they trust you and show you some of their vulnerability back. 'Expert by experience' is very abstract. It's just like the reciprocity that we have with people, that people feel. It's just as difficult to explain to someone what humour is or what love is.
>
> I think it's a perfect combination, because I notice that a lot of people, once you start talking, like to tell their story. There's indignation or sadness in it and they can express that to us, without having to be afraid of anything. Then I notice that they like the fact that there is an expert by experience, and then they think: okay, there is a bit of reciprocity and familiarity in that, but also that there is, let's say, this sounds very strange, but a 'normal' person who is interested and wants to hear their story.

Peer researchers perform emotional labour to make participants feel at ease and comfortable enough to share their story (Hardt & Negri, 2004; Voronka, 2017). While interviewing can be emotionally draining for academic and peer researchers alike, for peer researchers, the stories often hit closer to home.

The above vignette shows that peer researchers practise self-disclosure in different ways. Our colleague above prefers to keep things 'concrete' by mentioning at the outset that she is an expert by experience and then only occasionally referring to her own experiences thereafter. She feels that sharing such personal information creates a bond of reciprocity with participants and appreciates the method of working in pairs consisting of a peer and academic researcher. The peer researcher creates reciprocity and familiarity, while the academic researcher is the 'normal' person whose openness to hearing the participant's story validates it.

Academic and peer researchers also often enter into relations of reciprocity. The continuation of the above vignette illustrates this in a telling way:

> I've heard so many sad stories. It sounds really lame, but I've become kind of immune to them. I've had one or two occasions where I just thought about it a bit. Then the two of us talked about it for a while and it was fine.

> I think it's the best work I've ever done. I wish it really was a normal job. I'm learning a lot, so there's a lot of knowledge transfer. I can go to conferences and meetings, so yes, I think that's really great. Yes, I'm really someone who is always very hungry for knowledge, so I try to absorb as much as possible.

> We are, so to speak, driven and we like it. Otherwise, most of the people I know say: 'I'm not going to do that for nothing'. And especially because it used to carry a bit of stigma. Experts by experience would come for a candy bar and a bouquet of flowers, you know? Yes, they want to get rid of that stigma.

Saara Greene (2013) observes that although academic researchers generally acknowledge the emotional risks of participating in research, this is less the case for the risks run by peer researchers. Greene calls on her fellow academics who work with peer researchers to better understand how they benefit from the emotional labour of community members, what impact emotional labour has on peer researchers, and their ethical and moral responsibility towards peer researchers, including supporting them in this role (Greene, 2013, p. 146).

While practices such as debriefing after interviews allow reflection and emotionally processing of what was said and heard, Greene argues that measures such as organising training and debriefing sessions only take the edge off more pernicious problems (Greene, 2013, p. 147). The gratitude expressed to her by one of her peer colleagues clearly revealed the imbalance of risks and benefits. While this colleague benefited from her peer research work in that she found it therapeutic and felt valued and appreciated, she ran considerable risks due to her position, with insider knowledge and being placed in situations rife with conflicts of interest (Greene, 2013, p. 145).

Our peer colleague had a different balance sheet, one with many benefits and no risks. She can attend meetings and conferences while she has developed 'immunity' to sad stories, while our practice of working in pairs enables immediate debriefing following interviews. At the same time, she wishes she could do this work as a normal job. Her reference to the refusal of other peer researchers to work voluntarily may be an indirect critique of the unpaid nature of her work. Either way, is it fair that an 'expert by experience' is rewarded with a candy bar and a bouquet of flowers? Academic researchers involve experts by experience in their research not only because they are committed to capacity building and social change but to gain privileged access to hard-to-reach populations (Greene, 2013, p. 142). Peer and academic researchers enter a web of intersecting relations with each other and with research participants; all need to be recognised as relations of ethical labour.

Working Out Procedural Ethics

Maintaining the 'privacy' of research participants was a central concern in the university's ethical guidelines. Members of the research ethics committee (REC) were especially concerned that research participants and peer researchers residing in the same city might know each other:

> It seems important that they (peer-researchers) come from the same place as the respondents. If that is the case, they may already know each other, or they may meet again later. This may not be desirable for privacy reasons. (Research Ethics Committee, 2018)

It was thus agreed that peer researchers would not interview participants in their city of residence. This had four negative consequences for our research. First, peer researchers' knowledge of the local context was lost, thereby undermining one of the primary reasons to work with peer researchers in the first place. Second, the agreement complicated established bureaucratic procedures, in this case concerning travel costs; one peer researcher ended her involvement in the project when the university administration provided wrong information to the tax office, which set off a highly stressful chain of events. The third was that a peer researcher who when he was himself homeless at the time resorted to using homeless services in almost any large Dutch municipality. Every other night, he would use the phonebook to call night shelters in other cities to ask if they had a place to stay that night. So, this researcher felt he would not be able to interview anywhere. Fourth, a peer interviewer who had been part of our team for three years conducting interviews in a given region moved to that region; he was formally no longer allowed to be involved in follow-up interviews.

Universities surmounting such administrative barriers through more tailored agreements with peer researchers would show some genuine appreciation for their efforts. But given the lack of flexibility and recognition of the bandwidth within which choices are made in daily practice, our team members only experienced the demands of the university's ethical review as a hindrance to research and collaboration. Ideally, the committee would simultaneously take a more distant stance and contribute to strengthening the team's everyday knowledge of ethical issues in research.

Morgan et al. (2023) describe how they worked with their institutional research ethics board to ensure that their workshops for peer research assistants met the necessary requirements. Our team training programme for both peer and academic researchers, developed by this chapter's author and an external advisor, focuses on basic principles of research and interviewing as well as on ethical dilemmas that can be encountered over the course of research. Developing this training in collaboration with the university's research ethics board would have guaranteed meeting changing institutional requirements as well as the practical needs of the team in pursuing research.

Reflecting on ethical guidelines is part of an ongoing process of training and intervision. Prompted by an incident and a training session on the extent to which peer researchers should offer support or counsel participants outside of interview settings, a recent meeting of four peer and academic researchers discussed ethical dilemmas posed by suicidal participants, the offering of advice during interviews, and how to respond to participants asking for help. The meeting led to an open discussion, with the range of viewpoints illustrating the importance of having these conversations. The meeting deepened mutual understanding and brought up more questions.

The meeting led to a preliminary framework for addressing ethical dilemmas, delineating a 'lower limit' (answering questions, staying friendly) and an 'upper limit' for researchers to become involved in the life of research participants (participants remain responsible for their own lives, researchers remain researchers and do not become social workers). Both limits are deliberately vague as not all situations can be codified. Our approach here aligns with that of relationship-based ethics, central to community-based research, which focuses on building relationships and trust (Banks et al., 2013). Banks et al. (2013) describe a process of 'everyday ethics' which acknowledges the 'dialectical tension between impartial principles and rules and the responsibilities that arise from relationships of trust and care and a commitment to working for a better world' (p. 274). Our aim is for the project's ethical framework to be a 'living document' that can facilitate further discussion of the many dilemmas encountered in conducting research among vulnerable persons.

Since all research ethics training to date has come from within the team, responsibility for the issues arising from the project remains with the team. While we have done our best to develop an ethical framework for research within the project, we are limited in our ability to review our own work. Here it would be helpful if the university's ethical review committee would, beyond focusing on the integrity of data, support the everyday ethics of doing research (cf. Carpenter, 2018).

CONCLUSION

This chapter critically examined the employment of peer researchers in a longitudinal research project on homelessness and sheltered living in the Netherlands. To analyse the possibilities and challenges of this methodology, we analysed a subsample of 30 interviews from this larger ongoing project, focusing on questions of both process and practical ethics.

We found that research participants appreciated the disclosure of personal experiences by both peer and academic researchers, which helped to build rapport and gain participants' trust in the interviews. The establishing of common ground by peer researchers – including their experiences of using the social or (mental) health services – validated participants' experiences, while the use of humour helped participants to feel safe enough to tell their stories. Devotta and colleagues see the demanding work of peer researchers – 'to be neutral yet personable, while using their discretion to go off script' (2016, p. 669) – as a craft, with peer interviewers responsible for sensing when it is suitable to share personal experiences and when to further probe participants.

Within this demanding craft, peer researchers run the risk of being too directive in their comments about policy, society, or the public services. In such instances, peer researchers can lead participant narratives and miss or blur the nuance in participants' experiences. Given the diverse intersections that shape individual experience, one risk is too easily assuming a commonality or a shared understanding of individual experience. Although acknowledging participants' experiences in interviews can help them to feel safe and encourage them to keep talking, we found that too readily offering a barrage of affirmations and compliments (arguably to place the researcher at ease) could get in the way of participants sharing their stories.

The motivation of researchers to disclose their personal experiences was often rooted in empathy for research participants and the wish to support or empower them. Peer researchers in particular struggled at times *not* to offer help or advice (cf. Devotta et al., 2016). Note, however, that in the analysed interviews, it was not only peer researchers who disclosed personal information or offered support, the institutional barriers towards being open about one's experiential knowledge as an academic notwithstanding. All this points to the conclusion that the binary opposition of peer versus academic researcher is ultimately unattainable.

This conclusion here is based on this particular research and not on specific other studies. The critical feminist literature has already successfully argued for 'Situated Knowledges' (Haraway, 1988). On the other hand, there have been experiences on several occasions, of academic team members, being warned by their teachers or colleagues – including by scholars with experiential expertise – not to go public with their personal experiences. This hints both at the widespread extent of relevant lived experience among academics and at the tenacious nature of this binary divide.

Peer and academic researchers engage in a web of intersecting, reciprocal relations, both with each other and with research participants. The ethical dimension of these relationships needs to be recognised. Peer researchers perform emotional labour to make research participants feel at ease, comfortable enough to share their stories (Hardt & Negri, 2004; Voronka, 2017). It is vital that academic researchers support their peer researcher colleagues in this role, and that power dynamics are acknowledged and discussed. While the ability to offer mutual feedback is crucial for the quality of research and collaboration, the university's ethical review board privileged the safeguarding of research participants' privacy above all else. Its 'solution' – that peer researchers do not interview participants in their city of residence – undermined one of the primary reasons to work with peer researchers in the first place: to access valuable local knowledge of context. At the time, ethical review boards were relatively new to Dutch universities, and it was not possible for researchers to have direct contact with this board and to have a dialogue.

Addressing the questions raised in this chapter remains an ongoing effort within our research project, in open discussions, and regular meetings focused on the 'everyday ethics' (Banks et al., 2013) of pursuing research. The dilemmas we encountered are not specific to peer research but can surface in any qualitative research project involving vulnerable participants. Having structures in place to address these issues – some of them predictable, others unexpected – is necessary. Within the team, reflecting on ethical guidelines is part of ongoing training and intervision, which unfortunately takes place without support from the university's current structures of ethics review.

While the external validity of this study is relatively high due to the large amount of data collected over a long period of time, the high number of participants, and the involvement of both peer and academic researchers, writing this chapter prompted useful reflection on the extent to which striving for data validity is compatible with the aim of peer research to achieve social justice. While the team offers training, support, and feedback sessions to reflect on interviewing practice, is this enough? It is my hope that the additional value of peer research is evident in this chapter. Still, I wish to highlight that peer research requires additional institutional support and is not for 'free'.

NOTES

1. See their website for more information: https://www.nivel.nl/en.

2. The research project is ongoing, which means that more interviews are being conducted. Also see: nienkeboesveldt.com.

3. Throughout this chapter, we refer to 'peer researchers' and 'academic researchers'. Some peer researchers are academically trained, while some academic researchers have lived experience of the phenomenon they are studying. Although these categories are problematic, we retain the distinction to refer to researchers' primary roles in the project.

4. One peer researcher has a formal labour agreement with the university, mainly because he worked more hours than allowed by regulations. This meant he was unable to receive financial compensation for his work.

ACKNOWLEDGEMENTS

Charlotte van der Veen joined me on the journey from validity to reflexivity, about which I learnt much from Thomas van der Molen. Marte Kuipers, Marcia Bochem, Robbert Brouwer and Sascha van der Dries were present at the 2019 *European Seminar on Peer Research and Understanding Homelessness* where the chapter's first ideas were presented. Maarten Davelaar was part of the team from its early years, developing with me the initial training programme for peer researchers. Peggy DeMilt and Thijs Kuiling provided valuable insights from their peer research. Finally, the comments of the anonymous reviewers provided valuable feedback for finalising this chapter, and I appreciate their time and attention. Takeo David Hymans edited the chapter.

REFERENCES

Banks, S., Armstrong, A., Carter, K., Graham, H., Hayward, P., Henry, A., Holland, T., Holmes, C., Lee, A., McNulty, A., Moore, N., Nayling, N., Stokoe, A., & Strachan, A. (2013). Everyday ethics in community-based participatory research. *Contemporary Social Science*, *8*(3), 263–277. https://doi.org/10.1080/21582041.2013.769618

Carpenter, D. (2018). Ethics, reflexivity and virtue. In R. Iphofen & M. Tolich (Eds.), *The SAGE handbook of qualitative research ethics* (pp. 35–50). SAGE.

Devotta, K., Woodhall-Melnik, J., Pedersen, C., Wendaferew, A., Dowbor, T. P., Guilcher, S. J. T., Hamilton-Wright, S., Ferentzy, P., Hwang, S. W., & Matheson, F. I. (2016). Enriching qualitative research by engaging peer interviewers: A case study. *Qualitative Research*, *16*(6), 661–680. https://doi.org/10.1177/1468794115626244

DeWalt, K. M., & DeWalt, B. R. (2002). *Participant observation: A guide for fieldworkers*. AltaMira.

Di Maggio, P. J., & Powell, W. (1983). The iron cage revisited: Institutional isomorphism and collective rationality in organizational fields. *American Sociological Review*, *48*, 147–160.

Edwards, R., & Alexander, C. (2011). Researching with peer/community researchers – Ambivalences and tensions. In M. Williams & W. P. Vogt (Eds.), *The SAGE handbook of innovation in social research methods* (pp. 269–293). Sage.

Elliott, E., Watson, A. J., & Harries, U. (2002). Harnessing expertise: Involving peer interviewers in qualitative research with hard-to-reach populations. *Health Expectations*, *5*(2), 172–178. https://doi.org/10.1046/j.1369-6513.2002.00158.x

Finlay, L. (2002). "Outing" the researcher: The provenance, process, and practice of reflexivity. *Qualitative Health Research*, *12*(4), 531–545. https://doi.org/10.1177/104973202129120052

Fortuna, K. L., Solomon, P., & Rivera, J. (2022). An update of peer support/peer provided services underlying processes, benefits, and critical ingredients. *Psychiatric Quarterly*, *93*(2), 571–586. https://doi.org/10.1007/s11126-022-09971-w

Greene, S. (2013). Peer research assistantships and the ethics of reciprocity in community-based research. *Journal of Empirical Research on Human Research Ethics*, *8*(2), 141–152.

Greene, S., Ahluwalia, A., Watson, J., Tucker, R., Rourke, S. B., Koornstra, J., Sobota, M., Monette, L., & Byers, S. (2009). Between skepticism and empowerment: The experiences of peer research assistants in HIV/AIDS, housing and homelessness community-based research. *International Journal of Social Research Methodology*, *12*(4), 61–373. https://doi.org/10.1080/13645570802553780

Groot-Sluijsmans, B. C. (2021). *Ethics of participatory health research: Insights from a reflective journey*. Ridderprint.

Guta, A., Flicker, S., & Roche, B. (2013). Governing through community allegiance: A qualitative examination of peer research in community-based participatory research. *Critical Public Health*, *23*(4), 432–451. https://doi.org/10.1080/09581596.2012.761675

Guta, A., Strike, C., Flicker, S., Murray, S. J., Upshur, R., & Myers, T. (2014). Governing through community-based research: Lessons from the Canadian HIV research sector. *Social Science and Medicine*, *123*, 250–261. https://doi.org/10.1016/j.socscimed.2014.07.028

Haraway, D. (1988). Situated knowledges. the science question in feminism and the privilege of partial perspective. *Feminist Studies*, *14*(3), 757–599.

Hardt, M., & Negri, A. (2004). *Multitude: War and democracy in the age of empire*. Penguin.

Ibáñez-Carrasco, F., Watson, J. R., & Tavares, J. (2019). Supporting peer researchers: Recommendations from our lived experience/expertise in community-based research in Canada. *Harm Reduction Journal*, *16*(1), 1–5. https://doi.org/10.1186/s12954-019-0322-6

Israel, B. A., Schulz, A. J., Parker, E. A., & Becker, A. B. (1998). Review of community-based research: Assessing partnership approaches to improve public health. *Annual Review of Public Health*, *19*, 173–202.

Johnson, B., & Clarke, J. M. (2003). Collecting sensitive data: The impact on researchers. *Qualitative Health Research*, *13*(3), 421–434. https://doi.org/10.1177/1049732302250340

Morgan, J., Neufeld, S. D., Holroyd, H., Ruiz, H., Taylor, T., Nolan, S., & Glegg, S. (2023). Community-Engaged Research Ethics Training (CERET): Developing accessible and relevant research ethics training for community-based participatory research with people with lived and living experience using illicit drugs and harm reduction workers. *Harm Reduction Journal*, *20*, 86. https://doi.org/10.1186/s12954-023-00818-6

Research Ethics Committee. (2018). Facultaire Ethische Toets Commissie Sociale Wetenschappen, personal communication, March 29, 2018 [Faculty Ethics Review Committee Social Sciences, personal communication, March 29, 2018].

Roche, B., Guta, A., & Flicker, S. (2010). Peer research in action I: Models of practice. *Community Based Research Working Paper Series*, *1*, 2–18.

Tseris, E., Franks, S., & Bright Hart, E. (2022). Beyond binaries: Complex roles and identities in critical mental health research. *Disability and Society*, *37*(4), 718–723. https://doi.org/10.1080/09687599.2022.2034111

Voronka, J. (2016). The politics of "people with lived experience': Experiential authority and the risks of strategic essentialism. *Philosophy, Psychiatry and Psychology*, *23*(3–4), 189–201. https://doi.org/10.1353/ppp.2016.0017

Voronka, J. (2017). Turning mad knowledge into affective labor: The case of the peer support worker. *American Quarterly*, *69*(2), 333–338. https://doi.org/10.1353/aq.2017.0029

Voronka, J. (2019). The mental health peer worker as informant: Performing authenticity and the paradoxes of passing. *Disability and Society*, *34*(4), 564–582. https://doi.org/10.1080/09687599.2018.1545113

Voronka, J., Wise Harris, D., Grant, J., Komaroff, J., Boyle, D., & Kennedy, A. (2014). Un/helpful help and its discontents: Peer researchers paying attention to street life narratives to inform social work policy and practice. *Social Work in Mental Health*, *12*(3), 249–279. https://doi.org/10.1080/15332985.2013.875504

Warr, D., Mann, R., & Tacticos, T. (2011). Using peer-interviewing methods to explore place-based disadvantage: Dissolving the distance between suits and civilians. *International Journal of Social Research Methodology*, *14*(5), 337–352. https://doi.org/10.1080/13645579.2010.537527

CHAPTER 4

INFORMED CONSENT IN QUALITATIVE RESEARCH: LESSONS ON RELATIONALITY FROM A TECHNOLOGICALLY DENSE CLASSROOM

Fride Haram Klykken

University of Bergen, Norway

ABSTRACT

This chapter examines the challenges that informed consent poses in qualitative research. Drawing on examples from a video ethnography in a technologically rich classroom in Norway, this chapter highlights limitations of the current emphasis on anticipatory approaches to informed consent. I explore how a nuanced processual understanding of informed consent can be added to these established procedures so as to navigate the intricate dynamics of conducting ethical research in a relationally constituted world. This chapter illustrates how, from a relationally situated approach, explicit and implicit negotiations of informed consent can be incorporated throughout the research process. Informed by sociomaterial and material feminist theories, this chapter reflects on the iterative and material effects of contemporary informed consent practices. Encouraging a rethinking of the role of informed consent within qualitative research, I argue that engaging in informed consent

Reframing Qualitative Research Ethics
Advances in Research Ethics and Integrity, Volume 12, 57–73

ISSN: 2398-6018/doi:10.1108/S2398-601820250000012004

practices is not only about formal procedures or written agreements but also entails a continuous relational negotiation that needs attention throughout the research process. In conclusion, I advocate that institutions and researchers should advance responsible research ethics by acknowledging ethical complexity, promoting trust, and building diverse and responsive ethical resource networks.

Keywords: Informed consent; relational ethics; research relationships; sociomaterial; educational research

INTRODUCTION

In this chapter, I explore the issues that the principle of informed consent poses for qualitative research. This ethical principle aims to safeguard human integrity, capacities, and free will, by protecting people's rights to receive information about what a research engagement will involve, as well as to be given real opportunities to choose whether or not to take part in the research (Alderson & Morrow, 2011). In Norway, the ethical guidelines for social research state that consent should, as a main rule, be informed, voluntary, and actively expressed, and researchers must be able to explain the consent process (NESH, 2021, pp. 18–21).

Researchers often report on their engagement with the principle of informed consent in the course of the planning and recruitment phases of the research. Consequently, many see the process as complete once consent has apparently been obtained through the signing of a form (Gallagher et al., 2010). This focus may result from the fact that informed consent requirements are, at least within the European Union (EU), connected both to privacy legislation and to research ethics. If researchers choose to primarily address informed consent by complying with legislative requirements, there is a risk of neglecting the ongoing and relational ethical quality of research. Instead of fostering the researchers' sense of ethical responsibility, a compliance approach may encourage box ticking, conformity, and ethical bureaucracy (Atkinson et al., 2024, p. 6). These practices of reducing ethical practices in qualitative research to formalise protocols, standards, rules, and procedures have been criticised as simplistic and institutionalised by many scholars (Caeymaex et al., 2023; Gillam & Guillemin, 2018; Hammersley, 2009; Murphy & Dingwall, 2007; Taquette & Borges da Matta Souza, 2022; Wynn, 2018).

While qualitative research has the potential to create understanding and knowledge about social phenomena, situations, and environments, such insights demand situated social interactions and are co-produced by all involved in the research (Denzin & Lincoln, 2018, p. 17). Because these relational perspectives are important, scholars call for ethical practices that are better aligned with the reciprocal, relational, situated, and processual nature of qualitative research (Atkinson et al., 2024; Bengtsson, 2020; Connor et al., 2018; De Poli & Oyebode, 2023; Stutchbury & Fox, 2009).

Drawing on these perspectives and based on empirical examples from a video ethnography in a technologically dense upper-secondary classroom in Norway, this chapter will explore approaches to informed consent as a relationally situated practice. The examples from the upper-secondary classroom are used to show how limiting the practice of ethical informed consent to giving information and asking individuals to sign a consent form before the fieldwork has commenced contradicts the unpredictable reality of qualitative research practices. Inspired by the study's sociomaterial and feminist materialist framework (Klykken, 2023c), I will first draw attention to the integral role of relationships in ethical informed consent practices. I will then discuss a more nuanced and relationally situated approach, incorporating explicit and implicit in-field negotiations of informed consent throughout the research process. Offered as an addition to the important practice of obtaining written informed consent at the outset, this approach aims to contribute to informed consent practices that are relationally attuned to ethical frameworks in qualitative research.

A VIDEO ETHNOGRAPHIC STUDY FROM AN UPPER-SECONDARY CLASSROOM

The research that this chapter draws upon is a video ethnographic study conducted in 2018 in a Norwegian upper-secondary classroom (Klykken, 2023b, 2023c). I followed one class for approximately 40 lessons over a period of three months. The participants were 23 students and their teacher in a second year within the study programme of 'Media and Communication'. Aiming to investigate sociomaterial practices comprising everyday teaching situations, I used two small video cameras and one audio recorder that I could easily move in response to the changing activities in the classroom. I collected audiovisual recordings and created field notes, and the use of these audiovisual tools allowed me to conduct a micro-level analysis and thus aided my exploration of both discursive and material aspects of the teaching situations. At the end of the fieldwork, I invited the participants to attend debriefing interviews, and 15 students agreed to take part. I also conducted a debriefing interview with the teacher. This allowed me to discuss the fieldwork and preliminary analysis with the participants and provided space to talk about any concerns or unresolved issues they might have (Brinkmann & Kvale, 2015).

As the students were enrolled in a media study programme, their immediate learning environment already included the presence of digital technology, with the students using audiovisual equipment as part of their course. They actively used a diverse range of screens and digital devices: in addition to cameras and audio recorders for school projects, they also used computers and mobile phones to access learning resources online. Since I used audiovisual equipment as part of the research, I also contributed to the density of digital technology in the classroom.

RETHINKING THE RESEARCH RELATIONSHIP

The study was framed by sociomaterial theoretical perspectives. As the name highlights, the social (e.g. human action and discourse) is argued to intertwine with the material (e.g. objects, artefacts, and technologies). Following Gherardi (2016, p. 686), practice is a situated and collective 'doing'. This sociomaterial approach emphasises relationships and gives both the human and the material key roles in stabilising practices (Gherardi, 2016, p. 685).

Objects and technologies are not seen as passive artefacts, subordinate to human intentionality, but as actively influencing social practices. They have productive capacities, meaning that by being involved in the sociomaterial ecosystem of relations, they contribute to the co-constituting and (re)producing of social order (Gherardi, 2016). Thus, from this perspective, the immediate environment, such as the classroom, but also artefacts such as digital devices (including the research tools), played an active role in the classroom activities that I researched, alongside the human agents, such as the participants and researcher (Santiago de Roock, 2020). From this stance, conducting social research is understood as a joint endeavour. Social and material actors, such as researchers, participants, tools, rules, and routines, are all seen as co-performing the relational arrangement of the research.

This sociomaterial framework resonates with situated and relational approaches to ethics (Gherardi, 2021). Having developed from feminist materialist scholarship and founded in our connections and concern for others (Denzin, 2003; Haraway, 1988), from this stance, interdependency is seen not as 'a contract, nor a moral ideal – it is a condition' (Puig de la Bellacasa, 2017, p. 70). Puig de la Bellacasa (2012) argues that situated knowledge entails 'that knowing and thinking are inconceivable without a multitude of relations that also make possible the worlds we think with' (p. 198). Through directing attention to the everyday relationality of the research engagement, these approaches enable our ethical consideration of the material components and consequences of scientific practice.

In the study, the students' situated interactions and their use of tools aided my understanding of their consent to – or dissent from – participating in the research project. In the following, the practical and physical dimensions of the research practice, such as recording devices and smartphones, and the use of informed consent forms can be understood as material artefacts with relational effects and consequences within the research practice.

ETHICS GUIDELINES AND PRIVACY LEGISLATION IN NORWAY

In Norway, researchers are required to follow both the research ethics legislation and guidelines and privacy legislations (Forskningsetikkloven, 2017; NESH, 2024). Ethical advice and guidelines for social research are provided by the National Committee for Research Ethics in the Social Sciences and the Humanities (NESH,

2021), an independent advisory body that provides both general and subject-oriented guidelines for ethical research conduct in Norway. Importantly, NESH provides guidelines but does not have authority to provide ethical approvals.

Informed consent is also connected to the protection of individuals' personal data. In Norway, the law requires that research participants must be informed about how any personal data will be handled in compliance with the General Data Protection Regulation (NESH, 2024). At the time that I was conducting my research, evaluations of how projects complied with data privacy requirements were conducted by the Norwegian Centre for Research Data, from now on referred to as NSD (2020).[1] Thus, the research described in this chapter needed a formal assessment of how personal data were treated from NSD. Consequently, I did not have to apply for any ethics committee review but only for data protection approval. Except for medical and health research,[2] there are no general systems for prior assessment of research in Norway. Meanwhile, more recently, several institutions have decided to establish their own internal ethical approval bodies (Fugelsnes, 2023). According to the Research Ethics Act, the overall responsibility for compliance with the recognised research ethics norms lies with the research institution (Forskningsetikkloven, 2017).

PLANNING AND IMPLEMENTING INFORMED CONSENT IN THE PRE-FIELDWORK PHASE

As described in the guidelines provided by NESH (2021), potential participants should be informed about the purpose of the project and about what participation will entail before making decisions about taking part in the research. Their consent needs to be clear and unambiguous, and the participants should have a real opportunity to decline the invitation. Additionally, the researcher needs to 'be able to explain how the ethical consent has been given and what information the consent is based on' (NESH, 2021, p.19).

I was a PhD candidate when I conducted the research and studied the ethical guidelines and the data protection requirements closely, as well as other relevant literature on research ethics. I planned to provide both written and oral information about the project to potential participants and created written information letters and consent forms using the officially recommended templates from NSD, adjusting the language to the age group (Busher, 2019). In the information letter, I described the interest and the aims of the project and explained that I intended to follow the activities of the students and their teacher, primarily focusing on ordinary whole-class situations and in-group interactions during everyday classroom activities.

Both the ethics guidelines and data protection legislation state that valid and ethical consent presupposes the capacity to give consent (NESH, 2021; NSD, 2020). In social science research, the capacity to consent is not tied directly to biological age but should be evaluated based on the nature of the research project (Backe-Hansen, 2023). For research in schools, if the research topic is not of a sensitive nature and no special category of personal data is collected, children who have reached 15 years are considered capable to consent on their own behalf

(Backe-Hansen, 2023). The proposed participants in my research project were between 17 and 19 years old, and the proposed research focus was on whole-class and group-level interaction in ordinary teaching situations. Hence, I planned for the students to consent themselves without approval from parents or guardians.

I submitted the research plan to NSD, with the information letter and consent form included, as well as a plan for handling personal data. I detailed the ways in which I planned to store and manage personal data and protect participants' confidentiality. As audio and video recordings contain identifiable personal information, this material would be stored on an encrypted disc throughout the project, with access restricted to myself and my PhD supervisors. I also provided information on how long the data would be stored and that data would be deleted at the end of the research project. On the consent form, the students could indicate if they wanted to take part in the study.

Once the project was formally approved by NSD, I could start recruiting participants for the study. I began the recruitment process by approaching gatekeepers, such as school leaders and department heads, giving them information on the project. The teachers who were interested then forwarded the information to the students, and I visited schools to speak to teachers and classes of students in person. In this way, information was distributed to potential participants in both written and spoken form. The students were then given time to read the information and consider taking part in the study. Some students decided quickly to participate, but others wanted more time to read and think about taking part in the research project. A few weeks later, one whole class of 23 students had agreed to participate.

INFORMED CONSENT AS RELATIONAL PROCESS[3]

An In-field Reframing of Pre-fieldwork Consent

In the pre-fieldwork phase of the research described above, the participants explicitly and formally consented to take part in the study. During the fieldwork, however, the students sometimes talked among themselves about the research and their participation in it and directly referenced the information I had given at the start of the project. Students talked, for instance, about who was going to watch the video recordings, and one student expressed a worry that he thought the teacher would see the recordings and that it would affect his grades (Klykken, 2022). I was surprised as I had been confident that I had informed everyone that this would not be the case: all the students had been present when I provided information to the class with both written documents and oral presentations. Still, during this and similar conversations, they did not always display this knowledge in such a way as I thought I had shared it. While in most cases the participants appeared to help each other and to correctly adjust each other's understanding about the study, these situations provided an opportunity for me as a researcher to learn about some of the limitations of pre-fieldwork consent.

First, as the example above show, engaging with the informed consent principle solely during the pre-fieldwork phase can be problematic. On a general level, understanding is a fluid concept, and as Gallagher et al. (2010) argue, research participants may forget or misunderstand the information given about the research project. Second, the students were in a mandatory educational setting, which creates further problems concerning a researcher's certainty of a shared understanding, as also been demonstrated by Gallagher et al. (2010). Young people in school contexts are frequently required to listen to teachers and then to repeat and have their answers assessed and graded and may therefore distrust adults, out of fear or from previous experience of such stigma; thus, they may hesitate to express their concerns to the teacher or the researcher if they do not feel they have a good understanding of the research (Gallagher et al., 2010, pp. 474–475).

Third, the idea of giving information and gathering authentic consent at one single point in time was challenged by the ways in which the information I had given about the research re-appeared in the conversations between participants. These occasions made it evident that the students continued to build on and reshape their understanding of the research project long after the recruitment phase (Klykken, 2022). Information about the research was also created in conversations, as students approached me during breaks, for instance, to talk about the research, casually asking me how my research was going, or what I was looking for in the study. These examples demonstrate some of the ways in which participants may continue to talk and reflect about a research project. Instead of a one-way communication process, where participants are on the receiving end, participants should be understood as actively and continuously constructing knowledge about the research, with the aid of others, through social sharing and their ongoing participation (De Poli & Oyebode, 2023; Klykken, 2022).

Fourth, what I learned from the above-mentioned situations was that pre-fieldwork engagement with informed consent can provide researchers with an in-field, relational affordance. Had I not provided the participants with information before the research started, with the plan for the research and the options on consenting, these participants may not have had any firm entry point for conversations about the research and their own participation in it. Information about the research can be interpreted as a shared material artefact that served as a catalyst for dialogue among participants themselves and between participants and researcher.

Recognising that participants' understanding of the nature of participating in a research project evolves highlights that engaging with informed consent during the pre-fieldwork phase is just the beginning of a process. In the following sections, I will explore how informed consent can be addressed as an iterative process throughout the research.

In-field Negotiations of Consent and Dissent

As ethnographic fieldwork takes place over some time, it entails carefully balancing planning with openness and flexibility to events taking new and unforeseen directions (Coffey, 2018). From this approach, social researchers are learners too, with ethical reflections being an integral part of this ongoing and relational inquiry (Atkinson et al., 2024). As Pink (2017) has argued, combining ethnography with video technology further instils a particular awareness of how the researcher must be responsive and responsible to emergent and unpredictable events and ethical challenges in the field. We cannot know what will happen as everyday activities unfold, which makes particularly evident the need for researchers' ethical competence to improvise around uncertainties as we step into a 'previously unknown, unseen and unexpected' future alongside our participants (Pink, 2017, p. 36).

Young people in education also report having a lot of school-related pressures and stress (Eriksen et al., 2017). Hence, asking to observe the everyday life of an upper-secondary class and creating audio and video recordings is potentially an intrusive request. Since the students were enrolled in a Media and Communications programme that incorporated the use of video and audio equipment into the curriculum, they were not only competent to operate but also likely to feel more comfortable being around recording devices. However, it was still important to me that research participation should not add to the pressures they faced.

Conducting social research means being involved in everyday relationships, which can change in nonlinear ways and are by their very nature opaque and untidy (Perez, 2019; Roulet et al., 2017). To show respect and awareness for the complex everyday lives of young people, I sought to communicate that their decisions regarding participation and involvement in the research – especially since it involved recordings – remained flexible and voluntary and could be accommodated and adapted according to, for instance, the need to talk in private about life events. Even though the students had been informed and had formally provided consent, this initial consent was granted several weeks before the beginning of the fieldwork, and their everyday life might have changed. To provide genuine opportunities to consent or withdraw from the research, I would – especially when I used the camera, and in the early days of the fieldwork – ask for permission to place the recording device with groups of students. Addressing their media competence, I would also inform them that they could themselves pause or stop the recording device at any point, if they should wish so (Klykken, 2023c).

As the fieldwork continued, I would frequently check in with the students to confirm their consent. For example, on the day of an important presentation, I encouraged the students – given their expressed worries in the days leading up to the event – to inform me if they did not want their presentation to be recorded. One student approached me and requested that I should not record his presentation. While it was clear from the conversation that his decision to withdraw participation was temporary, and that he only requested that his presentation did not become part of the empirical data, this serves as an example of informed dissent after an explicit dialogue about the research participation (Klykken, 2022, p. 801). The same student also chose to take part when invited to a debriefing interview.

This shows how the participants continued to become 'informed' through their experiences of the unfolding research relationship. In this way, while in the field, I initiated 'explicit (re)negotiations' with the participants on their informed consent and dissent status (Klykken, 2022, p. 801). By providing real openings for participants to withdraw from the research, we can demonstrate that we as researchers see the integrity of participants as more important than the research itself. This can be one way to signal respect and that engagement in research is an authentically open-ended and voluntary dialogue and to contribute to a continuous building of trust (Smette, 2019).

When attending to informed consent over a longer period of time, it may be practical and relationally appropriate to be receptive not only to explicit but also to implicit ways of consenting and dissenting, through attending to both 'what is said and unsaid' (Bourke & Loveridge, 2014, p. 153). In this context, some kinds of positive interactions, cooperation, and engagement in the research can be interpreted as implied or 'implicitly (re)negotiated consent' (Klykken, 2022, p. 802). By directing attention to the more subtle reciprocal gestures, I learned from the relationality of the classroom. This reflexive engagement represents a form of relational attuning and aligning with participants about their understanding of the boundaries of the research participation (Klykken, 2023a).

In one situation, after I had placed a camera next to a table where a group of students were sitting, one of the students left the table and moved to another part of the classroom (Klykken, 2022). One interpretation of this situation was that the student moved away from the camera, and this could indicate he did not consent to take part in the research that day. I chose to consider this a case of 'implicitly (re)negotiated dissent' (Klykken, 2022, p. 803). After this situation, I adapted my recording strategies and the way I engaged within the class, so that I could keep a considerate distance from that student. As the fieldwork evolved, through my interactions in the classroom and by looking through and analysing the empirical material, I learned more about the students, the teachers, and the classroom's patterns, arrangements, and enactments.

Post-fieldwork Constructions of Informed Consent and Dissent

Due to the availability of digital devices, our everyday lives are increasingly characterised by constant connectivity and availability. Especially for young people, this may result in a blurring of the distinctions between what is traditionally understood as 'online and offline', 'formal and informal', and 'in and out of school' (Erstad & Silseth, 2023). Such digital connectivity also characterised the classroom practices I was studying.

When working on school tasks, the students would often seamlessly interweave their work on school tasks with more socially motivated peer interactions (Klykken, 2023b). School-oriented and socially oriented activities intertwined tightly, not only in the 'physical' space of the classroom but also on the screens of the students' digital devices. For instance, smartphones were used by students to access both learning platforms and social media. The students also frequently shared and communicated with their co-students via the phone, either by showing each other the screens of their phones or by communicating digitally via social media apps. This took place even though they were sitting next to each other. Students could, for instance, demand that a co-student should: 'Check your Snap!' or 'Open my snap!' This way of communicating corresponds with a growing practice among young people where physical meetings often are complemented by online interaction (Sjolie et al., 2024).

During the analysis of the visual recording, I became interested in the students' digital switching between on-task and off-task activities (Klykken, 2022). In the video recordings, I could sometimes see screens of devices such as on the students' computers and their mobile phones. However, as I had not foreseen this activity, I had not stated that I would make any notes about on-screen activities in the information sheets I distributed. Nor had I mentioned this in the debriefing group interviews I had conducted upon leaving the field. This put me in an ethical dilemma. I had not explicitly informed the participants, and they had not been made aware or been specifically informed that their on-screen activities during the fieldwork could be recorded and analysed. It is important to find ways to check back with participants – wherever possible and appropriate – to explore whether they endorse our understanding of their consent or dissent. However, at this time in the analytical phase, over a year had passed since the data collection. The class had graduated from the school, and I was no longer able to discuss these issues with them.

I wondered if I could, from a research ethics perspective, conduct an analysis of the students' on-screen activity in the video recordings, considering that the participants had not explicitly consented to this specific component? When these situations became a point of interest in my analysis, I began a process of re-considering the participants' informed consent and evaluating if their digital interactions could become part of the video ethnographic corpus (Klykken, 2022). I reviewed and searched through the video corpus, the interviews, and the field notes to look for indicators of informed consent or dissent to the recording of their on-screen activities. In some cases, I could see, for example, that students deliberately held the screens of their mobile phones to display to the camera, hence providing open access to their screen-based activities. Such episodes could suggest that, for many students, the presence and visibility of screens was ubiquitous and an ordinary and well-known part of the classroom (Klykken, 2022).

However, as I continued to search the video data to look for events that could inform me concerning participants' consent to sharing their screen-based activity, there were other signs of students limiting access. For instance, in this situation, while the students were speaking, parts of their exchange were communicated solely through the phone screen:

Student 4: Shall I show you what he said?

Student 3: Can I read?

Student 4: Yes [Hands over phone to Student 3]

Student 3: [Looks at the screen and then returns it to Student 4]

Student 4: But it was this that happened [Displays screen to Student 3 again]

Here, parts of the dialogue were conducted in a cautious way, as one student was showing their mobile phone screen to another. In similar situations, the students were sometimes using their smartphones while not actually speaking to each other. Their eye contact, however, suggested that they might be in dialogue, communicating with each other through their digital devices. This nonverbal and screen-based communication could be an indication that the students were deliberately creating a private space within the classroom, withholding and protecting their conversation from others.

This mode of communicating created boundaries between what I viewed as public and what I understood to be private in the classroom: I interpreted this as an indication that they wished to safeguard their private sphere by using the digital device to keep the conversation out of the reach of the researcher and the research camera. The students' subtle gestures thus indirectly signalled dissent regarding sharing their on-screen practices, and consequently, I believed it would be unethical for me to make notes about the content of those on-screen activities in the classroom. If I had created research accounts about the students' on-screen practices, this could be conceived as a betrayal of the trust they placed in me by consenting to the research and allowing me into the classroom. This, in turn, could also cause damage to research integrity by decreasing public trust.

When I combined my understanding of the above observation with the fact that I had not explicitly asked the students for approval to analyse the on-screen activity, I concluded that this was a case of the students implicitly renegotiating the terms of their involvement (Klykken, 2022). Tracing the participants' interactions with the research at different stages thus informed the post-fieldwork boundaries for the research, and reframing the principle of informed consent provided a useful way to deal with this ethical dilemma. Thus, the participants' interactions and my broader knowledge about the research relationship became a guide to inform my ethical decisions in situations in which consent status was ambiguous (Klykken, 2022).

This post-fieldwork example illustrates how the researcher's responsibility to seek informed consent can continue after leaving the field, guided by the relational knowledge gained from the research engagement. As explained above, I began to navigate concepts of informed consent by imagining the meanings of the students' behaviours in relation to using their screens, and in this case, based on their actions and gestures, I came to understand their status as informed dissent. To follow up these issues directly with participants, after the fieldwork, would be best, as there are multiple pitfalls in navigating the boundaries of the research relationship through a speculative 'thinking-with' the participants' actions in this way (Puig de la Bellacasa, 2017, p. 85). Importantly, we can say that pre-fieldwork practices of informed consent also involve trying to predict the consequences of qualitative research, and so they are equally acts of speculation and creativity (Cassell, 1982, cited in Flinders, 1992, p. 103), because it is effectively impossible for any of those involved to create an unambiguous account of how the research process will unfold.

DISCUSSION: INFORMED CONSENT ONGOING AND RELATIONAL ETHICAL PRACTICE

The principle of informed consent aims to protect the human integrity and freedom of research participants, and research guidelines detail that participants should be provided with clear and unambiguous information about research before deciding on whether to take part or not (NESH, 2021). Meanwhile, living relationships are changing, flexible, and never fully controllable, and the boundaries between research practices and the practices under study are fluid. Representing research engagements which involve everyday social interaction consequently entails accounting for processes that inevitably are nonlinear and complex (Klykken, 2022; Wang, 2013).

This chapter has provided an account incorporating the informed consent principle as a way to ethically consider and account for the research relationship and its boundaries. The boundaries of consent are at the core of what researchers wish to communicate to the participants when detailing the research process in informed consent documents (Hamilton, 2009). However, as I have argued, these boundaries are continuously re-negotiated and co-created during the fieldwork.

Requirements for approval and documentation demand direct focus, requiring that the researcher actively comply with these principles and procedures (Traianou, 2019). In the Norwegian context, the data protection assessment necessitated my active attention in order to obtain the necessary approval. Reflecting upon the actions and elements of the pre-fieldwork phase of my study and its informed consent practices, we see that navigating ethical guidelines and the formal procedures of approval were prioritised in this phase. Decentring the focus on human agency foregrounds how ethical regulatory guidelines, information sheets, and other information about the project stand out as material entities that enact relational agency in the practice of research ethics (Gherardi, 2017). As has been argued, the pre-fieldwork procedures were productive, and the use of clear and understandable communication suited for the target group remains crucial for initiating the research relationship. Yet when ethical practices are primarily informed and guided by obligatory standards, there is a risk that they may become moral recipes (Puig de la Bellacasa, 2017) or 'game-like' activities to solve (Atkinson et al., 2024, p. 2). A consequence, in turn, is that the more complex in situ ethical work may be left with less focus or even unattended (Guillemin & Gillam, 2004; Traianou, 2019).

The nature of conducting fieldwork is rife with ambiguity and uncertainty (Atkinson et al., 2024). In this study, the participants' explicit responses and implicit cues, as well as my own evolving social and ethical sensitivities, shaped my in-field decisions. For instance, I adjusted my behaviour, including who to follow and my ways of interacting, and continuously evaluated situations to consider if they were inside or outside the consent boundaries of the research relationship. Post-fieldwork, the students' use of digital devices arose as one example of how the participants had established clear boundaries to the researcher's access. Importantly, this relational sensitivity, informed by sociomaterial perspectives, highlights how 'in field' situated interactions were joined by material entities, such as digital devices and informed consent documents, and all contributed to collectively shaping the everyday practice of research ethics.

Safeguarding participants' integrity involves recognising their agency and their capacity for making decisions about their involvement in research. From a relationally situated and continuous understanding, the processes of informed consent should move beyond emphasising explicit, direct, and verbal consent and should acknowledge indirect and implicit interpretations of consent and dissent when trying to develop a shared understanding of the research relationship. Instead of trusting the written word, incorporated into a warrant of 'ethics in advance' (Strathern, 2000, cited in Pink, 2017, p. 34), ethics needs to be an ongoing practice, with informed consent considerations accompanying the researcher throughout the research process, valuing both explicit and implicit dialogues about consent (Klykken, 2022, p. 807).

When evaluating and reporting on informed consent processes, the qualitative research community emphasises the pre-fieldwork responsibility to *give* information to research participants and *obtain* consent. Current practices of pre-fieldwork consent reflect an over-reliance on ethical approvals, as well as undue trust in the written words, which can work against the fundamentals of qualitative research which is necessarily a co-constituted practice. In research articles, the ethical considerations sections are often so general that they resemble a chatbot-style response such as: 'Ethical approval for this study was obtained from [relevant ethics committee]. All participants provided informed consent prior to their involvement'. This seems to reflect a lack of trust (and perhaps even a lack of interest) in the participants and the research process.

Trust is at the core of being able to carry out research, so trustful relationships need not only to be established but also maintained (Riese, 2019). I would argue that by providing a more nuanced and transparent account of informed consent processes, for instance, by accounting for ambiguous and complex cases of informed consent and dissent, researchers can produce more authentic and trustworthy reports on ethical practice. Reflexive attunement and alignment with participants about their understanding of the boundaries of the research participation remains key for taking responsibility for the integrity of research and building societal trust in research.

If researchers go on ethical auto-pilot, putting all their trust in simplistic informed consent procedures, not only do they risk inauthentic ethical reporting, but they also miss out on engaging in ethical deliberation and the ongoing development of professional practices necessary for high-quality and ethical research engagements (Stutchbury & Fox, 2009). Ethical deliberations provide opportunities to reflect and develop the skills to navigate demanding decision-making, necessary to conduct ethically sound research (Smette, 2019). For instance, looking more closely at situations with uncertain and ambiguous consent status can provide opportunities to develop skills related to relational awareness and sensitivity to context when evaluating the limits to informed consent (Homan, 1991, 2001). As part of this agenda, researchers should also explore ways of following up with participants to reflect on their views about ethical issues if new questions about these emerge, even after the fieldwork.

CONCLUSION

From a procedural point of view, the researcher's responsibility to inform and to obtain consent lies on the threshold between research ethics and privacy legislation. Personal data have become more valuable than ever before (Pangrazio & Selwyn, 2019), and it is arguably therefore more important to handle participants' data with care. For researchers, this may lead to increasing emphasis on data practices and data management. This emphasis is seen, for instance, in that some researchers struggle to distinguish legal perspectives from ethical practices (NESH, 2021). This can be one of the reasons that 'legal' approaches to ethics, including informed consent, are prioritised over attending to important situated ethical responsibilities when conducting qualitative research (Atkinson et al., 2024; De Poli & Oyebode, 2023). The informed consent principle is there to protect human subjects from harm, but if the focus stops at documentation and ethical bureaucracy, these efforts appear to be primarily aimed at protecting the researchers and the research institutions from negative sanctions, rather than protecting the participants from harm (Caeymaex et al., 2023; Gallagher et al., 2010; Homan, 1991).

Research education, and other training organised by institutions, could therefore play an important role in equipping future researchers to be able to carry their ethical responsibilities and be equipped to work ethically within real spaces and processes which inevitably are uncertain and unpredictable (Mercieca & Mercieca, 2013). Reflexivity is key to developing skilful ethical practices that will enable the researcher to adjust to unexpected research developments and ethical challenges and to respond adequately to circumstances that arise (Caeymaex et al., 2023; Guillemin & Gillam, 2004). In a similar vein, Fox and Mitchell (2019) argue that spaces for thinking together with other researchers are key to support researcher reflexivity and the application of ethics.

Many research institutions and ethical committees emphasise anticipatory and risk-based approaches which, as shown above, are insufficient when it comes to qualitative research. It is vital that these bodies also take an interest in ethical practices as processes in addition to requiring formal informed consent at the outset of research (Beach & Arrazola, 2019; De Poli & Oyebode, 2023). Given that ethical issues in qualitative research are diverse and unpredictable (Pink, 2017), institutional support for diverse resource networks and environments is essential in this context: this should include providing opportunities for professional development in research ethics as well as offering opportunities for research communities to develop understandings of relational ethics.

NOTES

1. In 2022, NSD became part of SIKT, a new Norwegian agency: https://sikt.no/en/home.
2. Medical and health research are covered by the Health Research Act and assessed by the Regional Committees for Medical and Health Research Ethics (REK): https://www.forskningsetikk.no/en/about-us/our-committees-and-commission/rek/.
3. Some of the empirical examples have previously been included in the article 'Implementing continuous consent in qualitative research' (Klykken, 2022).

ACKNOWLEDGEMENTS

The writing of this chapter was made possible by financial support from the Trond Mohn Research Foundation through the EduTrust AI project (TMS2023TMT03).

REFERENCES

Alderson, P., & Morrow, V. (2011). *The ethics of research with children and young people: A practical handbook* (2nd ed.). SAGE Publications Ltd. https://doi.org/10.4135/9781446268377

Atkinson, P., Cataldi, S., & Wästerfors, D. (2024). For an ethics of generosity: Values for ethnography in a time of regulatory ethics. *Qualitative Research, 23*(1), 1–17. https://doi.org/10.1177/14687941241259978

Backe-Hansen, E. (2023). *Når barn og unge deltar i forskning [When children and adolescents participate in research]*. National Research Ethics Committees. https://www.forskningsetikk.no/ressurser/fbib/bestemte-grupper/barn/

Beach, D., & Arrazola, B. V. (2019). Ethical review boards. Constitutions, functions, tensions and blind spots. In H. Busher & A. Fox (Eds.), *Implementing ethics in educational ethnography: Regulation and practice* (pp. 32–47). Routledge. https://doi.org/10.4324/9780429507489

Bengtsson, T. T. (2020). *Informed consent as a situated research process in an ethnography of incarcerated youth in Denmark* (1 ed., pp. 130–142). Routledge. https://doi.org/10.4324/9780429424489-10

Bourke, R., & Loveridge, J. (2014). Exploring informed consent and dissent through children's participation in educational research. *International Journal of Research & Method in Education, 37*(2), 151–165. https://doi.org/10.1080/1743727X.2013.817551

Brinkmann, S., & Kvale, S. (2015). *InterViews. Learning the craft of qualitative research interviewing.* SAGE Publications Ltd.

Busher, H. (2019). Ethical research practice in educational institutions. In H. Busher & A. Fox (Eds.), *Implementing Ethics in Educational Ethnography: Regulation and Practice* (pp. 64–76). Routledge. https://doi.org/10.4324/9780429507489

Caeymaex, F., Wenger, C., de Heusch, F., & Lafleur, J.-M. (2023). "Ethics ready"? Governing research through informed consent procedures. *International Journal of Qualitative Methods, 22*, 1–11. https://doi.org/10.1177/16094069231165718

Coffey, A. (2018). *Doing ethnography*. SAGE Publications Ltd. https://doi.org/10.4135/9781526441874

Connor, J., Copland, S., & Owen, J. (2018). The infantilized researcher and research subject: Ethics, consent and risk. *Qualitative Research, 18*(4), 400–415. https://doi.org/10.1177/1468794117730686

Denzin, N. (2003). *Performance ethnography*. SAGE Publications, Inc. https://doi.org/10.4135/9781412985390

Denzin, N. K., & Lincoln, Y. S. (2018). Introduction: The discipline and practice of qualitative research. In N. K. Denzin & Y. S. Lincoln (Eds.), *The SAGE handbook of qualitative research* (5th ed., pp. 1–26). Sage.

De Poli, C., & Oyebode, J. (2023). Research ethics and collaborative research in health and social care: Analysis of UK research ethics policies, scoping review of the literature, and focus group study. *PloS One, 18*(12), 1–28. https://doi.org/10.1371/journal.pone.0296223

Eriksen, I. M., Sletten, M. A., Bakken, A., & Von Soest, T. (2017). *Stress og press blant ungdom. Erfaringer, årsaker og utbredelse av psykiske helseplager* [Stress and pressure amongst young people: Experiences, causes and prevalence of mental health problems]. Report, no. 6, Norsk Institutt for forskning om oppvekst, velferd og aldring (NOVA), June 2017. https://hdl.handle.net/20.500.12199/5115

Erstad, O., & Silseth, K. (2023). Rethinking the boundaries of learning in a digital age. *Learning, Media and Technology, 48*(4), 557–565. https://doi.org/10.1080/17439884.2023.2260977

Flinders, D. J. (1992). In search of ethical guidance: Constructing a basis for dialogue. *International Journal of Qualitative Studies in Education, 5*(2), 101–115. https://doi.org/10.1080/0951839920050202

Forskningsetikkloven. (2017). *Lov om organisering av forskningsetisk arbeid [Research Ethics Act] (LOV-2017-04-28-23)*. Lovdata. https://lovdata.no/dokument/NL/lov/2017-04-28-23

Fox, A., & Mitchell, R. (2019). Ethical learning from an educational ethnography. The application of an ethical framework in doctoral supervision. In H. Busher & A. Fox (Eds.), *Implementing ethics in educational ethnography: Regulation and practice* (pp. 110–125). Routledge. https://doi.org/10.4324/9780429507489

Fugelsnes, E. (2023, September). Higher demand for prior approval. *Research Ethics Magazine*, pp. 4–7. https://doi.org/https://www.forskningsetikk.no/globalassets/dokumenter/2-bladet-forskningsetikk/alle-utgaver/the-research-ethics-magazine-2023.pdf

Gallagher, M., Haywood, S. L., Jones, M. W., & Milne, S. (2010). Negotiating informed consent with children in school-based research: A critical review. *Children & Society*, *24*(6), 471–482. https://doi.org/10.1111/j.1099-0860.2009.00240.x

Gherardi, S. (2016). To start practice theorizing anew: The contribution of the concepts of *agencement* and formativeness. *Organization*, *23*(5), 680–698. https://doi.org/10.1177/1350508415605174

Gherardi, S. (2017). Sociomateriality in posthuman practice theory. In A. Hui, T. R. Schatzki, & E. Shove (Eds.), *The nexus of practices: Connections, constellations, practitioners* (pp. 38–51). Routledge.

Gherardi, S. (2021). A posthumanist epistemology of practice. In C. Neesham (Ed.), *Handbook of philosophy of management* (pp. 1–21). Springer International Publishing. https://doi.org/10.1007/978-3-319-48352-8_53-1

Gillam, L., & Guillemin, M. (2018). Reflexivity: Overcoming Mistrust between Research Ethics Committees and Researchers. In R. Iphofen & M. Tolich (Eds.), *The SAGE handbook of qualitative research ethics*. (pp. 263–274). SAGE Publications Ltd. https://doi.org/10.4135/9781526435446

Guillemin, M., & Gillam, L. (2004). Ethics, reflexivity and "ethically important moments" in research. *Qualitative Inquiry*, *10*(2), 261–280.

Hamilton, J. A. (2009). On the ethics of unusable data. In G. E. Marcus & J. D. Faubion (Eds.), *Fieldwork is not what it used to be. Learning anthropology's method in a time of transition* (pp. 73–88). Cornell University Press.

Hammersley, M. (2009). Against the ethicists: On the evils of ethical regulation. *International Journal of Social Research Methodology*, *12*(3), 211–225. https://doi.org/10.1080/13645570802170288

Haraway, D. (1988). Situated knowledges: The science question in feminism and the privilege of partial perspective. *Feminist Studies*, *14*(3), 575–599. https://doi.org/10.2307/3178066

Homan, R. (1991). *The ethics of social research*. Longman.

Homan, R. (2001). The principle of assumed consent: The ethics of gatekeeping. *Journal of Philosophy of Education*, *35*(3), 329–343. https://doi.org/10.1111/1467-9752.00230

Klykken, F. H. (2022). Implementing continuous consent in qualitative research. *Qualitative Research*, *22*(5), 795–810. https://doi.org/10.1177/14687941211014366

Klykken, F. H. (2023a). 'Are we going to do that now?' Orientations and response-abilities in the embodied classroom. *Pedagogy, Culture & Society*, *31*(5), 1079–1095. https://doi.org/10.1080/14681366.2021.1998794

Klykken, F. H. (2023b). The teaching apparatus: A material-discursive entanglement of tasks and friendship in the upper-secondary classroom. *Critical Studies in Education*, *65*(1), 1–19. https://doi.org/10.1080/17508487.2023.2207607

Klykken, F. H. (2023c). *The teaching apparatus: Understanding the material entanglement of practices in the upper secondary classroom* [Doctoral thesis, University of Bergen].

Mercieca, D., & Mercieca, D. P. (2013). Engagement with research: Acknowledging uncertainty in methodology. *International Journal of Research & Method in Education*, *36*(3), 228–240. https://doi.org/10.1080/1743727X.2013.806470

Murphy, E., & Dingwall, R. (2007). Informed consent, anticipatory regulation and ethnographic practice. *Social Science & Medicine*, *65*(11), 2223–2234. https://doi.org/10.1016/j.socscimed.2007.08.008

NESH. (2021). *Guidelines for research ethics in the social sciences and the humanities*. National Committee for Research Ethics in the Social Sciences and the Humanities. Retrieved May 1 from https://www.forskningsetikk.no/globalassets/dokumenter/4-publikasjoner-som-pdf/nesh-guidelines-en-2024

NESH. (2024). *Spørsmål og svar: Ny lovgivning om personopplysninger – Hva betyr det for forskning? [Q&A: New legislation on personal data - What does it mean for research?]* National Research Ethics Committees. Retrieved August 1, 2024, from https://www.forskningsetikk.no/ressurser/gdpr/

NSD. (2020). *Norwegian centre for research data: Data protection in research*. Retrieved April 18, 2020, from https://www.nsd.no/personverntjenester/oppslagsverk-for-personvern-i-forskning

Pangrazio, L., & Selwyn, N. (2019). 'Personal data literacies': A critical literacies approach to enhancing understandings of personal digital data. *New Media & Society*, *21*(2), 419–437. https://doi.org/10.1177/1461444818799523

Perez, T. S. (2019). In support of situated ethics: ways of building trust with stigmatised 'waste pickers' in Cape Town. *Qualitative Research*, *19*(2), 148–163

Pink, S. (2017). Ethics in an uncertain world. In S. Pink, V. Fors & T. O'Dell (Eds.), *Theoretical scholarship and applied practice* (pp. 29–50). Berghahn Books. https://doi.org/10.1515/9781785334177-004

Puig de la Bellacasa, M. (2012). 'Nothing comes without its world': Thinking with care. *The Sociological Review*, *60*(2), 197–216.

Puig de la Bellacasa, M. (2017). *Matters of care. Speculative ethics in more than human worlds*. University Of Minnesota Press.

Riese, J. (2019). What is 'access' in the context of qualitative research? *Qualitative Research*, *19*(6), 669–684. https://doi.org/10.1177/1468794118787713

Roulet, T. J., Gill, M. J., Stenger, S., & Gill, D. J. (2017). Reconsidering the value of covert research: The role of ambiguous consent in participant observation. *Organizational Research Methods*, *20*(3), 487–517. https://doi.org/10.1177/1094428117698745

Santiago de Roock, R. (2020). Digital selves, material bodies, and participant research tools: Towards material semiotic video ethnography. *International Journal of Social Research Methodology*, *23*(2), 199–213. https://doi.org/10.1080/13645579.2019.1669926

Sjolie, H., Olsen, C. F., & Hempel, M. F. (2024). Attachments or affiliations? The impact of social media on the quality of peer relationships – A qualitative study among Norwegian high school students. *Youth & Society*, *56*(4), 673–692. https://doi.org/10.1177/0044118x231171180

Smette, I. (2019). Ethics and access when consent must come first. Consequences of formalised research ethics for ethnographic research in schools. In H. Busher & A. Fox (Eds.), *Implementing ethics in educational ethnography: Regulation and practice* (pp. 51–63). Routledge. https://doi.org/10.4324/9780429507489

Stutchbury, K., & Fox, A. (2009). Ethics in educational research: Introducing a methodological tool for effective ethical analysis. *Cambridge Journal of Education*, *39*(4), 489–504. https://doi.org/10.1080/03057640903354396

Taquette, S. R., & Borges da Matta Souza, L. M. (2022). Ethical dilemmas in qualitative research: A critical literature review. *International Journal of Qualitative Methods*, *21*, 1–15. https://doi.org/10.1177/16094069221078731

Traianou, A. (2019). Phrónēsis and the ethical regulation of ethnographic research. In H. Busher & A. Fox (Eds.), *Implementing ethics in educational ethnography: Regulation and practice* (pp. 32–47). Routledge. https://doi.org/10.4324/9780429507489

Wang, X. (2013). The construction of researcher–researched relationships in school ethnography: Doing research, participating in the field and reflecting on ethical dilemmas. *International Journal of Qualitative Studies in Education*, *26*(7), 763–779. https://doi.org/10.1080/09518398.2012.666287

Wynn, L. (2018). When ethics review boards get ethnographic research wrong. In R. Iphofen & M. Tolich (Eds.), *The SAGE handbook of qualitative research ethics* (pp. 248–262). SAGE Publications Ltd. https://doi.org/10.4135/9781526435446

CHAPTER 5

ETHICAL CONSIDERATIONS DURING PHOTO-ELICITING TRAJECTORIES WITH MIGRANTISED WOMEN FOCUSED ON 'GENDER EMPOWERMENT' IN CIVIL SOCIETY ORGANISATIONS

Lore Van Praag[a], Amal Miri[b], Kaya Klaver[b] and Neda Deneva[c]

[a]*Erasmus University Rotterdam, The Netherlands*
[b]*University of Antwerp, Belgium*
[c]*SYNYO GmbH, Austria*

ABSTRACT

This chapter explores ethical considerations that arose when conducting photo-interviews about concepts of gender empowerment, inclusion and gender equality with members of Civil Society Groups and with women from migrant groups. We explore insights from the Horizon Europe ReIncluGen project, which was conducted in Austria, Belgium, Italy, Poland and Spain. Drawing on this research, we discuss the negotiation of ethical issues before, during and after photos were taken. We then explore the diverse challenges

Reframing Qualitative Research Ethics
Advances in Research Ethics and Integrity, Volume 12, 75–94

ISSN: 2398-6018/doi:10.1108/S2398-601820250000012005

that arose in relation to the use of these visual methodologies. We show how ethical concerns were encountered in relation to the emotions that were evoked, for some, by participating in these activities – notably in relation to discussing the photographs – and consider questions of safety and safeguarding that also had to be addressed in this context. We reflect on our experiences of interacting with ethics committees and advisors prior to entering the field and show how we addressed issues of anonymisation, negotiating access and informed consent throughout the project. Based on these experiences, we recommend that ethics boards and ethics advisors should implement a more processual approach to ethics at several points in time of a research project and develop clear reflection guidelines. We hope that by shedding light on these experiences, we will inspire future researchers to (better) reflect on ethics when designing and executing research using visual methods.

Keywords: Photo-eliciting methods; migration; gender; empowerment; visual methods

INTRODUCTION

Visual methods, such as photo-voicing and photo-eliciting methods, are becoming increasingly popular in social sciences. These visual techniques are used to conduct research when working with participants who are stigmatised, vulnerable, oppressed, or who find it difficult to articulate ideas solely in a narrative or interview format (Clark, 2019; Milne & Muir, 2019; Teti, 2019; Wang, 1998; Wang & Burris, 1997). Photo-voicing can be used to discuss and conceptualise difficult questions and to express ideas beyond language (Teti, 2019). The value of using such methods lies in their high level of flexibility and in the possibility of adapting them for use with particular target groups and communities (Wang & Burris, 1997). In doing so, researchers aim to generate insights that they would not have access to through other approaches, and likewise participants can raise aspects the researcher would not have thought of as relevant (Cooper & Yarbrough, 2010; Wang & Burris, 1997). This facilitates the discussion of controversial topics or topics where the researcher and the interlocutor have diverging takes on what is being discussed (Wang & Burris, 1997).

Despite the growing popularity of visual methods (Hannes & Parylo, 2014; Milne & Muir, 2019; Rosemberg & Evans-Agnew, 2020; Teti, 2019), less attention has been given to the ethical challenges and questions related to these visual methods (Clark, 2019). These difficulties concern the uniqueness of visual methods, which complicate possibilities for maintaining anonymity and confidentiality, jeopardising the approval of ethical boards at universities or funding bodies. This chapter reflects on the ethical considerations that we encountered when working with visual research methods in our research focused on migrantised groups.[1] This is relevant since, in contrast to audiovisual/narrative techniques, some additional questions arise. These issues range from safeguarding the participants despite their higher visibility through photo-voicing, exhibiting photos, problems about ownership of these images, the potential for photos or images provided by the participants to be misinterpreted, as well as issues of anonymity and pseudonymisation. In exploring these issues, we support the idea that ethics are not set in stone but constantly evolve over time and are adjustable to the context (Liebenberg, 2018).

In the following sections, we provide an overview of photo-voicing and photo-eliciting methods and consider the existing literature on ethics related to visual methods in social sciences. Afterwards, we reflect on the ethical issues and considerations related to visual methods made throughout the ReIncluGen project.

PHOTO-VOICING AND PHOTO-ELICITING METHODS

Since Collier and Collier (1967) introduced photography as a research method, coining the concept of visual anthropology, researchers have used, experimented and reflected upon how visual methods – in particular photographs – can go hand in hand with research. There are several visual methods, ranging from journey mapping, photo-voicing and photo-eliciting, used in social research. While both photo-elicitation and photo-voicing involve the use of photographs to gather qualitative data, the key difference lies in who selects and takes the photographs.

Photo-voicing involves participants taking their own photographs to share their perspectives. The core of the photo-voicing methodology is that the studied group receives photography training and is instructed to take pictures of anything they deem important regarding a specific subject. Afterwards, the photos are shared and discussed individually or in a group in the format of a focus group discussion. Photo-voicing can be used as a technique, primarily focused on the pictures, or as an auxiliary technique to assist with interviews on complicated topics (Duffy, 2011; Wang & Burris, 1997). Wang and Burris (1997) argue that the use of photo-voicing techniques enables participants to (1) amplify their voice, (2) bring to the fore less acknowledged types of knowledge, such as tacit and experiential knowledge, (3) be a catalyst for social change and/or be a tool for the development of critical consciousness, and (4) change existing dynamics in relationships between communities, researchers and policymakers. However, Milne and Muir (2019) have added some critical perspectives, highlighting the pitfalls that such methods may encounter and questioning whether photo-voicing as such will necessarily result in such positive social changes. Rather, they suggest, these could lead to unanticipated effects, including suspicion of the researchers, and negative portrayal of the communities that participants belong to.

Photo-elicitation involves researchers providing photographs to participants. Photo-eliciting techniques are defined as follows by Harper (2002, p. 1): 'Photo elicitation is based on the simple idea of inserting a photograph into a research interview'. According to Harper, the use of images, such as photos, drawings and cartoons, helps to evoke more distinct kinds of information than would have been retrieved using interviews. This technique heavily relies on the idea that visual information enables the voices of participants to be amplified (Luttrell, 2010; Milne & Muir, 2019).

In our project, we aimed to consider the diversity among our participants. This influenced the choice of one method over another. We focused on the ethical considerations when using visual research techniques. In doing so, we sought to create an environment in which participants use photos or objects, which could be older or more recent ones, taken or chosen by participants to denote their understanding of 'empowerment' in general and to further specify their thinking about gender in this context. Using and selecting these typically led in two different directions: (1) the use of photographs or objects to gauge meanings of empowerment in consecutive interviews, and (2) to voice the views and experiences of participants in relation to empowerment to a larger audience in a photo-exhibition, accompanied by a small text or story told by the participants on the significance and symbolisation of the photograph. This supported the viewers of the photos to better interpret or (re)imagine the meaning of the photograph. Participants were first asked to participate in the interview and afterwards to give permission to share their photographs and narratives in the exhibition.

VISUAL METHODS AND ETHICAL CONSIDERATIONS IN LITERATURE

When reflecting on ethical considerations regarding the usage of visual methods, it is important to distinguish between the ethical concerns that arise across diverse target groups and research settings. The formulation of the questions to be asked about images or the demand to bring along or take pictures also requires some cultural sensitivity.

Many studies using visual methods focus on vulnerable groups in society, including children (Epstein et al., 2006; Glaw et al., 2017; Gube, 2022), which need additional care and attention. For instance, in a study by Epstein et al. (2006), in which photos were used to elicit children's perspectives, the authors highlight that some ethical concerns arose in relation to who takes the picture (whether researchers or the children) and the extent in which they are involved in research. In that study, children who were attending a camp were given a camera at particular moments in time (after the camp activities), so they would not always be in charge. In another study, by Glaw et al. (2017), the researchers wanted to compare photos taken by those who suffer from mental health complaints, with those taken by a group of scholars. However, as 'people in an acute care setting may be very ill and may struggle to participate in research of this type', they opted to select solely people in a community setting (Glaw et al., 2017, p. 4).

A second theme is that visual methods could be of added value, especially in specific, often sensitive, settings (Gautam et al., 2018). This may be so where target groups are less easy to reach through other research inquiries, such as quantitative surveys. For example, Gautam et al. (2018) conducted research with sex-trafficking survivors in Nepal. Based on their experiences, they suggested using photovoice during rehabilitation.

Third, some projects, like the SEXHUM project led by Nicola Mai, seek to ensure that more efficient and ethical policies and social interventions are developed to address the needs of the research participants, in this case sex workers in strategic urban settings in Australia, France and the United States.[2] The methodology for this research draws upon several qualitative methods like art-science ethnographic filmmaking in which research participants partake in the ethnographic filmmaking to narrate their realities and to address the relational and performative dimensions of their experiences.

Finally, it needs to be clearly defined who will eventually see these pictures after the research has been conducted. These decisions will necessitate clear communication and discussion with the participants – and sometimes an additional ethics review may be needed to clarify these boundaries.

RESEARCH DESIGN OF THE REINCLUGEN PROJECT

In our project, which is still in progress, photo-eliciting methods were deployed to help us understand the concept of 'gender empowerment' by migrantised women in an emic, inductive and collaborative way. Asking women to bring pictures and using them as an entry point allowed the interview to be led by the ideas and concepts of the women, rather than to have preconceived questions and indicators of gender empowerment imposed from outside by the researcher. In narrative interviews, the questions, their formulation and the order of how they are asked can predefine the way interlocutors formulate their answers. By using photo-elicitation, we wanted to avoid this and let conceptualisations of gender empowerment stem from the participants and their views. In this way, it was the participants who led, decided and selected the topics, the approaches and emphases. This enabled us as researchers to understand more deeply why the photos were chosen or taken as they were, what was being expressed and why this was important to them and the group. Although we initially focused on photographs during the preparations for our fieldwork, and during the interviews themselves, we realised that not everyone is familiar or comfortable with taking photographs, and that they could feel burdened to capture a sensitive and broad concept in a specific photograph. Because of this, we opened up our methodology so that participants could also, if they wished, bring objects to the interviews.

By directly including participants in several steps of the research process, this research project aimed to be highly co-creative (Liebenberg, 2018). This participatory dimension can be seen first of all in the inclusion of civil society organisations (CSOs) within our project consortium and second by our use of participatory research methods, such as photo-eliciting interviews resulting in an art exhibition. Furthermore, our commitment to participatory approaches was reflected in our use of evaluation methods to assess promising practices of gender empowerment and inclusion in CSOs using an intersectional approach. As such, we found that these approaches could be empowering, shifting some of the control over the research process and the main categories and definitions from the researcher to the participants (Budig et al., 2018).

Through the creative process of selecting pictures and attributing meanings to them, participants took the lead in defining and crafting meanings, which allowed for inductive and collaborative research. Hence, the selected or produced picture, combined with an explanatory quote or essay, could also result in more ownership, especially when making them public (Wang & Burris, 1997). As visual methods are exploratory, inductive methods, we aimed to deconstruct the meaning of the concept 'gender empowerment' and to stimulate debates about what this concept could mean, how it could be (re)interpreted in society, and how it is applied in the CSOs that participants are involved with.

During this project, for each of our case study countries (Austria, Belgium, Italy, Spain and Poland), we selected three CSOs and invited 10 migrantised women who participated in the CSOs' activities to conduct approximately three consecutive interviews (30 participants in five countries: 150 participants in total). We realised this goal, although some participants preferred only to have a brief contact or dropped out, especially for the third round of interviews. Before the interviews, the team conducted around 20 days of ethnographic fieldwork in each of the CSOs. This helped to build up trust between the researchers and the participants and to encourage participants to engage in the three consecutive interviews. During the first interview encounter, ethical aspects were explained and discussed, and the researcher asked about their initial ideas on the concept of 'empowerment', and especially 'gender empowerment', beginning to build a rapport with the participant and then explaining the 'photo assignment' and discussing together what the photos should depict. This is a crucial step in encouraging participants to share photos, as many are hesitant or feel inadequate at first, and to discuss how a relatively vague concept such as 'gender empowerment' could be portrayed in photos.

Participants were then asked to bring around three to five photos to the next interview, which we hoped would be less stressful than having to select only one. Some prompts were also given to ease the respondents who felt inadequate to use pictures to tell their views (for example, 'bring a picture of a moment where you feel strong, encouraged or like yourself'). It was, however, emphasised that these guidelines were only suggestions and that they were free to bring whatever felt right. In this sense, participants could also bring a personal or symbolic object. In the third interview, participants were asked about their opinion on photo-elicitation how they felt after having reflected in such a manner on their processes of empowerment and whether they would still like to add something to their narratives. Additionally, participants were asked whether they would be willing to showcase one of their photos or objects, initially used during the interviews, in a travelling art exhibition and photo-essay book, in which they would present a short explanatory essay or quote to set out their ideas concerning these photos and their message. At this point, they would be asked to select only one photo together with the researcher. Although the interview data were processed in an anonymous way for analysis, for the photo-exhibition, in contrast, participants are asked whether they want to add their name to the photo or prefer to use a pseudonym, and if they would like additional changes to be made for reasons of privacy, such as blurring parts of the photo. From our perspective, the choice to see all participants at consecutive moments over time, even after extensive ethnographic fieldwork, was needed to develop trust. This reflects the importance of helping people to feel at ease before being involved in 'creative' activities of this kind, which is also mentioned by Shobiye (2023), who asked refugee women to make simple drawings at the end of the interview on mothers' social spaces.

Next to the photo-voicing interviews with women who participated as part of the collaborating CSOs, we also launched a photo-essay contest in order to widen our scope to a broader public and reach other migrantised women in society. Through their participation in the contest, other women's photos and objects could also become part of the international travelling exhibition. Another rationale behind the contest was to raise awareness and to promote our project with society as we diffused the contest call using different channels, including via social media, newsletters, emails, project and CSO websites. In the following section, we discuss the four main themes of our ethical reflections during the fieldwork.

ETHICAL REFLECTIONS ON PHOTO-ELICITING TRAJECTORIES

As explored below, undertaking this research involved us in negotiating ethics before, during, and after the photo-eliciting trajectories within CSOs and with their participants.

Ethics Committees

Before we started the fieldwork, all university partners asked for approval from their research ethics committees (RECs). We found that doing this took quite some time and so slowed down the work of reflecting on ethical issues as a team. Given that the research funder had also required the appointment of an Independent Ethics Advisor to provide advice, support and monitoring of the ethical issues arising in the project, the appointed Advisor also provided feedback on reports to the funder as well as on the submissions to the local ethics committees.[3] In view of the detailed attention paid to these processes, this all took quite some time.

Some reflections can be made that may be useful for ethical boards at research institutions or for university networks. First, before submitting, the researchers were obliged to discuss their proposals with an ethics officer and a data manager. These discussions led to the joint development of a 'decision tree' on anonymisation and pseudonymisation (below) presenting ethics more as an ongoing discussion that needs to be continuously considered and adjusted to the actual needs of researchers and research participants, as well as to the changing requirements and developments in society and the research project itself. Similarly, the requirement to discuss ethics with an external Independent Ethics Advisor obliged us as a team to discuss our ethical concerns in some depth. This resulted in further reflections on trauma-informed research competencies, highlighting the need, from our point of view, for ethics committees to take account of these issues (Goodwin & Tiderington, 2022). This caused the researchers to organise a lecture on this topic by Goodwin and Tiderington (2022). These are good examples of seeing ethics in terms of an ongoing discussion about issues that are not 'set in stone', a perspective that we feel is not sufficiently adopted in academia, where there may not be much space for these debates.

Second, we found reflecting on ethics and submitting protocols to the ethics boards to be a time-consuming process, with diverging speeds and demands across universities that could be simplified by collaborative ethics networks, in which the same ethical requirements were shared per university, avoiding duplicating work for ethical boards. As these steps are time-consuming, we would argue that (1) protocols and related documents such as informed consent forms (ICFs) should be evaluated as swiftly as possible by ethics committees, consistent with their duty to scrutinise these carefully; (2) where appropriate, requirements for ethics reports across research institutions should be standardised, and a clear timeline for acknowledgements of these reports should be introduced; and (3) a processual approach to ethics should be included, in which at several moments in time, researchers have the opportunity to discuss and evaluate their ethical considerations with an ethics officer.

Third, collaboration and unification of participant information across research institutions may yield benefits. During the course of the project, a standardised form in 'simple language' was developed. Especially for participants who are not aware of these ethics procedures, who do not trust governmental bodies, do not speak the local language and are suspicious of signing formal documents, the language and content of ICFs can be burdensome. The use of simplified ICFs can be helpful here. Collaboration across ethics boards could further facilitate the development of ICF templates in different languages, to which only small changes may need to be added regarding the content and objective of the research. This can facilitate awareness of ethics and makes sure all participants are *really* informed about the ethical procedures followed.

Entering the CSOs

Of the three CSOs involved in our research, one is actually part of the research consortium and the other two were selected later on. The process of negotiating access depended on whether or not they were included in the consortium and their size, which had an impact on how many people in the CSO were already aware of the research and its objectives. In addition, some people working with the CSOs felt that their organisations were understaffed, which would complicate their participation in a research project. Gaining access to the field therefore demanded much effort, and the project members had to take care not to ask for additional time and effort from the CSOs. Once the researchers were immersed in the fieldwork, and trust was built, we heard and experienced less reluctance as we continued to reflect on how to 'give back to the CSO', which in some cases resulted in our giving token gifts to interview participants, such as vouchers, or paying for a drink or a meal or buying chocolates.

As this project consists of a nested structure – namely recruiting participants that take part in activities organised by a specific CSO – additional care was needed to ensure safety, privacy and the application of ethical guidelines. Some CSOs work on very specific topics (such as gender-based violence or poverty) with a particular target group, which may be newcomers from a specific region, people confronted with violence, or refugees. To reflect on how we would deal with ethical considerations, especially to guarantee and safeguard anonymity and pseudonymisation of the data when desired, we used a 'decision tree'. This decision tree was followed by researchers to understand the level of anonymisation and pseudonymisation needed to be used to safeguard anonymity – even if names of individuals and organisations are not disclosed. This was needed due to the selection of the CSOs in our sample which may be easily recognisable by virtue of their work in a particular context and country. In addition, given that many of them were relatively small, functions of participants (for example, CSO director) or socio-demographic information (for example, an older Pakistani woman working in a bakery) could immediately identify participants. Hence, further measures were taken to not disclose the personal and sensitive information of participants and CSOs involved. Another precaution taken was to ensure that if participants wish to disclose information about themselves, this would not impact the anonymity and pseudonymisation of other participants. The latter is especially important concerning the photo-trajectories and to avoid a paternalistic approach to anonymisation (Kara, 2022).

In Fig. 5.1, we give an overview of the considerations that the researchers, and the consortium, followed to decide on how CSOs and their participants will be discussed and referred to in our research outputs.

This figure shows that the following elements are considered: (1) the size of the CSO, (2) the specificity of the data, (3) being able to track down the quote to one person and (4) the position of the participant in society.

1. *Is the CSO large in size?* The size matters to ensure people cannot be identified based on their demographic data when revealing the name of the organisation. This could mean, for instance, that approximately 10 persons with similar demographic data are needed to not automatically disclose information when participants do not wish to. If not, the quote used for a participant may be anonymous on its own but not when the name of the CSO is mentioned.
2. *Is the quote itself very specific?* If the information revealed from the quote is very specific, you may immediately guess the organisation this person is part of.
3. *Is the quote clearly tracked down to one person?* Discuss this with the participants first (and thus discuss their anonymity) or write it in such a way it is not formulated in a quote but part of a larger chunk of text.
4. *Does the participant hold a vulnerable position in society?* Discuss the differences between anonymity and non-anonymity with the participant. Discuss the risks they could face and support them when making decisions on participation and/or anonymity.

Regarding anonymisation of CSOs, we have not, so far, encountered any major challenges. However, we have reflected on the need to consider this when talking about the ethnographic process in conferences or even to our advisory boards. Given the diversity of CSO landscapes in all the countries involved in our consortium, it is also relatively easy to identify organisations based on their characteristics, scope and target population. Particularly in relation to smaller countries

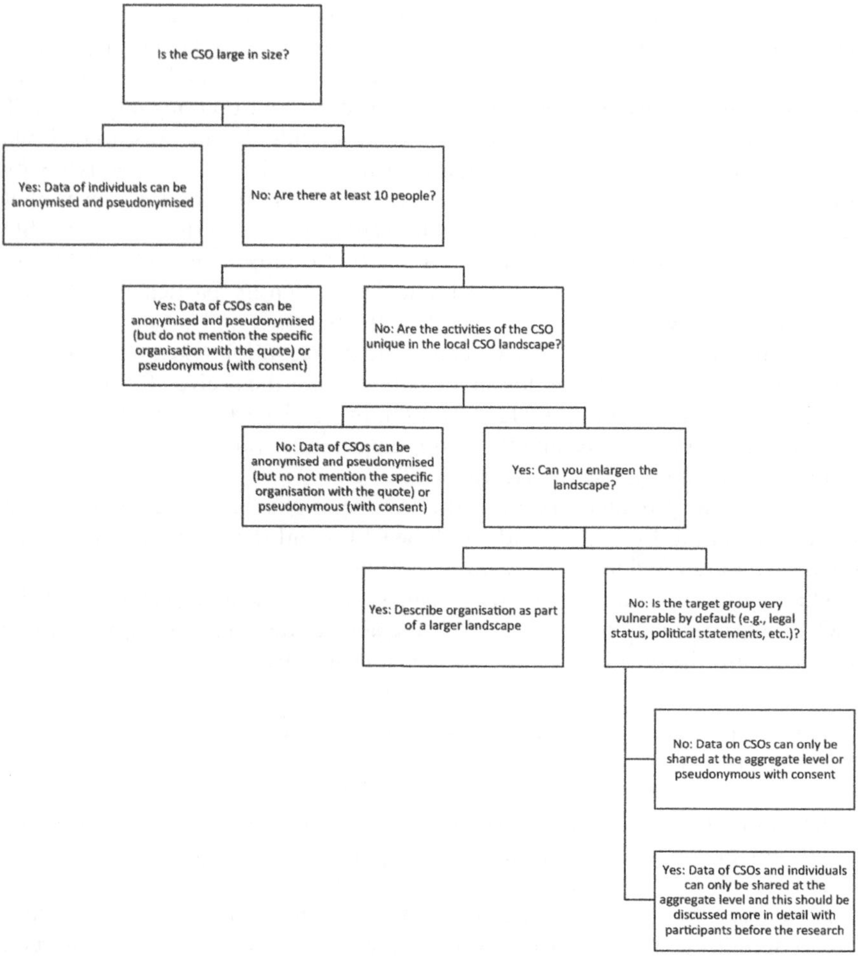

Fig. 5.1. Decision Tree on Level of Pseudonymisation and Anonymisation Possible per CSO and Their Participants.

like Austria and Belgium, we have decided to talk about CSOs in more general terms, always being aware to not give away any information which could identify these organisations. Anonymisation of the CSOs was considered essential both for the analysis and presentation of findings about the opinions and discourses of their staff members, as well as for better anonymisation of participants from the migrantised groups with whom these organisations work. As for women from the target groups who took part in in-depth photo-elicited interviews, we found that it was essential for us to spend some time together with them, even before doing the interviews, to explain the aim of the research better and gain their trust. In other words, anonymising organisations was deemed to be necessary for photos to be shared – especially when these touched on gender empowerment, which is a sensitive and highly debated topic in society.

NEGOTIATING ACCESS AND INFORMED CONSENT

Our negotiations with participants – often combined with their participation during the interviews – usually followed a stepwise process. Already in our consent form, participants had the option to agree to either one or several aspects of the project. This ICF included an option to stay anonymous, to use photos during the interview and to use the photos for the art exhibition and/or photo-essay book. Given that this was already quite detailed, somewhat academic in nature and formulated in the dominant language of the country, presenting and explaining the ethical procedures took quite some time. As participants were not fully aware of what would be entailed at the outset, a stepwise approach to participation in the research project was agreed, with participants first being asked which elements they wanted to participate in: this felt reassuring and helped to overcome initial barriers to participation. It often helped that the researcher took part in some activities organised by the CSO before conducting the interview, building rapport with the participants and gaining mutual trust. Additionally, we found that having WhatsApp groups for researchers, participants and CSO staff was another medium to build rapport and provided a way for participants to get in touch using direct messages to raise questions concerning the use of their photos or objects and potential references to their name. Within these groups, only members of the same CSO were included, and no sensitive data were shared. Rather, practical questions about the research were shared. We also noticed that researchers with a migration background experienced less difficulty with reaching participants. One Belgian researcher with a migration background also mentioned that speaking the same mother tongue or having the same ethnic or religious background as the participants made it easy for them to be open and make connections. After getting to know the researcher and showing their first photos during the interviews, it seemed easier to also agree to contribute to the art exhibition at a later stage. During the first interview, the researcher explained the assignment and which kind of photos or objects the participants were expected to bring during the next interview.

Using an interpreter, as we did in Austria, offered another approach to establishing rapport and facilitating a clear understanding of the consent forms. Interpreters were also from migrant backgrounds and shared both language and cultural background with the participants. They explained both the process and the different steps of the interviews, as well as the implications of agreeing to participate with quotes, pictures and sharing the pictures publicly. This was treated as a separate stage, before the interview, and was conducted directly in the language of the participant, explaining and replying to questions, without translating them back to the researcher. This helped to create a sense of intimacy and trust. Some of the participants shared after the interview that they felt comfortable to ask further questions about the use of photos, for example, at a later stage during the interview, without feeling embarrassed that they did not understand the idea for the exhibition during the first explanation, because they already trusted the interpreter.

Using an interpreter, however, does raise additional questions pertaining to ethics and power relations and to levels of sharing and opening up during an interview. As also noted in other analyses (Bowlby & Day, 2018), using interpreters during interviews can change the dynamics and sometimes even partly the content of the interview. We found that interpreters with a similar background to that of the participants built a different type of rapport with the participants than researchers who do not speak the same language. The use of interpreters can also create ease and more openness in the interview, since it avoids the sometimes intense dynamics of a one-to-one interview. Overall, we have found that having an additional person present during the interview with shared cultural and linguistic knowledge with the interviewees created a different setting and changed the power relations and positions in that context. A shared cultural background and language is, of course, just one of the possible common denominators. In our case, gender between the participants and the researchers was also the same during all interviews, having only female interpreters. But other socio-demographic factors, such as social class, educational background, rural/urban location and age are all potential additional points of difference that varied and impacted the flow of the interview. Another contentious point about having interpreters involved relates to the way in which interviews are translated, whether immediately (literally) or after a duration of time: these dynamics can affect the flow of an interview or in some cases leave the interviewer in a position of partial understanding. Although we did not translate them afterwards for further triangulation, this would have further added to insights into the concepts used. While in some interviews, this could have facilitated the interview, it might, in others, have disrupted the flow. Despite these difficulties, this does not necessarily undermine the quality of data obtained (Bowlby & Day, 2018).

Given that our research project takes a very personal and even intimate look into each participant's understanding of womanhood and empowerment, our approach to the interviews was to give participants a large role in deciding which research topics they wanted to delve into. In setting-up the interviews, we offered them space to reflect and discuss freely their selected topics, to go in directions that they felt are important and to share life details only to the extent that they felt were relevant for the topic. Since this is at the core of the participatory approach we aim to take, we found that the changed dynamics brought about by the interpreter contributed to a direction of participants feeling comfortable and well understood, even if the flow between questions and replies might have been influenced. To ensure the reliability of the information shared, we tried out several methods for presenting a shorter and a longer translated version of the ICF, a short description of the project and of the interview process, that can be taken home by the participants. We also analysed the translations of the interviews afterwards. In addition, we used the same interpreters for each language, to ensure consistency.

Depending on the background of the participants, the time taken to explain the project and sign the consent forms varied. Completion of the consent forms took less time for the CSO organisers, compared to the other participants. For some of the women with lower education, or lower levels of literacy, it was overwhelming to read this document. What came across as difficult in some cases was that while, on the one hand, we explained that we will keep their anonymity and privacy and we will not disclose their names, unless they explicitly agree, on the other hand, we asked them to identify themselves when signing the consent form. We spent time carefully explaining the way we stored the consent forms, and that they would not be connected to the analysis in any way.

We explained that signing is a way of guaranteeing that we would share only the information that they agree upon, which kept the researcher responsible. For instance, in Vienna, one woman asked whether she could see the answers of other women, and we explained that this was not possible, precisely because of privacy issues, which, in fact, convinced her that we would not disclose sensitive information. This, we found, was particularly important for women who were going through divorce procedures and feeling vulnerable. Overall, it felt that taking the time to explain and reassure participants that their answers would remain anonymous and to explain the process of analysis was beneficial for trust building. This was particularly important in the cases where women shared traumatic life stories.

In the case of our work in Belgium, participants experienced it as discouraging if we presented the consent form right away – as this might seem to be putting too much emphasis on 'concerns' rather than on what this could also mean in terms of 'safety' and 'opportunity' for the women. For this reason, the researchers in Belgium sometimes presented the consent form at the end of the first interview after providing general information on ethics. In Austria, the researchers found that taking the time to explain the project, to describe the interview process and to explain how anonymity and privacy would be secured was a step towards establishing trust. While this did take significant time at the beginning of the first interview, it demonstrated to the participants the two-way engagement and the willingness of the researchers to invest their time to reassure and make them feel comfortable. This discussion was used as a time to discuss possible concerns and worries about sharing personal stories and details. Thinking of the informed consent procedure as a significant step in the interview process, rather than as a formality, allowed researchers and participants both to understand the details and to better understand the meaning of research.

OWNERSHIP AND PROFESSIONALISM

Questions about ownership and power relations in visual research methods emerge even before the research project starts. While claiming that the usage of visual methods can result in more empowerment, awareness and ownership by so-called 'hard to reach' groups or vulnerable groups in society, many research projects design their research questions without consulting their target group. This brings in some power imbalances, as the research questions do not always resonate with the questions, demands and voices of the people involved (Milne & Muir, 2019). Within our project, CSOs were involved in the proposal writing and helped to recruit participants who in some cases already had a desire to discuss gender and empowerment in society. When the broader research design was set up, the interpretations of the civil society partners and their participants were warmly welcomed, albeit that this could have resulted in some selection bias of participants. Hence, solely those attracted to the theme, or the specific CSO focusing on this topic, engaged with this time-intensive project and met several times with a researcher to further develop the interview questions.

Concerning the usage of visual methods, many debates arose regarding how we should prepare participants when taking and discussing photos on gender empowerment. These debates concerned professional support for training when using visual methods or even hiring a professional photographer to re-enact the photos with the participant. Arguments that were in favour of professionalisation stated that everyone deserves to showcase photos of high quality in an art exhibition, and this would also be a benefit from participating in this research project. Concerns were related to the impact that the art exhibition might have on the participants if we did not manage to come out with photos which, when exhibited, made them feel proud of their process and work, making them feel exposed or vulnerable. For many participants, the process was experienced as rewarding, so instead of focusing on the end result, many focused on this participatory experience as being reflective and meaningful. After one of the final interviews, a participant informally discussed with the researcher that she wanted to edit or change some details about her picture because 'after knowing the project better and understanding the bigger purpose of representation' she learned that she wanted to 'pass on the message to society of different generations of migrant women and that all have made a difference' (ORG3_BE_10). This conversation continued with the participant stating that, for her, the message or story behind the photo is more important. Arguments against professionalising the process of taking photos underlined that the participants should be valued in their own right, and that seeing the photos they had taken themselves in an essay book, art exhibition or when discussing them with a researcher was empowering in itself. In the end, both strategies were experienced as 'empowering'. In addition, many participants wanted to show their names when presenting their photo in the art exhibition, although this did cause additional efforts for the researchers in terms of anonymising both the organisations and participants' quotes in academic publications. Finally, during the selection of photos for the photo-contest, we differentiated between those who enjoyed training, workshops or had a professional background in photography.

PHOTO-ELICITING TRAJECTORIES: EVOKING EMOTIONS AND SAFEGUARDING EQUALITY

The procedure and impact of the photo-eliciting trajectories also prompted some ethical reflection. Participants showed photos of themselves during turning points in their lives – working, obtaining a degree, marriage, first child, migration – and reflecting important aspects of their identities and cultures, such as a book or an inspiring individual, and life philosophies. In some cases, photos felt very personal and were therefore harder to bring to the interview moment.

For this reason, we opened up an option for participants to also bring objects, as this may feel safer and so make the selection easier. Some brought (a photo of) an old but special newspaper or a memory box. This corresponds to the remarks made by Luttrell (2010) and Milne and Muir (2019), who question the notion that all research participants welcome the use of camera technologies to express their stories and ideas.

While we emphasise the participatory nature of our project, we must acknowledge that only one 'side' is asked to provide photos (both as a research tool and as an output). One could question this approach, arguing that it does not provide an equal context to participate together in one research project (Van Praag, 2021). Following the conventions of interviewing, the researchers did not provide photos, nor did they discuss their views and ideas on 'empowerment'. Even though we tried to personally engage with the photos and the corresponding narratives, we are aware that less attention had been paid to reciprocity during our interviews. In some cases, we tried to balance this by discussing the challenges and the different ways of approaching the task, with the researcher and/or the interpreter sharing what they would bring to such an interview and what it would mean to them, with the aim of creating more of a shared space of exchange and reciprocity.

Second, given the contextual difference between the photo-eliciting interviews and the art exhibition, we encountered some difficulties when participants used photos of themselves and/or their family members. As using the photos or objects during the interviews – so as to show how proud they are of their family – had less ethical considerations than exhibiting these photos or objects for the public, this further complicated reflections on the limits to anonymity in this context. Added to this, minors were often included in the photos, which we only displayed in the exhibition if explicit consent had been given by one of the parents for their display. As for others shown in the pictures, direct consent was also obtained from these people.

Third, trauma often came up for the researchers during the photo-eliciting interviews for various reasons. For instance, migrantised researchers felt that some topics made them emotional, for example, when discussing first generation parents and their similar struggles. Both in Belgium and in Austria, it was noted that participants appreciated it if the researchers expressed and shared some of their experiences. In this respect, the sharing of some personal details by the researcher or by interpreters provided a sense of reciprocity and better understanding. On some occasions, the researcher experienced emotional challenges to process the often painful stories told by the participants.

Importantly, and related to the third point, many participants also experienced emotions and trauma when selecting and sharing their photos. For instance, one participant mentioned liking these kinds of challenges to their creativity, which helped her to reflect on what this concept really meant to her, to visualise it and to discuss some of her emotions:

> I always find such a conversation very therapeutic. I say that, but I guess it is like that. You feel relieved and you are sure that they will do some things with it. If you create 'awareness' with the exhibition, and then you think that you will reach somewhere with that information, that you will reach an audience, something will happen. (CSO3_BE_4)

Showing photos and simultaneously having the opportunity to engage in a conversation around that photo was well received by the participants. As other interviewees put it:

> It was good to reflect a bit about the past. (CSO1_BE_6)

> I enjoyed talking about myself with someone (...) it does not occur that often (...) that I could talk about my life and what I did. (CSO1_BE_8)

> Yes, it brought up a lot in me, also the choosing of the three objects [the interviewer provided the option to give 3 objects instead of photos if that was easier]. That was something I had never thought of before ... in the end I ended up with 'water'. How do you get there? Yes, it did something with me. (CSO3_BE_2)

The choice of photos often resulted in some stress to pick the 'correct' photo or to put into photos what a vague concept such as 'gender empowerment' means. One person said jokingly that she encountered difficulties picking one photo: 'Oops, which photo, this one is good or that one', adding afterwards that she didn't find it easy to express herself using photos 'maybe I can present myself better' (CSO1_BE_7). Yet, she said that hadn't had much time to prepare, which affected her choices and the experience in general. On a similar theme, other participants said that 'it was interesting but at the same time also difficult as I couldn't find what I mean myself' (CSO2_BE_6) and commented on the wider meanings of such difficulties:

> Difficult, because I had to answer a couple of questions. Allez, I found it difficult, especially, there was one question ... A photo that reminds you of a specific moment in your life when you overcome a difficulty. I found that very difficult, I wouldn't know which photo. (CSO_BE_9)

While the experiences with photo-eliciting interviews varied between participants, we can say that in many cases, these interviews did bring up some valuable reflections, both for the participants and for the researcher.

Some participants wanted to show even more and others deliberately searched for photos that represented specific moments in their lives. One found that 'for me, it's easier with photos, as you will focus more on searching for specific moments in time. And at the same time, memories come up, that goes easier with photos for me' (CSO1_BE_5). As reflected in the following quote, this shows the complexity of affect and emotion, as both nostalgic feelings and also more traumatic experiences came up.

> I thought about my mother, my family, what we said, and things that have been going on for a very long time - not like the things in my country but it came back, yes. (CSO2_BE_3)

Participants wanted to make sure that several photos were included as part of their narrative of empowerment. A 'before and after' was indicated by selecting a photo illustrating the way the participant felt before and after a significant event, such as separation, which illustrated a path towards empowerment. This participant insisted her photos only made sense together and must be used as two parts of one illustration. Taking into account such a requirement was also considered part of our ethical responsibilities.

Finally, some comments were made about 'selecting photos that can be shown to someone else'. This suggests that some participants considered representations of themselves, or the group they belong to, when selecting the photos, as described in the following conversation with a participant (CSO1_BE_3):

Interviewee: 'I wanted to add more photos, but found that there were sufficient photos'.
Interviewer: 'That's very good, I was just wondering why you didn't include personal photos from yourself or your life?'
Interviewee: 'I think I would then have to give information about my personal social contacts, for instance, I have the impression that if I tell about my own life, that I also have to talk about theirs and they will look at me in a different way'.
Interviewer: 'You don't like it that people look at you differently?'
Interviewee: 'I don't have any issues telling things, but photos – also not those of my children – I don't like that. I don't mind when it doesn't hurt anyone, I don't have a problem with [people sharing theirs] but if I have to choose myself, I prefer not to do so, privacy'
Interviewer: 'How did you feel after our first interview?'
Interviewee: 'Relieved'.

This extract reminds us that there is a huge variety of ways that photos can provoke emotions and stimulate the conversation, as well as sometimes limiting the sharing between the participant and the researcher.

CONCLUSION

This chapter sheds light on the use of visual methods when conducting research with migrantised women in five European Union (EU) countries as part of our comparative project. Visual methods are often used to reach out to specific groups and discuss sensitive topics or topics that demand fresh and novel insights (Duffy, 2011; Epstein et al., 2006; Glaw et al., 2017; Gube, 2022; Wang & Burris, 1997). In our case, we aim to deconstruct the concept of 'gender empowerment' by using a so-called empowering technique, in which participants are free to show a novel perspective on this concept, with time to reflect on the topic. This concept is frequently used in research – and recurs in many policy initiatives – and yet is hard to translate or 'capture'. Using photo-eliciting techniques could therefore provide an elegant way to further define and conceptualise this concept, by exploring visual materials with participants.

In the course of our project, we realised that at different stages, ethical considerations came to the fore, which needed careful thought and often did not have clear-cut solutions. We realised that these ethical aspects needed to be negotiated before, during and after the photo-eliciting trajectories with interviewees. Furthermore, debates about who owns the research, and about the photos and the people in them, were held, reflecting on the need to include a sense of ownership into this research trajectory as well as the role professionalism plays in this context. These debates reflect the critical insights offered by Milne and Muir (2019), which highlight that giving voice to so-called vulnerable or 'hard to reach' groups in societies may challenge existing ideas about ownership and how social action takes place.

Finally, the use of visual methods, accompanied by the time that we invested in this project, was associated with participants and researchers becoming emotionally engaged with the project. This raised concerns about peoples' well-being, which continue throughout the research and will remain even after it ends. We hope that by shedding light on the experience gained by our project, we can further inspire future researchers to (better) reflect on the ethics when designing and executing research using visual methods.

Some future research recommendations can be formulated, especially for university ethics boards. We recommend that research institutions should, where possible, have similar ethical forms and requirements for ethics review and should formally acknowledge the decisions made by ethics committees from other institutions. Second, this collaboration should facilitate the development and sharing of a set of ICFs in simplified language and in different languages across research institutions, to avoid overburdening participants with unnecessarily complex material (Crow et al., 2006). Finally, ethics boards and advisors should implement a processual approach to ethics in several moments in time of a research project and develop clear reflection guidelines. Although the literature on ethics may already point to these solutions, they are not widely implemented in research institutions, albeit that the demands and ideas of ethics boards vary considerably.

NOTES

1. We deploy the term 'migrantised' to describe a group of people in society who are considered as 'migrants' in society due to their migration history, regardless of whether they have migrated or not themselves.
2. https://sexhum.org
3. The appointment of an Independent Ethics Advisor may be required by the EU research agencies, when EU-funded research is considered to raise potentially serious or complex ethical issues (European Commission, 2023).

ACKNOWLEDGEMENTS

We would like to thank the reviewer for the thorough feedback on this chapter. We are very grateful for the language edits made by Helen Busby, which significantly improved the quality of this chapter. Lore Van Praag would like to thank Elien Colman for her reflective insights on the use of art for research and mental well-being purposes and on how photographs can say more than a thousand words. This chapter is based on the findings of the Horizon Europe ReIncluGen project, which has received funding from the European Union's Horizon Europe Research and Innovative Action under Grant Agreement No. 101093987.

REFERENCES

Bowlby, S., & Day, C. (2018). Emotions, disclosures and reflexivity: Reflections on interviewing young people in Zambia and women in midlife in the UK. In T. Loughran & D. Mannay (Eds.), *Emotion and the researcher: Sites, subjectivities, and relationships (Studies in qualitative methodology, Vol. 16)* (pp. 127–142). Emerald Publishing. https://doi.org/10.1108/S1042-319220180000016009

Budig, K., Diez, J., Conde, P., Sastre, M., Hernán, M., & Franco, M. (2018). Photovoice and empowerment: Evaluating the transformative potential of a participatory action research project. *BMC Public Health*, *18*(432), 1–9. https://doi.org/10.1186/s12889-018-5335-7

Clark, A. (2019). Visual ethics beyond the crossroads. In L. Pauwels & Mannay, D. (Eds.), *The SAGE handbook of visual research methods* (2nd ed., pp. 682–693). SAGE Publications.

Collier, J., & Collier, M. (1967). *Visual anthropology: Photography as a research method*. Holt Rinehart and Winston.

Cooper, C. M., & Yarbrough, S. P. (2010). Tell me – Show me: Using combined focus group and photovoice methods to gain understanding of health issues in rural Guatemala. *Qualitative Health Research*, *20*(5), 644–653. https://doi.org/10.1177/1049732310361894

Crow, G., Wiles, R., Heath, S., & Charles, V. (2006). Research ethics and data quality: The implications of informed consent. *International Journal of Social Research Methodology*, *9*(2), 83–95. https://doi.org/10.1080/13645570600595231

Duffy, L. (2011). "Step-by-step we are stronger": Women's empowerment through photovoice. *Journal of Community Health Nursing*, *28*(2), 105–116. https://doi.org/10.1080/07370016.2011.564070

Epstein, I., Stevens, B., McKeever, P., & Baruchel, S. (2006). Photo elicitation interview (PEI): Using photos to elicit children's perspectives. *International Journal of Qualitative Methods*, *5*(3), 1–11. https://journals.sagepub.com/doi/10.1177/160940690600500301

European Commission. (2023). *Ethics advisors and ethics advisory boards roles and function in EU-funded projects*. https://ec.europa.eu/info/funding-tenders/opportunities/docs/2021-2027/horizon/guidance/roles-and-functions-of-ethics-advisory-ethics-advisory-boards-in-ec-funded-projects_he_en.pdf

Gautam, A., Shrestha, C., Tatar, D., & Harrison, S. (2018). Social photo-elicitation: The use of communal production of meaning to hear a vulnerable population. *Proceedings of the ACM on Human-Computer Interaction*, *2*(CSCW), 1–20. https://doi.org/10.1145/3274325

Glaw, X., Inder, K., Kable, A., & Hazelton, M. (2017). Visual methodologies in qualitative research: Autophotography and photo elicitation applied to mental health research. *International Journal of Qualitative Methods*, *16*(1). https://journals.sagepub.com/doi/10.1177/1609406917748215

Goodwin, J., & Tiderington, E. (2022). Building trauma-informed research competencies in social work education. *Social Work Education*, *41*(2), 143–156.

Gube, J. (2022). Photo-eliciting technique as an integrated meaning-making practice: An introspective look at diversity, identities, and voice-giving. *Visual Studies*, *37*(1–2), 116–127. https://doi.org/10.1080/02615479.2020.1820977

Hannes, K., & Parylo, O. (2014). Let's play it safe: Ethical considerations from participants in a photovoice research project. *International Journal of Qualitative Methods*, *13*(1), 255–274. https://doi.org/10.1080/1472586X.2020.1854053

Harper, D. (2002). Talking about pictures: A case for photo elicitation. *Visual Studies*, *17*(1), 13–26. https://doi.org/10.1080/14725860220137345

Kara, H. (2022). Doing research as if participants mattered. *Impact of Social Sciences Blog*. https://blogs.lse.ac.uk/impactofsocialsciences/2022/07/11/doing-research-as-if-participants-mattered/

Liebenberg, L. (2018). Thinking critically about photovoice: Achieving empowerment and social change. *International Journal of Qualitative Methods*, *17*(1), 1–9. https://doi.org/10.1177/1609406918757631

Luttrell, W. (2010). 'A camera is a big responsibility': A lens for analysing children's visual voices. *Visual Studies*, *25*(3), 224–237. https://doi.org/10.1080/1472586X.2010.523274

Milne, E.-J., & Muir, R. (2019). Photovoice: A critical introduction. In L. Pauwels & D. Mannay (Eds.), *The SAGE handbook of visual research methods* (2nd ed., pp. 282–296). SAGE Publications.

Rosemberg, M. A. S., & Evans-Agnew, R. (2020). Ethics in photovoice: A response to Teti. *International Journal of Qualitative Methods*, *19*. https://doi.org/10.1177/1609406920922734

Shobiye, L. (2023). "I survive on people": (Mis)recognising the value of social learning for mothers seeking sanctuary in Wales. PhD Thesis, Cardiff University. https://orca.cardiff.ac.uk/id/eprint/164130/1/FINAL%20COPY%201469982%20%20L%20Shobiye%20PhD%20Thesis_Redacted.pdf

Teti, M. (2019). The murky ethics of visual qualitative methods: Picturing a clear path forward. *International Journal of Qualitative Methods, 18*. https://doi.org/10.1177/1609406919884810

Van Praag, L. (2021). *Co-creation in migration studies: The use of co-creative methods to study migrant integration across European societies*. Leuven University Press. https://doi.org/10.2307/j.ctv1qhstr1

Wang, C., & Burris, M. A. (1997). Photovoice: Concept, methodology, and use for participatory needs assessment. *Health Education & Behavior*, *24*(3), 369–387. https://doi.org/10.1177/109019819702400309

Wang, C. C. (1998). Photovoice: A participatory action research strategy applied to women's health. *Journal of Women's Health*, *8*(2), 185–192. https://pubmed.ncbi.nlm.nih.gov/10100132/

CHAPTER 6

AUTOETHNOGRAPHY: AN ETHICS CHALLENGE FOR RESEARCHERS AND REVIEWERS

Nicole Brown

University College London, UK

ABSTRACT

Autoethnography has gained significant traction in qualitative research due to its introspective nature and its ability to connect personal experiences with broader societal and cultural contexts. In this chapter, I explore the ethical challenges inherent in autoethnographic research, where the researcher is both the subject and object of inquiry. While this approach offers opportunities for deep reflection and the creation of new knowledge, it also presents unique ethical dilemmas, which result in conventional research ethics guidelines falling short in addressing these. I propose an expanded ethical framework that includes relational and contextual ethics, as well as an ethics of the self, which emphasises self-care for researchers as they navigate emotionally charged topics. Additionally, I suggest that an attitudinal shift is required regarding the role of research ethics committees (RECs), which often prioritise procedural governance over meaningful ethical reflection. I advocate for more flexible review processes, while also suggesting social fiction as an alternative solution for researchers to ensure that autoethnographic research is conducted ethically.

Keywords: Autoethnography; ethics; ethical considerations; methodology; social fiction; reflexivity; research ethics committees

Reframing Qualitative Research Ethics
Advances in Research Ethics and Integrity, Volume 12, 95–110

ISSN: 2398-6018/doi:10.1108/S2398-601820250000012006

INTRODUCTION

In the 2020s, autoethnography as a qualitative inquiry is thriving, with many books outlining the method to be applied on an individual (Chang, 2016) and collaborative basis (Chang et al., 2016). This trend towards autoethnographic work does not come as a surprise, however. For decades, qualitative researchers have queried the purpose and nature of research and have inquired conscientiously about their relationship with chosen topics and research participants. With this increasing interest in reducing power dynamics and hierarchical structures in research, a more egalitarian and participatory approach to doing research has emerged, and so researchers' understanding of their role in research has developed, too. Knowing that positionality would have a significant impact on how research agendas are set, and how data are collected, analysed, and disseminated, researchers have more consistently looked inward; so much so that a reflexive turn within qualitative research became recognisable (Foley, 2002). The consequence of this emphasis on reflexivity is that researchers have looked to research approaches that would support a systematic turning inwards for the benefit of the research process.

At the same time, qualitative researchers as a collective have also pursued the potential of doing research differently. In the spirit of fostering inclusion and equality, researchers have emphasised the important role that participants play in the research process. Rather than seeing research participants as passive subjects, they now see them as becoming empowered to be active producers of new knowledge. Ultimately, they have lived experiences to draw on. It is this specific focus on lived experience and profound insider knowledge in connection with the increased work of reflexivity, especially in the context of marginalisation within the academy and society, that has led researchers to look inward even more. Autoethnography has emerged as one of the collective answers to the conundrum of embedding the self in qualitative research. Against this backdrop then, it is not surprising that autoethnography continues to gain traction within qualitative research despite the fact that critiques of autoethnography abound.

I contend that autoethnography is not an easy choice methodologically, and I use this chapter to explore some of the practicalities and pragmatics of this approach, in particular where ethical considerations are concerned. I begin my contribution with an outline of the challenges and opportunities that autoethnography as a research approach brings before examining some ethical considerations surrounding autoethnographic work. I conclude my chapter by offering potential solutions for individual researchers and research ethics committees (RECs) to ensure that autoethnography can be undertaken ethically.

AUTOETHNOGRAPHY IN QUALITATIVE RESEARCH

Autoethnography is a process of research predominantly through writing (-graphos) that requires individuals to focus on introspection (autos-) in order to make sense of cultural and societal phenomena (-ethnos-) (Chang, 2016; Ellis, 2004). Autoethnography, therefore, has the potential of being as close to a lived experience as possible because it relates to the researcher's own lived experience,

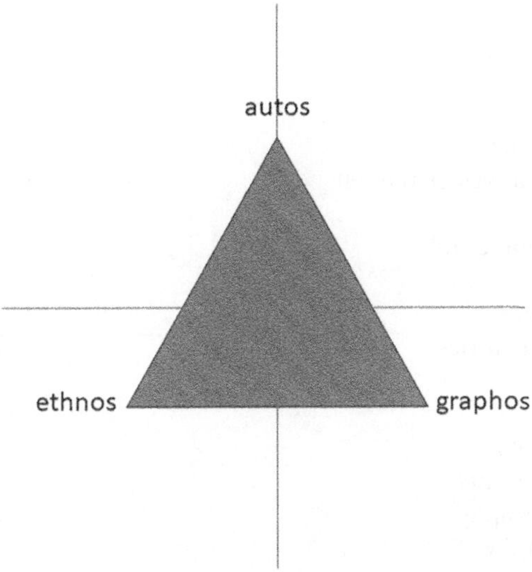

Fig. 6.1. Triad of Autoethnography.

while also connecting to wider cultural and societal circumstances and contexts. Autoethnographers therefore do not aim for objectivity and distance from their research focus, as they agree that such an endeavour would not be achievable anyway. Instead, autoethnographers embrace their closeness to and familiarity with the research data, and their own lived experiences, which enable them to then engage meaningfully and critically in the triad of self (autos) – other (ethnos) – research process (graphos). The foundational principle of autoethnography is not the uncovering of existing knowledge but the construction or active generation of new knowledge in the researcher's specific context. These specificities about personal context tend to have an impact on the individual researcher's emphasis when it comes to the three elements within autoethnography.

Good autoethnography should be balanced and therefore 'ethnographic in its methodological orientation, cultural in its interpretive orientation, and autobiographical in its content orientation' (Chang, 2016, p. 48). See Fig. 6.1, which I have created for a visual representation of the autos-ethnos-graphos triad.

In practice, autoethnographic work comes in different forms and formats, from personal narratives (Group, 1989), narratives of the self (Richardson, 1994), personal experience narratives (Denzin, 1989), and personal essays (Krieger, 1991) to ethnographic short stories (Ellis, 1995), writing stories (Richardson, 1997), self-ethnography (Van Maanen, 1995), emotionalism (Gubrium & Holstein, 1997), and radical empiricism (Jackson, 1989). The vast range of autoethnographic works becomes evident, when considering the types Ellis and Bochner (2000, pp. 739–740) list:

autobiographical ethnography
autobiology
auto-observation

autopathography
collaborative autobiography
complete-member research
confessional tales
critical autobiography
emotionalism narratives of the self
ethnobiography
ethnographic autobiography
ethnographic memoir
ethnographic poetics
ethnographic short stories
evocative narratives
experiential texts
first-person accounts
impressionistic accounts
Indigenous ethnography
interpretive biography
literary tales
lived experience
narrative ethnography
native ethnography
new or experimental ethnography
opportunistic research
personal essays
personal ethnography
personal experience narrative
personal narratives
personal writing
postmodern ethnography
radical empiricism
reflexive ethnography
self-ethnography
self-stories
socioautobiography
sociopoetics
writing stories

The common thread through all forms of autoethnography relates to questions about the legitimacy and context-specificity of qualitative inquiry. Instead of amplifying the myth of an objective researcher, autoethnography deliberately seeks to disrupt conventionally accepted norms of research practices. In this sense, autoethnography is not radically different from other ethnographic research approaches where insider-researchers are connected with their research foci and research participants before the research formally begins. However, autoethnography develops that disruption through the researcher's political engagement with their self and the society they inhabit. Autoethnography therefore does not aim at allowing for easy access to data but rather at fostering cultural and societal understanding, which in turn is experienced as transformative for the researcher as well as the audience (Chang, 2016, pp. 52–54). These benefits can be encouraged further in autoethnography that is undertaken as a collaborative effort with other researcher-participants. The joint sense-making and critiquing in collaborative autoethnography leads to deeper and richer explorations of researcher subjectivity in a process that enables power-sharing in a more efficient research process offering a sense of community, which all bring about an intense learning about the self and other (Chang et al., 2016, pp. 25–30).

Yet, this form of qualitative inquiry is only possible if we challenge or potentially suspend our beliefs in traditionally foregrounded dichotomies, such as 'self and other, subject and object, humanities and social science, process and product, personal and political, emotional and rational, passionately involved and neutral and evocative and analytic' (Ellingson & Ellis, 2008, p. 448). Rather than trying to navigate these dichotomies, the autoethnographer sees their work as a social constructionist project, which means embracing vulnerabilities to highlight and thereby challenge existing societal conventions. This is particularly important for researchers who may be marginalised and for whom engagement with their protected characteristics represents an opportunity to empower themselves and their communities and to have their voices heard (e.g. Gandhi, 2021; Kelly et al., 2024; Teman, 2019). Therein also lie some of the criticisms which autoethnographic work has to contend with. Autoethnographers themselves are often called narcissistic navel-gazers who do not spend sufficient time on fieldwork or theory (Delamont, 2009; Fine, 2003; Soyini Madison, 2006). Additionally, the autoethnographers' use of literary tools to tell their stories and disseminate their research findings positions them between autobiography and ethnography, where autoethnography is sometimes considered as too artistic to meet the standards of good ethnography (Ellis, 2009).

When it comes to judging the quality of autoethnography, the criteria typically used to assess quality in qualitative research are therefore not sufficient. For example, the eight 'big-tent' criteria of (a) worthy topic, (b) rich rigour, (c) sincerity, (d) credibility, (e) resonance, (f) significant contribution, (g) ethics, and (h) meaningful coherence (Tracy, 2010) disregard autoethnography's endeavour to express and illuminate experiences while evoking particular kinds of responses in audiences. At the same time, however, autoethnography is often seen as too scientific for the artistic criteria of autobiography or other related literary fields (Ellis, 2009). Yet, within the scope of autoethnography as a social constructionist project, autoethnographers must engage their readers, who are seen to be co-constructing social truths with them (Poulos, 2020). Therefore, the qualities of audience response, expression, illumination, and evocation along with the use of creativity must be included, to achieve the right balance between autos-ethnos-graphos. Although good quality in autoethnography remains linked to the autos-ethnos-graphos triad, for many the criteria are too vague, because who is to judge what makes something 'a sterile and boring read' (Adams & Herrmann, 2023, p. 5). In this respect, it may help to see autoethnography connected with arts-based approaches in qualitative research, which, in turn, can be judged according to the criteria that are relevant. For Barone and Eisner (2012, pp. 148–154), the criteria relate to (a) incisiveness, (b) concision, (c) generativity, (d) social significance, and (e) evocation and illumination, whereas Leavy (2015, pp. 268–285) lists (a) methodology, (b) usefulness, significance, or substantive contribution, (c) public scholarship, (d) audience response, (e) aesthetics or artfulness, (f) personal fingerprint or creativity, and (g) ethical practice.

Although it can be argued that these criteria, like any and all criteria, are also based on subjective judgements, these criteria offer a sense of critical transparency and systematicity that many autoethnographers and their audiences will find helpful. A key element within the criteria offered by Leavy (2015, pp. 268–285) is ethical practice within the research, which we shall turn to in the next section.

AUTOETHNOGRAPHY AND ETHICS

Autoethnography in many ways appears to be a study of one, where the researcher is their own participant. Unfortunately, this is a drastic oversimplification. Our contemporary understanding of self and identity formation highlights that as human beings we inhabit many different social spaces within which we co-construct a variety of social realities (Giddens, 1991). We are cultural agents, who experience a certain level of sharedness, common understanding, and/or repeated actions binding us together to groups, and we can be members of a variety of different organisations or cultural groups at the same time and indeed quit these groups at will (see Chang, 2016, pp. 21–23). In short, as individuals we do not exist in a vacuum. The following autoethnographic fiction I have written highlights some of the conundrums an autoethnographer faces when attempting to write about their experiences.

The Writer

For weeks she had been thinking about writing the story. It seemed such an easy task, enjoyable even. But then every time she sat down at the computer, she would stare at a blank page. Eventually she would close the computer down having done nothing at all. How could she call herself a writer, when she didn't write?

Thank goodness, today feels different, as if she'd woken up from a deep sleep. Her characters speak to her now, tell her the story, explain how they behave and move, and what they think and feel. There is Tracy insisting that she is a woman of mixed heritage, so she cannot be stereotyped as neither too white nor too black. Then there is John who knows that his diagnosis is unusual for a bloke, that it really is a woman's illness, but no, he doesn't feel emasculated. And finally, there is Karen, strong Karen, who conveys everything without saying anything.

'Focus on how we speak to you and grow with us', Tracy and John encourage the writer, as she puts down her first sentence.

Karen shakes her head.

'Not my sentence', Tracy says.

'Well, it's not my sentence either', John sighs.

The writer deletes the sentence. She feels the weight of truthfulness pressing down on her shoulders, the responsibility for the truth overwhelming.

Karen's disapproval, Tracy's dismissal, and John's disappointment reverberate in her mind. Spinning. The writer inhales sharply, holding her breath as her fingers hover over the keyboard. One sentence. Just one sentence. She types, deletes, retypes.

Tomorrow, she thinks. Tomorrow might be different.

In this brief section, we see a writer struggling to express their autoethnographic truth because the characters, who are all composites and fictionalisations of 'real' people, have a strong voice and want to be heard in a way that is appropriate to them. The writer is guided by a strong sense of self that interweaves and interferes with their concern of duty to and care for the other(s). This brief interlude highlights how, within autoethnography, ethical issues that are relevant for conventional qualitative inquiries continue to be at play alongside certain dimensions that are unique to this particular form of research: issues of confidentiality, anonymity, and consent and the role of the self. Ethics guidelines from across all disciplines in the academy refer to confidentiality, anonymity, and consent but only in relation to participants. What often happens in practice in autoethnography, when there are no formal participants that are asked to be interviewed, is a 'muddling through' (Dilger, 2017, p. 192), which can be described as dealing with ethical issues on '*individually* applied criteria and rarely the outcome of *institutionally or disciplinarily shared efforts*' (Dilger, 2017, p. 192, emphasis in original). And yet, by writing about the self, the researcher-participant implicates others. Edwards (2021, p. 3), for example, talks of 'how it feels to be included without permission in someone else's work'.

For autoethnography to be done ethically, therefore, the ethics standards and approaches need to be adjusted. Rather than merely seeing ethics as a tool for and of institutional governance, the researcher has to engage ethically throughout the entire research process. Ethics in autoethnography therefore is not just procedural, it has three additional dimensions: it is contextualised to the situations (Fletcher, 1966) while also accounting for relationships with other(s) (Ellis, 2007) and the self (Edwards, 2021) as these are all affected by the research project. Considerations of anonymity, confidentiality, and consent can be mitigated if ethics is viewed as a continuous process throughout the research rather than as a one-stop snapshot. The researcher should then approach everyone implicated in the research to ask for consent when it comes to including particular storylines to the entire autoethnographic narrative. The solution sounds simple. Yet, solving the full ethical conundrum is not quite as easy as that.

Many autoethnographies are written long after the fact. For some autoethnographers, the writing of their own stories would be too painful, sensitive, and raw, if they were written immediately. A certain distance is often needed in order to be able to address the issues that need to be explored in those deeply reflected manners that autoethnography demands. With that distance come two complicating factors: the fallibility of memories and the changed relationship with other(s). A world that we see as socially constructed already harbours many versions of truth, with each individual's perspective shaping meaning further. When time lag is added because the autoethnographer does not approach the writing immediately, that shaping of an individual truth is subject to further reinterpretation. We select, reinterpret, reselect, and reconfigure events to form our very individualised memories, which form the basis of 'abstraction, explanation and analysis' (Freeman, 2015, p. 927). This is ultimately the autoethnographer's task. The issue is that during that process of reconfiguring the past, other individuals may become implicated in ways that are unfair to them because the final narrative does not take into account that person's truth or perspective.

Additionally, relationships between the autoethnographer and the persons implicated in the narrative may have changed in such a way that it is impossible to reconnect over questions of truth and consent. In the most extreme case, the person implicated in the narrative may even be deceased (see Ellis, 2018). In such circumstances, ethics can only be navigated in that haphazard way where the individual autoethnographers use their moral compass to decide what to include and exclude, and apply their values, in short they are 'muddling through' (Dilger, 2017, p. 192). In such situations, the autoethnographers' relationships with other(s) are affected, as well as their sense of their own selves. The proposition to expand the autoethnographic ethics framework by a fourth dimension to include an ethics of the self (Edwards, 2021) is therefore only logical: within the scope of autoethnography, the researcher must account for their own health and well-being. In this respect, an ethics of the self is a form of self-care and self-preservation from the point of view of self-compassion.

As human beings we generally are empathetic and compassionate when it comes to the experience of others but tend to remain critical, strict, and stringent in the connection with our own experiences. An ethics of self upends this commonly applied balance to such an extent that the autoethnographer's own self is foregrounded. The criticism of being narcissistic and too focussed on the self comes back to mind. Yet, being an autoethnographer is often not so much a choice as it is 'a mode of knowing and a way of being' (Sparkes, 2016, p. 516), irrespective of any personal and professional consequences that may arise. Most notable is the account by Carol Rambo, a renowned academic and professor of sociology, whose professional reputation is somewhat tarnished because of her autoethnographic writings about 'childhood sexual abuse at the hands of my father and mentally disabled mother, or [...] experiences as an exotic dancer' (Rambo, 2016, p. 6). The ethics of self in this context is perhaps less one of self-preservation and more self-compassion, in that her engagement with the topic leads the autoethnographer to make cultural and societal connections, which in turn enables her to make sense of and process her own experiences. It is this interplay between the self and the other that makes autoethnography 'difficult' for RECs.

AUTOETHNOGRAPHY AND RESEARCH ETHICS COMMITTEES

RECs play an important role in the contemporary higher education sector. For many institutions, the REC is the gatekeeper for and of any research that is carried out under an institutional banner and branding. In our contemporary society, which unfortunately is quite litigious, such a protective layer is welcome. In reality, then, the role of the REC therefore is often not only to ensure that research is undertaken ethically but also to confirm compliance with institutional systems and regulations. For this reason, ethics committees are often viewed as being too removed from the practice of research and too focussed on legal and reputational issues such as those surrounding data protection and cyber security. As a consequence, researchers and committee members are often at odds with one another, as the committees focus on the procedural aspect of ethics, while researchers try to implement situational or relational ethics processes in their projects (e.g. Brindley et al., 2020; Lanzerath, 2023). I have written elsewhere about the impact of our changing social sciences landscape on the practices and processes of RECs (Brown, 2023). Suffice it to say here that the one-stop snapshot approach prevailing across many RECs does nothing to alleviate researchers' fears when it comes to applying for ethics approvals. In the context of autoethnography, this them–us division is further compounded. The following is a fictionalised example of an ethics review that has been completed in response to an ethics application form proposing an autoethnographic study.

The Reviewer

Ethics Review Checklist

This checklist is to help reviewers to:
guide their feedback to ensure they address key areas within the application
support reviewers in accessing the latest guidance on each area through web links.

Actions required:
Complete checklist by clicking 'Choose an item' under each question and selecting an option from the drop-down.
Highlight in the section under each question any areas that the Principal or Co-Investigator have not adequately addressed
Add a grade and highlight any other ethical concerns that need clarifying at the end (if applicable)

1. Has the applicant provided an ethics application form with all relevant sections completed and signed?
There are no consent forms and information sheets.

2. Ethics application supporting documents
2a. Are appropriate participant information sheets provided? If participants include children, is an appropriate information sheet provided for them?
There are no participants per se.

2b. Do the information sheets include an appropriate privacy notice, as per GDPR guidelines? Do the information sheets include a statement regarding ethics approval number and data protection number?
There are no information sheets.

2c. Are appropriate consent forms provided for all participants? If participants include children, is an appropriate consent form provided for them?
There are no consent forms.

3. Is Section 7, concerning Data Storage and Security, adequately completed?
3a. Has the applicant clarified whether personal and/or special category data will be collected?
I am not entirely sure, but it looks like all data is personal and special category data.

3b. Has the applicant clarified whether data will be anonymised or pseudonymised?
Data will not be anonymised, and pseudonymisation is only partial.

3c. Has the applicant provided appropriate details of data storage that satisfy our institutional requirements?
No. The applicant wants to use their private journals, some of them digital, some of them handwritten notebooks.

3d. Has the applicant provided appropriate details of how long the data will be stored for?
Applicant says data will not be destroyed.

4. Is Section 8, concerning ethical issues and risk, adequately completed, including details of how the researcher plans to mitigate any risk factors?
Yes. This section is very detailed.

5. Are there any philosophical or theoretical issues that you wish to raise in relation to the ethical dimensions of this research?
I cannot see which theoretical framework(s) will be applied.

6. Are there any issues that you wish to raise on the methodology or design, specifically in relation to the ethical dimensions of the research?
This is an autoethnography, a study of one. How is this applicable and generalisable to the general public? What is the value of this research for the wider society?

Decision on application (grade): REJECTED.

This fictionalised completed ethics review form highlights the methodological problems posed by autoethnographic methods, which do not fit neatly within any existing theoretical frameworks. For autoethnographers, this is a strength. For ethics reviewers, the intersectional potential of autoethnography and the often rather loosely justified relationship between autoethnography and theory (Silverman & Rowe, 2020) raise the concern that research may be done badly or poorly, and that society ought to be protected from that (Gelling, 1999). Based on these and similar concerns, some scholars argue quite forcefully and strongly against autoethnography, in general. Sara Delamont, for example, raises the following six objections to autoethnography:

1. It cannot fight familiarity
2. It cannot be published ethically
3. It is experiential not analytic
4. It focuses on the wrong side of the power divide
5. It abrogates our duty to go out and collect data
6. Finally and most importantly 'we' are not interesting enough to write about in journals, to teach about, to expect attention from others. (Adapted from Delamont, 2007, pp. 4–5)

In addition to this methodological challenge of an atheoretical approach to research, the researcher's focus on the self often leads to the conclusion that there are no research participants involved in autoethnography. Consequently, many institutions, especially in non-English-speaking countries, do not require institutional reviews for autoethnographic work because, strictly speaking, autoethnographers do not 'collect' data. This is somewhat problematic. As has been said before, the autoethnographer does not exist in a vacuum and therefore there should be some review process to ensure that institutions, ethics committees, and researchers fulfil their duty of care towards the researchers, any persons implicated in or affected by the research, and the institution itself. A lack of formalised procedures for this kind of research means that, paradoxically, for researchers who would like to have their autoethnographic research proposals reviewed, there are often no processes or systems in place. However, anyone engaging in and with autoethnographic work in their research is very much aware of the need to be reviewed, receive constructive feedback, and enter a conversation about ethical considerations and conundrums. Unfortunately, in many institutions in the United Kingdom and beyond, ethics committees have become regulatory boards, for whom the institutional protection is the primary objective (Guillemin et al., 2012). Consequently, feedback loops or conversations about ethics are not commonly built into existing review processes.

Finally, there are issues relating to the institutional organisations of RECs themselves. Within higher education institutions in the context of the United Kingdom, reviewers and members of REC boards commonly undertake these roles voluntarily. This puts RECs in the position of relying on the goodwill of individuals, and so it becomes difficult to place additional demands and burdens on members. Any additional methodological training can therefore only be offered but not be made mandatory. Consequently, reviewer expertise cannot be considered routinely when it comes to assigning ethics reviews for approval, even though we would have thought that the specificities of autoethnography, or other special forms of qualitative inquiries for that matter, would require the specialist knowledge of experts in the field. With the current lack of reviewer expertise when it comes to the intricacies of autoethnographic work, there is the danger that an ethics review reverts to the scope of compliance and governance rather than really focussing on the specificities of autoethnographic ethics matters.

SOLVING AUTOETHNOGRAPHIC ETHICS MATTERS

So far in this chapter, I have outlined opportunities, challenges, and ethical tensions afforded by and with autoethnography. In this section, I would like to propose two potential solutions for some of the ethical concerns mentioned above: one for the applicant and one for the RECs and their reviewers. Let me begin with the latter.

As I have argued elsewhere (Brown, 2023), RECs and institutional review boards need to become more accepting of our changing social sciences landscape. And that includes keeping up-to-date with methodological developments. Autoethnography, although not necessarily mainstream within the context of qualitative inquiry, is certainly not a new approach to doing research. It therefore seems inconceivable that institutions do not yet have systems in place to enable individuals undertaking this form of research to have the protection and support of RECs and their members through meaningful approval processes. These existing, often rigidly fixed systems, need to be overhauled to allow for more flexible and malleable procedures. We need to allow researchers to apply for ethics reviews at various stages of their research to enter a constructive dialogue with the members of the ethics committees about ethical issues and how to navigate those as they occur during the course of the autoethnographic work. RECs should also build a database of reviewers with specific expertise, such as intimate knowledge of autoethnography, for these dialogues to be rigorous and purposeful. Capacity-building activities in and across RECs, and a significant attitudinal shift from compliance to an interest in ethical practices, would not only support autoethnographers with their research but could also significantly improve institutional research cultures. Such capacity-building activities should include ethics training sessions that provide time, space, and opportunity to engage with meaningful discussions around difficult scenarios, like Carol Rambo's (Ronai, 1996), whose mother's voice was never heard, or like Alice Goffman's (2014) whose book *On the Run: Fugitive Life in an American City* has been simultaneously praised for its audacity and sociological insights (Newburn, 2014) and condemned for its inaccuracies and ethical shortcomings (Lubet, 2015).

At an individual level, autoethnographers themselves can take steps to alleviate some of these ethical concerns, by educating themselves about autoethnography and about writing social fiction. There is a risk that autoethnography is deployed as a 'lazy' approach (Delamont, 2007) rather than as the rigorous research endeavour that it can and should be. Guidelines and advice about how to do autoethnography meaningfully, well, and ethically, abound (e.g. Ellis, 2004, 2007, 2009; Gibbs, 2018; Tolich, 2010; Tullis, 2013). It is therefore up to each and every autoethnographer to educate themselves and to engage deeply with the literature so that they may do justice to the research approach and to the story that is to be told. This brings me to social fiction writing. Many autoethnographers, especially those in vulnerable situations and contexts, engage with fictionalisations or vignette writing to create a much-needed artificial distance to their true-life accounts. Not every autoethnographer will be able to 'other' their experiences to such an extent that individuals are no longer recognisable (Edwards, 2021). 'Strange accounts' (Rambo, 2016) allow the autoethnographer to write in intentionally ambiguous ways which result in neatly controlled sharing of information and details that will maintain individuals' secrets and protect them from potential harm. Yet, this form of storytelling merely makes strange and others what is familiar with the risk of recognisability remaining intact. Social fiction is slightly different. Writing fiction as a research practice is not new. It emerges from the context of arts-based research methods and practices and is closely connected with poetic inquiry (Faulkner, 2019; Prendergast, 2009) and other forms of learning and making sense through writing (Richardson, 2000). What connects these approaches to inquiry is the focus on the generation of truth in a form that is abstracted from reality so that individuals are no longer recognisable, but that is so generally applicable that the story resonates with its readers. Social fiction writers build a relationship and develop a conversation with their readers to ensure that they engage with the topics presented in the narratives, through the application of literary tools. As such, social fiction writers need to hone the craft of writing, and apply their writing selves as interlinked with culture and society. The difference between fiction and social fiction then lies in the embeddedness of rigorous research. The difference between autoethnography and social fiction lies in the actuality of truth. This is not to say that the social fiction writer is more of a lyricist or inventor than the autoethnographer. Rather, the social fiction writer's role is to mould a multitude of realities into one coherent narrative so that there is a meaningful message for the reader. If we return to the autos-ethnos-graphos triad, the social fiction writer may be leaning a bit further towards the ethnos-graphos than the autos. I have created an adjusted new figure to represent this different orientation (see Fig. 6.2).

The methodological orientation here is still ethnographic, and the interpretive orientation is still cultural. But with the slight slant away from the autos of autoethnography comes the opportunity to incorporate the lives, stories, activities, and experiences of a wider group of people. In conventional research, these may be seen as research participants. And indeed, the social fiction writer may well wish to engage with other(s) more formally and as per the commonly applicable

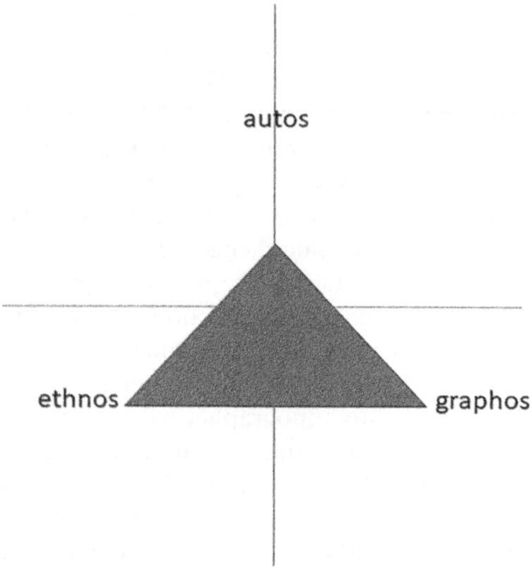

Fig. 6.2. Triad of Social Fiction.

research ethics processes to ensure generativity of the fiction pieces. Let me finish therefore with a flash fiction, which emphasises the role of the audience when it comes to autoethnographies, and which therefore focusses on the wants and the needs of the reader of autoethnographic work.

The Reader

Let me open your book, read your story.

As I begin to read you take me to another world.

Where I feel your feelings.

Where I laugh, when you laugh.

Where I hurt, when you hurt.

Where I can learn, and grow.

Where I can understand what it means

to be you.

REFERENCES

Adams, T. E., & Herrmann, A. F. (2023). Good autoethnography. *Journal of Autoethnography*, *4*(1), 1–9.

Barone, T., & Eisner, E. W. (2012). *Arts based research*. Sage.

Brindley, R., Nolte, L., & Nel, P. W. (2020). We were in one place, and the ethics committee in another: Experiences of going through the research ethics application process. *Clinical Ethics*, *15*(2), 94–103.

Brown, N. (2023). Research ethics in a changing social sciences landscape. *Research Ethics, 19*(2), 157–165. https://doi.org/10.1177/17470161221141011

Chang, H. (2016). *Autoethnography as method*. Routledge.

Chang, H., Ngunjiri, F., & Hernandez, K.-A. C. (2016). *Collaborative autoethnography*. Routledge.

Delamont, S. (2007). *Arguments against auto-ethnography, paper presentation*. https://archive.org/details/delamont-arguments-against-autoethnography/mode/2up

Delamont, S. (2009). The only honest thing: Autoethnography, reflexivity and small crises in fieldwork. *Ethnography and Education, 4*(1), 51–63.

Denzin, N. K. (1989). *Interpretive biography* (Vol. 17). Sage.

Dilger, H. (2017). Ethics, epistemology and ethnography: The need for an anthropological debate on ethical review processes in Germany. *Sociologus, 2*, 191–208.

Edwards, J. (2021). Ethical autoethnography: Is it possible? *International Journal of Qualitative Methods, 20*, 1609406921995306. https://doi.org/10.1177/1609406921995306

Ellingson, L. L., & Ellis, C. (2008). Autoethnography as constructionist project. In J. A. Holstein & J. F. Gubrium (Eds.), *Handbook of constructionist research* (pp. 445–465). Guilford.

Ellis, C. (1995). Speaking of dying: An ethnographic short story. *Symbolic Interaction, 18*(1), 73–81.

Ellis, C. (2004). *The ethnographic I: A methodological novel about autoethnography*. Altamira Press.

Ellis, C. (2007). Telling secrets, revealing lives: Relational ethics in research with intimate others. *Qualitative inquiry, 13*(1), 3–29.

Ellis, C. (2009). Telling tales on neighbors: Ethics in two voices. *International Review of Qualitative Research, 2*(1), 3–27.

Ellis, C. (2018). *Final negotiations: A story of love, loss and chronic illness* (Revised and expanded ed.). Temple University Press.

Ellis, C., & Bochner, A. (2000). Autoethnography, personal narrative, reflexivity: Researcher as subject. In N. K. Denzin & Y. S. Lincoln (Eds.), *Handbook of qualitative research* (Vol. 2, pp. 733–768). Sage.

Faulkner, S. L. (2019). *Poetic inquiry: Craft, method and practice*. Routledge.

Fine, G. A. (2003). Towards a peopled ethnography: Developing theory from group life. *Ethnography, 4*(1), 41–60.

Fletcher, J. F. (1966). *Situation ethics: The new morality*. SCM Press.

Foley, D. E. (2002). Critical ethnography: The reflexive turn. *International Journal of Qualitative Studies in Education, 15*(4), 469–490.

Freeman, J. (2015). Trying not to lie … and failing: Autoethnography, memory, malleability. *The Qualitative Report, 20*(6), 918–929.

Gandhi, R. S. (2021). Being brown: An autoethnographic exploration of internalised colonisation. *Psychodynamic Practice, 27*(2), 127–143.

Gelling, L. (1999). Role of the research ethics committee. *Nurse Education Today, 19*(7), 564–569. https://doi.org/10.1054/nedt.1999.0349

Gibbs, A. (2018). Ethical issues when undertaking autoethnographic research with families. In R. Iphofen & M. Tolich (Eds.), *The Sage handbook of qualitative research ethics* (pp. 148–160). SAGE Publications.

Giddens, A. (1991). *Modernity and self-identity: Self and society in the late modem age*. Polity.

Goffman, A. (2014). *On the run: Fugitive life in an American city*. University of Chicago Press.

Group, P. N. (1989). *Interpreting women's lives: Feminist theory and personal narratives*. Indiana University Press.

Gubrium, J. F., & Holstein, J. A. (1997). *The new language of qualitative method*. Oxford University Press.

Guillemin, M., Gillam, L., Rosenthal, D., & Bolitho, A. (2012). Human research ethics committees: Examining their roles and practices. *Journal of Empirical Research on Human Research Ethics, 7*(3), 38–49.

Jackson, M. (1989). *Paths toward a clearing: Radical empiricism and ethnographic inquiry*. Indiana University Press.

Kelly, B. T., Castillo-Montoya, M., Varghese, R., & Zúñiga, X. (2024). Braids and bridges: A critical collaborative autoethnography of racially minoritized women teaching intergroup dialogue. *Journal of Diversity in Higher Education, 17*(1), 1.

Krieger, S. (1991). *Social science and the self: Personal essays on an artform*. Rutgers University Press.

Lanzerath, D. (2023). Research ethics and research ethics committees in Europe. In T. Zima & D. N. Weisstub (Eds.), *Medical research ethics: Challenges in the 21st century* (Vol. 132, pp. 423–439). Springer.

Leavy, P. (2015). *Method meets art: Arts-based research practice* (2nd ed.). The Guilford Press.

Lubet, S. (2015). Ethics on the run. *The New Rambler*. https://newramblerreview.com/book-reviews/law/ethics-on-the-run

Newburn, T. (2014, July 10). *Book review: On the run: Fugitive life in an American city by Alice Goffman*. LSE Blog. https://blogs.lse.ac.uk/lsereviewofbooks/2014/07/10/book-review-on-the-run-fugitive-life-in-an-american-city-by-alice-goffman/

Poulos, C. N. (2020). The perils and the promises of autoethnography: Raising our voices in troubled times. *Journal of Autoethnography*, *1*(2), 208–211.

Prendergast, M. (2009). "Poem is what?" Poetic inquiry in qualitative social science research. *International Review of Qualitative Research*, *1*(4), 541–568.

Rambo, C. (2016). Strange accounts: Applying for the department chair position and writing threats and secrets "in play". *Journal of Contemporary Ethnography*, *45*(1), 3–33. https://doi.org/10.1177/0891241615611729

Richardson, L. (1994). Nine poems: Marriage and the family. *Journal of Contemporary Ethnography*, *23*(1), 3–13.

Richardson, L. (1997). *Fields of play: Constructing an academic life*. Rutgers University Press.

Richardson, L. (2000). Writing: A method of inquiry. In N. K. Denzin & Y. S. Lincoln (Eds.), *Handbook of qualitative research* (2nd ed., pp. 923–948). Sage.

Ronai, C. R. (1996). My mother is mentally retarded. In C. Ellis & A. Bochner (Eds.), *Composing ethnography: Alternative forms of qualitative writing* (Vol. 1, pp. 109–131). AltaMira Press.

Silverman, R. E., & Rowe, D. D. (2020). Blurring the body and the page: The theory, style, and practice of autoethnography. *Cultural Studies ↔ Critical Methodologies*, *20*(2), 91–94. https://doi.org/10.1177/1532708619878762

Soyini Madison, D. (2006). The dialogic performative in critical ethnography. *Text and Performance Quarterly*, *26*(4), 320–324. https://doi.org/10.1080/10462930600828675

Sparkes, A. C. (2016). Introduction: Autoethnography as a mode of knowing and a way of being. In T. E. Adams, S. Holman-Jones, & C. Ellis (Eds.), *Handbook of autoethnography* (pp. 512–668). Routledge.

Teman, E. D. (2019). Autoethnographic poetic inquiry: Therapeutically engaging with violence toward queers. *Journal of Poetry Therapy*, *32*(2), 63–77.

Tolich, M. (2010). A critique of current practice: Ten foundational guidelines for autoethnographers. *Qualitative Health Research*, *20*(12), 1599–1610.

Tracy, S. J. (2010). Qualitative quality: Eight "big-tent" criteria for excellent qualitative research. *Qualitative Inquiry*, *16*(10), 837–851.

Tullis, J. (2013). Ethics in autoethnographic research. In S. Holman-Jones., T. E. Adams, & C. Ellis (Eds.), *Handbook of autoethnography* (pp. 244–261). Left Coast Press.

Van Maanen, J. (1995). An end to innocence: The ethnography of ethnography. In J. Van Maanen (Ed.), *Representation in ethnography* (pp. 1–35). Sage.

CHAPTER 7

WHOSE ETHICS AM I CONCERNED WITH? PERSPECTIVES FROM QUALITATIVE RESEARCH WITH RETIRED EDUCATORS IN BOTSWANA

Hildah L. Mokgolodi

University of Botswana, Botswana

ABSTRACT

This chapter outlines some unanticipated ethical issues that arose in the course of conducting qualitative research for my doctoral research on the experiences of retired educators in Botswana. I describe how, in the course of conducting the fieldwork, I encountered ethical dilemmas in terms of my subjectivity as a researcher, role-conflicts between my professional roles as a counsellor and as a researcher, and tensions around power and cultural dynamics. I indicate how, as I analysed these dynamics, I began to understand the problems I encountered in a wider context. This entailed framing ethical issues in a different way than was done during the research ethics review at the outset of my research. Whereas the review drew on established ethical codes to focus on practices related to informed consent, confidentiality and anonymisation, protection from harm, and justice, it became clear in the course of my fieldwork that less recognised ethical

Reframing Qualitative Research Ethics
Advances in Research Ethics and Integrity, Volume 12, 111–125

ISSN: 2398-6018/doi:10.1108/S2398-601820250000012007

issues may emerge at later stages. Although such issues cannot always be anticipated, research ethics committees may benefit from reflection and training on broader perspectives on ethics – such as on understanding the significance of Indigenous knowledge, researcher subjectivity, and cultural and power dynamics. In conclusion, I recommend that ethics training for researchers too should be extended beyond the established track of familiarisation with key tenets of conventional research ethics to include opportunities for reflection and discussion about wider issues arising from fieldwork in community settings.

Keywords: Ethical research; ethical principles; Indigenous research; qualitative research; Indigenous knowledge

INTRODUCTION

Indigenous knowledge creation emerging from research cannot be the preserve of the researcher but should be seen to be constructed by participants and their environment together with the engagement of the researcher. Indigenous research fits well within the qualitative research paradigm as it encourages qualitative methodologies that are participatory and, in my case, could be seen as following a key African philosophy known as Ubuntu. 'Ubuntu' is sometimes translated as 'I am because we are' or 'I am because you are' (Chilisa, 2020, p. 99). It is concerned with 'humanity towards others'. As such it becomes central to how Indigenous research is conducted among those who follow or believe in Ubuntu, respecting the participants as the key knowledge holders. However, a major ethical challenge remains in indigenising counselling research and thinking about it from Indigenous peoples' perspectives, away from commonly used post-positivist paradigms and methodologies. For example, while such approaches may recommend the use of pseudonyms or complete anonymisation, an ethical issue remains when the participants themselves wish to have their names out there to have the world know their thoughts and how they personally added to the creation of this knowledge. In my own work (as reported below), I continue to feel ethically conflicted as I reason through the power dynamics between myself as a researcher and my participants. To avoid several ethical dilemmas experienced in research, as a counsellor educator and researcher, I have tended to prefer using secondary data in my studies rather than collecting primary data especially from my students. Another ethical concern highlighted when dealing with secondary data, especially within Indigenous studies, is the potential for interpretation to be a long way from what the participants meant about what was written down by the primary researcher. This may then constrain my use of secondary data as I wished to immerse myself in the participants' experiences firsthand. Dilemmas such as these must be confronted when conducting all qualitative and counselling research, but perhaps more so in Indigenous research as this chapter aims to show.

> Qualitative research can easily become both a vehicle and a target for ethical, political, and methodological attack. Moral conflicts surface in even the most systematically organized study. (Karagiozis, 2018, p. 19)

Some argue that ethical research requires completing research in a standardised 'right' way that follows 'universal principles that are norms that apply to all people in all places, times and contexts' (Msoroka & Amundsen, 2018, p. 2), in addition to protecting not only the participants but also researchers and their institutions (Alderson & Morrow, 2020; Yip et al., 2016). Ethical guidelines for research are available to be followed in the professions of psychology and counselling, from, among others, the American Psychological Association, the British Psychological Society (Mcleod, 2023), and the American Counselling Association (2014). While most academic institutions follow such guidelines, distinctive ethical concerns arise where Indigenous or cultural ethics are deemed to be stronger or even more important, as I came to learn when I was collecting data for my PhD study. Rossman and Rallis (2010) have reflected on how following the kinds of ethical procedures outlined in institutional human subjects review regulations is not in itself sufficient to address issues that emerge when working with Indigenous people. Throughout this chapter, I address issues of subjectivity, role-professional conflict, power, and cultural dynamics as some of the ethical concerns I experienced as a researcher.

RATIONALE FOR THE STUDY

The rationale for the study was to harness the experiential knowledge and soft skills of retired educators, which they had acquired over decades of work, to inform career development programs in Botswana (Mokgolodi, 2015, 2022). These retirees were not necessarily staying home but could have retired as educators and could have formal or informal employment beyond retirement. Career construction was central to this study as a theoretical base. Career construction theory proposes that individuals' careers are lifelong personal and social constructs, while focusing attention on how they interpret processes, how they interact with society and the meaning they make out of these interactions (Savickas, 2005, 2011; Schreuder & Coetzee, 2011; Wang & Li, 2024). Furthermore, people's life stories and lived experiences are central to the development of their careers as they look at their past, present and future to construct, deconstruct and re- or co-construct these to make meaning of their careers (Maree, 2015; Watson, 2013). In other words, career construction is about developing one's career from making reflections on one's behaviour and interaction with the environment as we try to make sense of who they are in relation to the world of work. I believed that the retirees had in effect 'constructed' their careers from lifelong reflections, hence could help young people do the same using retirees' developed knowledge and skills. A mixed-method, sequential and explanatory design based upon assumptions of pragmatism was used: both quantitative and qualitative methods were used as they came across as the best way to answer the research questions from a pragmatic point of view (Hall, 2013). In this case, the first phase of the study involved gathering quantitative data through a survey, to explore participants' biographical data and constructs on themes including career guidance and counselling, self-awareness, mentoring and soft skills (Mokgolodi, 2015). The weightier and second phase of the study was qualitative and phenomenological, and this phase was used to answer in depth the question of what skills the retirees acquired and how – and how these might serve others – from the perspective of the retirees' experiences.

Qualitative paradigms and constructivist perspectives shaped the ontological and epistemological assumptions underlying my PhD study (Mokgolodi, 2015). Purposive sampling was used to select key participants for the qualitative phase through respondent directed and snowball techniques. All the study participants were referred to me either by colleagues who knew about my study or by other participants, were Batswana (meaning they are from Botswana) and had worked in Botswana. In-depth interviews, focus group discussions, observations, a reflective journal, and reiterative member checks were used for data collection throughout my study. Sixteen retirees (seven males and nine females) were interviewed, and three focus group discussions were also a data source. The focus groups took place in different regions which included the capital city of Botswana, a big village and a small one, with the aim of drawing on different experiences that retirees had because of their backgrounds. Data were analysed thematically. Several ethical decisions were made and addressed within the study following the host institution's requirements in relation to procedures for informed consent, privacy and confidentiality, protection from harm and justice. The institutional review board (IRB) required that I highlight my position and role as a researcher, which meant I needed to reflect on how being a counsellor would affect or be likely to influence the study. These ethical concerns covered mainly the process of conducting the study and were required to be addressed primarily before collecting data. It was only later that I realised several dilemmas arose during the study that posed ethical challenges, and which had not been considered at the institutional level, some of which are discussed below.

SUBJECTIVITY

I collected data from retired educators while I still worked for the Ministry of Education and Skills Development in Botswana and was nearing early retirement. Although it is common to address ethical issues such as informed consent, privacy and confidentiality, protection from harm and justice and so on, I was concerned that formal ethics review could not anticipate important issues that would arise during the fieldwork. Perera (2018, p. 2) highlights this and points out that 'ethical issues can and do arise when formulating research questions, preparing data for analysis, conducting analysis, and when writing up one's findings'. To avoid bias in data collection, researchers may reiteratively check with their supervisor and with their participants during the engagements. I felt that some skewed conclusions were likely, due to my personal interpretation of what participants said, given that I also was an educator who was nearing retirement and with views of my own on this life transition.

Scholars such as Karagiozis (2018) argue that the interrelations and interactions that take place between the researcher and participants in qualitative interviews effectively construct new knowledge and that one should not assume the existence of objective knowledge somehow separate from that engagement. I reflected on researcher proximity throughout the study and considered my role as a researcher consistently, including an awareness of the influence and or power dynamic I could be bringing to the study, that came with being a researcher. I was a Motswana (a person from Botswana) woman nearing retirement, which could affect the outcomes of the study as I shared a lot in common with the participants (Mokgolodi, 2015). While I conducted member checks and closely worked with my supervisor, I could not shake off the feeling that there was a lot more of me in the data collected than met the eye. The comfort came from appreciating that although a qualitative study is necessarily subjective, transparency about the methods used to collect and analyse data will provide a more rigorous account. I asked myself then, why was I worried about the study being subjective, because the narratives indeed had to be subjective and both retirees and researcher interpretations were subjective. I also wondered whose ethics I was worried about? It seemed to me that I had become more worried about adhering to the set research standards rather than considering what was most relevant to the participants. I felt that institutions perpetuated rather than challenged set standards. For instance, both the institutions where I conducted my PhD and the guidelines for research at my current institution primarily emphasised consideration of ethical aspects before the study, with only minimal attention being paid to them during and after the fieldwork. I therefore wondered whether my ethical focus should be more on conducting the study or on addressing the 'conventional' issues arising from the ethics review? As the study progressed, the balance between these approaches continued to challenge me.

Ethical standards often require the use of pseudonymisation or even complete anonymisation, especially when the research is on a sensitive topic, or the participants are considered to be especially vulnerable. However, I found this problematic when the participants themselves wished to have their names out there to have the world know their thoughts and of their contribution to the creation of this knowledge in my study. Iphofen (2011, p. 98) summarises this dilemma as follows:

> If a subject wishes their identity to be disclosed as part of the research report, the researcher then has some dilemmas – principally the effect this might have on other subjects of their research (knowing the identity of one participant might help identify others who desire continued anonymity).

Some subjects may wish their identities to be disclosed to maintain some link to the data they provided, however, gatekeepers for participants who are susceptible to abuse may want to be known to appease donors of the studies (Grinyer, 2002). Further to this, Iphofen (2021) explores the complexities of public and private spaces and anonymity which, depending on the research, may create some dilemmas. Therefore, the fact that the participants want to be disclosed is not enough to make their names public, nor is it an ethical requirement for participants to be anonymous, as studies require people's real stories to share. Hence, a balancing act may be necessary to reach a decision as to whether participants should remain anonymous or not.

I strongly agree with Shaw et al. (2019, p. 14) that

> researcher positionality and the researcher's status as an insider/outsider has implications for the topics we choose to study, the way we do research and engage with our research participants, how we analyse our data, and how we communicate our findings.

Thus, the interpretation of the data and the subsequent knowledge created cannot be separated from the researcher's engagement. Their assessment is that even those conducting sensitive participatory research cannot be boxed into a specific category of 'ownership', as long as the researcher's values are not in conflict with the participants of the study. Shaw et al.'s position reduces the likelihood of ethical conflict one would experience when conducting a qualitative study with lots of unexpected dynamics between one as a researcher who is expected to follow ethical standards of research and the desires of their participants. For as long as both the researcher's and the participants' values are not conflicting or trampled upon, the process of conducting the study is likely to attain the desired goals – accurate and truthful accounts of authentic experience. For some case studies, it might be appropriate that participant names can be published, but I still think that at the end of the study, it is not about an individual person but rather about a synthesis of thoughts and answers. For many studies, individuals have a right to allow their actual names to appear subject to the disclosure caveat raised by Iphofen above. On balance, for my study, I felt that I should not publish participants' names given that only some participants, not all, wanted their names acknowledged.

RESEARCHER ROLE-PROFESSIONAL CONFLICT

Retirement and its problems were a big issue for the participants. Many of the participants did not undergo counselling in order to adequately come to terms with the reality of the loss brought about by retirement. I came across participants who, though having retired a few years back, still grieved for loss of their jobs and the ill treatment they suffered at the hands of their supervisors, which was what had led to early retirement for some educators. I was not only almost at early retirement, but I was also a professional counsellor during both the periods of data collection and analysis. At times, I could not help but be empathic to the research participants and offered brief counselling when the participants were overwhelmed. Iphofen (2011) highlights the pressures brought about by multiple roles played by professionals, when conducting research, including which role should be taking precedence. In my case, the counsellor role kicked in when there were emotional challenges brought about by grief. However, I referred participants to other counsellors as my focus had to be on the research due to my institutional ethical requirements. It is important to acknowledge that as far back as 1986, Woolsey (1986, p. 84) contended that the 'major source of the practitioner-researcher split is the conflict of values between the underlying assumptions of the traditional methods of research and theories of counseling'. Throughout the study, I had to consciously remind myself not to blend the roles as it would be unethical (for who may be a moot point) to do so. While I appreciated the danger of biased data that may be collected from a participant who at some point became a client, I still thought allowing this brief relationship brought out the best in terms of participation and sharing of perspectives. Thus, some of the skills of counselling may be entirely appropriate for the gathering of qualitative data. I also understood that disclosing one's professional position may have methodological consequences, as the participants may be influenced to behave differently because of the information about the researcher's 'other' role (Iphofen, 2011). However, I was also aware that some participants may want to please and overcompensate. With practice, I learnt that my ethical behaviour could improve through 'respecting core human values; respecting local traditions; and the belief that context matters when deciding what is right and what is wrong' as pointed out by Donaldson (2016, p. 403). At the same time, one must take a balanced approach, so that these concerns do not completely overwhelm the possibility of achieving meaningful and important research, notes Iphofen (2011, p. 59).

EXISTING POWER DYNAMICS UNKNOWN TO THE RESEARCHER

Indigenous research methodologies adjust existing methods to 'perspectives and methods that draw from Indigenous knowledges, languages, metaphors, worldviews, experiences, and philosophies of former colonized, historically oppressed, and marginalized social groups' (Chilisa, 2020, p. 72). I may have been naïve, but I expected the research to go as smoothly as I had been taught it would. I had not anticipated experiencing ethical challenges relating to cultural issues. Being a professional counsellor prepared me to work on multicultural issues when counselling, but in preparation for research, I had adopted the approach that counselling should not be part of it because of potential role conflict as outlined above. Yet during the fieldwork, I had a sense that there seemed to be latent power dynamics among the participants aside from the issue of researcher dominance in the setting and I had the strong feeling that participants in one of the focus group discussions seemed not to be genuine in their answers. It might be 'counsellor's intuition'! Muhammad et al. (2015) discussed issues of positionality for researchers within communities, where social, ethnic and economic inequalities could be addressed if collaborative relationships are formed between the researcher and the researched. Simultaneously, highlights of inherent power struggles within the community itself are referred to in the article, which led me to address my relationships with caution.

There was no obvious prior positional hierarchy, but that someone appeared to have worked longer or produced commendable results as an educator was enough to intimidate others, as I came to understand the focus group better. As a novice researcher, it was a bit difficult to deal with this observation at first, fearing that if I talked about it, it would further increase the risk of some participants staying in their shells, or of embarrassing those who were 'fearful' or inflating those who seemingly were pleased. Those apparently in power were less talkative or stayed silent most of the time unless asked directly to comment on what was being discussed. I found group facilitation using counselling skills quite helpful in this regard, as eventually there seemed to be some collegiality among the participants. While I asked my own questions, I was also open to asking participants how they related to what another person said. Understanding group dynamics was very helpful as, with a little nudge, eventually all participants seemed to talk freely. So, I found myself applying counselling skills as well as research skills which meant that I could not easily separate my professional self from the emerging researcher role.

Given such power dynamics, and as a new researcher, I doubted my confidence when it came to interviewing people who had been my superiors and had been in very high positions at some point as educators. For instance, while it was not taboo to go and see the permanent secretary to the Minister or the Ministry of Education, these people were not easily accessible for ordinary employees. Muhammad et al. (2015, p. 1047) asserted 'the need for more explicit attention to power as it relates to identity and intersectional positionality of researchers, based on gender, sexual orientation, ability, and multiple cultural, racial/ethnic, educational, and other forms of identity'. I considered myself an ordinary employee, while they knew me or had heard about me; I wondered whether my questions would solicit what I was looking for when interviewing them or might they turn the tables and 'interrogate' me instead. Whether we were co-constructing knowledge or if my interpretations of their answers led to the creation of new knowledge remains a moot point. Power dynamics were at play here for which I was not prepared. I sought to avoid these, but the snowballing sampling methodology prevented me from running away from the situation. With the snowball technique, referral meant that participants would give me names of people I could invite for interviews, who were known to be retired educators who might contribute to my study, and I would get in touch with them. For example, at one point, I was referred to the vice president (VP) of the country who at some point in his life had been an educator. The referrer pointed out how valuable as a key informant the VP would be given his varied experience in relation to my study. I was scared out of my wits; I started worrying about how he would respond to me and if he would see value in my study and if I really needed to call him for an appointment. Eventually, I called and he accepted my call. However, the interview could not take place, as his interpretation of the request for an interview was that he was still an educator and had not yet retired as one. Reflecting on it now, even though it is accepted that participants must be able to choose whether to participate or not or withdraw from it during the process, from a personal point of view, it felt like a rejection if someone declined: I was not prepared for a refusal or for the possibility of a participant leaving a study midway. Another example of a power dynamic that I was unprepared for was a referral to a retired educator with a PhD. With this participant, I felt like a student in class. The participant answered my questions, then turned the tables to mentor me on the process of getting a PhD. Dealing with someone who is more informed and knowledgeable was also different from dealing with someone who was in a high position of responsibility. I found these to be subtle ethical issues that do not often get talked about in accounts of qualitative research ethics. Yet the level of engagement of participants or community partners may affect how the benefit of the study and how knowledge from the study is constructed or may affect the outcomes of the study (Edwards & Brannelly, 2017; Muhammad et al., 2015).

CULTURAL DYNAMICS

Donaldson (2016) reminds me that I am a product of my cultural education; hence, ethical issues in my qualitative research studies are likely to be strongly influenced by my Indigenous background more than my training, which I need to be aware of at any given time in the research process. Cultural forces and ethics were intertwined in my world while I was conducting my PhD study. I was not prepared for some of the experiences I had. In my culture, the power dynamics that played above when I had to interview my supervisors, some of whom mentored me, and was referred to the VP of the country, were all overwhelming, and I could not tell where research ethics met cultural ethics and which took precedence. I felt that I needed to continue respecting that the participants were not only retired educators, supervisors or leaders but also my elders and deserved a different form of reverence. Not that my current position as an IRB member and my prior knowledge and experience could answer all the issues that arose and may continue to arise. Insider privilege as a local made me appreciate that different cultures bring different ethical and moral dilemmas to research practices. While it may be a rule of thumb to side with the participants when experiencing ethical dilemmas and/or universal principles, I concur with Msoroka and Amundsen (2018) that one size does not fit all. That is, standard principles of ethical research cited in institutional guidelines cannot and would not address all ethical issues that arise during a study. For example, I was instructed to separate my professional stance as a counsellor from that of myself as a researcher. I found it difficult to not provide brief counselling to a participant who was distraught on how the education system ill-treated them during their many years as a teacher. First, there was no way we could continue with the interview, unless I provided brief counselling. Second, even though I had liaised with a clinic to provide mental health support during my study, counselling could not be made available immediately. My view then was that my profession should facilitate my research; hence, I needed to acknowledge that my skills as a counsellor had a role to play in my study. I believe that sometimes a researcher may need to follow their gut when addressing ethical issues, as long as they are convinced that they are not making decisions detrimental to the well-being of the participants and the study. Further to this, being in the helping professions, I believe that ethical decision-making can be achieved by involving the client at every stage where a decision has to be made (Corey et al., 1998), and qualitative studies present such an opportunity.

Such opposing cultural dynamics point to the fact that universal principles may have their own limitations as mentioned earlier. This highlights the need for qualitative methodologies to embrace the world views of Indigenous people, where applicable. In this chapter, I am attempting to show that indigenisation and decolonisation of qualitative research methods can be used interchangeably, where indigenisation brings in Indigenous knowledge systems into the practice of research and decolonising means challenging and replacing some long-standing and colonial systems and ideologies with Indigenous ones. Thambinathan and Kinsella (2021, p. 1) articulate ways to decolonise qualitative research and propose 'four practices that can be used by qualitative researchers: (1) exercising critical reflexivity, (2) reciprocity and respect for self-determination, (3) embracing "Other(ed)" ways of knowing, and (4) embodying a transformative praxis' (p. 1). As researchers, we must emphasise the need to be cognisant of the axiology and philosophical underpinnings of Indigenous knowledge.

WHOSE ETHICS?

My experience in qualitative research during my PhD study led me to ask the question, whose ethics should I be worried about? Edwards and Brannelly (2017, p. 272) asked questions such as

> who owns the research issues, who initiates them, in whose interests the research is carried out, who has control of research, how power relations and decisions are negotiated in creating knowledge, who the research is for, what counts as knowledge, who is transformed by it, and whose is the authorial voice.

Ubuntu philosophy may help us to explore these questions. As mentioned earlier, Ubuntu philosophy is a concept that emphasises 'we' more than an 'I' and is practised widely in most African societies. The philosophy of Ubuntu acknowledges the relationality of Indigenous people and the communality of knowledge, that is, knowledge does not belong to a single individual but to multiple people. Seehawer's (2018, p. 453) study explores Ubuntu as an Indigenous paradigm, drawing from experiences of a participatory action research and concludes that 'Ubuntu research agendas contribute to strengthening community and methodologies are community based, relational and participatory'. Furthermore, citing UNESCO (1996), Chilisa (2020, p. 72) asks whose reality counts and highlights that 'Research institutions and practitioners are called upon to commit themselves to undertaking research that is relevant, participatory; based on Indigenous culture and language of the people and that would serve the needs of the local communities'.

Additionally, both Seehawer (2018) and Marovah and Mutanga (2023) support Ubuntu as an epistemological paradigm with the potential to broaden ethical principles when conducting qualitative research with a focus on participatory research. Chilisa (2020) and Edwards and Brannelly (2017) look to ask these critical questions when conducting a qualitative study. It is clear that the above researchers are looking at new ways and transformational ways of conducting research. My institutional advisor and my continuous training, which focused on ethical concerns such as informed consent, doing no harm, separating roles as a professional counsellor and the researcher role, made me appreciate some of the above issues during my study. However, in my view, the issue of Indigenous culture did not come through adequately at that stage (if it did at all) as those other aspects of the research process, yet the characteristic of Indigenous culture seemed to play a bigger role when I was collecting data. Consequently, as a new scholar, I felt I was not adequately equipped to conduct the kind of qualitative study as mentioned in the quotation above. Hence, prior to being engaged as an IRB member, and post my PhD, I preferred to use secondary data rather than primary data on the assumption that it is less risky to the participants and less likely to cause harm. However, that did not take away my ethical concerns. Rather, I occasionally experienced conflicting ideas about not getting permission from the participants, for me to conduct a new study using their contributions. Metcalf and Crawford (2016) highlight the misconception posed by this supposition, given that data combinations from different sources may pose risks to individuals and communities that participated in such studies. Although permission may have been sought from the primary participants by the first researcher, I still worried that secondary use could pose some ethical concerns when it came to further interpretation of the data. Metcalf and Crawford (2016) give accounts of how unanticipated uses of data can be invasive and harmful and highlight the question of whose ethics we should be considering when using secondary data or when funded to conduct a study. I now appreciate that regardless of which data are being used, ethical concerns will arise depending on how the study is conducted. Secondary data being brought into the public eye can still bring harm to those who originally supplied it.

My outlook has changed since I read more on ethics and joined the IRB of my university. I continue to ask 'whose ethics' and 'whose reality' should I be concerned with when I am conducting a qualitative study.

HOW MY EXPERIENCES AS A MEMBER OF AN IRB BOARD INFORMS MY EXPERIENCE OF QUALITATIVE RESEARCH ETHICS AND MY DECISIONS ABOUT MY OWN RESEARCH PRACTICE

Being an IRB board member has changed my outlook on ethics and continues to influence my practice of qualitative research. As an IRB member, I went through several training workshops to discuss not only administrative issues but to learn the following: the application of ethical principles; to understand local and global regulations and guidance on research ethics and their appropriate application in review of research studies; to analyse and apply ethical principles, regulations and guidance during case study discussions; to demonstrate overall comprehension, understanding and knowledge for research ethics (World Health Organization African Region, 2021). In addition, I went through an Introductory Research Ethics Module offered by Training and Resources in Research Ethics Evaluation (TRREE) which can be accessed at https://elearning.trree.org/. This module took me through the history of ethics and helped me to go through case studies for certification. I had to read my university's policy documents on ethical conduct in research, and consequences relating to misconduct. These aimed to establish ethical codes of practice and mechanisms for ensuring compliance with the ethical standards and values of the university, the international research society and civil society, as well as establish the framework for developing and implementing codes of conduct for ethical behaviour in research and consultancy and guided practice. I was taken through the history of ethics development and in addition to institutional documents, I had access to, among others, the Declaration of Helsinki adopted in different regions at different times, Nuremberg Code and the Standards and Operational Guidance for Ethics Review of Health-Related Research with Human Participants (WHO, 2011). Central to all these documents is understanding that issues of values, beneficence and maleficence play a critical role in ethics. There is also an attempt to appreciate local values and ethical principles which may not necessarily be universal. Appreciating local values or Indigenous ways of knowing speaks directly to qualitative methods of conducting research if we consider participatory and/or community involvement strategies (Thambinathan & Kinsella, 2021). However, knowledge of all of these ethical codes is expected of all active members of IRBs, who not only assess study proposals but conduct qualitative studies as well.

CONCLUSION

In my experience, membership of an IRB offers support that one does not get when conducting a study because decision-making in the ethics review process is collective rather than individual. One cannot go through the above experiences as an IRB member and remain the same. The Standards and Operational Guidance for Ethics Review of Health-Related Research with Human Participants (WHO, 2011), which members of my institution's IRB must be familiar with, alone gives a lot of guidance on ethical processes for instance. As a result of familiarising myself with these key documents, my appreciation of ethical considerations commonly used as standard in ethical evaluations of qualitative research has heightened. This is because ethics plays a critical role in ensuring that while benefits are attained from research studies, participants are not exploited intentionally. I must hasten to say that these treatises on ethical research standards also made me appreciate that not only participants but researchers, research teams, entities such as institutions conducting research and countries need to be protected and their vulnerabilities not exploited. One critical aspect that I learnt about concerns the multiple identities and roles which participants as well as researchers bring to bear to qualitative studies. Muhammad et al. (2015) posit that the multiple identities which researchers bring to community participatory studies may impact epistemologies and methodologies. Furthermore, while counselling itself encourages qualitative studies and client-informed methodologies, being an IRB member crystalised my support for constructivism as a paradigm, and so I advocate strongly for participatory methodologies in qualitative research. Participatory methodologies, as discussed by Hall et al. (2021), involve a close working relationship between the researcher with both participants and communities in designing and conducting the research. Broader ethical concerns are likely to be addressed earlier on if participants and the community have a say in decision-making of the processes of the research. Relational paradigms and philosophies of research and participatory methodologies address important ethical dimensions and allow the counsellor-researcher to be immersed within a community where their study is being conducted.

My conclusions align with those of Chilisa (2020) and Thambinathan and Kinsella (2021), who believe that if ethical concerns are based only on universal principles and conventional issues in qualitative methods, and do not acknowledge Indigenous cultures, some important aspects are bound to be overlooked. Failure to recognise Indigenous knowledge systems underscores the question of whose ethics research is concerned with and without this dimension, ethical concerns written on a proposal might seem to be superficial and missing a crucial element. In order for research relating to counselling to bear fruit for those the study is being conducted for, I continue to advocate for participatory and relational qualitative methodologies because 'Relational models of evaluation encourage evaluators to reconsider the philosophical foundations of their practice, which can be used to decolonize the theory, methods, and practice of Indigenous guidance and counseling' (Mokgolodi, 2023). For counselling to address problems of society, the research methods used in social, psychological and counselling research need to be ethically sound and resonate and in tune with the people research is being conducted for. Lastly, both procedural and practice ethics are important components of a study as all participants in a study are vulnerable to some form and level of ontological exploitation (Shaw et al., 2019). While global ethical standards are there for participatory research, they should, however, not be limiting and continue to marginalise Indigenous approaches. I am appreciative of my advisors for my PhD study as I came to understand that there were many ethical considerations that went into the study – although I may not have realised it at the time. I certainly learned that ethics should be studied beyond the preparation for a proposal but should be studied throughout one's conducting of the research.

Based both on the experiences of conducting the study which I have shared here, and my reading of the literature, I conclude that research ethics studies should involve more than a discussion, or individual reading, and should extend to a whole course to be taken by all students who are planning to conduct research at the graduate level. Ethical issues in conducting research need to be interrogated in depth before, during and after the conduct of the study. Considering Indigenous knowledge and participatory methods – including Ubuntu and relational viewpoints – that encourage community empowerment and or benefits, may help researchers to be open to making decisions about ethics informed by these important dimensions. Institutional ethics committees may need to take account of communal decision-making in awarding or not awarding ethical clearance and to encourage qualitative researchers to address ethical dilemmas with the participants rather than on their own. Finally, it is essential for researchers to involve participants in addressing difficult situations, as to do otherwise implies that they are vessels from which knowledge is collected rather than co-constructors of knowledge in this context.

ACKNOWLEDGEMENTS

I would like to acknowledge Ron Iphofen's and Helen Busby's editorial guidance from the first to the final drafts of this book chapter: their encouragement, expertise and guidance was much appreciated. Finally, I would like to acknowledge that the University of Botswana IRB and Professor Chilisa have played a significant role in influencing my resolve to understand and write on research ethics and Indigenous methodologies, respectively. I would like to thank them immensely.

REFERENCES

Alderson, P., & Morrow, V. (2020). *The ethics of research with children and young people: A practical handbook* (2nd ed.). SAGE. ISBN 1529736676, 9781529736670.

American Counselling Association. (2014). *2014 ACA code of ethics*. https://www.counseling.org/docs/default-source/default-document-library/ethics/2014-aca-code-of-ethics.pdf

Chilisa, B. (2020). *Indigenous research methodologies* (2nd ed.). SAGE.

Corey, G., Corey, M. S., & Callahan, P. (1998). *Issues and ethics in the helping professions* (5th ed.). Brooks/Cole.

Donaldson, T. (2016). Values in tension: Ethics away from home. In B. S. Reiche, G. K. Stahl, M. E., Mendenhall, & G. R. Oddou (Eds), *Readings and cases in international human resource management* (6th ed., p. 13). Routledge.

Edwards, R., & Brannelly, T. (2017). Approaches to democratising qualitative research methods. *Qualitative Research*, *17*(3), 271–277. https://doi.org/10.1177/1468794117706869

Grinyer, A. (2002). The anonymity of research participants: Assumptions, ethics and practicalities. In N. Gilbert (Ed.), *Social research update* (Issue 36). Department of Sociology, University of Surrey. https://sru.soc.surrey.ac.uk/SRU36.PDF

Hall, J., Gaved, M., & Sargent, J. (2021). Participatory research approaches in times of Covid-19: A narrative literature review. *International Journal of Qualitative Methods*, *20*, 1–15. https://doi.org/10.1177/16094069211010087

Hall, J. N. (2013). Pragmatism, evidence, and mixed methods evaluation. *New Directions for Evaluation*, *138*, 15–26. https://onlinelibrary.wiley.com/doi/10.1002/ev.20054

Iphofen, R. (2011). *Ethical decision making in social research: A practical guide*. Palgrave Macmillan.

Iphofen, R. (2021). *Research ethics in ethnography/anthropology*. European Commission, DG Research and Innovation. https://ec.europa.eu/info/funding-tenders/opportunities/docs/2021-2027/horizon/guidance/research-ethics-in-ethnography-anthropology_he_en.pdf

Karagiozis, N. (2018). Complexities of the researcher's role. *The International Journal of Interdisciplinary Educational Studies*, *13*(1), 19–31. https://doi.org/10.18848/2327-011X/CGP/v13i01/19-31

Maree, J. G. (2015). Career construction counseling: A thematic analysis of outcomes for four clients. *Journal of Vocational Behavior*, *86*(2015), 1–9. https://doi.org/10.1016/j.jvb.2014.10.001

Marovah, T., & Mutanga, O. (2023). Decolonising participatory research: Can Ubuntu philosophy contribute something? *International Journal of Social Research Methodology*, *27*(5), 501–516. https://doi.org/10.1080/13645579.2023.2214022

Mcleod, S. (2023, December 7). *Ethical considerations in psychology research*. Simply Psychology. https://www.simplypsychology.org/ethics.html

Metcalf, J., & Crawford, K. (2016). Where are human subjects in big data research? The emerging ethics divide. *Big Data & Society*, *3*(1), 1–14. https://doi.org/10.1177/2053951716650211

Mokgolodi, H. L. (2015). *Harnessing experiential knowledge and skills of retired educators to inform career development programmes in Botswana* [Doctoral dissertation, University of Pretoria]. https://repository.up.ac.za/bitstream/handle/2263/44142/Mokgolodi_Harnessing_2015.pdf?sequence=1

Mokgolodi, H. L. (2022). Retired educators' career transition as a new life role of underwriting career development in Botswana. *Population Ageing*, *15*(2022), 891–905. https://doi.org/10.1007/s12062-020-09303-5

Mokgolodi, H. L. (2023). Decolonizing evaluation of indigenous guidance and counseling approaches: A review of selected evaluated programs. *Journal of Multidisciplinary Evaluation*, *19*(44), 231–246. https://doi.org/10.56645/jmde.v19i44.779

Msoroka, M. S., & Amundsen, D. (2018). One size fits not quite all: Universal research ethics with diversity. *Research Ethics*, *14*(3), 1–17. https://doi.org/10.1177/1747016117739939

Muhammad, M., Wallerstein, N., Sussman, A. L., Avila, M., Belone, L., & Duran, B. (2015). Reflections on researcher identity and power: The impact of positionality on community based participatory research (CBPR) processes and outcomes. *Critical Sociology*, *41*(7–8), 1045–1063. https://doi.org/10.1177/0896920513516025

Perera, K. (2018). The ethical concerns of writing in social science research. In N. Emmerich (Ed.), *SAGE research methods cases* (pp. 1–8). SAGE. http://dx.doi.org/10.4135/9781526437020

Rossman, G. B., & Rallis, S. F. (2010). Everyday ethics: Reflections on practice. International Journal of Qualitative Studies in Education, *23*(4), 379–391. https://doi.org/10.1080/09518398.2010.492813

Savickas, M. L. (2005). The theory and practice of career construction. In S. D. Brown & R. W. Lent (Eds.), *Career development and counselling: Putting theory and research to work* (pp. 44–20). Wiley.

Savickas, M. L. (2011). Career counselling. In J. Carison & M. Englar-Carlson (Eds.), *Theories of psychotherapy series*. American Psychological Association.

Schreuder, A. M. G., & Coetzee, M. (2011). *Careers: An organisational perspective*. Juta and Company Ltd.

Seehawer, M. K. (2018). Decolonising research in a Sub-Saharan African context: Exploring Ubuntu as a foundation for research methodology, ethics and agenda. *International Journal of Social Research Methodology*, *21*(4), 453–466. https://doi.org/10.1080/13645579.2018.1432404

Shaw, R. M., Howe, J. H., Beazer, J., & Carr, T. (April, 2019). Ethics and positionality in qualitative research with vulnerable and marginal groups. *Qualitative Research*, *20*(3), 146879411984183. doi:10.1177/1468794119841839

Thambinathan, V., & Kinsella, E. A. (2021). Decolonizing methodologies in qualitative research: Creating spaces for transformative praxis. *International Journal of Qualitative Methods*, *20*, 1–9. https://doi.org/10.1177/16094069211014766

Wang, D., & Li, Y. (2024). Career construction theory: Tools, interventions, and future trends. *Frontiers in Psychology*, *5*(15), 1381233. https://doi.org/10.3389/fpsyg.2024.1381233

Watson, M. (2013). Deconstruction, reconstruction, co-construction: Career construction theory in a developing world context. Indian Journal of Career and Livelihood Planning (IJCLP), *2*(1), 3–14.

Woolsey, L. K. (1986). Research and practice in counseling: A conflict of values. *Counselor Education and Supervision*, *26*(2), 84–94. https://doi.org/10.1002/j.1556-6978.1986.tb00700.x

World Health Organization. (September, 2011). *Standards and operational guidance for ethics review of health-related research with human participants*. WHO Document Production Services. https://www.who.int/publications/i/item/9789241502948

World Health Organization African Region. (2021). *Training for ethics review of clinical research: A virtual training course for Africa*. https://www.afro.who.int/health-topics/immunization/avaref/training

Yip, C., Han, N. L. R., & Sng, B. L. (2016). Legal and ethical issues in research. *Indian Journal of Anaesthesia*, *60*, 684–688. https://pubmed.ncbi.nlm.nih.gov/27729698/

CHAPTER 8

ETHICAL PRACTICE IN QUALITATIVE RESEARCH INVOLVING USER-GENERATED ONLINE CONTENT: QUESTIONS, CHALLENGES, AND OPPORTUNITIES

Helena Webb

University of Nottingham, UK

ABSTRACT

Massive amounts of user-generated content (UGC) are posted online daily across the globe on social media sites, Internet discussion forums, blogs, and more. This content is a valuable source of data for qualitative researchers seeking to conduct detailed analyses of how individuals describe their experiences and perceptions, how they present themselves online, and how they interact with others in online spaces. However, working with UGC presents ethical challenges. These particularly relate to questions regarding whether online content should be treated as public or private, whether the informed consent of users is necessary, and what anonymity and privacy look like in the online landscape. This can leave researchers uncertain over the correct course of action to take. This chapter provides an overview of the ethical challenges faced when working

Reframing Qualitative Research Ethics
Advances in Research Ethics and Integrity, Volume 12, 127–143

Published under exclusive licence by Emerald Publishing Limited
ISSN: 2398-6018/doi:10.1108/S2398-601820250000012008

with UGC and describes different ways researchers in this area have attempted to address them as well as highlighting elements of current guidance. The aim is to help researchers, particularly those new to working with UGC, prepare to deal with these issues in their own work. The overview shows that there are no fixed procedures for ethical practice with UGC and instead decisions are often made flexibly, dependent on context. I argue that a useful way forward in this space is dialogue between researchers and ethics committees/advisors. Dialogue can recognise the challenges researchers face, acknowledge the importance of context for ethical decision-making plus likely future changes in the UGC landscape, and promote deeper discussion on fundamental issues regarding research ethics.

Keywords: User-generated content; social media; informed consent; privacy; data access

INTRODUCTION

The contemporary Internet creates opportunities for individuals across the world to post their own content online. As online users, people can write blog posts, join in on discussion forums, make comments on news articles, and share news and opinions on social media sites. This user-generated content (UGC) has quickly become of interest to qualitative researchers. Analysing UGC can help us to understand how individuals describe their experiences and perceptions, how they present themselves online, and how they interact with others in online spaces. UGC is therefore of significant interest across various academic disciplines including social science, psychology, human–computer interaction, linguistics, media and cultural studies, and health sciences. However, while finding this a very fruitful area for study, researchers have also often discovered that work involving UGC raises significant ethical dilemmas. These particularly relate to questions regarding whether online content should be treated as public or private, whether the informed consent of users is necessary for research to take place, and what anonymity and privacy look like in the online context.

In this chapter, I describe the ethical challenges typically faced by researchers conducting qualitative work involving UGC. I begin by outlining the characteristics of UGC itself, to demonstrate how the unique landscape of UGC and online spaces undermines many familiar ethical practices around data access, privacy, and consent. I then focus on the research stages of site access, data collection, and dissemination to describe the challenges researchers might encounter as they work through projects. The aim is to provide an overview that can help researchers, particularly those working with UGC for the first time, to prepare for these challenges. I use examples from existing research around the world to illustrate the specific ethical questions that UGC poses and how researchers have sought to address them. It is intended that these examples can aid researchers across the globe. The popularity of platforms and practices of use do vary in different countries; however (local data protection regulation notwithstanding), the ethical challenges arising from research involving UGC have many similarities regardless of where data are collected and where users are posting from. I also highlight passages from ethical guidelines that have been developed in response to the challenges of UGC. I specifically provide examples from research organisations in the United Kingdom. This current guidance is flexible rather than fixed; this is indicative of an absence of set procedures across research in this area more generally.

In the final part of this chapter, I focus on the importance of dialogue between researchers and ethics committees/advisors. I argue that discussion is a productive way forward to determine ethical practice, in particular as it can allow for consideration of context in ethical decision-making and acknowledge the impact of ongoing changes relating to UGC. Additionally, dialogue presents an opportunity for more fundamental discussion about what research ethics means when working with user-generated online content.

BACKGROUND – UGC AND ITS CHARACTERISTICS

UGC on the Internet refers to content that is created by individuals rather than companies, institutions, or brands (Naab & Sehl, 2017). The individuals who post the content are (typically) unpaid, and the content itself may take the form of text, photographs, audio, videos, etc. The contemporary web 2.0 era has facilitated the posting of UGC on a massive scale. Online users can contribute content by, for instance, posting in discussion forums, adding comments on online news articles, and responding to online polls and research. Web 2.0 is particularly exemplified by the rise of social media platforms. Facebook, Instagram, X (formerly Twitter), LinkedIn, YouTube, TikTok, etc. allow users to post content about themselves, share news and opinions, build up networks, and interact with each other. Mobile-based apps such as WhatsApp are also often included within the definition of social media as they use Internet technology to facilitate the sharing of content between users. Social media platforms have become highly prevalent in contemporary life across the globe, as shown by Facebook usage statistics. The most popular platform in the world, Facebook, has, as of April 2024, an estimated 2.11 billion daily users and 3.07 billion monthly users (Shewale, 2024).

UGC can take a variety of forms, and the platforms it is posted on differ too. However, both content and platforms tend to share certain characteristics. First, UGC can often be posted anonymously. Platforms require users to have some form of identity when posting content, for instance, a username. However, this does not necessarily need to match the 'real world' identity of the user. Many usernames on X, Instagram, discussion forums, and so on are obvious false names or pseudonyms. Facebook does have an ostensible 'real name' policy, but this was watered-down following civil liberties concerns and is hard to enforce in practice (Hern, 2015). The anonymity afforded by platforms means that, if they choose to, users can post content without revealing their name, location, job details, etc. Second, much UGC can be seen and even shared by large numbers of other people simultaneously. Some platforms are open by default; for instance, the comments sections of many online newspapers and discussion forums such as reddit. On these platforms it is necessary to have an account to post content but anyone with an Internet connection can read what is posted. Depending on the settings used, contents on Facebook, Instagram, You Tube, and X can also be seen publicly. In addition, some platforms allow content to be shared by users with an account. Posts on X can be 'retweeted', some posts on Facebook can be shared, and some messages in WhatsApp can be forwarded. Sharing increases the visibility of a post, and content propagation can be massive in both volume and speed (Haralabopoulos et al., 2017). In 2019, a Japanese billionaire posted on X about a money giveaway; this content was reposted 3.8 million times[1] – a record for most reshared content. The rapid spread of UGC has been associated with the spread of misinformation and has consequences for individual and collective behaviours (World Economic Forum, 2013).

A further characteristic is that UGC can often be deleted. Several platforms, including Facebook, X, and Instagram, allow users to change their minds about content they have posted and remove it. Platforms themselves might delete posts or stop them being posted as part of their moderation procedures. Many use filtering technologies to identify and redact inappropriate language and images, and reporting mechanisms are also common. Platforms vary a great deal in the strictness of their moderation policies (Cai et al., 2024) and some online discussion forums have become famous, or infamous, for their relaxed approach to moderation – for instance, 4chan and Kiwi Farms. Another, connected, characteristic is that negative or harmful UGC is seen to be increasing in volume. Large amounts of problematic content are posted online in the form of hate speech against demographic groups, harassing content targeted towards individuals, political extremism, conspiracy theories, and misinformation and disinformation (Keipi et al., 2016; Millwood Hargrave & Livingstone, 2009; Scheuerman et al., 2021; Schmid et al., 2024). It is often theorised that the anonymous and asynchronous nature of UGC has deindividuation and disinhibition effects, which embolden users to say things in more inflammatory terms than they would do in face-to-face interactions (Lowry et al., 2016; Suler, 2004). Even where content falls foul of moderation policies, platforms may not deal with it quickly or consistently (Common, 2020; Díaz & Hecht-Felella, 2021). Consequently, harmful online behaviours such as harassment and the spread of inflammatory content have, to some extent, become normalised (Awan, 2014; Lumsden & Morgan, 2017).

The final characteristic to note is that the platforms UGC is posted on are constantly changing in use and form. Platforms rise and fall in popularity. TikTok has become hugely popular with young people over a short period of time (Geyser, 2024) while Facebook is dropping in popularity among the same demographic (Gottfried, 2024). Meanwhile WhatsApp has become the default mobile app of use for many in the Global South (Wodinsky, 2021). Platforms also change. New features such as livestreaming or personalisation features are added, moderation policies change, and monetisation policies change. The existence of features on platforms which allow access to third parties, such as researchers, also changes over time – as will be discussed below.

The combination of these characteristics creates a unique sociotechnical landscape. This underpins why UGC is of such fascination to researchers across academic disciplines. It is also the cause of many of the ethical challenges that arise for researchers when they conduct this work. Familiar understandings around data access, informed consent, and privacy are undermined, particularly so in the case of qualitative research. These challenges are discussed next.

ETHICAL ISSUES ARISING FROM QUALITATIVE RESEARCH INVOLVING UGC

The ethical challenges arising from qualitative research involving UGC largely centre around privacy, informed consent, and the potential harms that may come to users (and researchers) if their identities are known. These challenges present themselves in different ways across the stages of the research process, but there is also overlap across them. In this section, I discuss three key research stages in turn: accessing the research site, collecting data, and dissemination. Examples from existing research and ethical guidance demonstrate how efforts are made to address these concerns. They also reveal that decisions about good practice are often context dependent rather than pre-established.

Accessing the Research Site

Accessing the research site when studying UGC can often be straightforward. When the content being studied is in an open online space with no password protection, then the relevant website, forum, or social media platform can be accessed easily through an Internet connection. However, there still may be a question of whether users posting content on these open spaces have an expectation of privacy. For instance, if I have a blog that I use to post about my niche hobby, I might normally only have a small number of readers and I might not expect that one of them is looking at my content to conduct research on it. Would it be reasonable to expect the researcher to contact me to ask if this is acceptable? Alternatively, should I consider my blog page to be equivalent to a public space and available for anyone to access? There are plenty of offline spaces which are theoretically public but in which I might rightfully expect protection from research intrusion. If I am in a park talking to a group of friends, it would not be considered ethically appropriate for a researcher to sit down with us and listen to our conversation. Accessing a conversation on an online platform without seeking consent could be considered equivalent to this. In its ethical guidance on Internet-mediated research, the British Psychological Association (2021) urges researchers to give careful consideration to this question and observes that 'the extent to which the research can be thought of as occurring within a private or public domain, may be difficult to decide, given that those boundaries are often blurred online' (p. 6). In 2015, the US Federal Policy (US Department of Health and Human Services, 2015) for the protection of human subjects (the 'Common Rule') categorised research involving public behaviour online as able to proceed without review: although the absence of a need for ethics review is not the same as the absence of ethical considerations.

Some platforms where UGC is posted are not open. It is therefore necessary for the researcher to take steps to access them, such as registering to make an account in order to gain a username and access to read and post content. This might require providing a name, email address, and potentially a phone number. Here, the researcher must decide whether to provide their real information or remain anonymous. Anonymity may be partial, i.e. a real name and email address for registration (information which will be seen by the platform but not by users) but a pseudonymous username. Or full anonymity may involve giving entirely non-identifying information during registration. In either case, the researcher is able to access the data site without other users being aware of their status. Ethical guidance generally cautions against covert practices of accessing data sites. For instance, the British Sociological Association Statement of Ethical Practice (2017a) observes that covert research methods 'violate the principle of informed consent and may invade the privacy of those being studied' (p. 5). It advises that the approach is taken only when overt methods are not possible – for instance, if awareness of being studied is likely to cause participants to change their behaviours significantly, and to the detriment of the research, or if it would be impossible to gain access to the research site overtly. Some researchers have argued that in certain kinds of online research, being overt provides academic benefit. Reflecting on the study of online fan cultures, Whiteman (2018) observes that when researchers openly share the particular enthusiasm of the fan group being studied (for a TV programme, celebrity, game, etc.), this can help to create a sense of connection and shared identity. As a result, the researcher is better able to understand the perspectives of the participants. Being overt can also facilitate participatory research activities, for instance, as conducted by Matias (2016) in a study of moderator protests on reddit.

There are various instances however of researchers choosing a covert approach. The justification given for this may relate to the impossibility of gaining access overtly. Semenzin and Bainotti (2020) conducted a study of the non-consensual dissemination of intimate images within private user groups on the online communication platform Telegram. When gaining access to these groups, they chose to conceal their status as researchers. Having identified potential groups to join, via lists found on an online pornography website, they chatted online with group administrators. When chatting, they deliberately chose gender-neutral nicknames and did not reveal that they were researchers – although they note they were not in fact asked to reveal their identities. The administrators then provided them with links to join the groups. Semenzin and Bainotti argue that this was the only viable way to gain access. If their status as researchers was known, they would not have been admitted and would not have had the opportunity to conduct research work of considerable public relevance.

Another rationale for a covert approach relates to the risk of harm to researchers if their presence is detected. This connects to the characteristic observed earlier regarding the prevalence of harmful content and behaviours on platforms with UGC. Researchers may choose to study online groups where hostile attitudes to 'outsiders' are common and for whom harassment (in online and offline forms) is a normalised behaviour. In these instances, anonymity may be a necessary protection. Askanius (2019) makes this point in a reflection on the ethics of studying organised racism in online environments. She notes that studying extremist nationalist groups may be safer to do online than offline, and that studying them covertly online can protect researcher safety. Massanari (2018) makes the same point in relation to the study of alt-right groups, observing that researcher safety can be an issue when conducting studies in politically extreme spaces. In these cases, it is argued, the importance of researcher safety might justify waiving the usual ethical preference for overt research.

Collecting the Data

The next research stage concerns collecting data. Qualitative researchers are likely to seek data in the form of observational material on user behaviours and forms of self-presentation, as well as the actual content of user-generated posts. A first ethical consideration is whether platforms hosting this content allow for data collection to take place. Platforms can be considered gatekeepers in this context. Their terms of service (TOS) set specific criteria through which third parties can access data, and they might also have further expectations regarding the conduct of academic research. For instance, some online forums allow recruitment messages for studies to be posted only in certain parts of the site and some forums or subforums explicitly ban the collection of posts as research data. Even where platforms are generally welcoming to third-party access, they may ban the practice of web scraping. Web scraping is a form of automated data collection in which a software tool gathers content posted online. It has come to be widely used in academic research (Luscombe et al., 2022) but may be considered ethically problematic due to the stress it can place on a website's servers and legally problematic due to issues around data protection. Many websites bar or limit web scraping as part of their TOS; in recent years, this has included the social media sites LinkedIn (LinkedIn, 2024), Facebook (Facebook, n.d.), and X (Vitaitis, 2024). While these bars are directed more towards blocking data access for commercial gain, they can be consequential to academic research. For example, in 2021, Facebook blocked access to a research team from New York University studying online disinformation, using the justification that their web scraping violated its TOS (Bond, 2021).

Over time, large platforms have increasingly closed down access to data through their application user interfaces (APIs). APIs enable different applications to interact with each other, for instance, facilitating the collection of data from a website. Once again, they are largely used for commercial purposes but can be valuable to research. Facebook restricted its API access following the Cambridge Analytica scandal (Constine, 2018). Prior to the Elon Musk takeover, X/Twitter had a very accessible API, which made it an extremely popular source of research data. This has been restricted and monetised from early 2023 onwards (Gotfredson, 2023). Both web scraping and APIs facilitate large-scale data collection, so their restriction impacts quantitative research more than qualitative.

Qualitative researchers may instead choose to collect data via notetaking plus screen shots of UGC and screen captures if video material is included. However, it is important to be aware of the ethical issues surrounding more automated forms of data collection and to note how these issues illustrate the frequency with which the landscape around UGC changes.

A final form of data collection arises via collaboration between academics and platforms. Given the gatekeeping role that platforms now play, initiatives such as Social Science One have emerged to establish models for collaboration and data sharing. Academic-platform collaborations can raise their own ethical questions. A famous example is the 'Facebook contagion study' of 2012 (Selinger & Hartzog, 2016). Collaborating with Facebook enabled researchers from Cornell in the United States to gain access to the newsfeeds of over 680,000 users. These users were separated into groups, some of which had their newsfeeds manipulated to emphasise either positive or negative content. The users' own posts were then monitored to assess whether this manipulation affected their emotional expression. The study was conducted without users being made aware at any point that they were taking part in an experiment, that their newsfeeds were being altered, and that their UGC was being monitored. The researchers justified this through the fact that Facebook's TOS (which users must agree to in order to create an account) allow for research to be conducted to improve its service. However, once the study was published, this was challenged very strongly by the academic community, and the journal has since placed an 'expression of concern' on the article. Although this is once again a piece of quantitative research, the lessons it provides apply equally to qualitative data collection involving UGC. Platform ethics are not research ethics. Even where an action is allowable by the TOS of a platform, this does not automatically mean it is ethically acceptable in research. Platform TOS do in fact frequently allow for research and development work to be conducted with user data, as in the case of the Facebook study. But researchers have also frequently argued (e.g. Williams et al., 2017a) that this alone does not make collecting user data ethical – not least because it is well known that users rarely read these, usually very lengthy, TOS in full. This brings us back to the issue of user consent.

Acknowledging that user agreement to platform TOS does not equate to genuine informed consent to take part in research makes it necessary to consider whether researchers must seek explicit consent instead. It is not uncommon for data to be collected on open platforms such as X (Zimmer & Proferes, 2014) or reddit (Fiesler et al., 2024) without consent being sought. In addition to the justification that such platforms may be equivalent to public spaces, it is also recognised, by the Association of Internet Researchers (Franzke et al., 2020) among others, that consent practices can be time-consuming and impractical. However, research on public opinion in the United Kingdom (Beninger et al., 2014; Williams et al., 2017b) suggests that a significant number of users feel researchers have a moral obligation to seek their consent when collecting data related to them, even on open platforms.

In some studies, researchers have used proxies for informed consent, such as seeking consent from a forum administrator or moderator rather than all its users

(Fiesler et al., 2024). Additionally, in online qualitative research, it is common to defer the question of informed consent to the stage of dissemination rather than data collection. That is, researchers collect data without consent but later consider whether it will be necessary to seek user consent to publish the data, or whether other protections such as anonymity might be sufficient. This position is put forward in the British Sociological Association (2017b) in its guidelines for digital research. It notes that 'Most, if not all ethical guidelines include exemptions to informed consent' and suggests that researchers think about how such exemptions might apply to their own project. The guidance argues that 'this is not an attempt to avoid consent … by identifying loopholes, rather it is a suggested initial pathway through a vast amount of information and complex issues' (p. 6).

The same considerations to waive or defer informed consent might be applied to research involving closed online spaces. However, where UGC is not publicly viewable, users are likely to have greater expectations of privacy and the ability to express an opinion about being involved in research. In a reflection on their qualitative research on Internet communities related to health, Eysenbach and Till (2001) note that members of chat rooms and mailing lists sometimes expressed discomfort or distress towards the idea of their posts being used as data and were occasionally even hostile to being approached about research.

There are some further ethical issues that may arise during data collection. One relates to the deletion of content. As noted above, many platforms allow users to delete UGC after posting it. Users may do this due to privacy concerns, a change of opinion, because the content received an inflammatory response or various other reasons. Platforms also delete content as part of their moderation procedures. Should deletion of content be regarded as equivalent to withdrawing from a study and therefore necessitate the removal of data from the dataset? This in fact may be a requirement that platforms put in place when allowing third-party access (Franzke et al., 2020) but checking for deletions can be time-consuming and impractical. The British Psychological Association (2021) guidance on Internet-mediated research argues that when data have been collected from a 'public' open space, it is acceptable to take a proportional approach to this question and not delete the data unless they 'included anything which could be deemed illegal or violating terms of use from its original space' (p. 14). As the quote also shows, another ethical issue relates to how researchers respond when seeing content/behaviours that are illegal or harmful. Online harassment is rife; should researchers attempt to deflect or stop it when they observe it during data collection? Much research involving UGC focuses on its more negative aspects – the spreading of harmful content, communities posting extremist or prejudicial viewpoints, etc. This can be distressing for the researcher to observe so self-care is another concern. It may seem that the online nature of data collection can provide a helpful barrier that protects the researcher from users and the immediacy of UGC. However, when data collection takes place in the office or at home rather than at a fieldwork site, there is a loss of 'travelling to' and the associated sense of separation this provides (Bengtsson, 2014). Data collection can blur with other activities and distress arising from research can invade other areas of life. Askanius (2019) describes this feeling in her own work on organised racism online. She writes that:

> Ultimately, exposing yourself on a daily basis to hateful, racist, anti-Semitic, misogynist and despotic language and imagery, … is, in the long run, hurtful on a personal level.

And, referring to Bengtsson's work, she adds that this exposure to hurt was amplified by the blurring of boundaries and

> consequently of having voluntarily invited national socialists into my home and my everyday life. (p. 884)

Dissemination

Ethical concerns in the dissemination stage connect to risks of harm to both researchers and participants. As already noted, researchers can receive a hostile response to their work, and dissemination is a critical point at which this might occur. If research has been conducted covertly, online users, and members of their communities, may react negatively to awareness they were unwitting research participants. In addition, research may receive a general hostile online response due to the subject matter it covers; for instance, Gelms (2021) describes how publishing work on online harassment risks researchers being harassed. While these risks are present for researchers studying various sensitive or controversial matters, they can be particularly resonant to researchers studying online communities. As mentioned before, some online communities treat the harassment of others as normal, perhaps even part of their standard behaviours (Colley & Moore, 2022). Members can be very adept at navigating the Internet to, for instance, find out private information about researchers, or even their family members, in order to make it publicly available ('doxing'), or to organise targeted campaigns of negative messaging. Some communities are known to actively monitor academic research in readiness to take action against projects which they perceive as antagonistic to them (Massanari, 2018). The experience of harassment can obviously have a very detrimental effect on researcher well-being, and the risk of it can even discourage researchers from conducting research and dissemination in the first place (Marwick et al., 2016). Female researchers, researchers of colour, and researchers in the LGBTQIA+ community are most likely to be affected (Gelms, 2021; Vera-Gray, 2017), and researchers often report that their institutions are unable or unwilling to deal with the problem decisively (Marwick et al., 2016). In addition to these issues, some researchers have expressed concern that dissemination can amplify harmful online content; this might produce further distress when the content is seen (Gelms, 2021) or bring extremist ideas to new audiences (Colley & Moore, 2022).

If the decision over informed consent has been previously deferred, it now becomes necessary at this stage to determine whether participants should be asked to agree to their UGC, and other data about them, to be included in dissemination. There may be a risk that individuals are identifiable in research outputs and that being identified can cause them harm. This is rarely an issue in quantitative research as data are generally aggregated, but qualitative projects are more likely to report data in potentially identifiable forms. Ethical guidance rarely states that informed consent is definitely necessary here and tends towards a case-by-case approach, dependent on factors such as the subject matter of the research and the openness of the research site (e.g. British Sociological Association, 2017b; The British Psychological Association, 2021; Townsend & Wallace, 2016). Many qualitative studies are published without informed consent, typically with steps taken to anonymise the data. As an extra protection measure, some researchers publish composite rather than real data (Markham, 2012), for instance, preparing synthesised posts that represent the patterns observed in the UGC they have analysed.

Informed consent and/or the anonymisation of data don't necessarily resolve these ethical considerations in full. The characteristics of UGC and online platforms insert complicating factors which can threaten the effectiveness of both. This is something my colleagues and I experienced in a study of the spread of hate speech on social media (Webb et al., 2017). We had collected large amounts of Twitter threads, each beginning with a post that might be considered sexist, racist, or homophobic. We then conducted both quantitative and qualitative analysis to understand how other users responded as the threads continued. The qualitative analysis was highly granular and when writing it up, we wanted to follow the convention of including actual posts in our dissemination. We had not sought consent at the point of data collection so now faced dilemmas over whether we should attempt to seek consent, and how we could anonymise the data. Publishing without consent seemed a substantial risk since the UGC we had collected was highly inflammatory and we were concerned that, if identified, it might embarrass the users who posted it or leave them open to repercussions from others. We also recognised that our ability to fully anonymise the content was limited. We could redact the username of the poster but if we included the real content of the post itself, this content could be pasted into Twitter's powerful search function, and the search result would reveal this information. So, if we included actual content of posts in our dissemination, anyone who wanted to could find the online identity of the users we had quoted. This is the case for various platforms in 'open' online spaces. We contacted the editors of some journals we were interested to publish in to ask whether using composite data would be an acceptable alternative that would allow us to present our analysis while also protecting user anonymity. We were told that this would not be possible as these journals emphasised the importance of naturalistic data, and synthesised posts would be classed as fabrication.

Having recognised the limitations of anonymisation, we decided to only include in our publications examples of potential hate speech posted by people already in the public eye (Procter et al., 2019). Our rationale was that the famous politicians, commentators, etc. included in our dataset had posted on Twitter knowing that their content would receive wide attention and usually as part of their work; our re-publishing these posts would be unlikely to amplify them or cause significant (further) harm. We then attempted to contact some of the users who had responded to these posts to ask if they would agree to us including their responses (typically ones expressing disagreement with the preceding hateful content) in our dissemination. As the only information we had about them was their Twitter account details, we sent messages to these users on Twitter to make the request and included a link which they could follow to read more details about our project and our intentions. We set up the messages as a reply to the particular post we wanted to publish so that users could see exactly what we were referring to. It was relatively quick to send these messages, and we received a small number of responses giving consent for publication. Although this gave us a sense of reassurance, we also realised a further limitation. All we knew about these users were details on their Twitter accounts. Some had clearly pseudonymous usernames and included little personal information. Others did include personal information but the anonymous nature of the Internet means that it was possible this did not mirror the user's 'real' offline identity. Even if we gained consent from a user who claimed to be a 30-year old, for example, we could not guarantee that this user was not in fact a young teenager posting pseudonymously or someone lacking capacity – and therefore not able to give consent. We could have of course searched through the user's other posts to try to establish their identity and work out whether they were genuinely able to consent. However, this would be an uncomfortably intrusive course of action to take. So, we were ultimately not able to address the issue of informed consent fully satisfactorily.

These experiences my colleagues and I had in our study of Twitter data exemplify the ethical challenges many researchers face when working with UGC. The characteristic properties of the Internet, in particular the public availability of some content while users can simultaneously retain anonymity, problematise established ethical practices and make it difficult to determine how research can avoid causing harm. This is particularly so when the online spaces and UGC being analysed are potentially harmful themselves. The lack of certainty over the best course of action to take means that a dialogue over ethics is highly desirable. Researchers across the community are already prompting this dialogue by including reflections on ethics in reports of their findings or as standalone articles. Many of their thought-provoking insights have been cited here. In the final section of this chapter, I argue that a dialogue between researchers and research ethics committees (RECs) and advisory groups can be equally beneficial, and that it presents a way forward for research in this area.

CONCLUSION

The preceding sections of this chapter have highlighted the ethical challenges that researchers might face when conducting studies involving UGC online. These challenges can arise across different stages of a research project – while accessing the research site, collecting the data, and disseminating the findings – and centre on issues regarding informed consent, privacy, and risks of harm to both participants and researchers. The unique characteristics of the Internet often mean that the effectiveness of traditional ethical safeguards is undermined. This can leave researchers in the position that my colleagues and I found ourselves in during our study of online hate speech: wanting to do the right thing but not knowing what that right thing was. During our study, we benefitted from the opportunity to talk through these issues with others. We presented our questions and concerns to ethics committees, members of ethics advisory groups, and other experts from research institutions across a number of countries. The reflections that these discussions prompted helped to shape the decisions we made in the project and have been written up to pass back to the community (Webb et al., 2017). Since that time, I have had further reasons to seek input from ethics committees on my research involving UGC, and I have also been invited to talk to ethics committees about my experiences. I have found these interactions to be very beneficial and believe that dialogue between ethics committees/advisors and researchers is crucial in the case of qualitative research involving UGC. This is due to the complexities of the issues involved plus the likelihood that they will keep growing and changing over time.

A first reason to advocate for ongoing dialogue between researchers and ethics committees/advisors is the context dependency of ethical considerations around research work involving UGC. The research examples covered in this chapter show that no clear 'one size fits all' solution has been found to successfully address all relevant challenges. Instead, researchers have drawn on contingent factors such as the openness of the online research site, the potentially harmful nature of UGC being collected as data, the capacity to interact with users, and the effectiveness of anonymisation to determine what constitutes a correct approach. This is mirrored in ethics guidelines, which similarly advocate a flexible approach rather than advocating for specific courses of action. I have focused on guidance produced in the United Kingdom to illustrate this, but similar flexibility can be observed in other countries and in guidance produced by globally focused organisations such as the Association of Internet Researchers. It is not uncommon for projects to move away from traditional ethical cornerstones such as informed consent. Doing so can feel very uncomfortable for researchers and raise concerns that research is prioritising what is practically accomplishable over ethical principles. Dialogue here can help to ameliorate this discomfort. It should be recognised that researchers have a valuable role to play in identifying ethical practice for their projects since they have in-depth understanding of the research context and awareness of how relevant factors such as those mentioned above will play out within it (Kohn & Shore, 2017). In return, ethics committees and other experts can provide guidance on how to acknowledge these factors while also paying due attention to ethical principles. The context of UGC can mean that there are sometimes no obvious 'good' or 'risk-free' decisions to make about ethical practice; ultimately a dialogue can ensure that researchers are given appropriate support and protection as they attempt to navigate the issues involved (Bloor et al., 2010).

A second reason why dialogue is necessary relates to the frequent changes that occur in the UGC landscape. In the relatively short period of time that UGC and the platforms it is posted on have grown popular, changes to platform organisation and user practices have impacted understandings of research ethics. We can expect this to continue. For instance, online forums and newspapers with comment sections are increasingly moving behind paywalls. They are becoming closed research sites for UGC but for reasons of monetisation rather than concerns about privacy. What does this mean for decisions over research site access and data collection? Additionally, governments around the world are attempting to introduce regulations that seek to hold platforms more accountable for content posted on them; this is likely to impact platform policies around third-party access, which in turn may have consequences for data collection. Finally, social media platforms are already being flooded with bots – automated programmes that mimic human users – and their presence is likely to rise further in the age of generative AI. This raises new ethical challenges. How can I get informed consent from a bot? How can I tell if the user I am seeking consent from is a human or a bot? Here researchers are well placed to advise ethics committees on the changes occurring to the UGC landscape and prompt reflection on what the changes mean for ethical research practice.

Finally, I would like to suggest that researcher and research committee/advisor dialogue can be an opportunity for more fundamental discussion about what ethics means in the context of UGC. It is clear that informed consent as a model struggles with UGC and in fact in the context of big data more generally (Froomkin, 2019; Luger, 2012). In addition to understanding that for some projects it might be ethically valid to waive seeking informed consent, we could open up discussion to consideration of alternatives to the model, seeking other mechanisms for protecting participants from harm and respecting their autonomy. Likewise, we could consider what it might look like to embrace practices informed by ethics of care, given that we can observe limitations to the application of deontologically informed principles in this space. This argument has been made by scholars in other contexts (e.g. Bell & Wynn, 2023; Hammersley & Traianou, 2014), who suggest we should not consider ourselves bound to ethical procedures inherited from biomedicine when they do not reflect the cultural, organisational, and behavioural contingencies of the specific areas we conduct research in. The unique landscape of UGC is a key exemplar of this difference. Researchers working in this field are therefore well-suited to undertake informed dialogue with ethics committees and advisors to discuss possibilities for change, and this can open up opportunities for exciting advances in research ethics that are both meaningful and radical.

NOTE

1. https://en.wikipedia.org/wiki/List_of_most-retweeted_tweets

ACKNOWLEDGEMENTS

The preparation of this chapter was supported by the UKRI under grant EP/T022493/1. No data were generated during the work to prepare this chapter.

REFERENCES

Askanius, T. (2019). Studying the Nordic resistance movement: Three urgent questions for researchers of contemporary neo-Nazis and their media practices. *Media, Culture & Society*, *41*(6), 878–888. https://doi.org/10.1177/0163443719831181

Awan, I. (2014). Islamophobia and Twitter: A typology of online hate against Muslims on social media. *Policy & Internet*, *6*(2), 133–150. https://doi.org/10.1002/1944-2866.POI364

Bell, K., & Wynn, L. (2023). Research ethics committees, ethnographers and imaginations of risk. *Ethnography*, *24*(4), 537–558. https://doi.org/10.1177/1466138120983862

Bengtsson, S. (2014). Faraway, so close! Proximity and distance in ethnography online. *Media, Culture & Society*, *36*(6), 862–877. https://doi.org/10.1177/0163443714531195

Beninger, K., Fry, A., Jago, N., Lepps, H., Nass, L., & Silvester, H. (2014). *Research using social media; Users' views*. NatCen. http://www.natcen.ac.uk/media/282288/p0639-research-using-social-media-report-final-190214.pdf

Bloor, M., Fincham, B., & Sampson, H. (2010). Unprepared for the worst: Risks of harm for qualitative researchers. *Methodological Innovations Online*, *5*(1), 4555. https://doi.org/10.4256/mio.2010.0009

Bond, S. (2021). NYU researchers were studying disinformation on social media. The company cut them off. *npr.org*. https://www.npr.org/2021/08/04/1024791053/facebook-boots-nyu-disinformation-researchers-off-its-platform-and-critics-cry-f

British Sociological Association. (2017a). *Statement of ethical practice*. https://www.britsoc.co.uk/media/24310/bsa_statement_of_ethical_practice.pdf

British Sociological Association. (2017b). *Ethics guidelines and collated resources for digital research: Statement of ethical practice annexe*. https://www.britsoc.co.uk/media/24309/bsa_statement_of_ethical_practice_annexe.pdf

Cai, J., Patel, A., Naderi, A., & Wohn, D. Y. (2024). Content moderation justice and fairness on social media: Comparisons across different contexts and platforms. In *CHI EA'24 Extended Abstracts of the CHI Conference on Human Factors in Computing Systems* (pp. 1–9). https://doi.org/10.1145/3613905.3650882

Colley, T., & Moore, M. (2022). The challenges of studying 4chan and the Alt-Right: 'Come on in the water's fine'. *New Media & Society*, *24*(1), 5–30. https://doi.org/10.1177/1461444820948803

Common, M. F. (2020). Fear the reaper: How content moderation rules are enforced on social media. *International Review of Law, Computers & Technology*, *34*(2), 126–152. https://doi.org/10.1080/13600869.2020.1733762

Constine, J. (2018, April 4). *Facebook restricts APIs, axes old Instagram platform amidst scandals*. techcrunch.com. https://techcrunch.com/2018/04/04/facebook-instagram-api-shut-down/#:~:text=Facebook%20restricts%20APIs%2C%20axes%20old%20Instagram%20platform%20amidst%20scandals,-Josh%20Constine&text=Facebook%20is%20entering%20a%20tough,part%20of%20the%20Instagram%20API

Díaz, Á., & Hecht-Felella, L. (2021). *Double standards in social media content moderation*. Brennan Center for Justice at New York University School of Law. https://www.brennancenter.org/our-work/research-reports/double-standards-social-media-content-moderation

Eysenbach, G., & Till, J. E. (2001). Ethical issues in qualitative research on internet communities. *BMJ*, *323*(7321), 1103–1105. https://doi.org/10.1136/bmj.323.7321.1103

Facebook. (n.d.). *What is web scraping and what can I do to protect my information on Facebook?* facebook.com. https://www.facebook.com/help/463983701520800

Fiesler, C., Zimmer, M., Proferes, N., Gilbert, S., & Jones, N. (2024). Remember the human: A systematic review of ethical considerations in reddit research. *Proceedings of the ACM on Human-Computer Interaction*, *8*(GROUP), 1–33. https://doi.org/10.1145/3633070

Franzke, A. S., Bechmann, A., Zimmer, M., Ess, C., & the Association of Internet Researchers. (2020). *Internet research: Ethical guidelines 3.0*. https://aoir.org/reports/ethics3.pdf

Froomkin, A. M. (2019). Big data: Destroyer of informed consent. *Yale Journal of Law and Technology*, *21*(Special issue), 27–54.

Gelms, B. (2021). Social media research and the methodological problem of harassment: Foregrounding researcher safety. *Computers and Composition*, *59*, 102626. https://doi.org/10.1016/j.compcom.2021.102626

Geyser, W. (2024). *The incredible rise of Tik Tok*. influencermarketinghub.com. https://influencermarketinghub.com/tiktok-growth/

Gotfredson, S. G. (2023). Q&A: What happened to academic research on Twitter? *Columbia Journalism Review*. https://www.cjr.org/tow_center/qa-what-happened-to-academic-research-on-twitter.php

Gottfried, J. (2024). *American's social media use*. Pew Research Center. https://www.pewresearch.org/internet/2024/01/31/americans-social-media-use/

Hammersley, M., & Traianou, A. (2014). An alternative ethics? Justice and care as guiding principles for qualitative research. *Sociological Research Online*, *19*(3), 104–117. https://doi.org/10.5153/sro.3466

Haralabopoulos, G., Anagnostopoulos, I., & Zeadally, S. (2017). *Viral content propagation in online social networks*. arXiv preprint arXiv:1712.02245

Hern, A. (2015, November). Facebook relaxes 'real name' policy in face of protest. *The Guardian*. https://www.theguardian.com/technology/2015/nov/02/facebook-real-name-policy-protest

Keipi, T., Näsi, M., Oksanen, A., & Räsänen, P. (2016). *Online hate and harmful content: Cross-national perspectives*. Taylor & Francis. https://doi.org/10.4324/9781315628370

Kohn, T., & Shore, C. (2017). The ethics of university ethics committees. Risk management and the research imagination. In S. Wright & C. Shore (Eds.), *Death of the public university: Uncertain futures for higher education in the knowledge economy* (pp. 229–249). Berghahn Books.

LinkedIn. (2024). *Prohibited software and extensions*. https://www.linkedin.com/help/linkedin/answer/a1341387/prohibited-software-and-extensions

Lowry, P. B., Zhang, J., Wang, C., & Siponen, M. (2016). Why do adults engage in cyberbullying on social media? An integration of online disinhibition and deindividuation effects with the social structure and social learning model. *Information Systems Research*, *27*(4), 962–986. https://doi.org/10.1287/isre.2016.0671

Luger, E. (2012). Consent reconsidered; reframing consent for ubiquitous computing systems. In *Proceedings of the 2012 ACM conference on ubiquitous computing* (pp. 564–567). Association of Computing Machinery. https://doi.org/10.1145/2370216.2370310

Lumsden, K., & Morgan, H. (2017). Media framing of trolling and online abuse: Silencing strategies, symbolic violence, and victim blaming. *Feminist Media Studies*, *17*(6), 926–940.

Luscombe, A., Dick, K., & Walby, K. (2022). Algorithmic thinking in the public interest: Navigating technical, legal, and ethical hurdles to web scraping in the social sciences. *Quality and Quantity: International Journal of Methodology*, *56*(3), 1023–1044. https://doi.org/10.1007/s11135-021-01164-0

Markham, A. (2012). Fabrication as ethical practice: Qualitative inquiry in ambiguous Internet contexts. *Information, Communication & Society*, *15*(3), 334–353. https://doi.org/10.1080/1369118X.2011.641993

Marwick, A., Blackwell, L., & Lo, K. (2016). *Best practices for conducting risky research and protecting yourself from online harassment (data & society guide)*. Data & Society Research Institute. https://datasociety.net/pubs/res/Best_Practices_for_Conducting_Risky_Research-Oct-2016.pdf

Massanari, A. L. (2018). Rethinking research ethics, power, and the risk of visibility in the era of the "Alt-Right" gaze. *Social Media + Society*, *4*(2), 1–9. https://doi.org/10.1177/2056305118768302

Matias, J. N., (2016). Going dark: Social factors in collective action against platform operators in the Reddit blackout. In *Proceedings of the 2016 CHI conference on human factors in computing systems* (pp. 1138–1151). Association of Computing Machinery. https://doi.org/10.1145/2858036.2858391

Millwood Hargrave, A., & Livingstone, S. (2009). *Harm and offence in media content: A review of the evidence*. Intellect Books. http://eprints.lse.ac.uk/id/eprint/49000

Naab, T. K., & Sehl, A. (2017). Studies of user-generated content: A systematic review. *Journalism*, *18*(10), 1256–1273. https://doi.org/10.1177/1464884916673557

Procter, R., Webb, H., Jirotka, M., Burnap, P., Housley, W., Edwards, A., & Williams, M. (2019). *A study of cyber hate on Twitter with implications for social media governance strategies*. Truth and Trust Online Proceedings. https://wrap.warwick.ac.uk/id/eprint/140877/

Scheuerman, M. K., Jiang, J. A., Fiesler, C., & Brubaker, J. R. (2021). A framework of severity for harmful content online. *Proceedings of the ACM on Human-Computer Interaction*, *5*(CSCW2), 1–33. https://www.semanticscholar.org/paper/A-Framework-of-Severity-for-Harmful-Content-Online-Scheuerman-Jiang/03e62d5f0265608c6ebdebba0870131b056b79a6

Schmid, U. K., Kümpel, A. S., & Rieger, D. (2024). How social media users perceive different forms of online hate speech: A qualitative multi-method study. *New Media & Society*, *26*(5), 2614–2632. https://doi.org/10.1177/14614448221091

Selinger, E., & Hartzog, W. (2016). Facebook's emotional contagion study and the ethical problem of co-opted identity in mediated environments where users lack control. *Research Ethics*, *12*(1), 35–43. https://doi.org/10.1177/1747016115579531

Semenzin, S., & Bainotti, L. (2020). The use of Telegram for non-consensual dissemination of intimate images: Gendered affordances and the construction of masculinities. *Social Media + Society*, *6*(4), 2056305120984453. https://doi.org/10.1177/2056305120984453

Shewale, R. (2024). *Facebook users statistics 2024 (worldwide data)*. DemandSage.com. https://www.demandsage.com/facebook-statistics/

Suler, J. (2004). The online disinhibition effect. *CyberPsychology & Behavior*, *7*(3), 321–326. https://doi.org/10.1089/1094931041291295

The British Psychological Association. (2021). *Ethics guidelines for internet-mediated research*. https://doi.org/10.53841/bpsrep.2021.rep155

Townsend, L., & Wallace, C. (2016). *Social media research: A guide to ethics*. The University of Aberdeen. https://www.gla.ac.uk/media/Media_487729_smxx.pdf

US Department of Health and Human Services. (2015). *NPRM for revisions to the common rule*. https://www.hhs.gov/ohrp/regulations-and-policy/regulations/nprm-home/index.html

Vera-Gray, F. (2017). 'Talk about a cunt with too much idle time': Trolling feminist research. *Feminist Review*, *115*, 61–78. https://doi.org/10.1057/s41305-017-0038-y

Vitaitis, J. (2024, March 18). *Twitter web scraping – End of an era?* https://iproyal.com/blog/twitter-web-scraping/

Webb, H., Jirotka, M., Stahl, B. C., Housley, W., Edwards, A., Williams, M., Procter, R., Rana, O., & Burnap, P. (2017). The ethical challenges of publishing Twitter data for research dissemination. In *Proceedings of the 2017 ACM on web science conference* (pp. 339–348). Association of Computing Machinery. https://doi.org/10.1145/3091478.309148

Whiteman, N. (2018). 'What if they're bastards?': Ethics and the imagining of the other in the study of online fan cultures. In R. Iphofen & M. Tolich (Eds.), *The SAGE handbook of qualitative research ethics* (pp. 510–524). Sage. https://doi.org/10.4135/9781526435446.n35

Williams, M. L., Burnap, P., & Sloan, L. (2017a). Towards an ethical framework for publishing Twitter data in social research: Taking into account users' Views, online context and algorithmic estimation. *Sociology*, *51*(6), 1149–1168. https://doi.org/10.1177/0038038517708140

Williams, M. L., Burnap, P., Sloan, L., Jessop, C., & Lepps, H. (2017b). Users' views of ethics in social media research: Informed consent, anonymity, and harm. In K. Woodfield (Ed.), *The ethics of online research* (pp. 27–52). Emerald Publishing Limited. https://doi.org/10.1108/S2398-601820180000002002

Wodinsky, S. (2021, October 7). *How WhatsApp swallowed half the world*. gizmodo.com. https://gizmodo.com/how-whatsapp-swallowed-half-the-world-1847805134

World Economic Forum. (2013). *Digital wildfires in a hyperconnected world*. http://reports.weforum.org/global-risks-2013/risk-case-1/digital-wildfires-in-a-hyperconnected-world/

Zimmer, M., & Proferes, N. J. (2014). A topology of Twitter research: Disciplines, methods, and ethics. *Aslib Journal of Information Management*, *66*(3), 250–261. https://doi.org/10.1108/AJIM-09-2013-0083

CHAPTER 9

THE ETHICS OF USING GPS IN QUALITATIVE RESEARCH WITH WAR-AFFECTED FAMILIES: EXPERIENCES OF MOBILITY FROM PALESTINE, LEBANON, AND CANADA

Bree Akesson and Karen Frensch

Wilfrid Laurier University, Canada

ABSTRACT

This chapter explores the use of global positioning system (GPS) technology as a qualitative research tool for studying the social and spatial experiences of war-affected populations. GPS technology has become increasingly accessible through integration into smartphones and wearable devices, allowing for more widespread application in research. While the use of emerging technologies like GPS offers valuable insights into the everyday experiences of marginalized populations, it also raises ethical concerns. This chapter focuses on three specific research contexts: Palestinian families living under political violence in the West Bank and East Jerusalem, Syrian families displaced in Lebanon, and war-affected families resettled in Canada. When triangulated with qualitative data, the GPS data provided a rich, comprehensive understanding of

Reframing Qualitative Research Ethics
Advances in Research Ethics and Integrity, Volume 12, 145–160

Published under exclusive licence by Emerald Publishing Limited
ISSN: 2398-6018/doi:10.1108/S2398-601820250000012009

war-affected families' experiences. However, detailed data generated from GPS methods presents a paradoxical situation, offering both research benefits and ethical challenges. While examining these ethical challenges, this chapter will also propose ways to address them while maintaining the rigor and sensitivity required when working with marginalized populations.

Keywords: Global positioning system; qualitative research; war-affected populations; research ethics; socio-spatial methodologies

INTRODUCTION

The precarious settings within which war-affected populations live pose challenges for collecting meaningful and rich data that accurately represents their everyday lives. Given these challenges, how can researchers learn about the social and spatial experiences of marginalized populations in a methodologically rigorous and sensitive way? And what are the ethical implications of using socio-spatial methodologies to capture peoples' interactions with their environments?

Emerging technologies to document human movement can be used as research tools to learn more about a range of issues impacting marginalized groups such as those impacted by war and displacement (González et al., 2024; Hinds et al., 2022; Palmer et al., 2013). GPS technology is one technology to map the movements of individuals in a range of contexts. More recently, GPS technology has been incorporated into smartphones or miniaturized as wearables (e.g., Fitbits and Apple watches) making their application much more accessible and broad especially for research (Apte et al., 2019, p. 1; Straczkiewicz et al., 2021). But the rapid inclusion of the technology in research warrants a thoughtful ethical discussion about its use.

This chapter will describe the use of GPS tracking as a qualitative research tool in three contexts: Palestinian families living in the shadow of political violence in the West Bank and East Jerusalem, Syrian families displaced from their homes and living in neighboring Lebanon, and war-affected families who have fled their countries of origin to resettle in Canada. The GPS technology produced visual mapping data that corresponded with and triangulated other qualitative data points, painting a comprehensive picture of the everyday experiences of war-affected families. Nevertheless, the inclusion of this technology raises several ethical questions, which Apte et al. (2019) refer to as a "double-edged sword": the detailed information that results from GPS-based methods represents both a value for research and the source of ethical issues. These ethical issues will be explored further in this chapter.

GPS AS A QUALITATIVE METHOD: THREE CASE STUDIES

To learn more about the experiences of war-affected families, our research team integrated GPS technology into qualitative research projects in Palestine

(2010–2014), Lebanon (2015–2019), and Canada (2020–2024). In all three cases, GPS was part of a multiple method approach that included participant observation, collaborative family interviews (CFIs), mapmaking and drawing, neighborhood walks, and daily diaries. We describe these studies in more detail below.

Palestine

The first study was conducted in 2012 with 18 Palestinian families living in the West Bank and East Jerusalem. GPS was not the primary method of data gathering in this study but was piloted in conjunction with other data collection methods to create a multifaceted and dynamic picture of people's lives. Upon receiving approval from our university's research ethics board, the research started with a CFI that discussed the family's everyday lives and their experiences. The CFI included elements of drawing and mapmaking, which encouraged children's voices in the research process.

After completion of the CFI and with their parents' permission, children were invited to lead the research team on a walk of their neighborhood community, while the research team carried a GPS device to record the walk (Akesson, 2018). The children were encouraged to explore places where, for example, they were allowed to visit, places where their daily activities occurred, and places where people they knew were located. With the children's permission, these places were photographed by the research team. Conversations about these places facilitated dialogue between the children and our research team, prompted by the people and places met along the way. The combination of the GPS with the neighborhood walk emphasizes the interaction between the micro-experience of the individual child and the macro-structures of the environment within which they walked (Sun & Zhu, 2024). In addition to observing the children in their natural environments where they expressed their multidimensional place experiences, the GPS technology yielded quantitative data on the length of the neighborhood walk in both distance and time, revealing a relationship between the level of violence in the family's community and the length of the neighborhood walk (Akesson, 2014). Combined with the other methods of data collection, the GPS data also served to better understand children's relationship to school. For example, some children showed us their school as a place of significance, elaborating upon stories related to traveling to and attending school. Combined with GPS, neighborhood walks are well-suited to children's natural ways of communicating, using a physical and mobile approach that is far more active than the traditional interview setting.

Lebanon

In light of the success of the method piloted with a small cohort of Palestinian families, we expanded the method to a larger sample size and in a different setting. In 2016, the second study – with 46 Syrian families who were displaced in Lebanon – made the GPS approach a more prominent part of the overall methodology. Like the study in Palestine, this research also received approval from our university's research ethics board. In addition to the CFI and the neighborhood walk used in the Palestine study, this research included geographic information system (GIS) technology to enhance an ethnographic approach to data collection. Family members were asked to carry a GPS device or "activity logger" that recorded their activity over a five-to-seven-day period. Family members were also asked to keep a daily diary of activities that we could use to determine the spaces and places they visited during the week. The activity logger and the daily diaries generated valuable data about individual family members' mobility and activities that expanded upon the data gathered in the neighborhood walk. We imagined the activity logger as a miniature ethnographic researcher being carried around in the pocket of research participants. The GPS data combined with the CFI data were used to create sensory maps of sights, sounds, and their corresponding feelings related to everyday mobility.[1]

Canada

In our third study, conducted at the time that Covid-19 pandemic lockdowns were being lifted in 2021, we incorporated the use of GPS methods to explore the resettlement experiences of 18 war-affected refugee families who were living in the Waterloo Region of Ontario, Canada. This study also received ethical approval from our university's research ethics board. Similar to Palestine and Lebanon, children in each family took research team members on a walk around their neighborhood. The researcher carried a GPS device which mapped the route taken. Points of interest (such as their school or favorite park) were noted utilizing the device, and the researcher took photos of these locations with permission. Additionally, three family members including a parent and two children (one older and one younger) in the family carried a GPS device during their daily routines for one week. Again, the activity logging data were accompanied by a written daily diary of events and locations. We used the geospatial software ArcGIS to generate visual maps of the neighborhood walk and weeklong activity patterns for family members.

THE VALUE OF GPS TECHNOLOGY AS A RESEARCH METHOD

When discussing ethics, we must first discuss the utility and strengths of a method, as these elements must be weighed against the risks. Of course, there are always risks in research. But to be ethical, such risks must be judiciously considered alongside the importance of the research.

Produces Visually Rich Data

In combination with multiple methods, the use of GPS in research creates visual representations of research participants' lives that other research methods alone might not be able to uncover. In all three studies, the GPS technology produced visual mapping data that corresponded with and triangulated other data points – such as narrative interviews, drawings, maps, and daily diaries – to paint a rich visual picture of the everyday experiences of war-affected families in contextual detail. As Šimon and colleagues (2020) remind us, "the GPS data are just bare geographic coordinates" (p. 14), and so research participants should be engaged in data elicitation methods that can provide qualitative information about the nature of these places and spaces. Additional qualitative approaches – such as our inclusion of neighborhood walks – deepen the researchers' understanding of participants' activities and interactions with space and place (Ho et al., 2021).

This triangulation supports what Cope and Elwood (2009) have noted as the importance of "bringing together multiple ways of knowing and making knowledge" (p. 6). For example, the data from both the Palestine and Lebanon studies revealed family members' engagement with education. From the multiple methods of data collection (e.g., CFIs, children's drawings, mapmaking, and neighborhood walks), we were able to determine which children attended school, which children only worked, and which children did both. We learned about the barriers that kept families from sending their children to school. We also discovered the importance that parents place on education.

As a product, GPS data can generate geovisualizations – or visual representations of geospatial data – that can complement, enhance, and/or deepen the overall analysis (Ho et al., 2021; Knigge & Cope, 2006; Pain et al., 2006; Preston & Wilson, 2014). It is one thing to say that a research participant has restricted mobility; but to see this phenomenon represented on a map – showing the dots of mobility and how that range is narrow – can be quite powerful and may be more impactful than statistical analyses alone. These geovisualizations can be integrated into visually rich and interactive "story maps" that serve as an effective means of knowledge sharing (Caquard & Dimitrovas, 2017; Kerski, 2019). As Buckle (2020) says, "Maps illuminate and share personal understanding of the world through visual communication" (p. 84).

Documents Experiences Difficult to Represent with Traditional Quantitative Methods

GPS can track experiences that are important but challenging to represent with traditional quantitative methods such as social networks (Aldrich & Sawada, 2015), local knowledge and experience (Ziervogel et al., 2016), and informal social infrastructure (Mitra et al., 2017). This speaks to the reality that human lives are complex, and it is therefore difficult to accurately capture all the facets of these lives with a quantitative survey or even a qualitative interview alone. GPS can visually depict the complexity of research participants' everyday lives in a visually appealing way. For example, in our studies with Palestinian and Syrian families, we found how important freedom of movement was during the qualitative narrative interviews and through the mapmaking and drawing exercises. But participant dreams conflicted with reality when we examined the GPS tracking data and found that research participants' worlds – the places they go and the things that they do in those places – were quite narrow and restricted due to a range of factors such as oppressive government policies, discrimination, age, and gender.

Due to the richness of the data, GPS approaches may also raise additional research questions that might not be the original focus of the research – and isn't the heart of research to not only find answers to questions but also to raise more questions? Pavlovskaya (2009) notes how GPS allows researchers to pose questions that might otherwise go unasked and reveal discrepancies that could remain hidden if only a single method were employed. Ho and colleagues continue: "Observed omissions and inconsistencies become opportunities for excavating power configurations and revisiting assumed knowledges" (p. 134). As an example, they describe Bagheri's (2014) research that combined ethnography and GPS to analyze the spatial dynamics of women's mobility in the public spaces of Tehran. The study revealed patterns of gendered access and segregation that would otherwise be invisible to planners and policymakers who decide how spaces are to be used. Likewise, Taylor and colleagues (2020) note that the different layers of research participant experience uncovered through GPS methods offer an opportunity for further discussion "rather than giving singular, objective answers, [and] acting as conversation openers rather than closers" (p. 3).

Eliminates Recall Bias and Error

Research has found that retrospective recollections of mobility tend to be unreliable (Šimon et al., 2020, p. 14). GPS technology helps eliminate recall bias and error that may occur in other research methods aimed at gathering data about mobility such as travel diaries. GPS technology provides accurate and objective data on location and movement without relying on participants' memory or subjective reporting. In traditional qualitative approaches, participants may not report something they deem to be "unimportant" or mundane; however, for research such as the three cases described above exploring families' everyday experiences, *everything* (especially the mundane!) is important.

GPS devices precisely record all movements and locations as they occur, reducing the chances of errors in reporting or recording. Of course, there may be instances where a participant's recollection of events differs from the GPS data. A mismatch between subjective experience and objective reality is a normal result of human memory, which qualitative research has proposed can be addressed by using multiple methods of data collection to increase the trustworthiness and authenticity of the data (Lincoln & Guba, 1985). Other researchers such as Flicker (2004) have suggested solutions to handling inconsistent data ranging from approaching future data cautiously to further ascertain the cause of the inconsistency to completely excluding the data from analysis. Based on a view that research participants have their own understanding of the world that research is trying to better understand, we would aim for caution and inclusion over exclusion.

To study movement over time – as our Lebanon and Canada research did – GPS technology can provide continuous tracking (if research participants decide they want to keep using the device, which will be discussed later in this chapter), thereby producing consistent data quality throughout the study duration. Ultimately, by leveraging GPS technology, researchers can significantly reduce biases and errors associated with traditional self-reporting methods, leading to more reliable research data.

Captures Longitudinal Data

Research is dominated by cross-sectional accounts of participants' experiences, capturing only one moment in time. Traditional ethnographic approaches require the researcher(s) to spend a considerable amount of time with the population of interest in order to accurately document research participants' movements. GPS provides an efficient alternative to cross-sectional and ethnographic methods by unobtrusively documenting spatial mobility over an extended period of time.

Is Accessible for a Range of Populations

Finally, GPS approaches may make research more accessible for certain populations. Engagement with GPS methods does not depend on participants' verbal accounts which may be impacted by their age, educational level, or language abilities. For example, in the Lebanon and Canada studies, the physical act of walking and talking during the GPS-tracked neighborhood walk method suited children and young people's developmental preference to "walk and talk". In fact, some children in the Lebanon study felt a sense of empowerment when participating in the research using GPS; one mother told our research team how her young children felt a sense of responsibility helping the research team by carrying and caring for the GPS devices. By giving control to the research participants and learning about their everyday engagement with their environments, the use of interactive methods such as GPS-tracked neighborhood walks can serve as a tool of empowerment for populations who are oftentimes erroneously described as only "passive victims" (Kinney, 2018; Sun & Zhu, 2024). Furthermore, GPS technology can capture details that some research participants may not be cognizant of, for example, routes and landmarks that they interact with but do not know the name of, as may be the case with children.

ETHICAL CONSIDERATIONS

Like any research method, while GPS technologies have a lot of promise as an approach to engage with research populations, they also pose ethical challenges. González et al. (2024) argue that there are two issues related to the ethics of human movement. First, because the notion of mobility is tied to issues of justice, discrimination, and marginalization, the study of mobility is inherently an ethical issue (González et al., 2024; Shannon, 2006). On the other hand, González et al. (2024) continue,

> [...] when undertaking psychological research that tracks where participants go, along what routes, to what destinations, staying for how long, and with what social and psychological consequences, we inevitably broach issues that are not yet fully encapsulated within the ethical guidelines of our field. That is, in creating opportunities to study human mobility using new technologies, we also create new risks of inadvertently harming the participants of our research. (p. 53)

In this section, we discuss issues related to consent, access, surveillance, privacy, confidentiality, spatial reidentification, and accuracy, with an eye toward how we addressed these issues in the use of GPS technologies across our three research studies.

Consent

Consent is essential for upholding ethical standards, protecting research participants, and maintaining the integrity of the research. Consent presents two issues: the first is selectivity, or who agrees to participate in the research, and the second is what participants agree to in the consent process.

Jacobsen and Kühne (2021) write about selectivity in research recruitment. In the case of multiple method studies such as those in the Palestine, Lebanon, and Canada, selectivity refers to the decision of participants to not participate in any one method or all of the research. Various studies have found that only about a quarter of potential research participants consented to the use of geotracking (Kreuter et al., 2016; Toepoel & Lugtig, 2014). We had higher rates of consent in our research projects. In Palestine, all 18 families agreed to the GPS-tracked neighborhood walks. In Lebanon, there were 2 out of 46 families who felt uncomfortable with carrying the standalone GPS loggers out of fear of surveillance and therefore opted out of that part of the research. In Canada, 3 families had members who did not consent to using GPS loggers. This is similar to other research with marginalized groups, such as Apte et al.'s (2019) study of care-seeking in rural west India where some study participants expressed concern that the GPS could record conversations or videos of their activities. Only one participant in Apte et al.'s study declined to participate due to confidentiality concerns.

Among research populations on the move, newly arrived migrants (González et al., 2024; Jacobsen & Kühne, 2021), those with residency permits (Jacobsen & Kühne, 2021), younger populations (Toepoel & Lugtig, 2014), and those living in cities (Apte et al., 2019) are more likely to consent to a GPS method of data collection such as a GPS-tracked neighborhood walk or weeklong GPS tracking. Anecdotally, we found a higher rate of consent in Palestine and Lebanon than we did in Canada, which aligns with consent trends for research more generally. Our Canadian study took place during COVID-19, which was a notably difficult time to recruit research participants for any study, whether using GPS approaches or not (Boelter et al., 2023).

Access to GPS Technology

Participants may be apprehensive to engage with a standalone GPS device, because they think they will lose or damage it. This may be an especially important point for participants with limited economic means, who may feel that they will be financially responsible for a lost or damaged device. In our Lebanon and Canada studies (when a standalone GPS unit was given to research participants for one week), we did not emphasize the value of the standalone GPS devices. Nor did we pressure families who lost devices. We did not want the perceived value of the device to make any research participant uncomfortable and perhaps less likely to engage with the device outside the home. In their study with low-income populations, Duncan et al. (2018) offered cash incentives to participants once they returned their GPS devices, which was a source of financial support for the research participants and contributed to a high device return rate.

The use of smartphone-based GPS technology (in contrast to a standalone GPS device) has revolutionized how research populations can participate in research. Research has found that participants regard smartphone-based GPS technology as more appealing and easier to use than standalone devices, because smartphones are familiar, inobtrusive, and ubiquitous (Hardy et al., 2018; Mathenjwa et al., 2023). Smartphones might be especially preferred where there is a risk of harm if the research participant is identified as being a part of a study. For example, in Mirzazadeh et al.'s (2014) study of injecting drug users, participants were concerned about carrying a standalone device (especially if such a device was labeled as being part of a research study), because they may be suspected as informants thereby putting their lives at risk within their community. But this kind of GPS tracking might not be available to participants who cannot afford a smartphone; therefore, they would be excluded from participating in smartphone-based data collection methods. This is an issue that is quickly becoming obsolete as reports indicate that a large percentage of refugee populations tend to own a smartphone.

While the practicality of smartphone-based GPS technology is obviously important for research participants, the research team is ethically responsible for advising on the risks of such devices. Namely, if a research participant uses a smartphone for research, the research data collected may be inadvertently shared with a variety of companies and other entities (Breslin et al., 2019) thereby representing yet another ethical issue.

Surveillance, Privacy, Confidentiality, and Spatial Reidentification

The precise tracking of participants' location through GPS raises concerns about surveillance, privacy, confidentiality, and spatial reidentification. These issues should first be addressed through the informed consent process. But with a multiple method approach to research, it might also require the research team to revisit these topics as different data collection methods are applied.

All our studies have used a standalone GPS device rather than smartphone-based GPS technology. During the informed consent process, our research team members informed potential participants that the standalone device would not transmit data back to us or anyone in real time. Therefore, we would not know what places they had visited until they give us back the device, and we transfered the data to a secure computer. We believe the use of a standalone GPS device versus the smartphone assuages participants' fears and leads to positive consent processes for more research participants. Nevertheless, in our Canada study, some participants expressed fear that the data would be used to report back to the government on the family's resettlement behaviors, especially if their residency status was still being processed.

Even after giving full informed consent, the monitoring of one's activities by researchers may still make a research participant feel like they are being watched (Dobson & Fisher, 2003). This is especially concerning for any vulnerable and marginalized groups who may have been surveilled by government bodies in their countries of origin or other contexts (Browne, 2015; Proulx, 2014). This was a very real concern for families in our Palestine and Lebanon research studies, both of whom have historically been subjected to surveillance by the government, including biometric mass surveillance (Paragi & Altamimi, 2022; Robins-Early, 2024).

As noted above, smartphones equipped with GPS sensing are more commonly being used in research to learn about the geolocations of research participants (Jacobsen & Kühne, 2021, p. 725). However, this raises ethical issues of surveillance. The dominance of smartphones in collecting GIS data through applications installed on the phone is making the separate hand-held GPS devices less desirable. Data can even be stored in the app until they can be uploaded to a server (a benefit in remote situations where there is no cellular service). While this seems to make data collection more accessible and seamlessly integrated into people's lives, it does open up additional ethical considerations facing big tech companies' collection and use of personal data. Therefore, the primary ethical concerns regarding GPS and privacy relate to what information is gleaned on a person's movements and how that information will be used (Michael et al., 2006).

There is limited capacity for researchers to anonymize movement data making breaches of locational privacy a possibility (Apte et al., 2019). In our three studies, we implemented careful processes for the storage and presentation of geolocation data we gathered from research participants. In addition to the ethical imperatives to store all data on secure computers, we took care to not publicly share mapping data unless it was impossible to identify locations. We have used heat maps, a visualization technique used to depict the intensity of data at certain geographical points. Therefore, if a research participant spent more time at home than school or work, then the heat map will depict a large red blob over that area, essentially obfuscating the actual location of the home. We have also zoomed out enough in our maps to make specific locations impossible to decipher.

Accuracy

Secondary to the risks to participants, issues related to surveillance, privacy, and confidentiality pose risks to the accuracy and therefore integrity of the study. If research participants fear that GPS technologies will record their conversations or behaviors, they may leave the devices at home when visiting certain places (Apte et al., 2019; Fuller et al., 2017; Haley et al., 2016; Mathenjwa et al., 2023; van Heerden et al., 2020) or change their habits due to awareness of being tracked (Borisoff et al., 2018). This means that the GPS data will not accurately capture participants' everyday lives.

In their study of immigrant adolescents in Canada, AlArasi and Buliung (2023) used smartphone-based GPS, noting that young participants "negotiated" (Giddens, 1999; Solberg, 1990; Williams & Williams, 2005) how they engaged with GPS independent of the research team. For example, some young people in their study used the GPS data to prove their location to skeptical parents who were questioning their whereabouts, while some others deliberately "forgot" their smartphones at home to avoid being tracked somewhere they didn't want others to know about. Mathenjwa and colleagues (2023) note that participants' non-use, or selective use, of GPS devices "should be expected and respected as part of participants' agency and ongoing respect" (p. 329). These examples also underscore the importance of taking a qualitative approach to GPS data collection, as these negotiations become a rich form of data that tell more of the story than GPS coordinates alone.

CONCLUSION

If care is taken to address the above ethical issues, GPS remains a promising qualitative approach to learn more about the everyday experiences of marginalized populations. The ethical challenges posed by GPS can be addressed through such measures as thoughtful informed consent processes, community participation, and engagement with research ethics committees (RECs). These measures will be discussed in detail below.

Thoughtful Informed Consent Processes

Informed consent upholds the principle that individuals have the right to make their own decisions about their participation in research without coercion or undue influence. Therefore, research participants must be fully aware of the purpose, procedures, risks, and benefits of the research, allowing them to make voluntary and informed choices to participate. In the case of GPS technology, participants need to be informed about how long the device needs to be used, what kind of data will be collected, and how the data will be used. These practical details must be explained in a way where participants can weigh the risks and benefits of participation.

Researchers – specifically the interviewers who facilitate the informed consent process – are crucial to ensuring that potential participants fully understand what they are being asked to do and upholding the integrity of the study (Jacobsen & Kühne, 2021). Researchers must therefore be cognizant of participants' different levels of literacy and technological knowledge regarding GPS so that informed consent processes can be effectively conveyed to the audience. During the informed consent process, researchers must also be prepared to address any misconceptions about GPS technology and research practices more generally (Addissie et al., 2016; Ndebele et al., 2014; Vallely et al., 2010). In their systematic review and meta-analysis, Tam and colleagues (2015) found that only between 52% and 76% of participants understood different components of informed consent. A more recent study (Wu et al., 2024) found 98% of participants understood the concept of confidentiality (98%) while 67% understood the concept of voluntariness. These findings have special resonance because they do not specifically address the nascent GPS methods that some participants may not have the technological knowledge to understand. Clearly, more should be done to ensure participants understand all of the components of the use of GPS technology in research.

Informed consent should ultimately safeguard participants from potential harm by ensuring they understand the risks involved and providing them with the opportunity to ask questions and seek clarification. By promoting transparency in the research process and demonstrating respect for participants' rights and welfare, consent has the potential to build trust between the research team and the participants. High-quality research really depends on the understanding and agency of participants. Engaged and informed participants are more likely to contribute meaningfully to the study thereby increasing its relevance and impact.

Community Engagement

Given the ethical challenges posed by consent, access, surveillance, privacy, confidentiality, spatial reidentification, and accuracy, a participatory approach to GPS technology in research could be quite effective. Rather than the traditional "tick box" informed consent process, González et al. (2024) suggest,

> an approach in which participants are invited to explore with researchers the nature of [GPS] data collection and analysis as a project unfolds, to consider its implications for privacy and confidentiality, and to have a greater sense of ownership and control over emerging, potentially sensitive, information. (p. 61)

This is aligned with recommendations from a range of researchers who have documented their success engaging with communities on GPS research. For example, Denwood et al. (2022) and Huck et al. (2014) are proponents of "participatory GIS," "a variety of systems through which groups and individuals can participate in GIS-based spatial analysis, planning, knowledge production, and decision making" (González et al., 2024, p. 54). In another example, Taylor et al. (2020) used arts-based workshop activities to create innovative and experimental map visualizations of resilience.

Research has found that the quality and impact of the research is enhanced by community engagement. Bradley and Vitous's (2021) research on health disparities and food deserts found that "involving research participants in the mapping process better reflects the lived experience of community members" (p. 416). Taylor et al. (2020) cite several studies that have engaged with communities to collect and use their own spatial data to negotiate for improvements in their cities (Dobson, 2017; Mulligan et al., 2017). Nevertheless, some researchers have also cautioned about the practicality of large-scale community consultation. For example, González et al. (2024) note that community approaches are less feasible in research involving a large number of participants due to limited resources.

Engaging Research Ethics Committees

For the three research projects described in this chapter, we received approval from our university's research ethics board (REB), otherwise known as institutional review board (IRB). Engaging with REBs is essential for us to ensure that our work adheres to the required ethical standards that help protect the rights and welfare of research participants. REBs are tasked with providing critical guidance on ethical elements such as informed consent, confidentiality, and balancing benefits and potential risks. This is particularly important in research that involves marginalized groups such as war-affected populations.

In all three studies employing GPS technology, we engaged in consultations with our REBs around this method and found the process to be collegial and helpful. The REBs have been able to ensure that we consider issues such as data privacy and the potential risk of participant identification in research that uses GPS technology. In working with these REBs, we have been able to anticipate and mitigate ethical risks, while still ensuring that participants' autonomy is prioritized.

Aside from submitting ethics applications, responding to REB queries, and revising ethics applications in light of REB feedback, we have hosted trainings for REB members, published a podcast episode (Moore-Kloss, 2021), and developed a training video that grapples with one of the central tensions within research ethics: protection versus inclusion (Akesson, 2022). The first author (Akesson) also sits on her university's REB which serves multiple purposes. First, this form of engagement provides an opportunity to deepen her understanding of the research ethics process, as well as to stay up-to-date on technological advances that may impact research. Second, she has been able to draw upon her first-hand expertise using GPS technology in research to advise other researchers across disciplines on the ethical challenges and best practices for mitigation. This allows for further collaboration and broadening of perspectives among researchers and ethical bodies (Drolet et al., 2023).

Researchers using GPS technology should continue to engage with their REBs to share best practices for collecting and securing data generated through GPS methods (Nebecker et al., 2015). REBs continue to grapple with technological changes that may impact participants, and researchers should approach REB engagement with the same energy as engaging communities. It is up to researchers and REBs to ensure that research participants are aware of potential risks and provide participants with the opportunity to contribute to research that has the potential to improve their lives.

NOTE

1. See www.outofplaceresearch.com for a sample of the maps that were created using the GPS data from this study.

REFERENCES

Addissie, A., Abay, S., Feleke, Y., Newport, M., Farsides, B., & Davey, G. (2016). Cluster randomized trial assessing the effects of rapid ethical assessment on informed consent comprehension in a low-resource setting. *BMC Medical Ethics*, *17*(1), 40. https://doi.org/10.1186/s12910-016-0127-z

Akesson, B. (2014). *Contradictions in place: Everyday geographies of Palestinian children and families living under occupation*. PhD dissertation, McGill University.

Akesson, B. (2018). "Every corner tells a story": Using neighbourhood walks and GPS to understand children's sense of place. In S. Kleinknecht, L.-J. van den Scott, & C. Sanders (Eds.), *The craft of qualitative research* (pp. 232–236). Canadian Scholar's Press.

Akesson, B. (Director). (2022, January 13). *International research ethical reviews* [Video recording]. Kindea Labs. https://www.youtube.com/watch?v=wZ7WJZwBQ0A&t=3s

AlArasi, H., & Buliung, R. (2023). Exploring the tactical mobilities and everyday activity of immigrant adolescents in a Canadian suburban city. *Children's Geographies*, *21*(5), 961–976.

Aldrich, D. P., & Sawada, Y. (2015). The physical and social determinants of mortality in the 3.11 tsunami. *Social Science & Medicine*, *124*, 66–75. https://doi.org/10.1016/j.socscimed.2014.11.025

Apte, A., Ingole, V., Lele, P., Marsh, A., Bhattacharjee, T., Hirve, S., Campbell, H., Nair, H., Chan, S., & Juvekar, S. (2019). Ethical considerations in the use of GPS-based movement tracking in health research: Lessons from a care-seeking study in rural west India. *Journal of Global Health*, *9*(1), 010323. https://doi.org/10.7189/jogh.09.010323

Bagheri, N. (2014). Mapping women in Tehran's public spaces: A geo-visualization perspective. *Gender Place Culture*, *21*(10), 1285–1301.

Boelter, J., Dennis, A. M., Vogel, L. K., & Croes, K. D. (2023). Recruiting hard-to-reach populations amid the COVID-19 pandemic. *Survey Practice*, *16*(1), 1–8. https://doi.org/10.29115/SP-2023-0011

Borisoff, J. F., Ripat, J., & Chan, F. (2018). Seasonal patterns of community participation and mobility of wheelchair users over an entire year. *Archives of Physical Medicine and Rehabilitation*, *99*(8), 1553–1560. https://doi.org/10.1016/j.apmr.2018.02.011

Bradley, S. E., & Vitous, C. A. (2021). Using GIS to explore disparities between the location of food deserts and vulnerability to food insecurity. *Journal of Hunger & Environmental Nutrition*, *16*(3), 406–422.

Breslin, S., Shareck, M., & Fuller, D. (2019). Research ethics for mobile sensing device use by vulnerable populations. *Social Science & Medicine*, *232*, 50–57. https://doi.org/10.1016/j.socscimed.2019.04.035

Browne, S. (2015). *Dark matters: On the surveillance of blackness*. Duke University Press.

Buckle, C. (2020). Touching, scrolling and swooping: Performing and representing migrant stories through geospatial technologies. *Geoforum*, *111*, 83–93.

Caquard, S., & Dimitrovas, S. (2017). Story Maps & Co. The state of the art of online narrative cartography. *Mappemonde. Revue Trimestrielle Sur l'image Géographique et Les Formes Du Territoire*, *121*, Article 121. https://doi.org/10.4000/mappemonde.3386

Cope, M., & Elwood, S. (2009). *Qualitative GIS: A mixed methods approach*. SAGE Publications Ltd.

Denwood, T., Huck, J. J., & Lindley, S. (2022). Participatory mapping: A systematic review and open science framework for future research. *Annals of the American Association of Geographers*, *112*(8), 2324–2343. https://doi.org/10.1080/24694452.2022.2065964

Dobson, J. E., & Fisher, P. F. (2003). Geoslavery. *IEEE Technology and Society Magazine*.

Dobson, S. (2017). Community-driven pathways for implementation of global urban resilience goals in Africa. *International Journal of Disaster Risk Reduction*, *26*, 78–84. https://doi.org/10.1016/j.ijdrr.2017.09.028

Drolet, M.-J., Rose-Derouin, E., Leblanc, J.-C., Ruest, M., & Williams-Jones, B. (2023). Ethical issues in research: Perceptions of researchers, research ethics board members and research ethics experts. *Journal of Academic Ethics*, *21*, 269–292.

Duncan, D. T., Chaix, B., Regan, S. D., Park, S. H., Draper, C., Goedel, W. C., Gipson, J. A., Guilamo-Ramos, V., Halkitis, P. N., Brewer, R., & Hickson, D. A. (2018). Collecting mobility data with GPS methods to understand the HIV environmental riskscape among young black men who have sex with men: A multi-city feasibility study in the deep south. *AIDS and Behavior*, *22*(9), 3057–3070. https://doi.org/10.1007/s10461-018-2163-9

Flicker, S. (2004). "Ask me no secrets, I'll tell you no lies": What happens when a respondent's story makes no sense. *The Qualitative Report*, *9*(3), 528–537.

Fuller, D., Shareck, M., & Stanley, K. (2017). Ethical implications of location and accelerometer measurement in health research studies with mobile sensing devices. *Social Science & Medicine (1982)*, *191*, 84–88. https://doi.org/10.1016/j.socscimed.2017.08.043

Giddens, A. (1999). *The runaway world*. Polity.

González, R., Lay, S., Huck, J., & Dixon, J. (2024). The use of GNSS technology in smartphones to collect sensitive data on human mobility practices: Ethical challenges and potential solutions. *American Psychologist*, *79*(1), 52–64. https://doi.org/10.1037/amp0001194

Haley, D. F., Matthews, S. A., Cooper, H. L., Haardörfer, R., Adimora, A. A., Wingood, G. M., & Kramer, M. R. (2016). Confidentiality considerations for use of social-spatial data on the social determinants of health: Sexual and reproductive health case study. *Social Science & Medicine (1982)*, *166*, 49–56. https://doi.org/10.1016/j.socscimed.2016.08.009

Hardy, J., Veinot, T. C., Yan, X., Berrocal, V. J., Clarke, P., Goodspeed, R., Gomez-Lopez, I. N., Romero, D., & Vydiswaran, V. G. V. (2018). User acceptance of location-tracking technologies in health research: Implications for study design and data quality. *Journal of Biomedical Informatics*, *79*, 7–19. https://doi.org/10.1016/j.jbi.2018.01.003

Hinds, J., Brown, O., Smith, L. G. E., Piwek, L., Ellis, D. A., & Joinson, A. N. (2022). Integrating insights about human movement patterns from digital data into psychological science. *Current Directions in Psychological Science*, *31*(1), 88–95. https://doi.org/10.1177/09637214211042324

Ho, E. L. E., Liew, J. A., Zhou, G., Chiu, T. Y., Yeoh, B. S. A., & Huang, S. (2021). Shared spaces and "throwntogetherness" in later life: A qualitative GIS study of non-migrant and migrant older adults in Singapore. *Geoforum*, *124*, 132–143. https://doi.org/10.1016/j.geoforum.2021.05.014

Huck, J. J., Whyatt, J. D., & Coulton, P. (2014). Spraycan: A PPGIS for capturing imprecise notions of place. *Applied Geography*, *55*, 229–237. https://doi.org/10.1016/j.apgeog.2014.09.007

Jacobsen, J., & Kühne, S. (2021). Using a mobile app when surveying highly mobile populations: Panel attrition, consent, and interviewer effects in a survey of refugees. *Social Science Computer Review*, *4*(4), 721–743.

Kerski, J. (2019). Types of story maps. In S. L. Arlinghaus, J. J. Kerski, Ann E. Larimore, & M. Naud (Eds.), *Spatial thinking in environmental contexts* (Ch. 17). CRC Press.

Kinney, P. (2018). Walking interview ethics. In R. Iphofen & M. Tolich (Eds.), *The SAGE handbook of qualitative research ethics* (pp. 174–187). SAGE Publications Ltd. https://doi.org/10.4135/9781526435446

Knigge, L., & Cope, M. (2006). Grounded visualization: Integrating the analysis of qualitative and quantitative data through grounded theory and visualization. *Environment and Planning A*, *38*, 2021–2037.

Kreuter, F., Sakshaug, J. W., & Tourangeau, R. (2016). The framing of the record linkage consent question. *International Journal of Public Opinion Research*, *28*(1), 142–152. https://doi.org/10.1093/ijpor/edv006

Lincoln, Y. S., & Guba, E. G. (1985). *Naturalistic inquiry*. Sage Publications.

Mathenjwa, T., Nkosi, B., Kim, H.-Y., Bain, L. E., Tanser, F., & Wassenaar, D. (2023). Ethical considerations in using a smartphone-based GPS app to understand linkages between mobility patterns and health outcomes: The example of HIV risk among mobile youth in rural South Africa. *Developing World Bioethics*, *23*(4), 321–330. https://doi.org/10.1111/dewb.12376

Michael, K., McNamee, A., & Michael, M. G. (2006). *The emerging ethics of human centric GPS tracking and monitoring* (p. 34). Institute of Electrical and Electronics Engineers (IEEE).

Mirzazadeh, A., Grasso, M., Johnson, K., Briceno, A., Navadeh, S., McFarland, W., & Page, K. (2014). Acceptability of global positioning system technology to survey injecting drug users' movements and social interactions: A pilot study from San Francisco, USA. *Technology and Health Care: Official Journal of the European Society for Engineering and Medicine*, *22*(5), 689–700. https://doi.org/10.3233/THC-140838

Mitra, S., Mulligan, J., Schilling, J., Harper, J., Vivekananda, J., & Krause, L. (2017). Developing risk or resilience? Effects of slum upgrading on the social contract and social cohesion in Kibera, Nairobi. *Environment and Urbanization*, *29*(1), 103–122. https://doi.org/10.1177/0956247816689218

Moore-Kloss, A. (Director). (2021, March 19). International research ethics: Dancing on a moving carpet [Broadcast]. *CRSP Talk*.

Mulligan, J., Harper, J., Kipkemboi, P., Ngobi, B., & Collins, A. (2017). Community-responsive adaptation to flooding in Kibera, Kenya. *Proceedings of the Institution of Civil Engineers – Engineering Sustainability*, *170*(5), 268–280. https://doi.org/10.1680/jensu.15.00060

Ndebele, P., Wassenaar, D., Masiye, F., & Munalula-Nkandu, E. (2014). Trial participants' understanding of randomization, double-blinding, and placebo use in low literacy populations: Findings from a study conducted within a microbicide trial in Malawi. *Journal of Empirical Research on Human Research Ethics: JERHRE*, *9*(3), 2–10. https://doi.org/10.1177/1556264614540592

Nebecker, C., Linares-Orozco, R., & Crist, K. (2015). A multi-case study of research using mobile imaging, sensing and tracking technologies to objectively measure behavior: Ethical issues and insights to guide responsible research practice. *Journal of Research Administration*, *46*(1), 118–137.

Pain, R., MacFarlane, R., Turner, K., & Gill, S. (2006). 'When, where, if, and but': Qualifying GIS and the effect of streetlighting on crime and fear. *Environment and Planning A: Economy and Space*, *38*(11), 2055–2074. https://doi.org/10.1068/a38391

Palmer, J. R. B., Espenshade, T. J., Bartumeus, F., Chung, C. Y., Ozgencil, N. E., & Li, K. (2013). New approaches to human mobility: Using mobile phones for demographic research. *Demography*, *50*(3), 1105–1128. https://doi.org/10.1007/s13524-012-0175-z

Paragi, B., & Altamimi, A. (2022). Caring control or controlling care? Double bind facilitated by biometrics between UNHCR and Syrian refugees in Jordan. *Society and Economy*, *44*(2), 206–231. https://doi.org/10.1556/204.2021.00027

Pavlovskaya, M. (2009). Non-quantitative GIS. In M. Cope & S. Elwood (Eds.), *Qualitative GIS: A mixed methods approach* (pp. 13–38). SAGE Publications Ltd.

Preston, B., & Wilson, M. W. (2014). Practicing GIS as mixed method: Affordances and limitations in an urban gardening study. *Annals of the Association of American Geographers*, *104*(3), 510–529.

Proulx, C. (2014). Colonizing surveillance: Canada constructs an indigenous terror threat. *Anthropologica*, *56*(1), 83–100.

Robins-Early, N. (2024, April 19). How Israel uses facial-recognition systems in Gaza and beyond. *The Guardian*. https://www.theguardian.com/technology/2024/apr/19/idf-facial-recognition-surveillance-palestinians

Shannon, T. (2006). The ethics of mobility: A framework for assessing mobility paradigms. *Transactions on Ecology and the Environment*, *93*, 569–578.

Šimon, M., Vašat, P., Daňková, H., Gibas, P., & Poláková, M. (2020). Mobilities and commons unseen: Spatial mobility in homeless people explored through the analysis of GPS tracking data. *GeoJournal*, *85*(5), 1411–1427.

Solberg, A. (1990). Negotiating childhood: Changing constructions of age for Norwegian children. In A. James & A. Prout (Eds.), *Constructing and reconstructing childhood: Contemporary issues in the sociological study of childhood* (pp. 139–156). Falmer Press.

Straczkiewicz, M., James, P., & Onnela, J.-P. (2021). A systematic review of smartphone-based human activity recognition methods for health research. *NPJ Digital Medicine*, *4*, 148. https://doi.org/10.1038/s41746-021-00514-4

Sun, Y., & Zhu, W. (2024). Using walking interviews in migration research: A systematic review of the qualitative research literature. *International Journal of Qualitative Methods*, *23*, 1–24.

Tam, N. T., Huy, N. T., Thoa, L. T. B., Long, N. P., Trang, N. T. H., Hirayama, K., & Karbwang, J. (2015). Participants' understanding of informed consent in clinical trials over three decades: Systematic review and meta-analysis. *Bulletin of the World Health Organization*, *93*(3), 186–198H. https://doi.org/10.2471/BLT.14.141390

Taylor, F. E., Millington, J. D. A., Jabob, E., Malamud, B. D., & Pelling, M. (2020). Messy maps: Qualitative GIS representations of resilience. *Landscape and Urban Planning*, *198*, 1–11. https://doi.org/10.1016/j.landurbplan.2020.103771.

Toepoel, V., & Lugtig, P. (2014). What happens if you offer a mobile option to your web panel? Evidence from a probability-based panel of internet users. *Social Science Computer Review*, *32*(4), 544–560. https://doi.org/10.1177/0894439313510482

Vallely, A., Lees, S., Shagi, C., Kasindi, S., Soteli, S., Kavit, N., Vallely, L., McCormack, S., Pool, R., Hayes, R. J., & Microbicides Development Programme (MDP). (2010). How informed is consent in vulnerable populations? Experience using a continuous consent process during the MDP301 vaginal microbicide trial in Mwanza, Tanzania. *BMC Medical Ethics*, *11*, 10. https://doi.org/10.1186/1472-6939-11-10

van Heerden, A., Wassenaar, D., Essack, Z., Vilakazi, K., & Kohrt, B. A. (2020). In-home passive sensor data collection and its implications for social media research: Perspectives of community women in rural South Africa. *Journal of Empirical Research on Human Research Ethics: JERHRE*, *15*(1–2), 97–107. https://doi.org/10.1177/1556264619881334

Williams, S., & Williams, L. (2005). Space invaders: The negotiation of teenage boundaries through the mobile phone. *The Sociological Review*, *53*(2), 314–331. https://doi.org/10.1111/j.1467-954X.2005.00516.x

Wu, C., Wang, N., Wang, Q., Wang, C., Wei, Z., Wu, Z., Yu, S., & Jiang, X. (2024). Participants' understanding of informed consent in clinical trials: A systematic review and updated meta-analysis. *PloS One*, *19*(1), e0295784. https://doi.org/10.1371/journal.pone.0295784

Ziervogel, G., Waddell, J., Smit, W., & Taylor, A. (2016). Flooding in Cape Town's informal settlements: Barriers to collaborative urban risk governance. *South African Geographical Journal*, *98*(1), 1–20. https://doi.org/10.1080/03736245.2014.924867

REFRAMING QUALITATIVE RESEARCH ETHICS: PROPOSALS FOR CHANGE

CHAPTER 10

THE CASE FOR DISCIPLINE-SPECIFIC ETHICS: A VIEW FROM SOCIAL ANTHROPOLOGY

Michael Herzfeld

Harvard University, USA

ABSTRACT

Anthropologists frequently find themselves perplexed by the requirements of ethical review. These requirements ignore the unpredictability of anthropology's central method (immersive long-term ethnographic fieldwork), suppress the agency of both anthropologists and their respondents, and fail to accommodate cultural differences among ethical traditions. Much of the existing process on both sides of the Atlantic ignores these aspects of ethics governance and therefore conflicts with anthropologists' culturally attuned sense of ethical responsibility. As a result, some researchers have been tempted to adopt evasive tactics through which they may superficially follow (or 'muddle through') the formal guidelines rather than strictly following the currently institutionalised ethical prescriptions. For these reasons, I argue that ethical review should be (a) discipline-specific and (b) consultative rather than regulatory. I also propose that review sessions in anthropology host members of one or two other social sciences as 'critical friends', with a view to improving communication and mutual understanding between anthropology and other disciplines. I suggest that moving to this combined reconfiguration of ethics review would help

Reframing Qualitative Research Ethics
Advances in Research Ethics and Integrity, Volume 12, 163–175

Published under exclusive licence by Emerald Publishing Limited
ISSN: 2398-6018/doi:10.1108/S2398-601820250000012010

to assure the survival and ethical transparency of ethnography as the core method of the discipline. While I am proposing this model for anthropology, its replication across the social sciences would improve transparency about ethical issues while simultaneously encouraging increased trans-disciplinary cooperation.

Keywords: Anthropology; ethnography; predictability; agency; cultural specificity of ethics; legalism; 'critical friends'; transparency; procedural reform; consultation vs regulation

ETHICS AND MANAGEMENT: AN ILL-MATCHED PAIR?

In this chapter, I offer a specifically anthropological perspective on social science ethics. I hope thereby to make a larger point but to make it by (anthropological) example. Ethical regulation of social science research does not usually make an explicit practice of distinguishing among disciplines. It does favour some discipline-specific methods over others, however, showing greater tolerance towards experimental and statistical methods with a high degree of procedural predictability and geared to the generation of predictive models and theories. Anthropology does not fit that bill, and its central method – immersive ethnography – must be able to follow paths of inquiry as they open up in the course of fieldwork. Its methods are thus predominantly exploratory and depend on the spontaneity of the casual encounter, in which local individuals knowingly exercise their agency in opening up or refusing access to intimate information. Concomitantly, anthropological theories, which Bruce Knauft (2006, p. 411) accurately described as 'mid-level', offer more in the way of explanation of facts discovered than of immediately usable generalisations. Nuance, adaptability, and serendipity play too large a part for some of the more formal ethics procedures to offer an empirically convincing means of assessment.

I write this on the basis of personal experience, so that a word of self-revelation is in order. Trained in the United Kingdom, with a long teaching career in the United States, I have watched with some consternation the spread of a largely American and Western European idiom of ethics governance to many parts of the world – a concern, following and also generating numerous conversations in several countries, that led me to accept the chance to guest-edit a special issue of *Anthropology Today* (April 2024). The increasing ubiquity of the relevant forms of ethics governance might give the impression that its culturally very peculiar idiom is in the process of actually becoming universal. That is a dangerous misapprehension. Any attribution of universality would simply reproduce the persistent hegemonic inequalities of the colonial global order. Such is the authority of bureaucratic governance in independent nation-states, however, that the resulting paradox has come in for astonishingly little comment.

Precisely because it stands out as a rare exception among the social sciences in this regard, anthropology, with its eclectic theory and situationally adaptive methodology, as well as a long history of sometimes lacerating self-critique and unceasing efforts to purge itself of a historically very real colonial burden of its own, may offer a useful foil to generic procedures considered appropriate in other fields. Anthropology also stands out in challenging universalist and legalistic assumptions that most ethics governance takes for granted (see, e.g., Fassin, 2014; Laidlaw, 2002) and in refusing to privilege philosophers' often rather hypothetical definitions over 'ordinary ethics' (see Lambek, 2010). Anthropologists insist on acknowledging the cultural understandings of ethics and morality that may not – and often do not – correspond to their own, and in the context of which the formal requirements of today's ethics bureaucracies make little sense. Anthropological critiques of ethics regulation therefore offer a useful perspective for disciplines less used to (or at least concerned with) challenging culturally familiar paradigms.

This chapter is absolutely not a plea for special treatment for one particular discipline alone. On the contrary, it is a plea to acknowledge the specific affordances and obligations of each of the social sciences and to seek mutual enlightenment. One size does not fit all, but all can learn from what makes each of the others distinctive. Later in this chapter, I offer a suggestion for opening up interdisciplinary dialogue. First, however, using anthropology as an example rather than as an authoritative model, I will attempt to suggest how all social science disciplines might develop a more thoughtful and less reactive relation to the automatism of form-filling that today often displaces real responsibility – the core of a genuine ethics – in the prevailing bureaucratic procedures of ethics governance and, by extension, in the way students are trained to deal with ethical issues.

To that end, we must recognise that, in discussing future options, too managerial a focus on the ethical conduct of social science research would foreclose discussion and, at the same time, too easily induce the self-censorship that current ethics regimes seem to foster. Research students in particular, intimidated by the minatory language of many of the regulations as well as by the abundant horror stories in circulation, are already policing their own projects and cutting out the more immersive aspects of method rather than making the specifically ethical case for such approaches (see, e.g., Budilová & Jakoubek, 2024; Simonsen & L'orange-Fürst, 2024). Such caution is self-defeating because, by effectively presupposing rejection, it pre-emptively increases the range of approaches that will be rejected in the future. It suppresses necessary discussion of potentially problematic aspects of research because students feel they will not be able to get them through ethics review. By acting so evasively, however, they effectively evade their own moral responsibility, ceding control to a managerial logic that thereby secures their complicity in maintaining a universalist model – one that is in reality often more concerned to protect the base institution from legal liability than to protect those unfortunately named 'human subjects' from harm (Herzfeld, 2023).

Another common approach, equally evasive of responsibility, is to adopt the pragmatic ethics of 'muddling through' that is often the hallmark of everyday life (see, e.g., Reed-Danahay, 1993). Some anthropologists, knowing that ethics committees lack the means to police research and enforce compliance, may even convince themselves that, when they get to the field, other cultural rules will affect their actions, while, back home, no one will know about the corners they may have cut. Both assumptions largely hold true, but acting in this way does not advance critique of the conditions that have made such evasive action seem necessary.

Neither of the two approaches I have just described, therefore, is helpful. Both weaken scholars' intellectual autonomy while substituting uncritical reflex responses for serious ethical cogitation and engagement. More important, perhaps, and certainly more damaging, is the inevitable consequence that such approaches deny potentially well-intentioned ethics committees the chance to engage reflexively with the ethics of their own methods of governance. Ethics committees often place assessment in the hands of colleagues with little or no understanding of what anthropologists do or of what interests them. It is all too easy to accept management, a technocratic procedure, as a substitute for seriously thinking about the potential ethical problems associated with unfamiliar practices. While some 'data managers' display a sensitivity far beyond what their title might imply, the managerial approach that the title implies often induces in anthropologists the complaisant responses I have just mentioned.

Social anthropologists rely on spontaneous interactions with their local interlocutors, who are generally aware that these scholars are engaged in research and usually achieve an informed understanding of the work's value. Anthropologists typically try to explain their intentions to their interlocutors, in large measure because field research is dependent on a high degree of mutual trust. That trust can founder when a scholar whips out a consent form and asks for a written signature. Trust is not something that can be built through bureaucratic process. It comes about through a culturally recognisable performance of friendship, a concept that itself has culturally variable implications, and that therefore is particularly susceptible to cultural variations in the very concept of ethics. For an anthropologist to engage in these formal assertions of ethical probity is thus, in many situations, trebly unethical. It causes distress to local interlocutors, it forces the researcher to betray the ethics of cultural respect, and it creates the dishonest impression that there is no further basis for ethical concern.

As I have already pointed out (Herzfeld, 2023, 2024), current procedures largely ignore the agency of our interlocutors as well as the resulting unpredictability of our research. The agency of both sides (anthropologists and their interlocutors) and the unpredictability of the research procedures are mutually entangled in ways that, as I hope to show here, shed a sharp searchlight on the logic of the ethical governance systems currently in use. In these systems, ostensibly designed to protect our interlocutors, ignoring the issue of agency is at best paradoxical. What kind of protection – other than the condescending variety we associate with colonial 'protectorates' – refuses to acknowledge, not merely the right but also the *capacity* of our so-called human subjects to push back at our impertinences, to decide what kinds of knowledge we should be allowed to have, and, most important of all, to decide for themselves whether and how far to trust us? I am arguing here for more engagement over ethics, not less. What most ethics regimes present is not really ethics at all. It is an arid exercise in legalism.

A CASE IN POINT: WHEN TO HIDE IDENTITIES?

Some debates about these issues go back a long way. Among these, perhaps the most frequent has been the question of whether to name persons and places. The late Ernestine Friedl wrote a book about a mainland Greek village whose name she made the title of her ethnographic study: *Vasilika: A Village in Modern Greece* (Friedl, 1962). Over a decade later, I overheard two young American women asking an Athens travel agent about travel to Vasilika. The travel agent was baffled; that is one of the commonest village names in Greece, so which one did they mean? They couldn't remember where it was (apparently their reading was none too thorough), but they'd read about this place in a book and wanted to experience it for themselves. At this point, I intervened, suggesting mildly that the villagers might not be so happy if unanticipated foreigners started descending on them, and that I was sure that Friedl herself might not have anticipated this outcome of her research publication. The agent did not have a profitable means of sending the two women to an obscure village he had never heard of, and so they soon decided to pursue a different travel option.

When I think back on that moment, I find myself critically reflecting that perhaps I had been rather presumptuous in thus second-guessing both Friedl's and the villagers' wishes. As far as I now recall, however, I was not dogmatically insistent that these young people should not visit the village under any circumstances, just mildly determined that the two Americans should think about the ethics of their intended tourism both towards the villagers and towards the anthropologist whose book had led them to consider the visit. It might have been useful to have a group of peers to discuss what the right approach would be. But the incident also speaks to an issue that is very much in play in current anthropology: are pseudonyms (for both names and people) appropriate? Are they even useful? And to what extent can we expect a code of conduct to help us deal with such moments?

Since we do not know whether the villagers of Vasilika would have welcomed curious tourists, or whether there was a breaking point at which an initial welcome might have soured, there is no easy answer in that particular case. I discussed the same issue with my interlocutors in the Cretan mountain village where I had worked on a range of topics including gender (especially ideas and practices associated with manhood), political performance, kinship, and resistance to state interventions. Initially, the majority seemed to favour a pseudonym (and liked the one I chose, which has connotations of merrymaking). Later, however, some villagers also agreed, especially as I said that my work would help to counter a negative media image of the community (Herzfeld, 2022, 177n80), that using the real name made better sense, and that is what I did. I continue to have an active relationship with the village, which awarded me honorary citizenship and thereby reassured me that thus far I had done no harm and had at least dignified the community by taking its values seriously.

I have also made it clear that if any official or other consequences of my work were to harm the village or its inhabitants in any way, I would speak out and take an active role in trying to reverse the damage. So far, the villagers and I have been fortunate in that no known harm has accrued. The hope is, instead, that my work may lead some readers to rethink their stereotypical ideas about supposedly uncivilised Cretan bandits – people who in reality are deeply courteous and whose indignant defiance of state power reflects what they see as an ethically justifiable stance, given the humiliations to which successive sources of official authority have subjected them. My sojourns among them have taught me more about the contingent character of ethics than any formal pedagogy could hope to convey. For their part, pleased that this Harvard professor speaks 'our language' (a dialect widely associated with negative stereotypes elsewhere in Greece) and has firmly resisted the sensationalism and exoticism that some journalists have exhibited towards them, the villagers have given me an ongoing but forever revocable licence to continue our affectionate and mutually respectful engagement.

THE HISTORICAL INSTABILITY OF ETHICS

My experience (over roughly half a century) of negotiating such issues with the villagers shows, moreover, that situations change over time. A bureaucratic declaration, designed with protecting one's home institution from legal consequences, treats an ethics committee's judgement as fixed for all time. To be fair, current institutional review board (IRB) protocols often do require that researchers update their plans regularly. That provision, however, is as toothless as it is impractical. It would be virtually unenforceable unless all journals and publishing houses were to require certification of all protocols, a requirement that would entail a huge expenditure of staff time and therefore also of money. Such a requirement would further burden an academic publishing industry already pushed to the wall. Moreover, anthropologists who remain 'research-active' throughout their careers typically work from ethnographic monographs towards more complex works of scholarship; these subsequent writings draw selectively on the earlier research, some of which will not have been previously published. It would be ludicrous to demand that those who have already enjoyed long and active research careers should renew all the IRB protocols obtained over several decades on the off-chance that they might need some as-yet unspecifiable data at some unspecified time. And what are they to do about research conducted before these protocols were invented?

Anthropologists have certainly committed ethical offences of various kinds. Some have done so within a *Zeitgeist*, most obviously that of European colonialism, of which they were barely cognisant precisely because they were part of it. Despite critiques of their alleged attitudes, some, at least, of these precursors were already critical, in inchoate but laudable ways, of the hegemonies in which they were enmeshed. It is fashionable to criticise the likes of Franz Boas, A.L. Kroeber, Bronislaw Malinowski, and E.E. Evans-Pritchard for their acquiescence in colonial rule and discriminatory governance, yet all four were also critical of the political powers that enabled and sometimes even financed their research.[1] Some of the critiques have been, perhaps inevitably, as 'chronocentric' as their targets had been ethnocentric. Without those targets' early misgivings, however, anthropology's ethical conscience – arguably one of its greatest epistemic *and* ethical strengths today – might never have awakened. The sobering retraction of charges against the late Napoleon Chagnon, whose work (like that of any social scientist) can certainly still be discussed for the ethical issues it raises, offers a particularly telling insight into the dangers of rushing to judgement – a move that arguably contradicted the discipline's own strongly anti-judgementalist ethics.[2]

Despite some reservations about particular approaches, I am emphatically not advocating the rejection of discipline-specific critique. To the contrary, critique contributes to the empirical – that is, grounded and experiential – methodology that allows anthropology today to claim some measure of moral high ground. I want instead to locate the debate in a greater degree of historical self-awareness. It is as fashionable to berate 'postmodernism' today as it was to promote it a mere decade or two ago. We should learn from this of the dangers that chronocentrism poses for a discipline that must, if it is to survive, adapt to a world in which culture itself clearly emerges as processual, evanescent, changeable, mercurial, indefinable, politically volatile, and conceptually fragile – as everything, in short, except for that fixed, bounded entity that a distressingly hardy strain of 'methodological nationalism' continues to imagine in everyday discourse.[3]

Early anthropologists were committed to the preservation of 'cultures', and their well-meant efforts have nourished much of the ethnic revivalism that has at least allowed groups of Indigenous people to maintain their dignity and, occasionally, some degree of independence. Yet it was also these same anthropologists who exhibited members of tribes as specimens and placed their considerable knowledge of Indigenous practices at the service of colonial administrations. Like cultural identities, these anthropologists, too, were in constant and sometimes confusing evolution. Reifying them as villains or saints is itself a chronocentric caricature. It forecloses serious consideration of the ethics they followed or failed to follow. To be sure, some did things that today we would consider so egregious as to merit exclusion from the discipline. Some acted in ways that were questionable even at the time. But these predecessors also paved the way for our realisation of where our current ethical obligations lie – and to a clear understanding that those obligations are necessarily always in flux, a conditionality that ethics bureaucracies seem unable to handle.

That observation brings me to the crux of my argument: that the static forms of bureaucratic oversight, well-intended though they may (in part) have been, do a disservice to the very concept of ethics. They not only posit a universal ethics; they posit an unchanging ethics. In so doing, they silence the very possibility of debate about what is appropriate when dealing with *this* moment in the history of *this* population and when considering how the criteria for such an evaluation might change in the future. The more benign operators of these ethics are indeed willing to contemplate a more flexible approach (see, e.g., Elfenbein & Hoffman, 2004). Their openness, however, entails a veritable Pandora's Box of possible evasive moves, and these have been the solutions with which many practitioners have had to be content. Such compromises belie the very claims to universality that motivate the entire system of ethics governance. Beating the system by 'fudging' the rules is hardly an approach that bespeaks ethical seriousness. But it is the intransigence and adherence to prescriptive norms on the part of ethics administrators that has favoured the widespread adoption of such tactical vagueness.

SEEKING ETHICAL CLARITY

What, then, *would* constitute ethical clarity? While a one-size-fits-all approach may give the impression of both realising a common ethical code for all social scientists and grounding it in incontrovertible values, and while such an approach may also come equipped with a ferocious array of vetted exceptions that still confirm the basic structure, one of its potential effects is to suppress intellectual independence. Since the claims of ethical governance are based on precisely an assumption that it has proved largely unable to document – that it respects academic freedom while also protecting the 'subjects' of academic research – the currently dominant design serves the interests of academic institutions, especially universities, that are predominantly concerned to protect themselves from possibly expensive legal misadventures. It serves the interests neither of the researchers nor, in many cases, of those whose lives the research examines.

Procedures, it is clear, have often become more influential than critical engagement in determining the shape of ethical governance. This tendency is by no means restricted to ethics regimes; it is pervasive. Visit a certain Danish university website, for example, and you will find bar diagrams that describe the output of each member of the professorial staff in a series of categories (research, writing, service). Other countries' evaluation systems attribute serious significance to the 'impact factors' of their faculty members' chosen publication venues and to published rankings of those venues. Treating academic output as grocery to be weighed by the pound, like 'culture' in tourism,[4] serves no purpose other than to simplify the work of assessment to the point of banality and to evacuate it of the capacity to challenge the intellect and the imagination. Similarly, while most ethics bureaucracies do operate more subtly, and while many staffers are conscientious and open-minded, the structuring of ethical knowledge in terms more appropriate to business accounting – 'audit culture'[5] – represents a huge temptation for the overworked functionary who does not really have a training in the discipline in question. Less well-funded institutions are clearly more vulnerable to this kind of problem than those able to pay for a sophisticated staff and extensive reference resources.

I am not critical of bureaucracy as such. I do nevertheless criticise mistaking bureaucratic efficiency for the presumed *object* – ethical clarity – of that efficiency. Sometimes, the practice of efficiency is remarkably inefficient in its effects; it is more a rhetorical form of action than an effective gauge of values. Treating ethics as reducible to an anticipatory declaration of intent is a serious error of collective judgement and may ultimately encourage researchers to shrug off ethical responsibility. It is all too easy to say, in effect, 'I've done what I had to do; now I'm free to get on with the job'. We all know that this happens and that it is an unfortunate aspect of the 'professional intimacy' of our discipline – a potential source of eventual embarrassment.[6]

The bureaucratisation of ethics suppresses agency. It suppresses the agency of the researcher (no guarantee of academic freedom there!), and it suppresses the agency of the researched (who are presumed to be passive objects incapable of making their own decisions about what to tell the researchers). Agency is, to be sure, a complex concept. Take the question of evaluating vulnerability. Bureaucracies such as the US IRB systems recognise some populations as particularly vulnerable *by definition*, but the criteria are often quite arbitrary. The age of majority, for example, is not the same in all countries,[7] so the requirement that 'minors' should receive special treatment looks like a catch-all device to ensure that a researcher's institution does not get sued by an opportunistic parent or guardian or even by the minor in question. There is no question that some categories – former prisoners, for example – do deserve special consideration, but what those categories are and how strict the criteria remain are issues that require constant revaluation. I have reason to believe that some of my informants are former prisoners, but, as I am not studying them as a category and have no way of knowing in advance whether they will reveal this part of their lives to me, I cannot anticipate the ethical questions that I will then have to resolve on the spot. Moreover, assigning them retrospectively to a single category ('former prisoners') may itself create new forms of vulnerability. An interesting new approach to the assessment of immigrants trying to enter Fortress Europe suggests that the selection of some restricted groups as legally 'vulnerable' has the effect of rendering all other migrants *more* vulnerable because of their exclusion from the special protections (Alexandridis et al., 2024). They are the ones who, merely by default, are more at risk of humiliation. Might not anthropologists who recognise the agency of such unexceptional sufferers actually provide them with the dignity that the officials would deny them? Might not such a consideration then extend to those defined as vulnerable by bureaucratic ethics regimes?

ANTHROPOLOGISTS AND THEIR DISCIPLINARY OTHERS: A NECESSARY CONVERSATION

None of what I have said obviates the need for some kind of ethical review process. The key term, however, is 'process'. Ethical review should not entail judgement by fiat. I am also not advocating for oversight committees exclusively drawn from one discipline alone. Such a move could prove disastrously self-isolating and might easily lead to the concealment of actions deserving of condemnation and correction. I am instead arguing for discipline-based committees in which external members would serve as 'critical friends'.[8] These committees would usually be organised within university departments where possible but could also benefit from the mixing of disciplines in some institutions and operate at a more inclusive level. In either situation, they would always include at least one or two 'critical friends' drawn from fields with different methods, theories, and epistemologies.

Departments or other appropriate units would be required to create and maintain these committees and include those vital extra-disciplinary voices. If such committees were operated at a national level, they could be constituted on the same principles that I have suggested here for departmental committees. No situation is so constituted as to preclude the formation of such hybrid arrangements.

This approach offers a double advantage. On the one hand, it should nurture greater mutual understanding among disciplines. Given their shared commitment to non-judgemental openness to new ideas and cultural differences, it is truly amazing – and distressing – that the social sciences often seem to experience great difficulty in talking to each other. Discussion of shared – or even divergent – ethical as well as epistemological questions (and the relation between them) could prove highly constructive. If it did not, there would be important conclusions to draw as well.

Each discipline has its own issues with ethics governance. Medical practice obviously requires clearly defined courses of action, although even here unexpected human situations face ethics committees with the need to make ad hoc judgements. The further we get from individual cases and unique groups, the more suited the research becomes to the existing instruments of ethical governance. Research with individual persons and unusual communities, however, is not lacking in theoretical significance. It is the commitment of ethical governance to a particular tradition of theory – and especially to its capacity to generate generalisations – that entraps the 'softer' social sciences in unsuitable procedures. The conception of science that animates most ethical bureaucracy comes from the more statistically and experimentally oriented social sciences and is poorly equipped to deal with the intentional unpredictability of social anthropology's preferred method of letting their interlocutors' preferences guide interaction. That approach fosters the necessary recognition of the local interlocutors' agency.

On the other hand, anthropologists would benefit from learning about why their more 'scientific' colleagues believe that surveys, formal interviews, and experiments might yield data more persuasive than those unearthed in anthropological fieldwork. All parties could usefully discuss their respective criteria of evidential sufficiency; for example, they might not agree on how many interviews would be enough to establish a convincing argument, but they would at least learn to appreciate each other's epistemological and ethical concerns and to state their evidential criteria in a manner comprehensible beyond their respective disciplinary boundaries. Understanding such differences and their intellectual implications would be a gain for all concerned. Including, for example, an economist and a sociologist in a committee designed to help anthropologists determine their ethical obligations would put pressure on the latter to maintain a consciously self-critical ethical standard. It would also induce the anthropologists to explain to the extra-disciplinary colleagues why it is important to develop less Eurocentric and universalistic concepts of ethics. Conflicting ideas about ethics would thus generate serious discussion. In short, such arrangements would provide the basis for an enriching and ongoing dialogue. The present arrangements do nothing of the sort, especially as confidentiality concerns mandate that the negotiations leading to committee decisions remain perpetually invisible.

Such departmental committees, crucially, would also be purely advisory, recognising that realistically they would lack the power to enforce compliance with protocols. That impotence is already the case with existing ethics committees, but the actions of these committees always seem to imply the vague threat of punitive responses to non-compliance in the field. Both sensibly and ideally, therefore, the committees would proffer recommendations, not demands, to the researchers. They would thereby avoid the major source of the (openly acknowledged) dishonesty generated by current practices.

An arrangement along these lines would seem to represent a considerable advance in terms that all concerned could recognise as ethical. Advisory sessions would ideally precede and follow the research. One clear result would be that researchers, instead of being hostages to their institutions' fears of liability, would be morally responsible and politically answerable for the local consequences of their research.

In practice, anthropologists already assume accountability in relation to their interlocutors. To do so, however, they have needed the freedom to improvise in response to their interlocutors' agency. If, for example, a researcher offers an interlocutor a consent form and the interlocutor refuses to sign the form but wants to continue the interaction, it is hard to see how refusing to continue a conversation could possibly be an ethical alternative to respecting the interlocutor's wishes. Indeed, the choice exposes the hypocrisy of *requiring* the signing of consent forms – an act that may be abhorrent to local interlocutors because it is associated with police or other forms of repression. There is no sense in which we can (or should) regard as ethical any action that is disrespectful or dismissive of our interlocutors' agency, their fears, or their own ethical standards. While some alternatives to the forms are possible under many ethics regimes – recorded oral consent is often an available option – none can obviate the deep sense of betrayal with which members of some societies respond to virtually any direct request for *explicit* consent. How do we deal with the implicit in situations where rendering it explicit would be viewed as tactless or even hostile?

For an anthropologist to explain such a dilemma to an economist, for example, might initially seem insurmountably difficult. Economists do not rely on the serendipity of particular moments of social interaction to generate their data. They rarely seek to learn major languages, let alone local dialects or Indigenous tongues, as a medium of research. They operate, in quite variable ways, with the expectation of generating predictive theory. Anthropologists operate in radically different ways and with radically different assumptions and expectations. That is all the more reason to have interdisciplinary conversations on a regular basis. It may be utopian to imagine the very possibility of improved mutual appreciation between disciplines with a long history of mutual distrust. Without such a vision, however, some disciplines – social anthropology among them – may die out, isolated from larger debates and crushed by the weight of an uncomprehending automatism. Current ethics procedures in the hands of uninterested or unsympathetic operators already threaten to destroy anthropology's key method of ethnographic fieldwork.

I am less concerned about the prospect that the formal discipline of anthropology might vanish than I am about the occlusion of the ethical debates that have long been at the heart of its epistemology. Those debates have a wider significance; they are immensely consequential. The discomfiting uncertainty and unpredictability of anthropology's methods, theories, and goals, on the other hand, are all aspects of what has animated the discipline's deep disquiet with today's technological reductionism – a reductionism that produces only *ersatz* ethics defined by numbers and forms. The disappearance of its practices and ideas would be a blow against the intellectual diversity that keeps productive debate alive. It would deprive the social sciences of an important, if sometimes rather annoying, critical voice. In the proposal outlined here, I have tried to offer a practically – and ethically – preferable alternative.

NOTES

1. See, e.g., Hitchens (1994) on Boas; Rosaldo (1986) (and cf. Herzfeld, 2016, pp. 160–161) on Evans-Pritchard; and Akkaraju (2021) on Kroeber; Weston and Djohari (2020, pp. 41–65) on Malinowski. For two assessments of the relationship between British colonialism and anthropology, see Asad (1973) and Kuper (1973).
2. Wong (2001) offers a useful, if brief, summary. See also Weston and Djohari (2020, pp. 126–146).
3. On methodological nationalism, see Wimmer and Glick Schiller (2002).
4. I borrow this phrase from Davydd Greenwood's (2012) superb and intellectually still relevant essay on the tourist industry's production of 'culture'.
5. See, most recently, and in the context of ethics governance, Shore (2024).
6. I originally suggested the term 'professional intimacy' as a variant of 'cultural intimacy' in the sense in which I developed that concept (Herzfeld, 2016, p. 180).
7. In Thailand, for example, the age of majority is 20 (but minors are emancipated on marriage).
8. I take this term from the British research assessment bureaucracy, in which I have served in that role for a university department.

ACKNOWLEDGEMENTS

I wish to express my appreciation, for their helpful comments on earlier drafts, to Helen Busby, John Carman, Martin Skrydstrup, and an anonymous reviewer of this volume.

REFERENCES

Akkaraju, M. (2021, January 28). *'Not so one-sided': Campus community reacts to unnaming of Kroeber Hall*. University Wire (Uloop).

Alexandridis, A., Giulia, S., & Dalakoglou, D. (2024). From Fortress Europe to border-filter: Vulnerability, biopolitics and the management of migration in Greece and EU after 2015. *Journal of Modern Greek Studies*, *42*, 139–164.

Asad, T. (Ed.). (1973). *Anthropology and the colonial encounter*. Humanities Press.

Budilová, L. J., & Jakoubek, M. (2024). Fieldwork? Better not: Ethics bureaucracy in Eastern Europe. *Anthropology Today*, *40*(2), 11–13. https://doi.org/10.1111/1467-8322.12873

Elfenbein, T. W., & Hoffman, A. S. (2004). Towards meaningful institutional change: Responsive bureaucracy and the governance of anthropological ethics. *Anthropology Today*, *40*(2), 4–7. https://doi.org/10.1111/1467-8322.12871

Fassin, D. (2014). The ethical turn in anthropology: Promises and uncertainties. *HAU: Journal of Ethnographic Theory*, *4*, 429–435. https://doi.org/10.14318/hau4.1.025

Friedl, E. (1962). *Vasilika: A village in modern Greece*. Holt, Rinehart and Winston.

Greenwood, D. J. (2012). Culture by the pound: An anthropological perspective on tourism as cultural commoditization. In V. L. Smith (Ed.), *Hosts and guests: The anthropology of tourism* (2nd ed., pp. 171–185). University of Pennsylvania Press.

Herzfeld, M. (2016). *Cultural intimacy: Social poetics and the real life of states, societies, and institutions* (3rd ed.). Routledge.

Herzfeld, M. (2022). *Subversive archaism: Troubling traditionalists and the politics of national heritage*. Duke University Press.

Herzfeld, M. (2023). Ethnographic responsibility: Can the bureaucratization of research ethics be ethical? *Anthropology Today*, *39*(3), 3–6. https://doi.org/10.1111/1467-8322.12811

Herzfeld, M. (2024). Introduction to ethics in ethnography: The practical politics of predictability. *Anthropology Today*, *40*(2), 3–4. https://doi.org/10.1111/1467-8322.12870

Hitchens, J. (1994). Critical implications of Franz Boas' theory and methodology. *Dialectical Anthropology*, *19*, 237–253.

Knauft, B. (2006). Anthropology in the middle. *Anthropological Theory*, *6*, 407–430. https://doi.org/10.1177/1463499606071594

Kuper, A. (1973). *Anthropologists and anthropology: The British School 1922-1972*. Pica Press.

Laidlaw, J. (2002). For an anthropology of ethics and freedom. *Journal of the Anthropological Institute*, *8*, 311–332. https://doi.org/10.1111/1467-9655.00110

Lambek, M. (Ed.). (2010). *Ordinary ethics: Anthropology, language, and action*. Fordham University Press.

Reed-Danahay, D. (1993). Talking about resistance: Ethnography and theory in rural France. *Anthropological Quarterly*, *66*, 221–229. https://doi.org/10.2307/3318065

Rosaldo, R. (1986). From the door of his tent: The fieldworker and the inquisitor. In J. Clifford & G. E. Marcus (Eds.), *Writing culture: The poetics and politics of ethnography* (pp. 77–97). University of California Press.

Shore, C. (2024). The bureaucratization of ethical integrity: Research ethics committees and imaginaries of risk. *Anthropology Today*, *40*(2), 8–10. https://doi.org/10.1111/1467-8322.12872

Simonsen, J. K., & L'orange-Fürst, E. (2024). Experiences of GDPR in Norway: Politics of autonomy and control. *Anthropology Today*, *40*(2), 18–20. https://doi.org/10.1111/1467-8322.12875

Weston, G., & Djohari, N. (2020). *Anthropological controversies: The 'crimes' and misdemeanors that shaped a discipline*. Routledge.

Wimmer, A., & Glick Schiller, N. (2002). Methodological nationalism and beyond: Nation-state building, migration and the social sciences. *Global Networks*, *2*, 301–134. https://doi.org/10.1111/1471-0374.00043

Wong, K. (2001, March 1). Controversial anthropologist Napoleon Chagnon, who chronicled the lives of the Yanomamö, has died. *Scientific American*. https://www.scientificamerican.com/article/controversial-anthropologist-napoleon-chagnon-who-chronicled-the-lives-of-the-yanomamo-has-died/

CHAPTER 11

IMPROVING FORMALISED ETHICS REVIEW: FIELD SENSITIVITY, BUNDLES OF USERSHIP AND DEVOLUTION

Margaret Sleeboom-Faulkner

University of Sussex, UK

ABSTRACT

This chapter illustrates how formalised requirements of research ethics and data management have affected social science research and anthropological research specifically. Examples of anthropological research of the experience of international and national science regulation in China show that, in practice, these requirements can lead to unnecessary complications in 'the field' and are apt to disregard the expectations and ethics of potential research participants. To counteract such inadequacies, this chapter suggests conceptual tools for the general improvement of requirements for research ethics and data management. It does so, first, by introducing notions of 'field sensitivity' and 'bundles of usership', which enable more appropriate ways of thinking about ethics in the field and the management of research materials; second, by explaining how the devolution of ethics review and its rooting in the educational curriculum could make ethics review more productive and more suitable to anthropological research specifically and social science in general; and, third, research is needed into the reasons for the great diversity in research ethics and data management requirements between and within countries in order to understand their impact in practice of fieldwork. Any changes will have to take the socio-cultural and political history of these institutions of governance into account.

Reframing Qualitative Research Ethics
Advances in Research Ethics and Integrity, Volume 12, 177–196

Published under exclusive licence by Emerald Publishing Limited
ISSN: 2398-6018/doi:10.1108/S2398-601820250000012011

Keywords: Formalised research ethics and data management; anthropology; field sensitivity; bundles of usership; devolution of ethics review

INTRODUCTION

Over the last decade, regulatory developments in ethics review and data management have affected social science research that relies on ethnographic fieldwork. The formalisation of research ethics in university bureaucracies tends to privilege research as defined by research ethics committees (RECs) rather than its negotiation with the ethics encountered 'in the field' (Sleeboom-Faulkner et al., 2017) This chapter asserts that, as a result of unsuitable systems of formalised ethics and data management, the research integrity of these disciplines is under threat (de Koning et al., 2019). This assertion is based on the presumption that an intimate link exists between the theoretical, ethical and practical dimensions of research. Ethics review, which was introduced in the social sciences in the United Kingdom in the 1990s (Caplan, 2003; Dingwall, 2008; Mills, 2003), has taken on organisational forms that vary across universities from centralised to devolved (Sleeboom-Faulkner & McMurray, 2018), while clear differences also exist between countries. For instance, while many countries in mainland Europe have institutionalised procedures of formalised ethics to accommodate funding requirements, in the United Kingdom, higher education institutions (HEIs) require all research to go through formalised ethics review (FER). Modes of ethics governance vary substantially. The German Anthropology Association only recently adopted European Research Council (ERC) guidelines after following the 'Frankfurt Declaration of Ethics' (Dilger et al., 2018), while in France, for a long time, mistrust towards Anglo-Saxon standardised research ethics has coloured ethics practices there (Vassy & Keller, 2008). In most cases, however, it tends to use a one-size-fits-all approach based on generalised notions of risk associated with the biomedical model of science, presuming a highly procedural form of research (Dingwall, 2008; Simpson, 2011). This situation has proven problematic for ethnographic fieldwork, as it covers a great variety of research designs ranging from open to tightly planned, various embeddings in local institutions and differential relations of power in the field (e.g., ranging from 'studying up' to 'studying down').

The introduction of the General Data Protection Regulation (GDPR) on 25 May 2018 (European Parliament, 2016) has created much confusion around its relation to FER. As the GDPR and its many clauses are open to various interpretations, HEIs within and across European Union (EU) countries have translated the GDPR into diverging systems of data management. This situation entails complications for social scientists, who need to negotiate with their respective universities regarding suitable guidelines for both ethics review and data management. The UK Research Councils emphasise the importance of data sharing through the UK Data Service, and after the coming into force of the GDPR, universities in the UK have started to develop data registries and archives for the social sciences. Across Europe, a number of data protection models have been implemented, yielding a motley patchwork of data management systems, varying from systems that require the storage of all raw research data, including ethnographic data (e.g., University of Utrecht) to more flexible systems that allow disciplines dependent on ethnographic fieldwork to manage their own data (e.g., University of Leiden) (Meyer et al., 2018). It is ironic that even though the GDPR recognises the need to protect confidentiality in the social sciences on a par with journalism (ICO, 2024), in practice, universities may not be sensitive to the diverse conditions under which research materials ('data') are created, including situations in which a researcher cannot share research materials with third parties without endangering research participants or without violating the relations of trust built up with them. A further issue concerns the presumption that anthropological research materials can be digitised and understood outside the context in which they were co-produced by research and interlocutors. In anthropology, even when accompanied by 'metadata', the translation of research materials into shareable 'data' is fundamentally questionable due to a lacking context and the problem of their inappropriate understanding and use by third parties (cf. Fabian, 1971; Geertz, 1993 [1973]; Meskel & Pels 2005; Pels, 1999).

Appraising questions of research ethics demands specialised knowledge, not just of formalised research ethics but also of 'real world' ethics, as the becoming of their interminglings unfolds. Furthermore, formalised requirements for research ethics and data management may well clash with the ability to achieve research aims and thwart ethical practices and the safety of co-researchers in the field. As shown in this chapter, clashes between ethical priorities and principles call for an exploration of new conceptual tools to understand the relation between regulation and ethnographic practices.

In this chapter, I speak of formalised requirements of research ethics and data management. As should be clear from the references to the diversity of ethics and data management governance, the term hides a complex range of processes around which requirements and practices of ethics review and appraisals develop. In this article, examples will mainly refer to formalised research ethics as regulated in the United Kingdom, where requirements seem to be more extensive compared to mainland Europe. As developments in research ethics seem to follow the general direction of those in the United States and the United Kingdom, I believe that they will be recognisable by most readers. However, there remains a need for more extensive understanding of the contexts in which the governance of research ethics has developed, as well as for new conceptual tools, such as those introduced in How to Improve Research Ethics in Anthropological Fieldwork: Conceptual Tools section, to improve practices of ethics review.

In the social sciences, a primary aim of FER in the United Kingdom is to regulate the ethnographic encounter between principal investigators (PIs) and interlocutors in the field, whereby the latter are usually regarded as the most vulnerable. In much ethnographic research, however, ethical issues envelop the research design as a whole. For example, my research on regenerative medicine and society in Asia aimed to understand the impact of international regulation on therapy provision in clinics and hospitals, given that many therapy providers are considered unauthorised. In other words, the ethics of research methods and the ethics of the research contents are intertwined: formalised requirements of informed consent and data management affect whether and how potential interlocutors attend to invitations to meet. In my research, their decisions were not just a matter of 'voluntary and informed decision-making by free individuals' but also matters of building trust and bridging conflicting positions and views. The effect of these requirements on conversations with research participants to a large extent depended on their interest in and influence on the research relevant socio-political circles. Research participants with 'deviant' views had been hesitant to meet and did not agree to consider informed consent. Formalised ethics requirements were experienced as an attempt to predefine the agenda of the meeting through information sheets and of taking ownership of the conversation by them consenting to take away potentially incriminating or controversial data (for similar observations, see Alvesalo-Kuusi & Whyte, 2018; Simpson, 2016). This thwarted the possibility of creating goodwill and the trust necessary for continued interactions.

If it is the aim of formalised research ethics to level the field of power differences between the PI and research participants by means of voluntary and freely given consent, then this clearly does not work. Meeting with potential research participants always presumes a minimum of interest and trust among people with a variety of vulnerabilities and powers, which frame the atmosphere, mood and potential for further meetings. In my research, rather than emerging from a contract of informed consent, trust grew through a shared intention to exchange experiences regarding questions that we all were grappling with: international research regulation and scientific reputation. Far from resolving inequalities through a formal contract, a recognition of the multitude of power differences among us was important to the course of our conversation and for the use of resultant research materials: it was *because* of a continued engagement with the conditions and reasons for structural inequalities and disagreements around science regulation that we shared aims of fairness, safety and the need for research, that it was worthwhile to continue the conversation. In other words, the experience of the conversation as a relational mode of being together in a shared world was crucial to how those involved in the conversation could learn from each other. It is the intersubjectivity underlying these meetings that enable us to explore each other's experiences (Fabian, 1971) and to reflect on and learn about our own and each other's assumptions and presumptions about the making, (non-)functioning and effects of science regulation.

In short, formalised requirements of ethics and data management in ethnographic fieldwork impact the way we create or 'co-produce' knowledge. Rather than arguing that no arrangements are needed to protect research participants and the research materials that result, I suggest that research participants are better protected by recognising the inequalities that pertain to those involved in the conversation, so that the provenance of research materials can be discussed in context. While a temporary bracketing of power relations is important to build the minimal trust needed to have a conversation, even if just to decide on a place to meet, it is essential to collectively establish hitherto unconsidered dimensions of power and to explicate how research materials emerging from the conversation may or may not be used by the PI.

In this chapter, I start with a discussion of some of the issues that I have encountered in my research on regenerative medicine and society in Asia, which cast doubts on the viability of the universalist tenets of formalised requirements of research ethics and data management. I will group these issues around questions raised by FER, data management requirements and the use of formalised research ethics in the field. Finally, I will outline the conceptual tools that I believe can improve research ethics: first, field sensitivity or the ways in which researchers relate to the authority, power and vulnerability of the people they work with/coproduce research materials with. The concept draws attention to the complexity of vulnerability, including that of the powerful. Second, bundles of usership, a concept that helps us think about 'research data' as research materials that are used conditionally and with different permissions, and third, the devolvement of RECs and re-rooting of research ethics in the curriculum to stimulate the simulation of research conditions.

FORMALISED RESEARCH ETHICS AND ANTHROPOLOGICAL RESEARCH

Compared to the feedback from the RECs on my past research projects, only one and a half decades ago, current feedback is less constructive. My former research aimed to shed light on how international cooperation in the life sciences deals with 'differences' between research institutions in countries with varying incomes and concepts of governance. I wanted to know how different health and financial circumstances in Asia and Europe shape international therapy provision and scientific research collaboration. In previous research, I had found that international standards and regulations governing scientific research and therapy provision played an important central role. Due to reputational politics, the research involved many politically sensitive questions related to research reputation, international exploitation of healthcare standards and poverty, the provision of experimental 'therapies' and the opportunistic exploitation of the research regulatory conditions in other countries through international science collaboration. I was keen to understand what those involved in networks of international science collaborations, in particular collaborative hosts and partners, considered to be 'good regulation', 'patient protection' and 'good' science'.

The feedback I had received from the university REC for these projects over a decade ago seemed to be aimed at creating awareness of particular ethical issues involved in the research. Though the use of informed consent and information sheets was required, it was also understood that in anthropological research oral means of 'consenting' may be considered more acceptable in many societies. By contrast, the rigid nature of feedback I have received more recently from RECs risked thwarting my relatively open research plan, which presumed and depended on mutual learning through conversation and experience. I explain this below.

Formalised Research Ethics and Planning Research

In this section, I consider current requirements for research ethics in the context of planning research locations and permissions, informed consent and information sheets and relations of power in the field.

Listing of Research Locations and Institutional Permissions in Advance

In general, RECs require that researchers seek informed consent from all individuals, though in the case of participant observation, a form of group consent given by a gatekeeper is sometimes recognised as acceptable. This is intended to ensure that human individuals enter research voluntarily having received full information (usually via information sheets) about what it means for them to take part, before consent is given. Over the last few years, anthropologists have been obliged to provide a list of research locations in ethics review applications, together with letters of research approval. Many find it hard to comply: viewing their research as 'open' rather than 'procedural', they partly rely on the research itself to prompt further research destinations. Others use snowballing methods to find relevant people and places to connect with. Many researchers, therefore, can only provide a list of places where they might go. But when the REC asks for letters of permission from institutions and gatekeepers, they cannot comply. Such requirements can create anxiety, sometimes leading to changes to research plans being made which are prompted by a fear of not receiving authorisation rather than based on research epistemology.

My research ethics applications had short-listed scientific institutions in China and Japan, where I had hoped to start my explorations, as I had connections with researchers who were happy to introduce me to relevant connections. Not knowing who they were beforehand, a request for 'institutional permissions' in advance would have been problematic and impolite. Further, a general, formal request for institutional access to, for instance, the Chinese Academy of Medical Sciences would have been inappropriate, as I was not applying for a position as visiting researcher. Had I been forced to acquire permission from all the scientific and health institutions I had been hoping to visit, there would have been no research. No matter how I would communicate my wish to converse about 'good regulation' and 'good science', I knew from previous experience that hospitals and clinics that are afraid of accusations of 'snake-oil' trade would not have the confidence to agree to a conversation formalised by informed consent, certainly not without seeing their guest in person or meeting them through an introduction by a trusted mediator. And, as discussed below, the GDPR does not require this where knowledge production serves the public good.

Institutional Permissions at Location

Had institutional consent at these sites been required at the time, I would not have known whom to approach in most of the institutions I planned to visit. In China, such favours from gatekeepers in hospitals or research institutions are usually accompanied by a bribe or a 'red envelope'. After all, exchanging favours with connections [guanxi] is one of the most accepted modes of organising anything that is not regulated (even when it is!) (Yang, 1994). But I would not expect this to provide protection to research participants. And as meetings involved a mélange of conversations, participant observation, discussions and auto-ethnography, I would have found anything less than a personal exchange and negotiation around what I was hoping for unacceptable: after all, partners in conversation need to have the opportunity and leeway to make up their mind.

Requesting institutional permission from bioethics committee members, regulators, entrepreneurs and patients would have been unwelcome and in some cases experienced as offensive. Much of anthropological research by its very nature involves a mixture of participant observation, interviews, conversations, being together (dining, smiling, waiting, sitting, etc.) and auto-ethnography. If not a part of the norms, rules and values of the research location, asking 'institutional permission' goes above the head of the people we are trying to approach: the norms, rules and values of the research location are in fact part of the research experience. Any member of a bioethics committee would have been displeased had I asked for the name of their line-manager to gain permission to speak with them; the science entrepreneurs I came across were hard to locate, and they would not have advised me to approach their company president without talking to them first (if I had insisted on applying for permission); the patients I met tended to approach me spontaneously as a researcher with knowledge of therapy providers. Asking them for institutional permission from the hospital would have baffled them, and requesting the name of their doctor would have defeated their hope of talking with me.

Information Sheets and Informed Consent

Usually, after arrival, colleagues introduced me to scientists who were interested in speaking with me. Alternatively, I approached potentially interested scientists and others by email. Sometimes, we arranged our own venue but occasionally a mediating secretary did. An initial explanation of my aims was always part of the intermediation and would be extended over the course of our conversations. As research participants know the appropriate ways of speaking with a guest themselves, they would not have been open to their guest handing them a list of ethical requirements!

Both written and oral informed consent from individuals can be problematic. For instance, it is widely known that in many communities, a signature or a spoken concession means that friendship or trust cannot be relied upon. As this does not make for a fertile ground for a meaningful conversation or relationship, oral consent is likely to be more suitable in those communities. However, an insistence on predefining the conversation and how it is going to be utilised (how data are going to be stored, banked and persons and locations are going to be named) is not welcome where those involved in conversations would like to have a say about issues discussed, whether conclusions are taken forward and how 'data' (research materials based on conversations) are going to be used. Without mutual exploration and acknowledgement, the encounter can become worrisome or even threatening. The latter happened, for instance, when a signing of the consent form in a Chinese state hospital was complemented the next morning by a Non-Disclosure Agreement, especially created for me! In some cases, even information sheets can be problematic, as carrying one can lead to unwelcome questions by others, and it is imaginable that research participants engaged in illegal activities are worried about being traced. One patient, who had approached me in a clinic, discarded the sheet directly, as the name of my university on it 'could lead to talk'.

The Bias of Formalised Research Ethics in 'Studying Down'

The 'Research and Governance' section on the website of School of Law, Politics and Sociology at the University of Sussex (2024) explains that ethics policies essentially aim to protect the subjects of research (and the researcher) from harm, though this can also involve legal protections. Many other universities also add that they aim to ensure responsibility and research integrity. In practice, the focus is usually on the vulnerability of research participants, such as minors, patients, other-abled people and people in developing countries. Although questions regarding 'safe countries' and secure places to conduct research are standard, RECs rarely show much concern for researchers who 'study up', that is, when they work with powerful research participants (Nader, 1972; Smith, 2006) such as members of the pharmaceutical industry. In my own research, I was often dependent on the goodwill of scientists, regulators, bioethicists and entrepreneurs for insight into their work and conversations about regulation and science. Though I might have been in a vulnerable position, it was misused only rarely. In one case, a widely criticised wealthy cell-therapy provider received me with an army of journalists, ready to photograph me when I visited. I later found one of the photographs of me shaking hands with the owner on their website, claiming that I was going to recommend their medicine to people in the United Kingdom. However, some powerful scientists made themselves vulnerable by speaking with me: in some cases, they put their reputation on the line, because they were concerned about international regulation. It was our conversation that persuaded them to do so, not an informed consent form. Some patients put themselves in a vulnerable position, too, though they usually approached me with the aim of strengthening their position through our conversation. Depending on the situation, patients can also be in a powerful position, especially when spreading rumours about certain hospitals or about the researcher. No informed consent form, website, business card or information sheet could prevent this kind of thing happening.

Thus, well-known scientists had a reputation to lose, while patients, just by pointing me in the direction of illegal or scandalous practices, could wreak much damage to hospitals. The power dimensions regarding the activities of unauthorised therapy providers are extremely complex. What these were exactly, in fact, was an integral part of the research itself! And as I shall argue in the How to Improve Research Ethics in Anthropological Fieldwork: Conceptual Tools section, awareness of its complexity through insight into what I call 'field sensitivity' is of greater importance than attempts to pre-regulate the PIs' responsibilities vis-à-vis research participants.

Unfortunately, requirements associated with FER can deter researchers from taking responsibility for their research actions rather than encouraging them to hold on to the integrity of their research. Thus, informed consent can turn into a license to treat mutually enriching conversations as research data controlled by the researcher. For example, uploading 'research data' in research archives allows the commodification of conversations that are not ours to trade. Calls have been made in support of alternative forms of research ethics that insist that the PIs of projects have to take responsibility for the 'data' or research materials co-produced with research participants (Dilger et al., 2018).

Data Management Requirements

In this section, I discuss data management requirements and the implications of making anthropological research materials subject to them for relations with research participants.

The 'anonymisation' of research participants is a longstanding practice in anthropology. There are various interpretations of its merits and of its feasibility (Berkhout, 2013), but a standard definition refers to 'keeping confidential the identity of research participants' (UK Data Service, 2024). In the case of my own research, effective anonymisation was never simple or without fallacies. Using pseudonyms, as is well known, does not mean that the research participant in question is not identifiable, as combinations of identifiers can reveal identities. Especially in anthropology, with its 'thick descriptions' (Geertz, 1993 [1973]), anonymisation might mean stripping research materials of much of their particularity, impeding their meaningful use in publication.

Anonymisation as a condition for informed consent cannot be guaranteed because circumstances and authorities may change (McMurray, 2024). Anthropologists, who receive stories and co-produce conversations with research participants, might refer to geographical names, institutions or companies, which at the time of research are uncontroversial but whose circumstances change over time. For instance, clinical scientists might tell us about a particular exciting but 'unproblematic' clinical application, which they or their competitors work on. Writing about the application or the hospital might actually endanger their job and freedom, when authorities at a later point of time decide to clamp down on hospitals using the particular application. Furthermore, anthropologists cannot *guarantee* anonymity, as legal authorities can demand research materials, for example, via a Law Enforcement Personal Data Request in the EU (LEPDR, 2024) and through other means elsewhere. For instance, anthropologist Martijn de Koning (2020) describes how he was obliged to appear as witness in a trial levied against his Salafi Muslim interlocutors. Especially with the increasingly widespread requirement of banking 'research data' in public registries and in university databases, it is important to ask how to think about 'data' in terms of ownership, gift and commoditisation. Rather than speaking about 'research data', I prefer to speak of 'research materials', as anthropology, unlike procedural sciences, rarely deals in 'research data' that can be passed on just with some explanatory 'metadata', as is requested by, for instance, the UK Data Service.

In anthropological research, interlocutors are crucial to what is referred to as the co-creation and co-production of knowledge (Meskel & Pels, 2005; Pels, 2000; Pels et al., 2018). For this reason, I often refer to them as research participants. Although in my research the focus was not the research participants themselves – after all, what brought us together was our interest in our common concern of international science regulation – their experience and the conditions of their experiences were essential to the conversation. The path along which the conversation developed, however, was one where we created and negotiated together, endpoints were redefined and the afterlife of research materials was negotiated to minimise potential harm to research participants. In other words, research participants had a say in the fate of what they contributed to the conversation; not so much in the sense of determining how the primary researcher should think or publish about their views – though our shared concern remained central to this – but more about how research materials were not to be used, curated or passed on to third parties.

Approaching people for a conversation requires goodwill and trust that we will not come to harm, even when fearing or disliking the other. It also requires some agreement about the aims and conditions under which we begin our conversation. In the 'field', I visit regulators, bioethicists, hospitals, laboratories and scientists who have radically different viewpoints on what is 'good regulation' and 'good science'. With the first two steps in place, it is possible for the vulnerable to express views that clash with dominant discourses. With just a basic sense of security, we could agree that we need to find out how scientific and regulatory practices evolve and play out unequally in a global context. We could then discuss how these insights could acknowledge various positions and views in a global context, reflect on the relation between regulation and international collaborative practices and discuss ideas for regulatory change.

Research participants knew that they had little say on my views in publications (with some exceptions), but they realised that I acknowledge the legitimacy of their position in their own terms, and that I wanted them to mould my understanding and influence my views. So, much effort went into making sure that we understood each other. Again, a certain amount of trust and security were necessary: I trusted that conversation partners would try to understand what I intended to say and that they would not intentionally misrepresent me to colleagues; in turn, research participants trusted that I faithfully understood the particular context that conditions their views and practices, thereby acknowledging the legitimacy of their position as explained in their terms. Indirectly, I knew that they trust that, whether I agree or not, I would not intentionally violate their trust by jeopardising this understanding, for instance, by passing on 'data' distilled from the conversation without the afore-mentioned qualifications.

What I took away was an integration of our worlds and thoughts on a particular topic. A decontextualised use would not just thwart the integrity of the project but also the integrity of all involved in its co-production. Its result is not so much a finished product that can be passed on as data but a new landscape.

It is the author that introduces this landscape and gives it their particular direction, but it is the partners in conversation whose 'gifts' need to be respected and protected in the spirit in which they were presented. Whether research materials should become part of careers, assessed by measures such as the Research and Excellence Framework (REF) in the United Kingdom, or databanks can legitimately be 'owned' by a university is therefore questionable.

The variety of circumstances and aims of research participants meant that I needed to consider my approach to anonymisation. Some scientists worried about attracting undesired attention, while others hoped for attention. Higher-level Heads of Laboratories usually show the 'public face of the lab' and encourage the use of their name in publications. But when talking of reputational risk, I would explain how I would deal with the issues in question. On the whole, this meant I followed a variety of strategies of anonymisation: in some cases, I would anonymise personal names and laboratories, but in others, the settings and circumstances had to be altered as well. All of this could not be explained in an information sheet or consent form, as many of the issues appeared along the path of our conversation. In fact, though keen for me to spread their views, quite a few scientists were not prepared to sign consent forms.

Anonymisation, then, is multiple. Each anonymisation needs to take into consideration a variety of factors, ranging from a person's vulnerability, that of their associates, the sensitivity of what was said, the political and social context, their international position, their finances and the uniqueness of their circumstances. In other words, I needed to know what constituted risk factors for them. This, I could only partly gauge in advance of our conversation. A fuller picture could only develop through our meetings. Careful consideration led me to include research materials using real names when these were already publicly available but not in all cases. Quoting depended on ramifications. In other words, I had to take into account the circumstances in which hundreds of conversations took place, but what I wrote transcended the separate conversations. For this reason, I consider my responsibility to be twofold: first, in relation to the way that 'raw' research materials could be accessed, and second, in terms of how the research would reach 'the public', as it concerned a bigger picture that none of us could have known beforehand. Although the latter can be problematic, I concern myself here with the former.

Since the coming into force of the GDPR in the EU in 2018, universities in the UK have introduced more prohibitive FER with a focus on 'informed consent'. Ironically, they usually use the legal ground of 'public interest' rather than 'consent' as the basis for processing data. According to the GDPR, scientific research that is in the public interest may apply various exemptions regarding a range of rights enjoyed by research participants: to be informed, to access, to rectification, to erasure, to restrict processing, to data portability and to object (ICO, 2024). The application of the exemptions must be necessary and proportionate and needs to be considered on a case-by-case basis. RECs are not very helpful in this regard, which is why most informed consent forms say that data will be stored and archived for a certain period of time or indefinitely in the archives of funders or universities, in the public interest. In addition, universities are often deemed to be the owners of the intellectual property 'in all items whether in paper, electronic or other form created or devised by their staff in the course of their employment', though, as is the case with the University of Sussex (2024), 'they are automatically assigned to the creator of an original work' (not to research participants). Together with the fact that no guarantee can be given that the researcher will not have to yield data to state authorities, there is much pressure on researchers to bank their data in university or other archives.

In short, given that I co-create research materials with hundreds of co-researchers, the use and publication of those materials need to be conditional. Some key concepts used in data management need to be reconsidered in the context of anthropology. First, the notion of 'research data' is not suitable for much social science research, as it refers to research materials that are turned into commodified information (Pels et al., 2018). These research materials, co-produced through various kinds of social and personal relations for certain academic and public aim, do not easily lend themselves to sharing with third parties without specified aims, and second, the notions of 'informant' and 'interlocutor' are problematic, as their various meanings indicate that a person gives or shares neutral information that can be stored, passed on or sold without causing ethical or other issues. This is because the meaning and significance of both raw and processed ethnographic materials are highly context dependent. I suggest, therefore, that anthropologists think about research materials in terms of 'bundles of usership', originally, a legal concept referring to who, how, when and for what research materials may be used. More about this below.

The Inadequacy of Formalised Research Ethics in Practice

Countries have different cultures of ethics review. While in the United Kingdom's research culture, it can sometimes feel as though a code of behaviour prevails based on 'guilty until proven innocent', ethics review in the social sciences is not institutionalised in all countries. If to protect the vulnerable in other countries, the enforcement of alien standards of FER might be viewed as patronising or 'colonial'. As a result, European researchers introduce their projects using information sheets that define the role of research participants in the research process and ask for an unnegotiable consent form, which explains the conditions under which their 'data' are taken and stored, to be signed. Such invitations describe the contents and scope of the conversation (often as a list of questions) and the direction of the process of interaction (e.g., a meeting plan; recording conditions; storage; a time limit for withdrawal). It is not surprising that anthropologists are tempted to stretch research ethics, are in denial of the grey area of covert research and attempt to adjust the research location to their requirements, odd adaptations that some researchers may make to 'comply' to the demands of FER.

In one example, the sheer embarrassment of the process of 'consenting' research participants led one junior researcher on a European project to ask a scientist for a signature only *after* they had ended their conversation. This, the researcher explained, was because their shared local identity had led the scientist to share his time and his views as a gift that could not be contracted. He was open to doing her a favour but not to contractual exchange.

Another example relates to the claimed differences between anthropologists who tend to have open, fiduciary relations and those who assume undercover roles in their research. For instance, anthropologists who walk into a shop to see if an illegal substance is for sale will not brandish their informed consent forms – they are assumed to conduct covert research. Under the influence of FER, the difference between 'open' and 'covert' research has become polarised, as 'open' anthropologists do not want to be burdened by the criticism received by 'covert' researchers. But in reality, between open and covert research, there exists a large grey area: even when shuddering at the idea of undercover research, an anthropologist openly conducting research on sexual harassment at rave events would not advertise this.

A last example concerns the adjustment of the location of fieldwork to meet the formalised requirements of research ethics. Impressed by the ethics requirements set by some RECs to gain ethics permission from a national ethics committee in developing countries, a junior anthropologist felt it necessary to prompt a well-known university in China to set one up so as to receive research permission. This could have far-reaching political consequences for large numbers of social science researchers.

These examples not only show the paternalistic attitude to the enforcement of FER in other countries; they also illustrate how anthropologists feel threatened by such requirements, making 'unethical' adjustments to the field location and trying to 'compromise' requirements of formalised research ethics with local norms and values. In the current atmosphere, notions of informed consent and discussion around covert and open research practices have become polarised and hidden.

In the discussion above, we saw that requirements of informed consent, information sheets and institutional research permissions are inadequate as they do not take into account the complex relations of power in which vulnerability is embedded. Furthermore, contracting of research participants, which enables the storing of 'research data' in data archives, commodifies data and can undo the identity protection measures that have been agreed as necessary in the course of the research. And finally, the paternalism inherent to defining what is best for 'the other' detracts from the ethical issues inherent at stake in the research. In short, FER tends to deskill PIs and remove important responsibilities from them when it comes to the protection of research participants and research materials. This trend could be somewhat reversed by ensuring that REC members are experts of the discipline and location of research. This, I argue, is best done through the devolution of research ethics and its re-rooting in the research curriculum.

HOW TO IMPROVE RESEARCH ETHICS IN ANTHROPOLOGICAL FIELDWORK: CONCEPTUAL TOOLS

In the sections above, I suggested that the conceptual tools of 'field sensitivity' and 'bundles of usership' and the devolution of RECs and their re-rooting in the discipline can help us to reflect on ethical issues occurring in research practice. Below I elaborate on how these concepts could help us in dealing with vulnerability, research materials and research ethics training. These concepts, I believe, are not only useful in the context of the ethics governance of social science in the United Kingdom, particularly when it concerns fieldwork but also elsewhere.

Field Sensitivity

As argued above, anthropological fieldwork characteristically has an open-ended research design, allowing for flexibility and contingencies, as relationships and ethics are typically negotiated 'in the field' and, often, over considerable time (Lederman, 2016). The human relationships involved in fieldwork vary too, ranging from the level of intimacy, trust and loyalty to the sensitivity and controversy of research issues concerned. The design of ethnographic research, then, varies considerably, can be based on close or loose collaboration and may involve powerful or vulnerable individuals or both. When working with powerful research participants, known as studying up (Alvesalo-Kuusi & Whyte, 2018; Armbruster & Laerke, 2008; Nader, 1972; Smith, 2006) such as military personnel, for example, or government officials, researchers may have to take into account different sensitivities compared to when engaging with vulnerable research participants (studying down). But it is important to go beyond our conception of power. We need to recognise the vulnerabilities of the powerful and the power of the vulnerable: they are part and parcel, not just of structures of power and systems of authority but of an unfolding densely patterned tapestry of relations in which our research is embedded.

I suggest that by using the notion of 'field sensitivity' one can chart the ways in which research may have to deal with different kinds of sensitivities related to the authority, power and vulnerability of the people researchers work with and co-produce research materials with. As the examples in Formalised Research Ethics and Anthropological Research section showed, these sensitivities affect how research ethics needs to be approached in the field as they are weighed against research aims, methodology, research impact and the management of research materials.

Bundles of Usership

Anthropological research materials are co-produced with individuals and groups (varying from co-researchers, interlocutors and strangers to friends, acquaintances and collaborators), sometimes by design and other times serendipitously. This does not only involve various degrees of trust, but it can also entail diverse regulatory bodies (as part of the institutions and phenomena we research in different countries), making for notions and practices of knowledge ownership and possession that cannot be generalised. An important question here is whether, how and when to store research materials, while trying to conform to the varying and sometimes clashing requirements of the data regulators, such as those associated with implementing the GDPR, universities, research funders and agreements negotiated with co-researchers. Further questions arise as a result of the various notions of how ownership relates to authorship and transnational research collaboration.

As indicated above, when taken out of context and without careful scrutiny of their use, sharing research materials can endanger the people involved in the research, attract the wrong kind of attention or lend itself to quasi-scientific use. For this reason, PIs have an obligation to use research materials in a suitable collaborative context (in accordance with arrangements made with co-researchers) to make the research materials available in the shape (raw data, data sets, processed data, article, pamphlet, briefing, etc.) that most suitably serves the research aim. For example, during participant observation, many relations formed with people are informal and serendipitous (and need to be so for research that is of public interest, e.g. research in oppressive countries, or of companies conducting clandestine practices). This need is recognised by the GDPR, which does not make informed consent a prerequisite for the processing of information (it is only one of its grounds) and makes allowances for researchers to protect their resources on a par with journalism (EU-GDPR, 2016/679).

To deal with the complexities around the use and ownership of research materials ('research data'), these notions can be understood in terms of 'bundles of usership arrangements'. 'Bundles of usership' is an amalgamation of 'bundles of rights', which ascribes certain rights invested in ownership and 'usership' (Dickenson, 2007, p. 13, citing Honoré, 1961). Dickenson, in her *Property in the Body* (2007), clarifies this by explaining the difference between being the owner or the user of something. In the car business, for example, 'car usership' (or leasing) is contrasted with car ownership, as it does not entail a large investment in buying a car and does not involve various responsibilities, such as paying taxes and servicing. I take the notion of 'usership' to indicate the many ways in which people can lay claims on something.

Thus, the use of project materials I worked with was restricted in at least four ways: first, classified information (*neibu*) received from a stem cell research department in a Chinese university: the materials are not for quotation nor for sharing with third parties. Second, knowledge given to me about an institute that I can also find in publicly available materials: I may quote and share it. Third, one original insight relevant to my research on the meaning of 'good regulation' which I can only use with permission and conditionally. Fourth, other original insights relevant to my research on the same, which I was encouraged to use. Usership, then, refers to negotiable bundles of various kinds of rights to usage, entailing responsibilities and duties regarding various groups of people, including funders, the university and a range of people involved in our research in diverse ways, including ourselves. In brief, viewing research materials in terms of 'bundles of use' allows us to become more aware about the conditions in which the research materials were gifted to us.

Devolved Research Ethics Rooted in the Curriculum

The complexity of research ethics and data management in relation to ethnographic research design, fieldwork and research materials necessitates training that can guarantee maximal ethnographic research integrity. Preliminary research shows that there is a connection between the administrative organisation of ethics review and how researchers are able to reflect on the ethical aspects of research (Sleeboom-Faulkner & McMurray, 2018). This connection, I believe, needs to be understood in the context of research ethics organisation, communication between REC and researchers and ethics training. First, the level of centralisation of RECs (centralised, devolved to faculty, devolved to department, etc.) is important to the kind of experts likely to review research submitted to a REC; second, appropriate methods of communication in discussing ethics review applications (whether solely digital, impersonal; in consultation with a committee; through personal guidance) are crucial to reflection on the suitability of REC feedback on research design; and third, suitable methods of research ethics training are crucial to the learning of both students and staff. Training through instructions on a website, in class practising filling out ethics review applications or in class discussions on how research ethics are an integral part of research epistemology (Fabian, 1971) is likely to result in different levels of understanding.

There are good reasons for having research ethics applications reviewed by experts in the field of the planned research, as they are likely to have a more in-depth understanding of the sensitivity of research materials involved. Whereas FER tends to place the emphasis on protecting the 'data' of research participants, a growing demand for data sharing by universities and funders across Europe puts pressure on researchers to share ethnographic research materials with third parties. This can lead to contradictory demands and confusion. At the same time, ethnographers are obliged to take into account different understandings of 'data ownership' and 'data sharing', i.e. bundles of usership, as the integrity of managing research materials largely depends on conforming to arrangements made during fieldwork with interlocutors.

Tailor-made training is needed to enable researchers to deal with the conflicting demands implicit in research ethics and research data management placed on PIs and research participants. Usually, there is little financial capacity available for such training, as investment in the area of research ethics often relates to software and the organisation of review systems. Here, it would be useful to have some reflection on what kind of coordinated embedding of research ethics and data management would be conducive to the integrity of ethical oversight and data management in ethnographic research. Such an effort could greatly benefit from more insight into the history and governance of regulatory variations across different countries. For anthropology, cross-border generalisations about training are hard to obtain, due to national and regional variations in models of research governance, risk assessment, data archiving, funding and educational institutions.

Devolution of ethics review in qualitative research in the social sciences, including participant observation, to the level of disciplines could be the beginning of a more adequate embedding of ethical training and dealing with research materials. The devolution of research ethics rooted in the discipline of the planned research, in particular when making use of ethnographic field methods, including participant observation and interviews, not only would allow ethics to be understood as part of research epistemology but could also provide opportunities for collective imaginary practices. For instance, by imagining the circumstances in which fieldwork takes place through role plays, discussion and mutual questioning, a more solid notion of fieldwork ethics will come within reach of student cohorts and staff.

CONCLUSION

Since formalised research ethics and generic models of data management have been introduced into the social sciences, a needless artificial separation has come about between FER and how ethical issues are constituted in the field. These regimes have also introduced various complications: first, their paternalist bias with a focus on 'studying down' has blunted sensitivity to the complexity of power relations in the field. The notion of 'field sensitivity' directs attention to the multiplicity of power relations and to the nuances that field experience adds to relations of power in practice. It is through these practices that the ramifications of power relations for the ethics of research activities and research materials need to be understood. It should be possible to take into account the expected 'field sensitivity' when dealing with research ethics submissions, so as to avoid a demand for the use of inappropriate measures of informed consent and permissions.

Second, informed consent forms and information sheets have facilitated the researcher in acquiring contractual consent to take away, store and use 'research data' from their co-creators. As indicated above, research materials in anthropological research have meaning in the context in which they were created and may be of great importance to those involved in their co-production. Where research materials are sensitive and matter to the lives of co-producers – not least because unauthorised access to them could cause direct harm or put them at risk – there needs to be agreement on their use. I have suggested that the notion of 'bundles of usership' allows researchers to think through the way in which research materials need to be discussed, stored and used conditionally. Conditions of, and permissions for, the usership of research materials might vary for storage in registers and archives, passing on to third parties and the use in publications. It should be possible for anthropologists to note the relevance of conditionality of usership on research applications for which data sharing may otherwise be a default requirement.

Third, as illustrated above, FER prescribes ethical procedures and requires permissions that clash with what is ethical and workable in the light of research epistemology. This has resulted in both the misleading of ethical review committees and a 'thin' reflexive engagement with ethical considerations by researchers. Preliminary research has shown that the severity of these clashes in the case of anthropological research partly correlate with the embedding of RECs in the institutional hierarchy of universities, whereby organisational distance tends to be accompanied by miscommunication, bureaucracy and inadequate ethics review (Sleeboom-Faulkner & McMurray, 2018).

Above, I have suggested that a devolution of ethics review to the discipline, together with a rooting of ethics training in the anthropological curriculum, would benefit research preparation and its ethics in its proper context. Research ethics training then would include reflection on the vulnerabilities of the powerful and the power of the vulnerable, including on the impact of research ethics on research participants and the research epistemology. Expert panels would collectively reflect on power dimensions (e.g., authorities, leverage, knowledge, tools, access) and vulnerabilities (e.g., poverty, secrets, employment, position, disability, resources) relevant to those directly and indirectly affected by the research, a practice already adopted, for example, by the devolved ethics board of the Amsterdam Institute for Social Science Research (2024). Here, the explication of concerns that are shared and not shared with research participants, and the necessity of basic forms of trust for the co-creation of any research materials, would be essential to judgements about the ethicality of research. And finally, the way in which co-produced 'research materials' are used and controlled needs to be thought through in a wider context beyond the primary sites of knowledge production. This, it needs to be pointed out, is best done in an awareness of the international diversity of the governance of research ethics and research materials in the social sciences.

ACKNOWLEDGEMENTS

The long-term research this chapter is based on was financially supported by the European Research Council (ERC: 283219), the Economic and Social Science Research Council (ESRC: RES-350-27-0002; ES/E00542X/1; ES/I018107/1) and the British Academy/Leverhulme Foundation (SRF20\200078).

REFERENCES

Alvesalo-Kuusi, A., & Whyte, D. (2018). Researching the powerful: A call for the reconstruction of research ethics. *Sociological Research Online*, *23*(1), 136–152. https://doi.org/10.1177/1360780417747O

Amsterdam Institute for Social Science Research. (2024). *Ethics, integrity and plagiarism*. https://aissr.uva.nl/our-research/ethics-and-integrity/ethics-and-integrity.html?cb#Ethical-Review-of-Research

Armbruster, H., & Laerke, A. (Eds.). (2008). *Taking sides: Ethics, politics, and fieldwork in anthropology*. Berghahn. https://doi.org/10.3167/9781845454210

Berkhout, S. G. (2013). Private talk: Testimony, evidence, and the practice of anonymization in research. *International Journal of Feminist Approaches to Bioethics*, *6*(1), 19–45. https://doi.org/10.2979/intjfemappbio.6.1.19

Caplan, P. (2003). Introduction: Anthropology and ethics. In P. Caplan (Ed.), *The ethics of anthropology: Debates and dilemmas* (pp. 1–34). Routledge. https://www.routledge.com/The-Ethics-of-Anthropology-Debates-and-Dilemmas/Caplan/p/book/9780415296434 de Koning, M. (2020). "For them it is just a story, for me it is my life". Ethnography and the security gaze: Academic research with "Salafi" Muslims in the Netherlands. *Journal of Muslims in Europe*, *9*(2), 220–239. https://doi.org/10.1163/22117954-12341418

de Koning, M., Meyer, B., Moors, A., & Pels, P. (2019). Guidelines for anthropological research: Data management, ethics, and integrity. *Ethnography*, *20*(2), 170–174. https://doi.org/10.1177/1466138119843312

Dickenson, D. (2007). *Property in the body. Feminist perspectives*. CUP, Law, Medicine and Ethics. https://doi.org/10.1017/CBO9780511618659

Dilger, H.-J., Pels, P., & Sleeboom-Faulkner, M. (2018, December 22). Guidelines for data management and scientific integrity in ethnography. *Ethnography*, *20*(1), 3–7. https://doi.org/10.1177/1466138118819

Dingwall, R. (2008). The ethical case against ethical regulation in humanities and social science research, *Twenty-First Century Society*, *3*(1), 1–12. https://doi.org/10.1080/17450140701749189

EthNav. (2019). *EthNav*. https://www.theasa.org/ethics/ethnav.html

European Parliament. (2016). Regulation (EU). *Official Journal of the European Union*, L 119/1 EU-GDPR 2016/679. https://www.privacy-regulation.eu/en/index.htm

Fabian, J. (1971). Language, history and anthropology, *Philosophy of the Social Sciences*, *1*, 19–47. https://doi.org/10.1177/004839317100100102

Geertz, C. (Ed.). (1993 [1973]). Thick description: Towards an interpretive theory of culture. In *The interpretation of culture* (pp. 3–30). Fontana Books.

Honoré, A. M. (1961). Ownership. In A. G. Guest (Ed.), *Oxford essays in jurisprudence*. Oxford University Press. https://dullbonline.wordpress.com/2020/08/19/a-m-honore-ownership-in-a-g-guest-ed-oxford-essays-in-jurisprudence-oxford-university-press-1961/

ICO. (2024). *A guide to the data protection exemptions*. https://ico.org.uk/for-organisations/uk-gdpr-guidance-and-resources/exemptions/a-guide-to-the-data-protection-exemptions/#ex16

Lederman, R. (2016). Fieldwork double-bound in human research-ethics reviews: Disciplinary competence, or regulatory compliance and the muting of disciplinary values. In W. van den Hoonaard & A. Hamilton (Eds.), *The ethics rupture* (pp. 43–72). University of Toronto Press. https://utorontopress.com/9781442626089/the-ethics-rupture/

LEPDR. (2024). *Law enforcement personal data requests*. https://www.sgul.ac.uk/about/governance/policies/law-enforcement-personal-data-requests

McMurray, J. (2024). The ends of consent: Professional ethics in the context of Xinjiang (2021). *Social Anthropology/Anthropologie Sociale*, *32*(2), 57–72. https://doi.org/10.3167/saas.2024.320205

Meskel, L., & Pels, P. (Eds.). (2005). *Embedding ethics*. Berg. https://doi.org/10.4324/9781003085249

Meyer, B., Moors, A., & Pels, P. (2018, January 23 and 24). Research seminar on 'Research ethics and data management'. University of Amsterdam.

Mills, D. (2003). "Like a horse in blinkers?" A political history of anthropology's research ethics. In P. Caplan (Ed.), *The ethics of anthropology: Debates and dilemmas* (pp. 37–54). Routledge. https://utorontopress.com/9781442626089/the-ethics-rupture/

Nader, L. (1972). Up the anthropologist-perspectives gained from studying up. In D. Hymes (Ed.), *Reinventing anthropology* (pp. 284–311). Pantheon Books. https://www.dourish.com/classes/readings/Nader-StudyingUp.pdf

Pels, P. (1999). Professions of duplexity: A prehistory of ethical codes in anthropology. *Current Anthropology*, *40*, 101–136. https://doi.org/10.1086/200001

Pels, P. (2000). The trickster's dilemma: Ethics and the technologies of the anthropological self. In M. Strathern (Ed.), *Audit cultures* (pp. 135–172). Routledge. https://www.routledge.com/Audit-Cultures-Anthropological-Studies-in-Accountability-Ethics-and-the-Academy/Strathern/p/book/9780415233279

Pels, P., Boog, I., Florusbosch, H. J., Kripe, Z., Minter, T., Postma, M., Sleeboom-Faulkner, M., Simpson, B., Dilger, H., Schönhuth, M., von Poser, A., Castillo, R. C. A., Lederman, R., & Richards-Rissetto, H. (2018). Data management in anthropology: The next phase in ethics governance? *Social Anthropology*, *26*, 391–413. https://doi.org/10.1111/1469-8676.12526

School of Law, Politics and Sociology. (2024). *Research and governance*. http://www.sussex.ac.uk/lps/internal/students/researchethics#:~:text=The%20University%20of%20Sussex%20requires,they%20also%20involve%20legal%20protections

Simpson, B. (2011). Ethical moments: Future directions in ethical review for ethnography. *Journal of the Royal Anthropological Institute*, *17*(2), 377–393. https://doi.org/10.1111/j.1467-9655.2011.01685.x

Simpson, E. (2016). Is anthropology legal? Earthquakes, blitzkrieg, and ethical futures. *Focaal*, *74*, 113–128. https://eprints.soas.ac.uk/22407/

Sleeboom-Faulkner, M., & McMurray, J. (2018). The impact of the new EU GDPR on ethics governance and social anthropology. *Anthropology Today*, *34*(5), 22–23. https://doi.org/10.1111/1467-8322.12462

Sleeboom-Faulkner, M., Simpson, B., Burgos-Martinez, E., & McMurray, J. (2017). The formalisation of social-science research ethics: How did we get there? *Journal of Ethnographic Theory*, *7*(1), 71–79. https://doi.org/10.14318/hau7.1.010

Smith, K. E. (2006). Problematising power relations in 'elite' interviews. *Geoforum*, *37*(4), 643–653. https://doi.org/10.1016/j.geoforum.2005.11.002

UK Data Service. (2024). *Anonymising qualitative data*. https://ukdataservice.ac.uk/learning-hub/research-data-management/anonymisation/anonymising-qualitative-data/

University of Sussex. (2024). *Data management*. http://www.sussex.ac.uk/library/researchdatamanagement/create/intellectualpropertyrights

Vassy, C., & Keller, R. (2008). Faut-il contrôler les aspects éthiques de la recherche en sciences sociales, et comment? *Mouvements*, *55*, 128–141. https://www.cairn.info/revue-mouvements-2008-3-page-128.htm

Yang, M. (1994). *Gifts, favors, and banquets: The art of social relationships in China*. Cornell University Press. https://www.cornellpress.cornell.edu/book/9780801495922/gifts-favors-and-banquets/#bookTabs=1

CHAPTER 12

ADVANCING INDIGENOUS HEALTH PARTNERSHIPS: ETHICAL APPROACHES TO QUALITATIVE RESEARCH AND HEALTH SYSTEMS IMPROVEMENTS

Lloy Wylie[a], Joyla Furlano[b] and Alana Kehoe[a]

[a] *Western University, Canada*
[b] *Queen's University, Canada*

ABSTRACT

Indigenous people and communities all over the world face significant barriers to healthcare and experience exacerbated health inequities. In this chapter, we reflect on the challenges that Indigenous health partnerships face including in the context of institutional research ethics processes, drawing on examples from a health services research project undertaken in Ontario. We focus on ways to improve Indigenous health partnerships, make suggestions as to how researchers and service providers can engage in meaningful partnerships that honour the role of Indigenous peoples, and suggest strategies for undertaking ethical qualitative research in such a way that it can contribute to transformative change that supports Indigenous peoples' health and well-being. We advocate that research should be conducted in partnership with communities to identify priorities. Such partnerships, we argue, are more successful when based on formalized guiding principles that are agreed upon between parties prior to the start of the research and oriented to actionable recommendations for change. Finally, these partnerships should be tailored to each Indigenous community and based

Reframing Qualitative Research Ethics
Advances in Research Ethics and Integrity, Volume 12, 197–215

Published under exclusive licence by Emerald Publishing Limited
ISSN: 2398-6018/doi:10.1108/S2398-601820250000012012

on collaborative co-decision-making. We conclude by proposing that university research ethics committees and boards should improve their own capacity to work in partnership with communities, and this should include working toward an understanding of Indigenous ethics. Ultimately, while successful partnerships are possible, they require re-evaluating the current systems in which we work: it follows that systems of ethical approvals based on colonial norms of control should be redesigned.

Keywords: Health; partnership; Indigenous; Canada; ethics

INTRODUCTION

Indigenous communities across the world experience poorer health outcomes relative to their non-Indigenous counterparts, and there are a range of social and Indigenous determinants of health that shape these poor outcomes (Adelson, 2005; de Leeuw et al., 2015; Reading, 2015; Reading & Wien, 2009). At the same time, Indigenous people face significant challenges in accessing appropriate and quality healthcare services, where healthcare systems are not culturally safe (Allan & Smylie, 2015; Allen et al., 2020; Browne et al., 2022; Wylie & McConkey, 2019). To address the challenges faced by Indigenous peoples in Canada, there needs to be a multifaceted approach. We argue that qualitative social sciences-based health research that follows Indigenous ethical protocols can be valuable in that partnership for change.

We have seen that although research and health service partnerships can be a way to support transformative change to better meet the needs of Indigenous people within healthcare systems, past negative experiences of research mean that many Indigenous communities are reluctant to participate in new research projects (de Leeuw et al., 2015; George et al., 2020). Whereas partnerships often fall short of ensuring Indigenous perspectives guide the work in both research and service, we propose that qualitative research that is undertaken in an ethical manner can support transformative change in this context. This chapter presents the potential role of qualitative researchers as agents of change, considers a range of challenges stemming from taking on research partnerships, explores navigating research ethics processes in this context, and discusses ethical issues that arose over the course of a health services research project undertaken in Ontario, Canada. In addition, we present ways that researchers and service providers can ensure that partnerships respect and honour the role of Indigenous peoples and create meaningful and successful partnerships which can lead to sustainable change and enhanced justice in Indigenous health and health research. We suggest strategies for ethical qualitative research to contribute to change that supports Indigenous peoples' health and well-being through supporting transformative health systems change. We then present recommendations for how research ethics boards can address the disconnection between university and community processes, to ensure that inclusive research ethics protocols are developed which emphasize the carrying out of social science research guided by Indigenous ethics.

PRINCIPLES OF PARTNERSHIP AND ETHICAL QUALITATIVE RESEARCH

In exploring the role of ethical qualitative research, we draw on an earlier study carried out by the first author, *Engaging for Change*,[1] which focuses on building partnerships between Indigenous communities and healthcare organizations in order to improve the experiences of Indigenous people when they access healthcare, as well as our general reflections as a team about ethical partnership research with Indigenous communities. Although partnerships are valorized as an important aspect of ethical practice and encouraged across government, public services, and university research, many barriers remain to ensuring that community voices inform the direction of those partnerships. In 1997, the *Canadian Journal of Public Health* published Scott and Thurston's framework for effective partnerships with vulnerable populations, noting that despite rhetoric, reality falls short (Scott & Thurston, 1997). Elliott et al. (2000) advanced this discussion by describing three types of partnerships: in this framework, cooperative partnerships are characterized by organizations setting the parameters, whereas coordinated partnerships involve a more consultative approach, and collaborative partnerships involve shared ownership, control, and implementation. Our qualitative research agenda has focused on how partnerships with Indigenous communities, including formalized agreements with defined deliverables, can address healthcare jurisdictional gaps and chronic underfunding that often mean life or death for Indigenous people, specifically those living in reserve communities (Wylie et al., 2020). The research project used as an example in this chapter focused on ways that research can support partnerships and knowledge brokerage, specifically aiming to ensure that Indigenous perspectives inform the expectations of partnerships with healthcare organizations. Building on this, we aim to explore how these partnerships can be created and sustained in ethical ways, and, specifically, in what ways research support health systems partnerships can facilitate the changes Indigenous people want to see in healthcare policy and practice.

As researchers of policy and organizational change, we often recognize a disconnect between what is said in policy documents and what is actually done in practice. Patient-centered care is a common mantra across healthcare organizations, despite the fact that protocols and practices are primarily driven by organizational and provider needs and preferences. Although policy mandates can support improved partnerships and patient-centered care, there is no guarantee that researchers and healthcare providers have the capacity and knowledge to be good partners and care providers, whose efforts lead to beneficial outcomes desired by Indigenous people. As an example, in the renewed Ontario public health standards of 2018, for which Indigenous organizations led important change to the language, the Ontario Ministry of Health and Long-Term Care (MoHLTC) created new standards mandating health units to develop collaborative partnerships between public health units and communities guided by five principles:

(1) *relationship-building* to foster trust and create safe spaces where Indigenous Peoples feel welcome and heard;

(2) *recognition, respect, and mutuality* to account for historical and cultural contexts and the unique social positions of Indigenous Peoples;
(3) *self-determination* by acknowledging rights of self-governance and enabling Indigenous Peoples' agency;
(4) *timely communication and knowledge exchange* for open and transparent communication;
(5) *coordination* to ensure effective and efficient collaboration (MoHLTC, 2018, pp. 16–17).

Despite this 2018 mandate, the COVID-19 pandemic showed the extent to which gaps and challenges continue as far as partnerships between public health agencies and Indigenous communities are concerned.

Even with the presence of both evidence-based recommendations and new political mandates, healthcare organizations' partnerships with Indigenous communities continue to be fraught with tension (O'Neil et al., 2016). When organizations attempt to develop these partnerships, they are often presented with challenges that they have not navigated before, including processes that are fraught with complex ethical issues that were not foreseen. The qualitative research project that this chapter will focus on aimed to support ethical partnerships to increase the voice of Indigenous partners in hospital decision-making, drawing on past experience from formalized partnerships between First Nations communities and healthcare organizations. Health systems researchers are well positioned to support Indigenous partners by, for example, collecting and sharing evidence around ethical and practical challenges that arise in healthcare partnerships that often prevent Indigenous Peoples' exercise of co-decision-making. Following ethical principles can ensure culturally appropriate implementation and integrated knowledge translation, in which the perspectives of Indigenous Peoples guide health systems improvements and so inform strategies for effective and meaningful partnerships to improve the healthcare system's ability to provide quality and culturally safe services for all Indigenous people.

Ethical qualitative research practices emphasize "the importance of relationship building, equitable partnerships, and equal distribution of benefits, among others to meaningfully engage with Indigenous community partners, and to implement both Indigenous and Western Ways of Knowing" (Stefanelli et al., 2017, p. 15). However, partnerships take time and resources to develop and can be strengthened through formalized agreements (O'Neil et al., 2016). Here, we provide key elements of successful partnerships, explore gaps, and recommend ways to build meaningful health system partnerships with Indigenous Peoples, drawing on principles and lessons from qualitative health research. Through this integration of Indigenous ways of knowing, researchers and decision-makers may come to understand that good research and practice seek to transform colonial systems in order to advance justice. While these are honourable goals that can support the process of truth and reconciliation in Canada, how can qualitative research advance this work, and what ethical challenges are faced along the way?

Community-based participatory research (CBPR) is an approach to increasing the participation and control of research by community partners, with the aim of ensuring that the outcomes of research are beneficial for the community. Following Indigenous research ethics, this approach creates "safety, by ensuring researchers work with and for Indigenous peoples themselves" (George et al., 2020, p. 5). At the same time, community participation benefits academia by including parallel and complementary insights from traditional knowledge as well as community experiences and expertise (Edwards et al., 2008). In general terms, qualitative research based in community partnerships starts with community engagement around the key areas and issues of concern, to ensure that the research aligns with the priorities of the community. This leads to a selection of the sites and people that will be focused on. Once that focus is decided, the next dialogue determines what we want to know and the themes to explore, which in turn inform the approach for data collection: the research interview questions, situations to observe, and documents to review. Once field research data collection has happened, interview transcripts are reviewed with respondents to ensure accuracy and consent, prior to the analysis of anonymized transcripts, observation notes, and organizational documents, to identify emerging themes (Denzin & Lincoln, 2011).

The next stage of ethical qualitative research is to share the findings. Community partners and research participants are engaged to help develop the analysis and understand the implications of the research findings and to determine how to share this information. Although universities often emphasize the value of peer-reviewed publications over other kinds of outputs, community partners are usually more interested in using the results to inform improvements in service provision and user's experiences. This engaged approach can be a promising way to bridge the gaps in translating research evidence into real-time healthcare settings, with the aim of addressing health disparities. Thus, CBPR approaches have been welcomed by communities due to the focus on collaboration that brings together community and academic-based knowledge and perspectives (Edwards et al., 2008). As George et al. (2020) note, ethical practice is based on values, as well as an acknowledgment that Indigenous people and their research allies value the knowledge that they bring to inform the research partnership. Related to this, research partnerships should ensure that an evidence-based approach is based on priorities set by the community, so that the research is able to respond to the specific needs of that community. Moreover, Oetzel et al. (2018) concluded that the CBPR conceptual model can explain key relational and structural pathways and so inform transformative change in health equity.

REFLECTIONS ON ETHICAL ISSUES IN HEALTH SERVICES RESEARCH

The research project began when I (first author) moved from British Columbia (BC) to Ontario. I had just completed an interdisciplinary PhD (political science, health services research, and nursing), where I drew on my training as a social scientist to take on health research. In addition to this academic training, I had been embedded in a transformative change process in BC, where significant political agreements and partnership work was being undertaken to address issues of Indigenous health, through transferring control of federally run health services to the First Nations of BC. In BC, trilateral agreements between the Government of Canada, the Government of BC, and the First Nations Health Society (representing all 203 First Nations communities in BC) included a mandate to improve health services for First Nations, specifically calling for First Nations people to be involved in the design and delivery of healthcare services. These agreements ensured that Indigenous health was on the agenda of the Ministry of Health, all health authorities, and every hospital. I was working for the BC First Nations Health Authority, as the senior advisor on health systems, responsible for facilitating and monitoring this work.

Ontario was a different place when I arrived in 2013. When I arrived at the hospital where I wanted to carry out research, there were blank stares when I asked about Indigenous health equity. I was even told that a hospital just provides clinical care, and that equity sounded like something from "the community," not relevant to a clinical institution. I was shocked to hear this but also knew that sharing what was happening in BC could support change in Ontario. My main priority was to explore how to support transformative work within the healthcare system in Ontario to advance Indigenous health equity. Thankfully, a colleague informed me of a fellowship from an agency that offered research funding aimed to advance compassion within the healthcare system in Ontario. I applied and was successful in getting funding to advance this research work.

My instincts were first to engage the community around the priorities that should be part of this research project, and so I sought advice from colleagues on how to initiate this research project, including ensuring an appropriate approach to get ethics approval from the university. This posed a chicken-and-egg problem for me: I needed to get ethical approval to speak to community partners about the issues, if I intended to formally collect this information and input to guide my research. While the ethics application required me to spell out the full details of the research project in order to be reviewed by the ethics board, I nevertheless tried to explain to the ethics officer that in community-driven research, community partners determine the research priorities, and therefore, I could not explain the full details of the research program without first engaging with Indigenous communities, which I was not allowed to do until receiving ethical approval. Unfortunately, my complications with the ethics process are far too common and demonstrate the institutional barriers that can be posed by an ethics review board with little experience in Indigenous ethics, a problem that researchers face when trying to work with Indigenous communities in a respectful and collaborative way. Recognizing that I was a human being first, I decided that I would simply meet with community partners in an informal capacity to get their guidance before writing up a research ethics protocol; even though I brought knowledge from working with Indigenous people in another part of the country, I knew that local Indigenous knowledge and experience had to guide the research. As stated by George et al. (2020), it is experiences like these that "highlight both the localised and global nature of Indigenous research, and especially ethics protocols, which in turn highlights the need to engage with Indigenous research participants during the design phases of research" (p. 3).

As someone deeply committed to advancing equity for people and communities excluded and marginalized by the healthcare system, I knew I had to orient myself to my new geographic and social realities. I met with leaders from Indigenous communities nearby, letting them know who I was and asking how I could support their goals for improving Indigenous people's experiences in the local healthcare system. I shared with them what things were like in BC, emphasizing the challenges as well as the commitments being made to advance culturally safe healthcare. People shared stories of poor experiences within the healthcare system, similar to those I knew of from BC. When I asked what was going on in the healthcare system that perpetuated those challenges, I was explicitly told: "Well that's your job to find out – it's your hospital. You go in there and find out why they treat our people so badly." Although I had never considered it "my hospital," I realized that I had an obligation to take some responsibility for the institution that I worked in. Thus, I had my direction and so developed a research program that focused on interviews with people working within the hospital about their knowledge, training, experience, and approach in providing care for Indigenous people. The community partners identified areas that were seen as priorities, where Indigenous patients were high users of the service, and/or where there was a history of poor experiences, including the emergency department, cancer care, mental health, maternity care, and diabetes. Once we had clarified the research plan, I submitted the ethical protocol accordingly.

My research project started off with a focus on the hospital environment. The first stage of the project involved interviewing 36 people who worked in or with the hospital, including 9 who identified as Indigenous. The interview guide focused on peoples' experience of providing care for Indigenous patients. Respondents were asked: what percentage of their patients were Indigenous; to share a positive and negative experience; what were the challenges they faced as care providers; what challenges did they think Indigenous patients faced; what support and resources did they have for providing quality care for Indigenous people; were there policies in place to support Indigenous care; and were they aware of and connected to Indigenous-specific community-based services for referrals and discharge. In addition, respondents were asked about the kind of training they had received in relation to Indigenous people, and what types of training did they want or need to feel more confident in providing care in this context.

In this project, we were able to identify a wide range of challenges, but at the same time, we discovered a desire among health professionals to improve the care and experiences of Indigenous people. Unfortunately, people were not sure how to do this, and the small amount of training they had undertaken only served to make them worried about saying the wrong thing when engaging Indigenous patients and families (Wylie & McConkey, 2019). The insights from this research have been published elsewhere (Wylie & McConkey, 2019; Wylie et al., 2020, 2021), and following this pilot project, I was funded for a further project that aimed to explore how to address the challenges that were discovered and how to build meaningful partnerships between Indigenous communities and healthcare organizations, specifically focusing on the hospital systems. Below we explore the challenges that this work identified, through the lens of ethical qualitative social science research in healthcare.

CHALLENGES AND PRINCIPLES FOR ETHICAL PARTNERSHIPS

Partnerships can increase health systems' ability to tailor care and integrate traditional practices, such as medicines, sweats, and smudging (Robbins & Dewar, 2011), improving Indigenous people's experiences and slowly combatting distrust toward medical establishments (Browne et al., 2016). Much work is needed to build trust in the healthcare system, as healthcare in Canada has an oppressive colonial history as well as systemic anti-Indigenous racism and structural violence to the present day (de Leeuw et al., 2015). Such distrust stems from racism that compromises patient care (seen in the high-profile preventable hospital deaths of Indigenous patients Brian Sinclair in 2008 and Joyce Echaquan in 2020) and historically from racially segregated Indian hospitals that were understaffed, underfunded, and used archaic and unjust practices, including enforced unnecessary hospitalization, physical restraints, and scientific experiments not permissible elsewhere.

Although further research would be valuable to explore the complexity, depth, and extent of challenges and solutions, qualitative research projects have helped us identify a range of gaps Indigenous people and communities experience working with healthcare organizations. The research work I had carried out previously about First Nations health governance in BC demonstrated some of the key challenges to partnerships. Even in the environment of a political commitment, signed into policy through a Framework Accord between federal, provincial, and First Nations governments, genuine partnership and co-creation of health systems and service delivery models remained a challenge (O'Neil et al., 2016).

I anticipated that the challenges could be even greater in the work I was to carry out in Ontario. No political commitments were in place to address these issues, and Indigenous health equity was not on the agenda of healthcare leadership or service providers at the start of the project in 2014. In addition, I was now working as a researcher, providing recommendations for change based on the evidence collected, whereas previously (in BC) I had been a representative of the First Nations Health Authority, mandated to advance the commitments made in the policy documents and to hold the partners accountable to those commitments. As the challenges in Ontario – where the role I held did not come with any authority to push for change – were very different, this would require a different approach, where I could not set the pace or approach of the institution's work to advance transformative change but rather was limited to providing evidence-based recommendations. Drawing on this research experience in Ontario, as well as our own experiences in Indigenous health research (L.W. in health services,

A.K. in emergency response, and J.F. in dementia), we collectively reflect on the rocky road of trying to support ethical, co-decision-making partnerships, and recommendations on strategies to overcome these challenges through ethically driven partnership research and practice in health systems.

Consultation Versus Representation

Indigenous Peoples regularly emphasize the importance of community control, which can ensure that the interventions and quality improvement processes are appropriate for their community as well as their teams of care providers. Community-driven approaches, that enable communities to set research and service priorities, are the best way to support tangible outcomes that will benefit Indigenous communities that partner with research or health services. Unfortunately, in this research, we saw a very different approach from the formal partnerships that existed in BC. Here, Indigenous people lacked a formal role in health governance and decision-making processes and instead were expected to operate in a consultative capacity, providing advice rather than taking part in a two-way, reciprocal partnership of co-decision-making. For example, when the hospital sought to recruit Indigenous people to participate in their committee on patient experiences, I was invited to share some of the findings from our research and was accompanied by an Indigenous student who was working with me to share her lived experience as a regular representative on this committee. After a short engagement with this group, the Indigenous representative explained to me that she did not consider this to be a safe space, as the "rules of engagement" were all defined by the institution, and the agenda for discussion was set: there was a greater interest in having Indigenous people share their negative hospital-based experiences, rather than on having them set direction for institutional change. Although sharing poor experiences could be an important part of increasing understanding about the issues, this also seemed to continue a process of pathologizing the Indigenous experience, rather than learning from Indigenous knowledge on ways to address the problems that stemmed from the healthcare system.

These experiences reflect how a consultation-based approach often produces more harm than good in this context, as it may undermine self-determination, empowerment, and trust (Harfield et al., 2018). In the early stages of this work in Ontario, we found that researchers or healthcare administrators were often looking for tokenistic participation and were reluctant to invest the time and resources that it takes to develop trust with Indigenous people so as to demonstrate that they are able to be good partners and willing to make changes accordingly. For many, community-driven research and community-based decision-making is seen as the only way to create sustainable benefits for Indigenous communities, as communities can make sure that any partnerships were focused on tangible outcomes for the community (Harfield et al., 2018). The fear that Indigenous healthcare leaders shared with us is that their efforts, if contained within an agenda set by institutions or non-Indigenous partners, would not produce results that the community would benefit from in the long term. Indigenous people whom we interviewed noted that although research and engagement can create opportunities for

Indigenous people and communities to share their stories, these stories are not meant to just evoke empathy; they are shared to inspire action that can advance Indigenous community goals of enhancing the health and wellness of their people. At this time, the institution we were researching was not engaging in partnerships to create change but instead used every engagement with the community to hear solely about the problems.

After the Truth and Reconciliation report was released in Canada in 2015, new directions and interest in addressing anti-Indigenous discrimination in the healthcare system stimulated a new approach to this work (The Truth and Reconciliation Commission of Canada, 2015). Moving away from uncoordinated one-off engagements, City Hospital[2] where we carried out research formed an Indigenous health circle that aimed to work with a wide range of Indigenous representatives, including from First Nations communities as well as urban-based Indigenous organizations. This body emphasized the need to re-evaluate the whole approach to consultation versus representation, as well as to bring a new perspective on how to advance Indigenous health equity. Although the group initially was able to advance meaningful discussions and consider the directions for change, decision-making power remained squarely in the hands of City Hospital leadership, and resource scarcity created tension between the goals of the group and the feasibility of advancing them.

Employment and Resources

The researchers working on this project and the Indigenous health circle both considered that there were not enough positions for Indigenous people within the healthcare system to create a safe space for Indigenous staff and patients. Including Indigenous people in the healthcare workforce and in leadership positions with decision-making power within the institution is a key strategy for meaningful change. Indigenous representation can enhance capacity and credibility for equity work that is happening in universities and healthcare organizations, as well as ensure strong advocates within those institutions. Benefits of ensuring employment of Indigenous people at the City Hospital include opportunities for knowledge sharing and to learn from the lived experience of other Indigenous people and communities. These knowledge-sharing opportunities are valuable ways to coordinate Indigenous approaches within and across healthcare organizations.

Approaches to increasing the presence of Indigenous people in the hospital were themselves contested: many felt that, if positions were created in City Hospital with the aim of achieving this, the community would not have a sufficient say about the work; on the other hand, if such positions were run by the community themselves, then the hospital would not build a strong base of Indigenous staff within the organization. As an elder noted in an interview for this research, seeing Indigenous people working in the hospital can help to create trust (Wylie et al., 2021). Indigenous partners may have a greater interest in being involved in research and health services engagement if they see that there are resources made available for the changes that they recommend. Unfortunately, that is often not the case, especially in health organizations that are operating in permanent austerity, as is the case across many Canadian hospitals. For example, at our research site, the views of members of the Indigenous health circle (made up of Indigenous and non-Indigenous people working in Indigenous health at City Hospital) and the research evidence both pointed to the necessity of providing cultural safety training for the hospital staff to improve Indigenous people's experiences, but it was difficult to secure the resources to provide the training and to pay for clinicians' time to attend this, which meant that these goals were not achieved.

In addition to health system resource challenges, Indigenous communities and organizations are regularly stretched thin with the high levels of need of their community and limited, unsustainable funding. Pressures of running the day-to-day operations of an Indigenous community health center make involvement in research and health service improvements a challenge. Resource pressures within Indigenous organizations (time, money, and staff) often hinder full engagement with research and quality improvement partnerships. Additionally, Indigenous organizations face challenges with hiring and retaining skilled staff for both on reserve and urban services. This problem can threaten both research and quality improvement initiatives, as sustainable participation is challenging. Increasing the numbers and breadth of Indigenous people working together across health and social services is key to ensure Indigenous people can support each other in settings that have not been a safe place to express themselves, often in an environment that misunderstands and excludes Indigenous people and knowledge. It is necessary to adapt health services engagement and decision-making processes to ensure they are guided by Indigenous ways and values and to create a culturally safe environment. Even when the hospital started to increase their engagement with the community, the recommendations were often not addressed. Community-engaged processes shared valuable information over and over again about what needed to change; rather than acting on these recommendations, the hospital seemed to stall the process, by continuously re-engaging the communities over the same issues, rather than reporting on what they were doing or intended to do about those problems.

Knowledge and Capacity

At the time of the initial *Engaging for Change* fellowship research project in Ontario in 2014, healthcare providers and leaders had inadequate knowledge and education around Indigenous health. This has been improving since the release of the Truth and Reconciliation report in 2015, which resulted in calls to action for improved training for health professionals around Indigenous health. Significant knowledge gaps remain, as training has often been approached as a check-box, rather than an ongoing journey of learning and engagement (Wylie et al., 2021). In addition, more Indigenous people are becoming health professionals, as educational and employment opportunities open up. The lack of education and understanding of the link between colonial history, historical trauma, and health that Indigenous people experience today can create healthcare environments that do great harm to Indigenous people (Allan & Smylie, 2015). Indigenous people want care providers to know colonial history and about the cultural practices and health issues of the Indigenous communities that they serve (Wylie et al., 2021). In our research project, we often saw that even when people had done some training, the situations where they had to problem-solve with Indigenous patients were more complex than people imagined (Wylie et al., 2020). Additionally, non-Indigenous partners need to demonstrate how they are bringing their expertise and skills to support Indigenous community-driven processes aimed to meet community-defined needs.

The ethical issue of who defines knowledge and capacity is significant in partnership work. It is important for researchers and health professionals to acknowledge the benefit that they receive in engaging and partnering with Indigenous people and communities, through the knowledge that is shared. In our research, we found that non-Indigenous partners often talk about ways to build the capacity of Indigenous people when they are building healthcare partnerships (O'Neil et al., 2016), usually meaning that Indigenous people have to learn to fit into the mainstream rules of engagement. Instead, hospital staff need to question their biases, acknowledge that Indigenous knowledge has a place in both patient care and organizational decision-making, and know how to create a safe space for that knowledge to be expressed. We witnessed again and again service providers, decision-makers, and researchers seeing Indigenous knowledge, reflecting the vision and voice of Indigenous people (Battiste, 2000), as only relevant to Indigenous issues, rather than valuing these perspectives as a way to improve the overall patient-centered and compassionate approach to healthcare delivery.

Indigenous participants in the research often felt the challenges that they raised were dismissed by hospital staff as an isolated incident or a biased interpretation. It was shared with the first author that having research outcomes that clearly state how these issues are systematic and have life or death consequences helped make the case to address these concerns. Expanding training on Indigenous health to include a wide range of hospital staff can be a key strategy to ensure the sustainability of any new initiatives, especially given the high level of staff turnover often experienced within healthcare organizations. Additionally, providing culturally safe health professional education for Indigenous people and expanding the numbers of Indigenous staff within healthcare organizations is foundational for ensuring that organizations have the capacity to meet the needs of Indigenous patients.

Research can create opportunities for Indigenous people to build the capacity of the university research team and to enhance Indigenous ways of knowing. At the same time, research and quality improvement processes can be of value by collecting and presenting the evidence in ways that inform effective strategies for implementing the recommendations from Indigenous communities. The Indigenous lead within the organization shared with the first author the value of research-derived evidence on Indigenous people's experiences, as often the personal stories of racism shared were dismissed as single incidents and biased accounts. This is a continuous process that should continue well beyond a particular research project, as health equity research, underpinned by ethics of transformative change, is committed to social change as a goal, regardless of how far off some things may seem.

Engaging with research participants both throughout and long after the research project is finished is an important approach for quality improvement. It is therefore problematic if ethics policies require qualitative researchers to specify how many people will be involved, how many times we will discuss issues with them, and when this dialogue will be finished – as this assumes a linear and finite process that rarely exists. When research shows that health systems change is a long-term process, then we must make space for researchers, healthcare providers, leaders, and the community as a whole to engage in ongoing quality improvement. Requiring protocols that mandate disengagement on a set schedule seems antithetical to community-engaged research and commitment to social change. Every time we complete an ethics application, we need to emphasize that in this case, there really is no clinical intervention, and that engaging people in dialogue about how we change healthcare systems will be ongoing. Our team continues to draw on this research to create resources that can support meaningful improvements in the healthcare system, even years after this work was completed, as many of the challenges identified persist.

Respect and Regard

Inadequate respect for elders and their knowledge is common, where researchers and health providers do not appreciate and value their expertise as community knowledge keepers. Integrating positions where elders advise and implement traditional healing practices alongside mainstream health services improves care and health outcomes (Allen et al., 2020). In our research, we found that there were real contradictions when it came to creating space and respect for Indigenous approaches to healing. Policies that outlined access to traditional healing practices, such as the right to burn indoors for smudging, were often disregarded, or there were logistical challenges to ensure the right to practice traditional healing within the hospital. This has improved with more Indigenous staff and an increasing awareness about processes to support traditional healers, yet staff attitudes still often made Indigenous people feel unwelcome to engage in traditional healing.

Indigenous healers are reluctant to establish partnerships with physicians due to fear of loss of autonomy and disrespect. This results in a lack of coordination between the teams that are providing support and care for Indigenous patients and families accessing mainstream health services. Clearly, the ethic of patient-centered care and "do no harm" requires a safe space for traditional healers to be engaged in the care plan of Indigenous people. In addition, Indigenous respondents in the research noted that their work to create a safe and humanistic space for their patients could help mainstream care providers reconnect with their own humanity. Many healthcare providers acknowledged that they often felt uncomfortable to have conversations with Indigenous patients and families, because they lacked the confidence in engaging with families about their Indigenous status or beliefs, as they were concerned that they would offend people. These difficulties demonstrated the need for ongoing training, to allow for explorations of complex and locally specific issues faced by the Indigenous communities served (Wylie et al., 2021).

Divergent Values

Differing worldviews and contrasting values between community obligations and mainstream healthcare norms can also cause tension in partnership work (Taylor & Thompson, 2011). Partnerships can agree to similar objectives yet lack agreement as to how to achieve them. We saw this in our work in the hospital, where there was often a lack of alignment between the interpretation of reconciliation, what that requires, and who defines its progress: important ethical questions about who defines reconciliation and how it should come about are often left unaddressed. In this research, we saw that often the processes of reconciliation were defined in drastically different ways between healthcare leaders in the hospital and those in the community. Ensuring that Indigenous values of holistic and relational care guide the work is an important way to support improved patient care. Research should support the development of new policies and processes to help embed a quality improvement approach that is guided by Indigenous aspirations for systemic change, rather than simply responding to problems as they arise, which we aimed to do by codifying and identifying the solutions recommended by Indigenous participants and community partners, as well as the problems.

Colonial history and past negative research practices have led to a strong mistrust of research, with Indigenous people feeling "researched to death" and continuously pathologized, rather than having the colonial roots of those problems recognized (Goodman et al., 2018). Consequently, researchers working with these communities need to make extra efforts to ensure they build trust and support projects with long-term benefits recognized by the community. When this research project began, community members shared a lot of concern with us about past research that had been done on communities: it was felt that values didn't align, and that the results of the research often presented a deficit approach to understanding Indigenous health, rather than focusing on the impact of colonization on health. Indigenous people also identified that even with respectful and beneficial research partnerships, expectations do not always align about how change should come about.

DISCUSSION

Although research has been seen as a dirty word in Indigenous communities across the globe due to past negative experiences and deficit-based portrayals of Indigenous people and their experiences, this is starting to change. Part of the challenge is that university research ethics boards may still frame research with a colonial mindset that puts control in the hands of the researcher, while at the same time forcing that researcher's hand to adhere to structures and rules that fail to properly support community-driven processes (George et al., 2020).

This chapter has sought to show that despite this deficit among ethics boards in understanding partnership approaches, researchers can still work in ethical partnership with communities. By bringing an approach of genuine collaboration, flexibility, feedback loops to ensure ongoing community oversight, financial support for community-driven quality improvements, and implementation research are valuable components to support comprehensive and sustainable partnership projects. While we hope that our description of the thorny challenges encountered in research projects with Indigenous communities will provide some insights into the types of issues that are unique to community-driven research, it is up to university-based researchers and ethics boards to build their capacity for supporting ethical community-based partnership research.

Amid the success of community-partnered research lie fundamental dichotomies between academic and community partners, in relation to agendas for research, power differentials in partnership, ownership of and identity of the research project, and the desired outcomes (Cottrell & Parpart, 2006; Israel et al., 1994). One way to mitigate such differences is to engage community members as meaningful partners in the research process throughout the life cycle of the project, from designing, data collection, analysis to dissemination (Dankwa-Mullan et al., 2010; Edwards et al., 2008). Ethics boards need to understand the complexity of building and sustaining relationships between researchers and Indigenous communities. As George et al. (2020) have emphasized:

> There are courageous Indigenous communities who know the value of their own knowledges and whose work demonstrates that research with Indigenous peoples can be a place of Indigenous sovereignty. Together with Indigenous researchers and non-Indigenous allies, Indigenous communities have reaffirmed ways of working that enable Indigenous agency in research to flourish. (p. 3)

Researchers and the ethics boards that support them must ensure that partnerships are formalized and guided by ethical principles that include Indigenous ethical approaches and should establish ways to be held accountable to these. Rather than adopting a "one-size-fits-all" approach, collaborative partnerships based on co-decision-making and open dialogue will help to ensure the creation of locally appropriate solutions, tailored to the specific needs and interests of each community partner.

This research has shown that ethical qualitative research approaches should aim to "establish meaningful relationships with community partners and to design research projects that have a shared benefit for both parties" (Stefanelli et al., 2017, p. 10). Meaningful relationships need to follow ethical standards and principles that support transformative change: "One of the key tenets of CBPR is that research resulting from CBPR frameworks should create knowledge that is actionable and meaningful to communities" (Gokiert et al., 2017, p. 15). This reinforces the key principle that researchers "need to partner with their communities rather than conduct research on the communities, as had been done in the past" (Moore et al., 2017, p. 9). Flexibility is required, as timelines of research projects do not always align with those of the community, and the relationship building that creates trust takes time, especially when starting from a deficit position of past mistrust. Institutions need to address the damage done by past researchers and service providers, in order to create positive space for future research partnerships with communities.

Given the diversity among Indigenous Peoples, it is also important to recognize that different groups have their own unique ways of communicating and understanding, and therefore no single intervention can meet the specific needs of each and every community. Needs and interests can and will change over the course of a research project; as researchers and ethics boards, we need to be prepared for unpredictability and be willing to change course. This is especially true when the research is engaged in transformative processes working with colonial institutions, like mainstream healthcare organizations.

Aligning funding models to support these sustained partnerships, as well as to fund the system improvements recommend by research would go a long way to address Indigenous inequities in the healthcare system. Too often, research is done that brings forward community voices when the institutions concerned have no commitment to act on those recommendations. In order to be a productive part of participatory research processes, we advocate that it is vital to educate ourselves as researchers in how to ethically engage in a process that will benefit the community and how to ensure that all players at the table are willing to engage in a process of co-decision-making to support transformative change.

As we have seen, ethical qualitative research that is committed to community-led initiatives raises a range of practical challenges. Nevertheless, the approaches set out above can guide future research to enable community members to be valued as experts with a view to creating effective synergy in community-based research.

Researchers and healthcare providers must ensure that scientific results are shared in a community-friendly way that has relevance. In addition, university-driven incentives for researchers need to better align with partnership work, rather than mainly focusing on peer-reviewed publications, which in many cases are the outputs primarily valued by universities. Feedback and guidance from community members on the analysis of the research findings strengthens the interpretation of results that reinforce community control. Genuine community partnerships can ensure the interpretation is shaped by a community perspective that has expectations of the research in terms of helping to strengthen future interventions and improve future dissemination strategies (Macaulay et al., 2007). Without that voice, research often perpetuates the norms of pathologizing Indigenous people, rather than acknowledging the harms of colonialism and the strengths of community.

Taking a systems approach to health services quality improvement processes that address the broader context (Bailie et al., 2013) is one way to create more sustainable and meaningful partnerships. Research is needed to ascertain whether and, if so, how current partnerships improve health services and outcomes for Indigenous people. This requires continuous collaboration with communities and must take a holistic Indigenous worldview (mind, body, emotion, spirit) for decolonized and culturally informed measures (Allen et al., 2020). This project has demonstrated that some of this initial work has to happen before developing a research plan, to ensure it is aligned with the priorities of the community partners. This of course means that engagement and relationship building, even though these are key aspects of research, should be able to take place, where appropriate, before applying for research ethics review.

In reflecting on this research experience, there are some key recommendations we can make about university-based ethics approval processes in Canada – and these may be applicable further afield as well. Support needs to be put in place within the university ethics community to ensure that their researchers have the capacity to engage in partnership research work. Non-Indigenous researchers and university-based ethics offices should build their capacity as good partners that aim to support transformative research that ensures Indigenous people guide the process and their own protocols are respected. The steps outlined here can improve these research processes by ensuring they are partnership driven, holistic in addressing structural and system-level issues, as well as being responsive to person, family, and community needs. Partnerships need to be reciprocal, clearly defined, and governed by ethical principles determined by both community and university partners. While the focus of this chapter has been on research with Indigenous communities, this work can and should be extended to other traditionally excluded groups to ensure a responsive culturally safe health system that meets the needs of everyone in society.

CONCLUSION

In conclusion, research ethics boards are well positioned to promote standards and guiding principles of sustained partnership research, if they are willing to decolonize the process of research ethics review. The work of ensuring community-driven processes cannot be placed solely on communities; partnerships must be *reciprocal* in nature. Capacity building within universities is needed to create partnership skills for working with Indigenous people and communities, which means knowing history, learning about the community, and letting go of colonial-driven models that haunt the echo chamber of the ethics office.

NOTES

1. *Engaging for Change* was L.W.'s Phoenix fellowship project funded by Associated Medical Services in Ontario.
2. This is a pseudonym for the hospital.

ACKNOWLEDGEMENTS

The authors acknowledge the participants in the research project as well as the editors and peer reviewers for their valuable recommendations. L.W. acknowledges Associated Medical Services, which funded the original Phoenix fellowship.

REFERENCES

Adelson, N. (2005). The embodiment of inequity: Health disparities in Aboriginal Canada. *Canadian Journal of Public Health, 96*(S2), S45–S61. https://doi.org/10.1007/bf03403702

Allan, B., & Smylie, J. (2015). *First peoples, second class treatment: The role of racism in the health and well-being of Indigenous peoples in Canada*. The Wellesley Institute.

Allen, L., Hatala, A., Ijaz, S., Courchene, E. D., & Bushie, E. B. (2020). Indigenous-led health care partnerships in Canada. *Canadian Medical Association Journal, 192*(9), E208–E216. https://doi.org/10.1503/cmaj.190728

Bailie, R., Matthews, V., Brands, J., & Schierhout, G. (2013). A systems-based partnership learning model for strengthening primary healthcare. *Implementation Science, 8*(1), 1–12. https://doi.org/10.1186/1748-5908-8-143

Battiste, M. (Ed.). (2000). *Reclaiming Indigenous voice and vision*. UBC Press.

Browne, A. J., Lavoie, J. G., McCallum, M. J., & Canoe, C. B. (2022). Addressing anti-Indigenous racism in Canadian health systems: Multi-tiered approaches are required. *Canadian Journal of Public Health, 113*(2), 222–226. https://doi.org/10.17269/s41997-021-00598-1

Browne, A. J., Varcoe, C., Lavoie, J., Smye, V., Wong, S. T., Krause, M., Tu, D., Godwin, O., Khan, K., & Fridkin, A. (2016). Enhancing health care equity with Indigenous populations: Evidence-based strategies from an ethnographic study. *BMC Health Services Research, 16*(1), 1–17. https://doi.org/10.1186/s12913-016-1707-9

Cottrell, B., & Parpart, J. L. (2006). Academic-community collaboration, gender research, and development: Pitfalls and possibilities. *Development in Practice, 16*(1), 15–26. https://doi.org/10.1080/09614520500450768

Dankwa-Mullan, I., Rhee, K. B., Williams, K., Sanchez, I., Sy, F. S., Stinson, N., & Ruffin, J. (2010). The science of eliminating health disparities: Summary and analysis of the NIH summit recommendations. *American Journal of Public Health, 100*(S1), S12–S18. https://doi.org/10.2105/ajph.2010.191619

de Leeuw, S., Lindsay, N., & Greenwood, M. (Eds.). (2015). *Indigenous determinants of health: Beyond the social*. Canadian Scholars Press.

Denzin, N., & Lincoln, Y. (Eds.). (2011). *The SAGE handbook of qualitative research*. SAGE.

Edwards, K., Lund, C., Mitchell, S., & Andersson, N. (2008). Trust the process: Community-based researcher partnerships. *Pimatisiwin, 6*(2), 186–199.

Elliott, S. J., Jolin, M. A., & Walker, R. (2000). Partnering in and for heart health promotion: Findings from a survey of community organizations. *Canadian Journal of Public Health, 91*(3), 229–233. https://doi.org/10.1007/bf03404278

George, L., Te Ata o Tu MacDonald, L., & Tauri, J. (Eds.). (2020). *Indigenous research ethics: Claiming research sovereignty beyond deficit and the colonial legacy*. Emerald Group Publishing.

Goodman, A., Morgan, R., Kuehlke, R., Kastor, S., Fleming, K., Boyd, J., & Western Aboriginal Harm Reduction Society. (2018). "We've been researched to death": Exploring the research experiences of urban indigenous peoples in Vancouver, Canada. *The International Indigenous Policy Journal, 9*(2), 1–20. https://doi.org/10.18584/iipj.2018.9.2.3

Gokiert, R. J., Willows, N. D., Georgis, R., & Stringer, H. (2017). Wâhkôhtowin. *International Indigenous Policy Journal, 8*(2), 1–20.

Harfield, S. G., Davy, C., McArthur, A., Munn, Z., Brown, A., & Brown, N. (2018). Characteristics of Indigenous primary health care service delivery models: A systematic scoping review. *Global Health, 14*(12), 1–11. https://doi.org/10.1186/s12992-018-0332-2

Israel, B. A., Checkoway, B., Schulz, A., & Zimmerman, M. (1994). Health education and community empowerment: conceptualizing and measuring perceptions of individual, organizational, and community control. *Health education quarterly, 21*(2), 149–170.

Macaulay, A. C., Ing, A., Salsberg, J., McGregor, A., Saad-Haddad, C., Rice, J., Montour, L., & Gray-Donald, K. (2007). Community-based participatory research: Lessons from sharing results with the community: Kahnawake schools diabetes prevention project. *Progress in Community Health Partnerships: Research, Education, and Action, 1*(2), 143–152. https://doi.org/10.1353/cpr.2007.0010

Ministry of Health and Long-Term Care. (2018). *Relationship with Indigenous communities guideline*. Queen's Printer for Ontario. https://files.ontario.ca/moh-guidelines-relationship-with-indigenous-communities-guideline-en-2018.pdf

Moore, C., Castleden, H. E., Tirone, S., & Martin, D. (2017). Implementing the tri-council policy on ethical research involving Indigenous Peoples in Canada: So, how's that going in Mi'kma'ki? *International Indigenous Policy Journal*, *8*(2), 1–19. https://doi.org/10.18584/iipj.2017.8.2.4

Oetzel, J. G., Wallerstein, N., Duran, B., Sanchez-Youngman, S., Nguyen, T., Woo, K., Wang, J., Schulz, A., Keawe'aimoku Kaholokula, J., Israel, B., & Alegria, M. (2018). Impact of participatory health research: A test of the community-based participatory research conceptual model. *BioMed Research International*, *2018*, 1–12. https://doi.org/10.1155/2018/7281405

O'Neil, J., Gallagher, J., Wylie, L., Bingham, B., Lavoie, J., Alcock, D., & Johnson, H. (2016). Transforming First Nations' health governance in British Columbia. *International Journal of Health Governance*, *21*(4), 229–244. https://doi.org/10.1108/ijhg-08-2016-0042

Reading, C. L. (2015). Structural determinants of Aboriginal peoples' health. In de Leeuw, S., Lindsay, N., & Greenwood, M. (Eds.)., *Determinants of Indigenous peoples' health in Canada* (1st ed., pp. 3–15). Canadian Scholars' Press.

Reading, C. L., & Wien, F. (2009). *Health inequalities and social determinants of Aboriginal peoples' health*. National Collaborating Centre for Aboriginal Health.

Robbins, J. A., & Dewar, J. (2011). Traditional Indigenous approaches to healing and the modern welfare of traditional knowledge, spirituality and lands: A critical reflection on practices and policies taken from the Canadian Indigenous example. *The International Indigenous Policy Journal*, *2*(4), 1–17. https://doi.org/10.18584/iipj.2011.2.4.2

Scott, C. M., & Thurston, W. E. (1997). A framework for the development of community health agency partnerships. *Canadian Journal of Public Health*, *88*(6), 416–420. https://doi.org/10.1007/bf03403918

Stefanelli, R. D., Castleden, H., Cunsolo, A., Martin, D., Harper, S. L., & Hart, C. (2017). Canadian and Australian researchers' perspectives on promising practices for implementing Indigenous and western knowledge systems in water research and management. *Water Policy*, *19*(6), 1063–1080. https://doi.org/10.2166/wp.2017.181

Taylor, K. P., & Thompson, S. C. (2011). Closing the (service) gap: Exploring partnerships between Aboriginal and mainstream health services. *Australian Health Review*, *35*(3), 297. https://doi.org/10.1071/ah10936

The Truth and Reconciliation Commission of Canada. (2015). *Honouring the truth, reconciling for the future: Summary of the final report of the Truth and Reconciliation Commission of Canada*. https://nctr.ca/records/reports/#trc-reports

Wylie, L., & McConkey, S. (2019). Insiders' insight: Discrimination against Indigenous peoples through the eyes of health care professionals. *Journal of Racial and Ethnic Health Disparities*, *6*(1), 37–45. https://doi.org/10.1007/s40615-018-0495-9

Wylie, L., McConkey, S., & Corrado, A. M. (2020). Colonial legacies and collaborative action: Improving Indigenous peoples' health care in Canada. *International Indigenous Policy Journal*, *10*(5), 1–27. https://doi.org/10.18584/iipj.2019.10.5.9340

Wylie, L., McConkey, S., & Corrado, A. M. (2021). It's a journey not a check box: Indigenous cultural safety from training to transformation. *International Journal of Indigenous Health*, *16*(1), 314–332. https://doi.org/10.32799/ijih.v16i1.33240

CHAPTER 13

IMPROVING THE ETHICS REVIEW OF QUALITATIVE HEALTH RESEARCH THROUGH INCREASED COLLABORATION BETWEEN RESEARCH ETHICS COMMITTEES, RESEARCHERS AND RESEARCH PARTICIPANTS

Sarah Potthoff[a] and Anke Erdmann[b]

[a]*University of Münster, Germany*
[b]*Kiel University, Germany*

ABSTRACT

Most qualitative health research is subject to ethics review and approval by a research ethics committee (REC). Numerous studies, though, have identified shortcomings with current ethics review practices and the challenges these present to qualitative health research. Now, researchers are increasingly calling for research to focus on possibilities for improving current ethics review practices. Practical suggestions or guidelines are needed for specific challenging methodological designs in qualitative research. The discussion here is based on

Reframing Qualitative Research Ethics
Advances in Research Ethics and Integrity, Volume 12, 217–233

ISSN: 2398-6018/doi:10.1108/S2398-601820250000012013

our reflections on, and experiences with, ethics review and our research experiences with people with dementia or psychiatric diagnoses and their families. We explore how to ensure that research participants are protected from harm but enabled to access participation in research. The inclusion of people with cognitive impairments or psychiatric diagnoses in research requires attentive consideration because they might be at a higher risk of being in a vulnerable situation. We suggest that to appropriately assess competence to consent and risks of harm, consideration must be given to the specific research design, the research participants' lifeworlds and their situational well-being. Recognising the need for increased collaboration between RECs, researchers and research participants is, we propose, one solution to better addressing ethical challenges and the shortcomings of current ethics review practices. We suggest that such collaboration would enable making research ethically 'safe' for participants and researchers by jointly developing appropriate protective safeguards.

Keywords: Dyadic interviews; confidentiality; capacity to consent; research ethics review; mental health; dementia research; ongoing consent; Germany

INTRODUCTION

The history of biomedical research has clearly demonstrated how important it is to protect research participants from harm. This applies in particular to the abuse and exploitation of people with psychiatric diagnoses, cognitive impairments and mental disability in research. Examples of this abuse include the hepatitis studies at the Willowbrook State School for Children (Staten Island, NY, USA), in which developmentally disabled children were deliberately infected with hepatitis A and B viruses, and the harmful research on people with psychiatric disorders at the Allen Memorial Institute in Montreal, Canada, without their informed consent (Bracken-Roche et al., 2016). In response, however, participants considered to be vulnerable due to a psychiatric diagnosis, cognitive impairments or mental disabilities have often been completely excluded from research for reasons of protectionism. In these cases, it was generally assumed that vulnerability is inherent in the diagnosis and that this would particularly impair free and informed decision-making (Bell et al., 2014). The strong protectionist stance of many RECs has led to limited inclusion of under-researched populations in research, meaning that there is insufficient health data relating to such populations, which is problematic (Friesen et al., 2023).[1] However, knowledge from the perspective of people with experience of mental illness and cognitive impairment is essential to tailor health and social care services to their needs. Research therefore requires involving people with severe mental illness and cognitive impairment, as they can best inform the study (Graor & Knapik, 2013; Reitinger et al., 2018). In recent years, there have been increasing efforts to redress this imbalance between necessary protection and benefit in accordance with the principle of justice.

The exclusion of population groups considered to be vulnerable has often been applied not only to high-risk biomedical research but also to quantitative and qualitative health research more generally. The exclusion of people deemed vulnerable from research has frequently been justified by an assumption that such participants have diminished decision-making capacity in relation to giving free and informed consent, especially for people with a psychiatric diagnosis. However, several scholars have highlighted that assuming limited or lacking decision-making capacity due to a person's psychiatric diagnosis is highly problematic and stigmatising (Allbutt & Masters, 2010; Bell et al., 2014; Bracken-Roche et al., 2016; Holland, 2007). Accordingly, a person's psychiatric diagnosis should not be interpreted as a sign of a lack of capacity to consent, but, rather, a presumption of 'capacity to consent' should prevail (Grisso & Appelbaum, 1998; Kim, 2010; Scholten et al., 2021). At the same time, conditions such as signs of acute psychosis or mania, impaired memory or spatial disorientations are risk factors for impaired consent capacity and must be considered by researchers (Kim, 2010).

In this chapter, we look at how RECs weigh up the potential future risks and benefits of qualitative health studies. Ethical challenges in qualitative research may result from the generally close relationship between researchers and research participants and from the deep insights that may be generated into the participants' lifeworlds (Peter & Friedmann, 2017). Ethnographic observation may raise concerns about privacy and consent, and in-depth interviews may implicate issues around potential identifiability and confidentiality (Peter, 2015; Tolich & Tumilty, 2020). Moreover, risks of harm can arise from methods of access and recruitment, data storage methods and the conclusions drawn from qualitative research (Tolich & Tumilty, 2020; Ummel & Aichille, 2016; Witham et al., 2015).

In the following discussion, we first problematise the concept of vulnerability, which is often used in the practice of research ethics review. Second, we explain the research ethics governance structure in Germany, where we conducted our research and gained our experience with research ethics review. We then draw on two cases from our own research to explore the ethical complexities and ambiguities that can arise and how we as researchers and the respective RECs dealt with these issues. These cases involved research with people with dementia and users of mental health services who had diagnoses of psychotic disorder, affective disorder, substance dependence and/or personality disorder – and their families. Based on our reflections on these two studies, we conclude by developing ideas for improving the management of potential future risks, versus benefits for research participants, within qualitative health research.

ASSESSING VULNERABILITY

Article 19 of the Declaration of Helsinki states that vulnerable groups and individuals 'may have an increased likelihood of being wronged or of incurring additional harm' and should therefore 'receive specifically considered protection' (World Medical Association, 2013). The guidelines of the Council for International Organizations of Medical Sciences (CIOMS) mention the following special protective measures: inclusion of individuals considered to be vulnerable only in studies that pose no more than minimal risks, supplementing the consent of the individual with that of their legal representative and the use of other tailored safeguards to minimise risk (CIOMS, 2016). Although the CIOMS (2016) guidelines recognise that 'vulnerability involves [...] also aspects of the ongoing participation in research studies' (p. 57), RECs generally require that the vulnerability of potential research participants be defined and determined prior to the beginning of a study (Allbutt & Masters, 2010; Friesen et al., 2023; Holland, 2007; Peter & Friedland, 2017). As individual research participants are not known at the stage of an anticipatory ethics review, RECs are likely to assess the vulnerability of potential research participants based on group characteristics (Bell et al., 2014; Potthoff et al., 2023). Several authors have pointed out that identifying vulnerability based on group characteristics can lead to enhancing the stigmatisation of, amongst others, people with a psychiatric diagnosis and those with cognitive impairments (Bell et al., 2014; Bracken-Roche et al., 2016; Carlsson et al., 2017; Øye et al., 2016; Schrems, 2014; Witham et al., 2015).

This discrimination should be avoided, and recent approaches to research ethics have accordingly argued that the term 'vulnerability' would benefit from a broader understanding rather than being used as a rigid, fixed label (Bell et al., 2014; Bracken-Roche et al., 2016; Racine & Bracken-Roche, 2019). Thus, Bell et al. (2014) and Bracken-Roche et al. (2016) argued for a relational understanding of vulnerability: according to them, relational sources of vulnerability include the educational level and health literacy of participants, as well as, from the research side, suboptimal study designs, dependencies and asymmetrical power relations between researchers and participants and lack of support for participants.

RESEARCH ETHICS GOVERNANCE STRUCTURE IN GERMANY

Whether a prior ethics review of a planned qualitative study including humans is mandatory, and which type of REC is responsible, depends on national regulations and their respective ethics governance infrastructure. There are different types of RECs in Germany, namely medical RECs, which are institutionalised nationwide, and non-medical RECs, which are affiliated with academic or professional associations. The latter can be further differentiated according to disciplines such as psychology and social sciences, although social science specialised RECs are relatively rare (RatSWD, 2017; Strobel et al., 2022; von Unger et al., 2016). Research involving humans is subject to approval by a medical REC located at a medical faculty or a medical professional organisation if one of the following conditions apply: the research is (1) conducted by a physician, (2) conducted at a medical faculty or hospital or (3) the participants are patients. Independent ethics review is not mandatory for qualitative health research involving humans that does not meet any of these criteria, although, in fact, this is relatively rare in practice (Dilger, 2017; Potthoff et al., 2024; von Unger et al., 2016). For social scientists working at a social science faculty, there is no nationwide legal or professional obligation to obtain approval from an independent REC for research involving human subjects (Strobel et al., 2022; von Unger et al., 2016).

Medical RECs are institutionally embedded in the medical faculties of universities, the German regional medical associations (*Landesärztekammern*) or the regional state office (*Kommissionen der Länder*). They are organised in The German Association of Medical Ethics Committees (*Arbeitskreis medizinischer Ethikkommissionen*), comprising 51 of the 54 medical RECs established under regional state law in Germany. While the general procedures for medical RECs are standardised, this is only partly the case for the composition of their membership: medical RECs are composed of physicians from different specialties and must by law also include at least one member with legal training (Gauckler, 2021). Typically, a REC's makeup also includes one member with expertise in ethics, and another with expertise in biometrics (Pigeot et al., 2019). Individual REC statutes also stipulate the membership of at least one layperson or patient representative. However, there are currently no statutes that require the membership of a person with expertise in qualitative research methods (Buchner et al., 2019; Gauckler, 2021). Individual REC statutes also regulate the responsibilities and working methods of the committee, such as the basis on which external experts can be called in to advise them. Involvement of the researchers submitting the application to explain the research and its methodology is not generally envisaged: on the contrary, if an applicant is a member of the REC, they are, according to the statutes, usually excluded from the committee's deliberations on this application. All the RECs are committed to the Declaration of Helsinki (World Medical Association, 2013). The members of the REC are usually listed on the university clinic's website.

For the two research cases that we present from our respective viewpoints and discuss below, obtaining an ethics review from a medical REC was mandatory. We are both social scientists and, therefore, not subject to the professional obligation to obtain an ethics review in Germany, but the research was conducted at medical faculties and some of the participants were patients.

CASE 1: IN-DEPTH INTERVIEWS WITH MENTAL HEALTH SERVICE USERS AND FAMILY MEMBERS

The present case is based on the first author's experience with ethics review by a medical REC during the design and implementation of a grounded theory study on informal coercion and psychological pressure in psychiatry (Potthoff et al., 2022). The first author designed and conducted the study together with colleagues in Germany between 2019 and 2020. The study aim was to explore mental health service users' and their relatives' experiences of psychological pressure in their social environment and in psychiatry. Psychological pressure encompasses communicative strategies used by professionals and relatives to influence service users' decision-making to increase their adherence to recommended treatment or social rules (Hempeler et al., 2024; Potthoff et al., 2022). Persuasion, interpersonal leverage, inducements and threats have all been described in the literature as examples of treatment pressures (Szmukler & Appelbaum, 2008). In-depth problem-centred interviews with service users and relatives of service users were planned for the data collection. Our inclusion criteria for service users were a self-reported psychiatric diagnosis and previous experience with formal coercion in mental health care. To avoid undue pressure to participate in the study, we excluded service users who were involuntarily detained at the time of the interview and included only service users who were undergoing voluntary inpatient or outpatient treatment or who were not undergoing treatment. The service users included in the study had self-reported diagnoses such as psychotic disorder, affective disorder, substance dependence and personality disorder. We generally assumed a 'capacity to consent' in order to avoid discrimination and stigmatisation based on psychiatric diagnoses (Grisso & Appelbaum, 1998; Kim, 2010; Scholten et al., 2021). Nevertheless, we were aware that conditions of acute psychosis or mania may impair a person's decision-making capacity and therefore carried out a structured capacity assessment if prospective research participants displayed symptoms of such conditions.

The ethics review of this project by the responsible medical REC resulted in a requirement that we must inform and obtain informed consent from service users before undertaking any interviews with their relatives. In the following, we will review the ethical considerations and challenges of our research project in light of this requirement. A distinction should be made between two options, which the REC did not do explicitly: (a) the inclusion of dyads consisting of a service user and their family member, and (b) the inclusion of service users and family members of other service users who did not know each other.

To understand the phenomenon of psychological pressure in mental health settings and the social environment of service users and relatives in depth, we had proposed the inclusion of dyads of service users with one of their personal relatives, so as to conduct a dyadic analysis (Eisikovits & Koren, 2010). We understand dyads to be 'individuals who have shared an intimate, common experience' (Ummel & Achille, 2016, p. 807). A dyadic analysis enables comparison of common experiences and situations narrated from the perspective of a service user and their relative. For each dyad, we had proposed to conduct two separate interviews (one with the service user, one with their relative) but not to do any joint interviews with the dyad members. This was because our main interest was in the experiences and perspectives of both parties on common situations and not their interaction in the interview situation (Voltelen et al., 2018; Zarhin, 2018). We saw a potential risk of negatively influencing the relationship of the dyads through participation, which could have caused emotional distress or mistrust. After the research ethics review, we chose to involve only service users and relatives of *other* service users who had also experienced coercion and had self-reported psychiatric diagnoses but who did not know each other. Zarhin (2018) calls this strategy involving 'social partners' (p. 851), that is, people who share similar experiences but are not connected as personal dyads. Responding to the constraints imposed by the REC, we decided to change our methodology: we were then unable to gain insight into shared experiences and perspectives of dyads on common situations and to compare them in the sense of a dyadic analysis. However, we were still able to understand psychological pressures from the perspective of service users and of service users' relatives while, according to Zarhin (2018), minimising the risk of harm to participants. Ultimately, the REC approved an amended study protocol involving option (b) as described above (Potthoff et al., 2023). With this adapted study design, we were not obliged to implement the requirement for double consent, because the situation of interviewing service users and their relatives did not arise. We reasoned that the purpose of interviewing relatives was to understand *their own* experiences and perspectives, which would likely also include some experiences they had shared with others. In our view, such narratives of relatives must be distinguished from the collection of personal data about service users from relatives, for which informed consent would have been required.

Afterwards, reflecting on the original requirement to seek consent from service users to interview their relatives, we considered that this kind of restriction could lead in an absurd direction: if narrating experiences which relate to other people already required their informed consent, interviewees would never be allowed to talk about their experiences relating to other people without first obtaining their informed consent. Therefore, we felt that the REC's requirement for us to obtain informed consent from service users if their relatives wished to participate was not justified – at least if conducting interviews with relatives only. This is not to say that conducting interviews with dyads does not raise ethical issues, but we did not see these as being addressed by a requirement for informed consent from the service users. We even envisaged some ethical issues that would have arisen if implementing such a requirement, as we would have had to collect names and contact details from service users to obtain their informed consent to our interviews with others, even if they themselves did not participate in the study. Furthermore, we would have had to contact the service user even if the relative had considered the relationship to be very problematic. Thus, in such a case, we could have exacerbated the situation and caused harm to the participants.

Nonetheless, qualitative research involving personal dyads of patient-relative, patient-caregiver or patient-healthcare professional is widespread (Collaço et al., 2021; Gumede et al., 2019), although the literature on ethical considerations for this research is still limited (Forbat & Henderson, 2003; Ummel & Achille, 2016). Accordingly, we turn now to discussing what appropriate safeguards could be put in place to ensure safe participation when involving dyads of family members in qualitative health research. Our suggestions result from ethical considerations based on a reflection of the recruitment practices and interviews conducted as part of the presented study. We will not address methodological questions and study results here.

Ethical Considerations – Internal Confidentiality

As Ummel and Achille (2016) pointed out, research in healthcare is likely to include individuals who are in crisis or whose time is limited and precious. In these often distressing circumstances, there is a fairly high risk of causing emotional harm to participants if they receive information about each other that is not intended to be shared. This is described as *internal* as distinct from *external confidentiality* (Tolich, 2004; Tolich & Tumilty, 2020). Internal confidentiality can be breached by interviewers if they intentionally or unintentionally disclose information from one interview to another and if study participants are able to identify each other when research results are disseminated. The risk of a breach of internal confidentiality is not limited to dyads but is higher in this model. It is almost impossible, though, to determine in advance what relatives will (or will not) share with each other, what secrets might be kept and which specific events or experiences lead to emotional distress (Gumede et al., 2019). However, pursuing our strategy of involving social partners instead of personal dyads also raised new ethical concerns. In one case, both a relative (the parent) and their adult child (the service user) wanted to take part in the study. We had to exclude one of them due to the limitations of study protocol as approved by the REC, even though this exclusion resulted in emotional distress for the dyad. The parent initially contacted me by phone and expressed her interest in taking part in the study. After speaking with the parent and confirming the interview and making an appointment, she called me again and asked if her child could also participate in an interview. Her child was very enthusiastic about the study and also wanted to express her point of view. The mother explained that they lived in the same household and that she supported her child's wish to take part in an interview. She believed that it would be good for both if they had the opportunity to contribute something from their perspective to the study.

This example shows the importance of going beyond *procedural ethics* to also take account of researchers' identification and treatment of ethical issues during the research process, which Guillemin and Gillam (2004) refer to as *ethics in practice*. In our view, this requires continuous reflection by researchers and a high level of ethical sensitivity together with a dialogue between researchers and REC that improves the basis for ethical decisions during research. In addition, to better prevent possible conflicts and emotional distress to participants, we recommend involving (potential) participants in certain decision-making processes. The present case concerns (1) the participation or non-participation of dyads and, if so, (2) the disclosure or blocking of personal information to the dyad partner. We develop these suggestions based on our reflections of our recruitment practices and interviews conducted with social partners of service users and relatives.

In one case, a service user wanted his partner, who was also a service user, to be present during the interview. He requested this before the appointment, explaining that it would make him feel more comfortable. In another case, I conducted individual interviews with two service users who were a couple living in the same household. During the first interview, the partner was in another room. However, the content of the interview did not appear to be confidential to the partner as the doors were open. At the end of this interview, the interviewee went to inform their partner (who had been resting) that it was their turn now to be interviewed. Then, she came into the room and spoke to her partner and me before I started the interview with her. The first interviewee then went into the kitchen and came back with coffee for us. During these moments when both participants were in the room with me, the atmosphere did not change; both seemed to know each other's stories. In contrast, in two further cases, relatives who had agreed to take part in an interview and shared their household with their partner (the service user) specifically wanted to conduct the interview without their relative knowing. Accordingly, they suggested a location outside of their home for the interview. For other participants, both service users and relatives, the question of confidentiality of the interview did not arise so directly as they did not live in the same household. This was particularly the case with parents and adult children. In some cases, parents explicitly stated that they would not share what they were saying in the presence of their children (including the service user and siblings). In other cases, service users explicitly stated that they no longer had contact with their family due to negative experiences. In one case, a service user who was an inpatient at that time spoke critically about his relationship with his wife. When informing him about the study, I pointed out the confidentiality of the interview, especially towards other patients and professionals in the clinic and also when disseminating the results, and he gave his informed consent to being interviewed. Nevertheless, the treating physician informed us the next day that this patient had major worries about his participation in the interview and the statements he had made. He felt uncomfortable and was restless. A team member then contacted the participant and explained to him (as I had already when informing about the study) that he had the option of withdrawing consent. This would mean that we would delete all of his data. This conversation assisted the participant's decision to withdraw. Afterwards he felt relieved. The last example shows that participants' well-being can be harmed not only by breaches of confidentiality but also by content shared with the interviewer when confidentiality is guaranteed.

In our view, the wide range of different relationship types and degrees of openness or privacy between people in close relationships shows that strict exclusion of personal dyads before the start of a study with the aim of causing no harm is not always proportionate. What is needed instead is a situational and relational assessment of the respective relationships and the wishes of potential study participants in combination with the development of protective safeguards.

The following are possible protective safeguards that can be put in place to ensure safe participation of dyads of service users and relatives (personal or social partners):

- Comprehensive advance, and ongoing, information from the researchers on internal confidentiality and possible breaches.
- Joint preliminary discussion by researchers and (potential) participants on their needs regarding internal confidentiality and possible negative consequences of breaches of confidentiality for the respective participant.
- Joint discussion on how to prevent a breach of internal confidentiality, e.g. the interviewee could explicitly flag up a potential concern during the interview or in the preliminary discussion.
- Researchers must maintain integrity and not use the knowledge gained in an interview for other purposes in contact with the other dyad partner.
- Ongoing joint reflection on informed consent and the possibility of withdrawing consent.

- If data analysis raises sensitive topics not previously known to a dyad, the results can be disseminated either at a general level to preserve internal confidentiality or not disseminated at all. The information from the preliminary separate discussion with the two dyad partners on how to deal with internal confidentiality must be considered and is a guide for the researchers' decision.
- If distress or conflicts arise from a dyad's participation in the study, counselling from a trained counsellor/therapist outside of the research team should be offered.

CASE 2: QUALITATIVE INTERVIEW STUDY WITH PEOPLE WITH DEMENTIA

The second author's PhD research in 2013 involved an evaluation study on integrative validation therapy (IVA) (Erdmann & Schnepp, 2016), an appreciative form of communication with people with dementia. In IVA, various communicative techniques are used to recognise the subjective reality of the person with dementia and not to correct them as would be the case with reality orientation training. For example, the emotions or motivations shown by a person with dementia verbally or nonverbally are validated with short sentences such as 'You are very worried' or 'You know your duties'. Emotions and motivations are also validated by mirroring the body language of the person or by using proverbs, wise sayings, songs or biblical sayings if these sayings are well known by the person. An important goal of IVA is to give the person with dementia the feeling that their situation and emotions are understood and that their identity is recognised (Erdmann & Schnepp, 2016).

In this study, we worked methodically with Fourth Generation Evaluation according to Guba and Lincoln's methodology (1989), which involves interviews with various stakeholders of the evaluation object. In the case of the IVA evaluation, relevant stakeholders were people with dementia, their relatives and experts on dementia. We therefore planned to involve people with early-stage dementia in the study. We wanted to show them conversational situations from an educational film in which IVA was being used and then ask them a few questions about what they thought and felt about these situations. The film showed conversational situations in which people with severe dementia were shown doing something that made sense to them but was nonsensical for healthy people. For example, one scene depicted a former shopkeeper who was physically re-arranging laundry that had been hung on a laundry rack to dry. Mentally, this person was organising goods in the shop where they had worked. A geriatric nurse positively recognised the (for others) nonsensical action – and thus demonstrated IVA (Erdmann & Schnepp, 2013). Interviewing people with dementia about how the nurse behaved in this situation and therefore including them in our research appeared to also be ethically appropriate, as some authors have been extremely critical of the systematic exclusion of people with dementia in research projects (Hellström et al., 2007; Wilkinson, 2007).

Despite several arguments in favour of involving people with dementia, the REC which reviewed the proposal recommended that this research project should preferably include relatives of people with early-stage dementia rather than those individuals themselves. The basis for this decision was a concern that when showing an excerpt from an educational film on IVA, people with dementia 'face the problem of possible uncertainty or provocation of emotional breakthroughs' (Erdmann & Schnepp, 2013). Although the REC did not specify what kind of emotions can occur, it can be assumed that unwanted emotions were meant, such as sadness, fear, worry or anger. The committee also proposed, as an alternative, an 'assessment of the individual risk situation by a familiar and gerontopsychiatrically experienced physician' (Erdmann & Schnepp, 2013) before any inclusion of a person with early-stage dementia. However, as people with early-stage dementia usually still live at home and are treated by various doctors who would have had to check the risk situation, this approach would have resulted in considerable additional work not only for the researchers but also for the people with dementia and the various doctors. Based on these considerations, we decided to exclude people with dementia and to interview relatives instead, despite knowing that those affected by dementia and their relatives do not necessarily always have the same interests (Erdmann & Schnepp, 2013).

The REC's recommendation in effect excluded people with early-stage dementia from participating, as the risk assessment by a physician with expertise in geriatric psychiatry appeared to be difficult to carry out in practice. The question is whether the ethics committee could have recommended other, more practical alternatives. In this context, the constitution of the REC is also interesting: the members of the committee were a clinical pharmacologist, a dentist, an ethicist (pastor), a lawyer/physician, a human geneticist, a radiologist and a mathematician. It is quite possible, then, that none of the members had any in-depth or specialised professional experience either with people with dementia or with qualitative research, and it is therefore questionable whether this committee had sufficient expertise to recommend other alternatives. But what alternative courses of action would have been possible and ethical? We make some suggestions below:

Ongoing Consent Instead of an One-off Consent and the Assessment of the Emotional Well-being

The recommendation of the REC in our example above suggests that its members assume that people with mild dementia cannot weigh up the risk (of an emotional breakthrough) posed by the research against the benefits themselves, but that only a doctor trained in geriatric psychiatry can do so. However, as dementia develops slowly, people with a dementia diagnosis are not immediately incapable of giving consent; rather, the ability to give consent depends on the progression of the disease and can vary depending on the time of day, concentration, motivation and general well-being (Gove et al., 2019). Considering that emotional breakthroughs can also occur in interview situations with participants suffering from other debilitating illnesses such as terminal cancer or motor neurone disease, it is inconceivable that people with dementia who are able to consent should be deprived of the opportunity to contribute to research. The questions that need to be answered are: in which cases, in which phase of the research process, and how, can the capacity to consent be determined, and who is responsible for this. We cannot assume that a person with a dementia diagnosis automatically has a limited capacity to consent, yet testing all such patients to assess their capacity, regardless of their clinical symptoms, may unintentionally stigmatise them and undermine their dignity. However, if researchers, the family or caregivers recognise clinical symptoms such as impaired memory, spatial disorientations, functional disability, poor concentration or communication, behavioural problems, fluctuation in mental performance or emotional dysfunction (Blossom & Brayne, 2014), then a structured evaluation of the capacity to consent may be appropriate. In addition, we should keep in mind that other reasons can cause a lack of capacity to consent, such as alcohol, medication, insomnia, etc. If we also cannot assume that the capacity to consent and the emotional resilience of people with dementia are not always equally good, they should not only be evaluated once prior to the start of the research but also during the research itself, for example, during the interview. However, this can only be done by the researcher themselves, unless an additional competent person is present at the same time. For this purpose, Dewing (2008) developed the 'process consent method', which entails as a first step generating biographical knowledge about how the person with dementia behaves when in a state of well-being. Taking this approach, a person's usual level of well-being should be recognised, and a description of their typical facial expressions for different levels of well-being should ideally be established to assess the person's emotional state. With this knowledge, a person's emotional state can be assessed at any time during the interview by the researcher themselves. Alternatively, a proxy who knows the person well could perform the role of tracking their well-being during the interview (Dewing, 2008). Should a person's well-being deteriorate significantly during their interview, the proxy could also act supportively.

Assessment of Capacity for Informed Consent

Assessing capacity to grant informed consent can be carried out with structured procedures. The most well-known and best validated questionnaire is the MacArthur Competence Tool for Clinical Research (MacCAT-CR) (Gilbert et al., 2017). This tool measures the capacity for informed consent on four dimensions: 1. understanding of the research project and procedures; 2. appreciation of the effects of research participation on the person themself; 3. reasoning about taking part in research; and 4. capacity to formulate a choice. Kim et al. (2001) tested the capacity for informed consent in a clinical trial with 37 people who had mild to severe Alzheimer's disease (AD) compared to 15 healthy elderly people who did not have AD. The proportion of people with AD who were unable to give informed consent depended on where the cut-off point was set. With a normative definition of the cut-off point (two standard deviations from the average of the comparison group), the incapacity on at least one dimension of the tool was 84% in the AD group. When the cut-off point was set by the judgement of three experts, however, the proportion of people with AD who were deemed not to have capacity in this context was only 62%. Conversely, this means that some people, despite their dementia, were competent in all four dimensions of capacity to consent (Kim et al., 2001). It would therefore be entirely possible to conduct studies with these people ethically, if the ability to give consent is checked with the MacCAT-CR when clinical symptoms are obvious and is continuously checked as part of ongoing consent. However, when obtaining informed consent, dementia-friendly methods should be used according to cognitive capacity. The information can also be communicated in plain language and possibly supplemented with pictures, objects or short videos (Dewing, 2008). Educational interventions for people with dementia could possibly improve their decisional capacity: Carpenter et al. (2000) used an abbreviated form of the MacCAT-CR to evaluate an educational intervention in patients with schizophrenia to improve their decisional impairment. During two 30-minute sessions, the study protocol was reviewed, information was provided, patients could ask questions and examples were given to illustrate the educational material. The authors tested the hypothesis that a reduced capacity for informed consent can be improved by the educational intervention. Indeed, the results showed a significant improvement in the understanding scores of patients participating in the educational sessions (Carpenter et al., 2000). This example shows that careful education can improve the informed consent process with people who are cognitively impaired.

CONCLUSION

Rather than excluding people with psychiatric and dementia diagnoses or intellectual disabilities from health research as a precautionary measure for their own protection, we strongly recommend enabling their access to research that is relevant to them. In any case, exclusion should never be based on diagnosis, as this would constitute discrimination (Bell et al., 2014; Carlsson et al., 2017; Øye et al., 2016; Schrems, 2014). However, enabling access to safe participation in research requires careful consideration. As our reflection on these cases shows, for a more appropriate assessment of the capacity to consent and the risks of harm, all three of the following dimensions should be considered: the specific research design (e.g. dyadic or non-dyadic interviews, participant-friendly study information, ongoing consent), the lifeworlds (e.g. dynamics in close relationships, dependencies, institutional settings) and the situational well-being of the research participants.

One way to achieve this, from our point of view, is to recognise and address the need for increased collaboration between RECs and researchers before, during and after research ethics review. Ethics review should not be one-sided, but a deliberative process between researchers and RECs, as this will allow for the development of a deeper understanding of the ethical challenges that research might raise. A deliberative process requires a spirit of collaboration and respect for each other's expertise (Brown et al., 2020; Carniel et al., 2023; Hickey et al., 2022). Prerequisites for developing respect for each other's expertise are that at least one member of the ethics committee has expertise in the field of research being reviewed, that the researchers perceive the ethics review as an opportunity for improvement and that both sides listen and communicate respectfully (Guillemin et al., 2012; Potthoff et al., 2024).

To enable consideration of knowledge about the respective lifeworlds of study participants, we propose two strategies. First, specific patient representatives should be included in REC meetings, where applicable, during the review process to sensitise committee members to the possible experiences of prospective participants, in our case of people with a psychiatric or dementia diagnosis. Second, the discussion should be extended to include (potential) study participants, as they know best about their personal situation including their personal relationships and situational well-being. Participant involvement in decisions that affect them should be continuously sought throughout the research process. In addition, researchers and, where appropriate, participants could be provided with specific guidelines containing information on particular research methods or participant groups. For example, the guideline 'Overcoming Ethical Challenges Affecting the Involvement of People with Dementia in Research: Recognising Diversity and Promoting Inclusive Research' (Gove et al., 2019) offers useful ideas for managing ethical challenges in the participation of people with dementia in research. Furthermore, when involving personal dyads of family members in health research, ethical considerations could be guided by the principle of preserving the 'pre-existing relationship between participants and their continuing relationship after the interview' (Voltelen et al., 2018, p. 9) in order to facilitate the best possible conditions for the future without causing distress to participants and endangering their well-being. A useful tool would be a joint preliminary reflection by researchers and (potential) participants on their needs regarding internal confidentiality. For example, interviewees could explicitly point out sensitive topics during the interview or in the preliminary discussion, which would assist researchers conducting the research.

Overall, we believe that our recommendations are also relevant to qualitative health research more widely, beyond the examples of individuals considered to be vulnerable that have been elaborated above, as health research often involves people who are in crisis, in a distressing situation or whose time is limited and precious.

NOTE

1. RECs are also known as institutional review boards (IRBs) and research ethics boards (REBs).

REFERENCES

Allbutt, H., & Masters, H. (2010). Ethnography and the ethics of undertaking research in different mental healthcare settings. *Journal of Psychiatric and Mental Health Nursing*, *17*(3), 210–215. https://doi.org/10.1111/j.1365-2850.2009.01493.x

Bell, E., Racine, E., Chiasson, P., Dufourcq-Brana, M., Dunn, L. B., Fins, J. J., Ford, P. J., Glannon, W., Macdonald, M. E., Mathews, D. J. H., & McAndrews, M. P. (2014). Beyond consent in research.

Revisiting vulnerability in deep brain stimulation for psychiatric disorders. *Cambridge Quarterly of Healthcare Ethics: CQ: The International Journal of Healthcare Ethics Committees*, *23*(3), 361–368. https://doi.org/10.1017/S0963180113000984

Blossom, S., & Brayne, C. (2014). Prevalence and projections of dementia. In M. Downs & B. Bowers (Eds.), *Excellence in dementia care. Research into practice* (2nd ed., pp. 3–19). Open University Press.

Bracken-Roche, D., Bell, E., & Racine, E. (2016). The "vulnerability" of psychiatric research participants: Why this research ethics concept needs to be revisited. *Canadian Journal of Psychiatry. Revue Canadienne De Psychiatrie*, *61*(6), 335–339. https://doi.org/10.1177/0706743716633422

Brown, C., Spiro, J., & Quinton, S. (2020). The role of research ethics committees: Friend or foe in educational research? An exploratory study. *British Educational Research Journal*, *46*(4), 747–769. https://doi.org/10.1002/berj.3654

Buchner, B., Hase, F., Borchers, D., & Pigeot, I. (2019). Aufgaben, Regularien und Arbeitsweise von Ethikkommissionen [Tasks, regulations, and functioning of ethics committees]. *Bundesgesundheitsblatt, Gesundheitsforschung, Gesundheitsschutz*, *62*(6), 690–696. https://doi.org/10.1007/s00103-019-02945-7

Carlsson, I.-M., Blomqvist, M., & Jormfeldt, H. (2017). Ethical and methodological issues in qualitative studies involving people with severe and persistent mental illness such as schizophrenia and other psychotic conditions: A critical review. *International Journal of Qualitative Studies on Health and Well-being*, *12*, 1368323.

Carniel, J., Hickey, A., Southey, K., Brömdal, A., Crowley-Cyr, L., Eacersall, D., Farmer, W., Gehrmann, R., Machin, T., & Pillay, Y. (2023). The ethics review and the humanities and social sciences: Disciplinary distinctions in ethics review processes. *Research Ethics*, *19*(2), 139–156.

Carpenter, W. T., Gold, J. M., Lahti, A. C., Queern, C. A., Conley, R. R., Bartko, J. J., Kovnick, J., Appelbaum, P. S. (2000). Decisional capacity for informed consent in schizophrenia research. *Archives of General Psychiatry*, *57*(6), 533–538.

Collaço, N., Wagland, R., Alexis, O., Gavin, A., Glaser, A., & Watson, E. K. (2021). Using the framework method for the analysis of qualitative dyadic data in health research. *Qualitative Health Research*, *31*(8), 1555–1564. https://doi.org/10.1177/10497323211011599

Council for International Organizations of Medical Sciences. (2016). *International guidelines for health-related research involving humans*. CIOMS. https://cioms.ch/wp-content/uploads/2017/01/WEB-CIOMS-EthicalGuidelines.pdf

Dewing, J. (2008). Process consent and research with older persons living with dementia. *Research Ethics Review*, *4*(2), 59–64.

Dilger, H. (2017). Ethics, epistemology, and ethnography: The need for an anthropological debate on ethical review processes in Germany. *Sociologus*, *67*(2), 191–208.

Eisikovits, Z., & Koren, C. (2010). Approaches to and outcomes of dyadic interview analysis. *Qualitative Health Research*, *20*(12), 1642–1655. https://doi.org/10.1177/1049732310376520

Erdmann, A., & Schnepp, W. (2013). Integrative validation (IVA) im Pflegeheim: Entwicklung eines Forschungsdesigns für eine qualitative Evaluationsstudie. *Pflegewissenschaft*, *15*(6), 325–332. https://doi.org/10.3936/1218

Erdmann, A., & Schnepp, W. (2016). Conditions, components and outcomes of integrative validation therapy in a long-term care facility for people with dementia. A qualitative evaluation study. *Dementia (London)*, *15*(5), 1184–1204. https://doi.org/10.1177/1471301214556489

Forbat, L., & Henderson, J. (2003). "Stuck in the middle with you": The ethics and process of qualitative research with two people in an intimate relationship. *Qualitative Health Research*, *13*(10), 1453–1462. https://doi.org/10.1177/1049732303255836

Friesen, P., Gelinas, L., Kirby, A., Strauss, D. H., & Bierer, B. E. (2023). Irbs and the protection-inclusion dilemma: Finding a balance. *The American Journal of Bioethics: AJOB*, *23*(6), 75–88. https://doi.org/10.1080/15265161.2022.2063434

Gauckler, C. (2021). Philosophers in research ethics committees-what do they think they're doing? An empirical-ethical analysis. *Medicine, Health Care, and Philosophy*, *24*(4), 609–619. https://doi.org/10.1007/s11019-021-10044-1

Gilbert, T., Bosquet, A., Thomas-Anterion, C., Bonnefoy, M., & Le Saux, O. (2017). Assessing capacity to consent for research in cognitively impaired older patients. *Clinical Interventions in Aging*, *12*, 1553–1563. https://doi.org/10.2147/CIA.S141905

Gove, D., Georges, J., Rauf, M., Broeke, J., Jongsma, K., Claeys, A., Berdai, S., Hellström, I, Tromp, K., Porteri, C., & Watchman, K. (2019). *Overcoming ethical challenges affecting the involvement of people with dementia in research: Recognizing diversity and promoting inclusive research.* Alzheimer Europe. https://www.alzheimer-europe.org/sites/default/files/2022-01/05706%20Alzheimer%20Europe%20ethics%20report%202019_92.pdf

Graor, C. H., & Knapik, G. P. (2013). Addressing methodological and ethical challenges of qualitative health research on persons with schizophrenia and bipolar disorder. *Archives of Psychiatric Nursing, 27*(2), 65–71. https://doi.org/10.1016/j.apnu.2012.10.006

Grisso, T., & Appelbaum, P. S. (1998). *Assessing competence to consent to treatment.* Oxford University Press.

Guba, E. G., & Lincoln, Y. S. (1989). *Fourth generation evaluation.* Sage Publications.

Guillemin, M., & Gillam, L. (2004). Ethics, reflexivity, and "ethically important moments" in research. *Qualitative Inquiry, 10*(2), 261–280. https://doi.org/10.1177/1077800403262360

Guillemin, M., Gillam, L., Rosenthal, D., & Bolitho, A. (2012). Human RECs: Examining their roles and practices. *Journal of Empirical Research on Human Research Ethics, 7*(3), 38–49.

Gumede, D., Ngwenya, N. B., Namukwaya, S., Bernays, S., & Seeley, J. (2019). A reflection on ethical and methodological challenges of using separate interviews with adolescent-older carer dyads in rural South Africa. *BMC Medical Ethics, 20*(1), 47. https://doi.org/10.1186/s12910-019-0383-9

Hellström, I., Nolan, M., Nordenfelt, L., & Lundh, U. (2007). Ethical and methodological issues in interviewing persons with dementia. Nursing Ethics, 14(5), 608–619.

Hempeler, C., Potthoff, S., Scholten, M., Juckel, G., & Gather, J. (2024). Strategies to promote treatment compliance: A grounded theory study with relatives of people with a serious mental health condition. *BMC Psychiatry 24*, 490. https://doi.org/10.1186/s12888-024-05907-9

Hickey, A., Davis, S., Farmer, W., Dawidowicz, J., Moloney, C., Lamont-Mills, A., . . . Maxwell, J. (2022). Beyond criticism of ethics review boards: Strategies for engaging research communities and enhancing ethical review processes. *Journal of Academic Ethics, 20*(4), 549–567. https://doi.org/10.1007/s10805-021-09430-4

Holland, K. (2007). The epistemological bias of ethics review. *Qualitative Inquiry, 13*(6), 895–913. https://doi.org/10.1177/1077800407304469

Kim, S. Y. H. (2010). *Evaluation of capacity to consent to treatment and research.* Oxford University Press.

Kim, S. Y. H., Caine, E. D., Currier, G. W., Leibovici, A., & Ryan, J. M. (2001). Assessing the competence of persons with Alzheimer's disease in providing informed consent for participation in research. *American Journal of Psychiatry, 158*(5), 712–717. https://doi.org/10.1176/appi.ajp.158.5.712

Øye, C., Sørensen, NØ., & Glasdam, S. (2016). Qualitative research ethics on the spot: Not only on the desktop. *Nursing Ethics, 23*(4), 455–464.

Peter, E. (2015). The ethics in qualitative health research: Special considerations. *Ciencia & Saude Coletiva, 20*(9), 2625–2630. https://doi.org/10.1590/1413-81232015209.06762015

Peter, E., & Friedland, J. (2017). Recognizing risk and vulnerability in research ethics: Imagining the "what ifs?". *Journal of Empirical Research on Human Research Ethics: JERHRE, 12*(2), 107–116. https://doi.org/10.1177/1556264617696920

Pigeot, I., Foraita, R., Frömke, C., Haller, B., Hoffmann, V. S., & Zapf, A. (2019). Ethische Bewertung von Studien am Menschen außerhalb des regulatorischen Rahmens: Nicht bindend, aber von großer Wichtigkeit. *Bundesgesundheitsblatt, 62*, 722–728. https://doi.org/10.1007/s00103-019-02947-5

Potthoff, S., Gather, J., Hempeler, C., Gieselmann, A., & Scholten, M. (2022). Voluntary in quotation marks: A conceptual model of psychological pressure in mental healthcare based on a grounded theory analysis of interviews with service users. *BMC Psychiatry, 22*, 186.

Potthoff, S., Hempeler, C., Gather, J., Gieselmann, A., Vollmann, J., & Scholten, M. (2023). Research ethics in practice: An analysis of ethical issues encountered in qualitative health research with mental health service users and relatives. *Medicine, Health Care, and Philosophy, 26*(4), 517–527. https://doi.org/10.1007/s11019-023-10169-5

Potthoff, S., Roth, F., & Scholten, M. (2024). Qualitative health research and procedural ethics: An interview study to investigate researchers' ways of navigating the demands of medical research ethics committees in Germany. *Research Ethics*, *20*(2), 388–410. https://doi.org/10.1177/17470161231202135

Racine, E., & Bracken-Roche, D. (2019). Enriching the concept of vulnerability in research ethics: An integrative and functional account. *Bioethics*, *33*(1), 19–34. https://doi.org/10.1111/bioe.12471

Rat für Sozial- und Wirtschaftsdaten (2017). *Forschungsethische Grundsätze und Prüfverfahren in den Sozial- und Wirtschaftswissenschaften*. German Data Forum (RatSWD). https://doi.org/10.17620/02671.1

RatSWD (Rat für Sozial- und Wirtschaftsdaten/German Data Forum). (2017). Forschungsethische Grundsätze und Prüfverfahren in den Sozial- und Wirtschaftswissenschaften. German Data Forum (RatSWD). https://doi.org/10.17620/02671.1

Reitinger, E., Pichler, B., Egger, B., Knoll, B., Hofleitner, B., Plunger, P., Dressel, G., & Heimerl, K. (2018). Research with people with dementia—ethical reflections on qualitative research praxis on mobility in public space. *Forum Qualitative Sozialforschung Forum: Qualitative Social Research*, *19*(3). https://doi.org/10.17169/fqs-19.3.3152

Scholten, M., Gather, J., & Vollmann, J. (2021). Equality in the informed consent process: Competence to consent, substitute decision-making, and discrimination of persons with mental disorders. *The Journal of Medicine and Philosophy*, *46*(1), 108–136.

Schrems, B. M. (2014). Informed consent, vulnerability and the risks of group-specific attribution. *Nursing Ethics*, *21*(7), 829–843. https://doi.org/10.1177/0969733013518448

Strobel, A., Zeiler, A., & Schaar, K. (2022). *Der Stand der Dinge zur forschungsethischen Begutachtung in den Geistes- und Sozialwissenschaften: Ergebnisse einer Umfrage unter Forschenden*. RatSWD Working Paper No. 278. Rat für Sozial- und Wirtschaftsdaten (RatSWD), Berlin. https://doi.org/10.17620/02671.67

Szmukler, G., & Appelbaum, P. S. (2008). Treatment pressures, leverage, coercion, and compulsion in mental health care. *Journal of Mental Health*, *17*(3), 233–244. https://doi.org/10.1080/09638230802052203

Tolich, M. (2004). Internal confidentiality: When confidentiality assurances fail relational informants. *Qualitative Sociology*, *27*(1), 101–106. https://doi.org/10.1023/B:QUAS.0000015546.20441.4a

Tolich, M., & Tumilty, E. (2020). Practicing ethics and ethics praxis. *The Qualitative Report*, *25*(13), 16–30. https://doi.org/10.46743/2160-3715/2020.4753

Ummel, D., & Achille, M. (2016). How not to let secrets out when conducting qualitative research with dyads. *Qualitative Health Research*, *26*(6), 807–815. https://doi.org/10.1177/1049732315627427

Voltelen, B., Konradsen, H., & Østergaard, B. (2018). Ethical considerations when conducting joint interviews with close relatives or family: An integrative review. *Scandinavian Journal of Caring Sciences*, *32*(2), 515–526. https://doi.org/10.1111/scs.12535

Von Unger, H., Dilger, H., & Schönhuth, M. (2016). Ethics reviews in the social and cultural sciences? A sociological and anthropological contribution to the debate. *Forum: Qualitative Social Research*, *17*(3). http://www.qualitative-research.net/index.php/fqs/article/view/2719/4033

Wilkinson, H. (2007). Including people with dementia in research: Methods and motivations. In H. Wilkinson (Ed.), *The perspectives of people with dementia. research methods and motivations*. Jessica Kingsley Publishers Ltd.

Witham, G., Beddow, A., & Haigh, C. (2015). Reflections on access: Too vulnerable to research? *Journal of Research in Nursing*, *20*(1), 28–37. https://doi.org/10.1177/1744987113499338

World Medical Association. (2013). *Declaration of Helsinki: Ethical principles for medical research involving human subjects*. https://www.wma.net/policies-post/wma-declaration-of-helsinki-ethical-principles-for-medical-research-involving-human-subjects/

Zarhin, D. (2018). Conducting joint interviews with couples: Ethical and methodological challenges. *Qualitative Health Research*, *28*(5), 844–854. https://doi.org/10.1177/1049732317749196

CHAPTER 14

RESEARCH INTEGRITY AND QUALITATIVE RESEARCH: TACKLING AND RESEARCHING UNETHICAL PRACTICES AT THE TOP

Nina Peršak

Institute for Criminal-Law Ethics and Criminology, Slovenia

ABSTRACT

Research integrity is an integral element of research excellence, of research ethics and trust in science. This chapter first examines the concept of research integrity, its different conceptions, evolution and possible distinctions between different fields of research. While many universities tend to tackle the problems in this area with research integrity courses aimed at early-stage scholars, I argue that the real responsibility lies also, or even primarily, at the top – with power-holders, institutions and structures. This chapter then addresses some problems with tackling such behaviour and researching this topic, particularly with regard to qualitative research. It concludes with some possible solutions or recommendations for ethical, integrity-respecting research.

Keywords: Research integrity; research ethics; qualitative research; power; structural factors

Reframing Qualitative Research Ethics
Advances in Research Ethics and Integrity, Volume 12, 235–251

ISSN: 2398-6018/doi:10.1108/S2398-601820250000012014

I. INTRODUCTION

Research integrity is an integral element of research excellence, a bedrock of public trust in research (Robishaw et al., 2019) and a key notion that lies at the heart of many discussions on research ethics, even though it often eludes concrete operationalisation in research ethics codes. This, on the one hand, allows research integrity to remain a rather abstract and amorphous notion in the eyes of many and, on the other, enables the concept of research ethics to stay largely disassociated from (wider) discussions about research integrity, limited to specific issues regarding the ethical handling of various matters occurring during actual research activities, such as research participant consent, personal data protection, handling of human cells and animals, possible misuse of data and similar issues that can be easily checked by institutional ethics committees prior to issuing approval.

Although research integrity is becoming more prominent at the university level, with committees, courses, training, guidelines and so on being established, these mechanisms still remain mostly narrow, and insufficiently address wider integrity-jeopardising conduct as well as the question of power (and those in powerful positions) and heightened research integrity risks that come from that. However, it is the latter, in particular, that strikes at the heart of research integrity and set the tone and tempo of how malpractices in this area are going to be addressed.

This chapter begins by examining the concept of research integrity, its different conceptions, evolution and possible distinctions between different fields of research. While many universities tend to tackle the problem, or deviations from the ideal, with various research integrity courses aimed at early-stage personnel or PhD students and by focusing on individual responsibility, I then argue that the real responsibility lies primarily at the top – with power-holders, institutionally and structurally. In doing so, I draw on real-life examples (reported under pseudonyms to protect the identities of those involved) and observations from several Western and Central European countries and their universities or research institutions, spanning the last two decades, in addition to other studies and literature. This chapter then addresses some problems with tackling such behaviour and with researching this topic, particularly within qualitative research. It concludes with some possible solutions or recommendations for ethical, integrity-respecting research, in this respect. While I mostly use the term 'research integrity', in light of its advocated broad conceptualisation, research integrity should be understood here as being coterminous with 'academic integrity' and 'scientific integrity' or with 'integrity *in* science and the 'integrity *of* science' (Mody et al., 2020, p. 373; emphasis in the original).

II. RESEARCH INTEGRITY: CONCEPTIONS, EVOLUTION AND QUALITATIVE RESEARCH

Conceptions: Narrow vs Broad

Research integrity, or rather the lack thereof, is often clarified in terms of avoidance of misconduct (Khanyile et al., 2006) or 'bad science', such as fabricated data, plagiarism, inappropriate use of statistical methodology, poor record keeping and data management, irresponsible authorship and similar (League of European Research Universities (LERU), 2020, p. 15), and so the emphasis on the need for research integrity in order to achieve 'excellence of, and trust in, research produced by universities' (LERU, 2020, p. 3) is understandable. Viewed from this perspective, research integrity is mostly about research production, that is, about research methodology and outcomes, not about research environments as such. One university definition (from Imperial College London) of research integrity, for example, explains it as

> conducting research in a way which allows others to have trust and confidence in the methods used and the findings in that result. It is not just a reflection of the individual research project, but of the institution, its researchers and the wider research community. Research integrity applies to the whole research lifecycle, from preparation and submission of grant and project proposals to the publication and dissemination of findings. (Imperial, n.d.)[1]

The European Federation of Academies of Sciences and Humanities' (ALLEA, 2023, p. 5) fundamental principles of research integrity, described in its European Code of Conduct for Research Integrity, include reliability, honesty, respect and accountability.

All these considerations are certainly extremely important and, in particular, the emphasis on the 'whole research lifecycle', considering that much discussion on research integrity revolves around issues such as consent and respect for respondents, robust data collection and analysis, proper data management, including respecting the General Data Protection Regulation, while forgetting critical stages such as preparation and submission of project proposals, which are often ridden with unethical, exploitative practices that seem in-built in the system and accepted by many. Unethical practices around applications for research funding, for example, include taking the credit or authorship for the proposal (as principal researcher and later, if successful, grant holder or project leader) while actually delegating the entire substantive work to junior research personnel or even students. As academic survival often depends on getting a grant to fund one's mostly precarious, fixed-term employment for the duration of the project, junior staff rarely dare to object, even if – in the long term – this practice does not serve them, as references for obtaining the grant go to the formally listed principal investigator (PI), not them, perpetuating their dependence on progressively successful professors who are award holders.

Despite the importance of the above-mentioned considerations for research integrity, these still amount to a rather 'narrow' definition of research integrity. In broader terms, research integrity should be understood as integrity in and of research, where 'research' is understood in terms of the broad activities of research institutions (and, in this way, as overlapping with terms such as 'scientific integrity' and 'academic integrity'), not merely linked to individual research project activities. This includes scrutinising practices that go against integrity in research settings, including, for example, (sexual) harassment, corruption, declaring and managing conflicts of interest, influencing results of public procurement and other abuses of power in research settings, as well as structural set-ups that impede research integrity. If research integrity were to be understood in this broader way, this would more clearly elucidate the interlinkages between, for example, the (purposeful) misattribution of authorship, gender dimension of research integrity, attrition of female PhD students and promotion of narcissistic and Machiavellian personalities into positions of leadership (Vaknin, 2008), as well as between structural frameworks (for example, relating to funding and evaluation) that undermine integrity and reticence at the top to interfere with status quo.[2] Such a broad definition of research integrity is bound to encounter certain opposition from those eager to embrace it as an unduly contemporary proclamation or virtue signalling which is supposed to demonstrate one's high commitment to ethics and responsible governance, yet whose secret aim beyond nominal adherence is not to radically change much, if anything, in the way the existing systems and structures operate.

Evolution: From Punitive to Educational, From Ethics to Competence

In the 1990s, when research integrity started appearing as an issue to be addressed more systematically in universities and other research institutions, ideas about adding training on it to the curriculum, at least as a lecture in the 'induction programme' for freshers and early-career scholars, appeared. The first approach to tacking practices that ran counter to it, conceived mostly as research (or scientific) misconduct, was controlling and punitive. Turnitin and similar plagiarism detection programmes were used (and still are) to check students' essays or other written work and, subsequently, penalise them if the software detected possible plagiarism. Students have progressively been warned in advance that this may follow, and in some cases, asked to sign a declaration of honour that what they are submitting is their own work.

With time, these approaches softened or broadened, acquiring a certain preventive, educational dimension as well. Training meant to clarify what is and what is not permissible was introduced, for example. Yet, the focus was on students and junior staff. This appears to have been based on the assumption that they are the ones most at risk of violating research integrity, be it because they do not know where the boundaries lie or be it because they are reckless or intentionally mischievous (for example, in order to get better marks).

Another observed shift involved the move from seeing research integrity as part of ethics to seeing it as a set of competencies. As the LERU writes:

> As it is a constitutive element of research literacy and of responsible scientific practice, it is important that the knowledge of and skills to develop research integrity are not seen as addenda to the core curriculum, but rather as an essential competence for future researchers. (2020, p. 15)

While this may make it more palatable to some, particularly to those averse to questions of ethics or those seeing ethics in relativist terms, such a representation of research integrity removes it from the question of values to something measurable and commodified. (One may put it on the CV as a 'skill' or 'competency'.) However, having a certificate in passing a course on research integrity does not 'a researcher of integrity' make. The notion of research integrity as a mere 'competency' devalues in some sense the meaning of research integrity, even if, in a system which drives students to work only to obtain some credit, this may indeed incentivise some to take up such a course, if it is not otherwise mandatory. Such a perspective can make research integrity be seen as a tool one learns how to handle, rather than as a value in itself.

Distinction: Natural vs Social Sciences, Quantitative vs Qualitative

The narrow understanding of research integrity as merely research ethics, dealing with misconduct during research production, or as a competency to be learnt, is not, however, the only problem. One only needs to scroll through various social media groups dedicated to research to observe a certain diversity if not a 'clash' of cultures related to different domains or disciplines, specifically along the natural/social science or quantitative/qualitative lines, or both, which permeates debates on what is ethical and what is respecting research integrity and what is not.

In the popular Facebook group 'Reviewer 2 must be stopped!', for example, there have been numerous occasions where problematic co-authorship practices have been brought up by a poster (often preferring to remain anonymous for fear of reprisal).[3] In the discussion that followed in the comments under the post, one could often spot scholars from the natural sciences pointing out the normalcy of, or even defending, practices that involve adding lots of co-authors to papers even if some of these authors had merely obtained the grant or allowed their lab to be used without having provided any substantive input to the manuscript itself. Their social science and qualitative research peers, conversely, often seem to be the ones pointing out that such practices are in conflict with, for example, the Committee on Publication Ethics (COPE) guidelines.

In social science (and humanities) qualitative research, it is often the case that no advanced statistical processing of data is required and so it is less usual for statisticians or junior scholars performing SPSS analyses to be included as co-authors of the paper purely by dint of having made some contribution with regard to statistical analysis of data (usually collected by someone else). In qualitative research, it is more common that the authors who collected the primary data are also the sole authors of the analysis and, finally, of the manuscript they produce in the end. On average, publications in the humanities have fewer co-authors than publications within other main research areas (Henriksen, 2016). Such differences in the way research is performed in different disciplines have been considered as a possible explanation for the reason why 'collaborative research among research performing organisations' was scored as having lower importance among various research integrity topics by humanities researchers than other researchers in focus group research (Sørensen et al., 2021, p. 5). Methodological differences across fields therefore impact on the perception of intra-field importance of various research integrity issues.

The above observation on co-authorship discussions does not mean, of course, that social scientists or qualitative researchers are any more integrity-proof than their natural science and quantitative research counterparts. It does, however, indicate that there may be different research cultures in which certain practices that may be seen as unethical and integrity-violating to some are either normalised or seen as unproblematic to others. Designing a one-size-fits-all approach regarding research integrity may thus encounter further obstacles if this is not taken into consideration. This observation may also be behind LERU's preference for an approach that is not top-down, one-for-all, but rather one 'that implements a tailor-made and often discipline-specific approach that is sensitive to the local context' (LERU, 2020, p. 15). The necessity for research performing organisations to consider disciplinary differences when framing research integrity policies so as to ensure that they are relevant was stressed by social science and humanities researchers in focus group research, with the latter explicitly critical of being held to standards that have nothing to do with their practice. In the view of many participants in Sørensen et al.'s research, a more differentiated approach would also help research organisations to legitimise their research integrity policies and procedures (Sørensen et al., 2021, p. 5).

Qualitative research may have its own specific risks and pitfalls. For example, 'qualitative research is sometimes defined as interpretive research, and as interpretations can be incorrect or biased, the findings may be controversial' (Sanjari et al., 2014). The dynamics of qualitative studies also often present new and unexpected ethical dilemmas in practice, for example, during interviews or fieldwork, which escape clear-cut solutions or examples provided in ethical guidelines and codes, requiring, instead, more 'situational solutions' (Taquette & Borges da Matta Souza, 2022, pp. 1–2). Roth, for example, has provided a very honest and graphic depiction of how the working conditions of survey fieldworkers (such as the tediousness of writing down numbers on pieces of paper, time-consuming transcription activities, having to ask embarrassing or nonsensical questions and time pressures) can easily become a source of misconduct. Starting from seemingly innocuous misbehaviour (not surveying throughout the full designated timeslot, leaving early), the questionable conduct of 'hired hands' (contracted for this task) 'soon boomeranged into a full cheating syndrome, where we would fake observations for some time slot which were never observed on the ward', lying to supervisors, cutting corners with inter-rater reliability checks, completing respondents' replies in the questionnaires or make them up and similar (Roth, 1966, pp. 190–191).

III. FOCUS ON 'THE BOTTOM' WITH LESS ATTENTION DEDICATED TO 'THE TOP'

While there are mandatory training courses in ethics aimed at junior scholars such as PhD students and early-career researchers, not enough focus is dedicated to 'the top', as if only those occupying the lower rungs of the academic ladder are at risk (or much more at risk) of violating research integrity, or as if the violation of research integrity by them is more serious. Recommendations that research integrity education should be 'mandatory' for 'PhD researchers and research students', while such training should only be 'offered' to 'more senior researchers' (LERU, 2020, p. 15), perpetuates the idea that those really in need of awareness raising on research integrity are junior researchers, while for 'senior researchers' – and it is unclear whether this also includes managers and heads of departments – training on awareness of these topics is optional.[4]

It is certainly important that younger people are socialised into integrity early on by developing the skills, knowledge, critical thinking and moral compass necessary for future integrity-respecting conduct (Lynch et al., 2022), and it is also known that job insecurity disproportionately affects younger researchers and may provide a certain stimulus for questionable research conduct (Dingwall, 1980). However, it would be unjustified to conclude that younger or more junior scholars are more prone to illegitimate, immoral, integrity-violating behaviour. So, whence does this viewpoint arise? The following small-scale study by Storr (2004) may provide some interesting insights. This study into the relationship between leadership and integrity, carried out in the United Kingdom and comprising 18 interviews, has revealed that *perceptions* of leadership character and leadership behaviour are used to evaluate the *effectiveness and integrity* of a leader. The author concludes that

> the findings suggest that leaders are not judged according to the ethical nature of decision making [...] but that the importance of integrity and ethical leadership correlated with higher levels of hierarchical status and that it is *assumed by virtue of status and success that leaders lead with integrity*. (Storr, 2004, p. 415; emphasis added)

However, such an assumption is clearly problematic and runs counter to the well-known adage that power corrupts and absolute power corrupts absolutely. Having this in mind, if anything should be 'assumed', it is that those with the most power who are the most 'at risk', as it were, to abusing power and acting without integrity if it serves their goals. And what are the goals or targets for those higher up? More publications, more research grants, more PhD students (PhD defences), academic promotions, rewards and so forth – goals that are considered indicators of 'success' and 'effectiveness' or lead to a higher status or allow the maintaining of their status, but which often stimulate bending of the rules, disregarding of work-life balance and normal working hours, and an increase of pressures and competition among 'subordinates' and similar. The fact that they often blame their junior staff and graduate students when their own misconduct is discovered is a testament to how salient and particularly pernicious are the violations of integrity when perpetrated by those in power.[5]

Furthermore, a lack of integrity at the top 'trickles down', as individuals read the conduct of leaders or those at the top as 'messages' and corporate values to be adopted in order to fit in. They are likely to mimic their superiors (supervisors, heads of departments, deans, other persons of authority) in order to get into their good graces and gain possible advantage, for example, in terms of being considered as a good candidate to be 'kept on' after their PhD, postdoc or project ends.

One typical, regular occurring example of such research integrity-violating conduct from the upper ranks of academic personnel is plagiarism. On the one hand, this encompasses the misconduct itself. Professors, like top government members,[6] have been found guilty of this prototypical academic misconduct, yet, as Bailey (2019) astutely observes, 'though we've seen our share of stories of professors and other academics being accused of plagiarism, there's still very little oversight over instructors, even as they put more and more pressure on their students to follow the rules'. While student work is often regularly monitored through plagiarism detection software, such as Turnitin, PlagiarismCheck and similar, professorial work – outside of submission to journals which use these as standard practice as well – rarely is.[7] On the other hand, the integrity story stretches beyond this, as it also includes (and must include) a visibly cavalier or nonchalant attitude of the perpetrator's colleagues towards such misconduct.

Another example is that of data fabrication, for example, of interviews being made up, surveys being replied to by the researcher's spouse and so forth, and supervisors' conduct towards it. In addition to clearly unethical research conduct, 'research misconduct' or 'academic dishonesty', research integrity-problematic behaviour related to this includes collegial pressures not to report the discovered misconduct, for example, of a PhD student (about to defend his doctoral thesis) of another professorial colleague who will receive a significant financial reward from the university for every successfully defended PhD thesis under their supervision. This also raises queries regarding the inherent risks (and possible mitigating measures or safeguards to be put in place) of a system that stimulates the acquisition of PhD students and rewards the supervisors for the successful completion of the formers' PhD trajectories. A professorial colleague, even if on an academic or hierarchical par with the supervisor, may feel strongly conflicted when they have to oscillate between what is the right/ethical thing to do and being a 'team player', maintaining collegiality, loyalty and support for their close-knit professional community, which may 'ostracise' them or seek revenge in a myriad of small ways, should they fail to do so.

Then, there is authorship (mis)attribution: even nowadays, in well-developed democracies and highly ranked universities, cases appear where supervisors unashamedly expect or dictate to their PhD students to list their name as co-authors of a paper, in the writing of which they had no substantive input. This is illustrated by the experience of 'Beth', one of several cases of researchers' experiences which have been made known to me and which are reported here under a pseudonym. In this case, Beth, who was in the advanced years of her PhD studies, her supervisor insisted she put him and his friend who 'needed some publications' among the authors of her paper. Coming originally from a different academic background, she was appalled by this, and confided in another departmental professor and friend, who was equally shocked and offered to alert the university's disciplinary body on her behalf. However, the next day, Beth realising that this could seriously hurt her standing and success at defending her thesis, which was coming up soon, begged the friendly professor not to say anything to anyone. With COPE standards and university policies on research integrity being progressively adopted, one hopes that such unethical conduct is diminishing. However, it has been around for decades, and left mostly unproblematised. Professors were and, to a large extent, still are seen as being untouchable – protected by their power, academic status, social standing and institution, which does not want dirty laundry discussed in public, particularly when this dirty laundry is just the tip of the iceberg or it gets them more funds, higher ranking and prestige.

While not considered plagiarism per se (as not based on a preceding publication) another kind of research integrity-violating conduct is the stealing of ideas, prior to publication. For example, 'Marina', a tenure-track Assistant Professor, invited a renowned British professor to contribute to her edited volume on a particular criminological topic. He respectfully declined for lack of time and, particularly, a preference for publishing in journals, but then this professor decided to edit a journal issue with a colleague on the same topic, and the central points of focus and rationale for this proposed special issue read as an almost verbatim copy of the content of the proposed edited volume that Marina revealed to him in her invitation email. (The only way Marina found out about this is because one of the chapter contributors to her volume had been asked to peer review the special issue proposal and alerted her to uncanny similarity between her invitation email and forthcoming book and their special issue which – journals being quicker in terms of publication, especially 'online first' – managed to come out a bit before Marina's book.) Nowhere in the journal special issue proposal or later introduction to this special issue is Marina's previous work on the topic or her forthcoming book referred to.

In these stories and examples, the gender dimension probably cannot be neglected. In many domains, particularly in social sciences and humanities, PhD students are predominantly female, while their supervisors and bosses are (still) predominantly male and often much older.[8] The power that the latter exert often extends to (sexual) harassment, which should in this setting also be regarded as a problem of the integrity of the research performing institution in question. For example, harassment has been found to disproportionally affect marginalised groups such as women, ethnic and sexual minorities (Lopez et al., 2009; Martin, 2003; McLaughlin et al., 2012; Naezer et al., 2019; Trotman Reid & Clayton, 1992). As exemplified below, young women with PhDs are still used for secretarial work that is not expected either from their male counterparts or (even) from male doctoral students. Similarly, they are expected (by senior male and female professors) to display more empathy and to perform 'traditional' female chores for them, such as babysitting. This, for example, is a story of 'Sara', who was completing her PhD during her visiting scholarship at Cambridge, when her senior colleague – for whom Sara was managing two research projects (proposals for which were also written by Sara) in her native country where both worked – came for a longer visit. After being there a while, she suddenly emailed Sara only to ask her directly to babysit her son, as she wanted to visit London. Sara being ill (in addition to being swamped with finalising her thesis due in a month, which her colleague knew about) excused herself but proposed to put up an announcement at her college, as many students are happy to take on some extra work. This, however, backfired. Her colleague never responded, sabotaged her communication with her boss regarding the projects Sara was managing for her and, in view of her colleague's influence at home, eventually succeeded in blocking her further employment prospects at the institution.

While field researchers are often trained to be aware of the power imbalances between themselves and their subjects, which requires particular sensitivity, self-awareness and care towards the latter, including the avoidance of situations in which their subjects would need to employ life-surviving strategies to negotiate their way out, regular work hierarchies rarely take such power differentials into account in the sense of obliging bosses of various types to pass an ethics/integrity training on similar power issues – these situations are rarely even perceived as raising an ethics or integrity issue. Nevertheless, as the above cases demonstrate, this is sorely needed.

IV. PRACTICAL PROBLEMS WITH ADDRESSING AND RESEARCHING THIS TOPIC

Practical problems with tackling behaviours, such as those mentioned above, start with people not coming forward, not reporting the unethical conduct out of shame or fear of reprisal (see, for example, Ahmed, 2021), distrust towards those to whom they should report (be they a person or an institutional body) or, simply, out of belief (or experience) that nothing will change. The same problem is encountered when trying to research the topic, particularly qualitatively (which requires in-depth interviews or surveys or focus groups), as respondents have to be willing to speak, to expose their identity and emotions. In interviews, for example, reliving such stories through telling them brings about discomfort, which may further impede the full disclosure of information.

Another problem is the reluctance on the part of authorities (for example, heads of departments, faculties) to tackle this issue for whatever reason. Sometimes the way things are is working for them, other times they are themselves facing reticence and reluctance among their subordinates, fellow professors and staff at the intermediate level of academic hierarchy to implement changes. In all cases, however, the most pressure lies on the most vulnerable – that is, the victim – to report and describe exactly what happened and implicate the usually more established and permanently employed persons at the institution. The victim, if not protected, has much to lose – as fictionalised beautifully in the 2020 film *The Assistant*, in which the protagonist, Jane, a hard-working young woman, finally decides to go to the human resource (HR) officer to report the improper, 'casting-couch' conduct of her boss, only to be met there with seemingly friendly advice, masked as a question, that follows upon the officer first complementing her skills and acknowledging that she has what it takes to make it there: 'So, why are you here trying to throw it all away over this bullshit?'

This brings us to the problem of reporting and whistle-blowing procedures, in which the victim is not really protected. In some cases, all that is available is a regular disciplinary (or even criminal) procedure, in which the victim is exposed from the outset, as they cannot remain anonymous. Many such proceedings end with the suspect being acquitted of charges, while the victim is ostracised, not only from the workplace but from similar workplaces or even the wider academic and research industry.

The power differential mentioned above and, more generally, distribution of power that is left without any checks and supervision, means that there is a lot at stake for those at 'the bottom' to come out. And even if or when they do, repercussions may be great, while rewards may be little or none. A culture of silence and complicity as well as concerns with corporate image often get in the way of tackling such unsavoury, unethical, integrity-violating workplace conduct. Some blame the procedures (for example, 'they didn't want to press charges (for sexual harassment), so we couldn't do much'), others normalise the situation by rationalisation ('everyone, everywhere does that') or justify it prospectively, in the long run ('someday it will be your turn'). This was Hannah's experience: she already had her PhD, wrote a few project proposals for her senior colleagues, but was also used for all kinds of administrative tasks, even typically secretarial work, while her male counterpart, still a doctoral student, was not. When she pointed out the inconsistencies and double standards to the head of institution – who otherwise seemed to like her, and particularly appreciated her 'still wearing skirts' not trousers, as he once told her – replied to this: 'don't worry, Hannah, someday your time will come and then you will have junior people doing such things for you'. This was apparently meant to appease her, while in reality this was when she realised there and then that this was not the place for her. The fact that one day she could be in a position to exploit her junior staff, which should make all of 'this' alright now (as well as her future exploitative conduct, apparently) repelled her on many levels.

In relation to certain other integrity-violating conduct, such as publication misconduct, wider systemic or structural stimulating factors also need to be inspected. Today's publish-or-perish academic culture demands a steady and quick production of new publications, of the right type and in the right outlets (for example, high-impact journals), which adds to academic pressure, increases the use of questionable research practices (Gopalakrishna et al., 2022) and provides a temptation for some to look for short-cuts, even when this entails unethical behaviour such as illegitimate attribution of (co)authorship or publishing in predatory journals with dubious peer-review practices, which, however, offer swift publication. Similarly, as noted by Organisation for Economic Co-operation and Development (OECD, n.d., pp. 11–12) in relation to scientific integrity, 'some individuals have a propensity (or susceptibility) to misbehaviour, which can be aggravated (and lead to concrete acts of misconduct) by external factors', among which they mention 'requirements to achieve significant positive results (and to publish extensively) in order to obtain and secure a staff position in a research institution, or to receive favourable consideration for future funding of research'. Moreover, open, consensus-building discussions must be had on what constitutes 'research', 'authorship' and 'ownership' in various fields, as misconceptions about, for example, the ownership of research still abound (Fields & Price, 1993).

V. CONCLUSION

This chapter has attempted to shed light on the bigger picture of research integrity, which goes beyond discussions on research ethics that tend to be narrowly conceived as relating to ethical practices employed during research activities. Various real-life cases have served as examples to highlight the integrity-violating practices of 'the powerful' within research institutions, be they senior researchers, professors or heads of various departments, deans, mid-level 'bosses' and so forth. While such anecdotal experience is coloured with self-perceptions, which is an acknowledged limitation, the aim was not to claim generalisability across all research settings but to highlight some fairly typical, symptomatic practices of those at the top or closer to the top, in order to stress the need to tackle misconduct in the upper echelons. This chapter has also pointed to the influence and effects of institutional structures and working conditions in encouraging or discouraging ethical and integrity practices. That structural conditions may generate unethical conduct, specifically in clinical research, has already been pointed out in pioneering work by Barber and colleagues (1973), emphasising the fundamental tensions between the values of scientific inquiry and its competitive practices, including disparities in allocation of recognition and reward (in Dingwall, 1980). Despite such persuasive early voices, however, half a century later, we are still insufficiently recognising these rather obvious factors in other fields of research and addressing them with inadequate attention and insufficient remediation.

Owing to the serious impacts that detrimentally affect not only the immediate victim (for example, psychological harm, reputational risks, loss of employment and career prospects) but also their colleagues and the working environment (for example, resentment, alienation from work, depression) and the overall integrity of the research and institution wherein such practices are carried out, monitoring of integrity risks and adopting of mitigating measures must be a continuous endeavour – not only from the viewpoint of quality research but also from the viewpoint of human rights and sustainability.

Possible solutions are manifold and they ought, ideally, to be pursued simultaneously. They could and should include mandatory training for *all*, including those at the top, which should also encompass a broader sensitivity training that could help build a more respectful, integrity-proof research environment. Contracts of employment and research project funding should automatically include a declaration of adherence to the ethical codes and standards of the institution (and to those of ALLEA, COPE and similar) and respect for research integrity or responsible conduct of research. Furthermore, considering the serious consequences of certain people coming to power, psychological evaluations of 'leaders' and screening for narcissists and Machiavellian personalities would likely be quite informative. Highly narcissist, manipulative types often make their way into positions of power; they are often very charming and seemingly 'cool' and relaxed on the outside but can be rather choleric, manipulative and abusive towards their subordinates behind closed doors. Vaknin (2008) notes that narcissists thrive in circumstances of 'awe, fear, subordination, admiration, adoration and obedience of their underlings' and achieve their goals of acquiring authority by any available means 'by making use of some outstanding traits or skills such as his intelligence, or through an asymmetry built into a relationship'. Researchers have been discovering that Machiavellian as well as narcissistic and psychopathic personality traits can play a part in research misconduct (Antes et al., 2007; Kennedy et al., 2023; Tijdink et al., 2016). The findings of another recent study (O'Reilly & Pfeffer, 2021), involving 699 individuals, demonstrate that 'people who rise to positions of power and influence often have high levels of narcissism and succeed at least in part because they are more willing to engage in organizational politics'. What puzzled the authors, however, is why people continue not only to tolerate but also to follow narcissistic leaders 'even after they have been shown to be self-interested, manipulative, and abusive'. Their proposed way ahead is to stop idolising narcissists who occupy positions of responsibility in organisations 'and start screening for them' (O'Reilly, in Dolan, 2021).

Sørensen et al.'s (2021) empirical study about diverging perspectives on the importance of various research integrity facets in different research fields and disciplines has underscored the significance of being open to designing research integrity measures and policies that are tailored to the realities of the research field in question. This, however, presupposes that sufficient research is being conducted on the nuances of these differential contexts. In this regard, it should be noted that research integrity in qualitative research appears to be under investigated in comparison with quantitative sciences. A recent report, commissioned by the UK Committee on Research Integrity (2024, p. 5), for example, notes that literature on research integrity 'is heavily skewed toward quantitative academic research', with qualitative research and research outside academia being 'underrepresented'. In its view, 'this quantitative bias appears partially a result of variance in the language used across disciplines to discuss overlapping goals or practices, and partly a result of differences in epistemic commitment and therefore the goals and practices themselves'.

Furthermore, there is also a need to 'shift away from individual blame and towards the need for structural and institutional changes, including organisations in the wider research environment, for example funding bodies and publishing companies', as noted by Kennedy et al. (2023, p. 471). Institutional policies and resource environments have been found to affect the integrity of researchers and, consequently, the occurrence of scientific research dishonesty (Zhao et al., 2022). In other words, all the main players in the research ecosystem, as *The Lancet* (2024) points out, 'need to ask themselves some tough questions about the underlying drivers'. This may also include rethinking the so-called league tables or, more specifically, major universities' decisions on the overall evaluation and ranking of world universities. In one recent study, 39% of all survey respondents (and more than half of the academic staff surveyed) identified the existence of league tables of institutions as having a negative impact on research integrity (Metcalfe et al., 2020, p. 27). Some world-renowned universities, such as universities of Utrecht and Zurich have thus decided to leave the Times Higher Education (THE) World Universities ranking. Utrecht (2023) explained their choice for not submitting their data for the said ranking by stating that, among things, these 'rankings put too much stress on scoring and competition, while we want to focus on collaboration and open science' and that 'the makers of the rankings use data and methods that are highly questionable', while Zurich maintained that rankings create false incentives, particularly the 'incentive to increase the number of publications rather than prioritise the quality of content' (Keystone-SDA, 2024). Sorbonne University, on the other hand, has decided not to renew its subscription to the Web of Science publication database and to Clarivate bibliometric tools in 2024 in order to free itself from proprietary bibliometric products and pursue its commitment to open research data and explore new open, free and participatory tools (Sorbonne, 2023).

LERU (2020, p. 17) also lists some useful ideas and best practices in this, broader, sense, such as its third recommendation, which stipulates that 'universities should ensure that institutional guidelines and support structures are put in place'. This entails developing institutional guidelines on good research practices, appointing personnel with special responsibility for research integrity, appointing confidential counsellors or advisors and appointing a committee or committees to handle allegations of research misconduct. Additionally, adequate safeguards should be implemented for whistle-blowers and victims (for example, victim representatives) to keep them safe, avoid any secondary victimisation and minimise risks of incurring negative consequences as a result of their coming forward.

While adopting guidelines, measures and codes of ethics is appropriate and necessary, so is a regular internal and external monitoring of institutional practices to check their implementation in practice. Unethical, integrity-violating behaviour at universities and other research institutions constitutes 'death by thousand cuts'. It thrives by not being addressed consistently, strongly, thoroughly, at all levels and by being silenced on all levels. By not speaking up one is implicated in its reproduction and becomes complicit in perpetuating unethical, corrupt practices. Speaking up, however, takes courage and high personal integrity, particularly in settings where whistle-blower protection is non-existent or in its infancy or its effectiveness is unclear.

It is through everyday, mundane workplace situations that one learns of a particular workplace culture or of the workplace community and its unwritten norms and expected standards of behaviour – and especially about how *not* to behave. The psychological impact of slight, seemingly insignificant but regular encounters is profound, as is the pressure to fit in, be part of the team, demonstrate loyalty and the group spirit. The latter often dictates to support the superior and/or the majority even if they are wrong and not to raise objections or contrary considerations in any shape or form lest one be labelled a troublemaker. In research environments where silence is normalised, it is particularly important to have a go-between or trusted person and effective protection of whistle-blowers, in addition to clear guidance, protocols and streamlined procedures for every stage of the research process if or when they are needed.[9]

NOTES

1. Nevertheless, from the listed 'commitments' in this regard, the Research Office of Imperial College clearly and adequately recognises that research integrity is not only about preventing and addressing research misconduct but also about 'upholding the highest standards of rigour and integrity in all aspects of research', compliance with ethical, legal and professional obligations and standards, as well as 'supporting a research environment that is underpinned by a culture of integrity and based on good governance, best practice, and support for the development of researchers' (Imperial, n.d.).

2. A recent study by Kennedy et al. (2023, p. 471), analysing data from 16 focus groups, discovered – or confirmed what many have been suspecting for a while – that 'structural frameworks for research such as funding, evaluation and publication were thought to both protect and, more commonly, undermine integrity. In addition, institutional systems, including workload and research governance, shaped participants' day-to-day work environment, also affecting research integrity'.

3. Reviewer 2 must be stopped (n.d.). Facebook (group page). Retrieved August 20, 2024, from https://www.facebook.com/groups/reviewer2/

4. Nevertheless, training may not be *the* solution for anyone. A recent study on 'questionable research practices' (QRPs) and 'open science practices' (OSPs) proposed by researchers and institutions as a solution to improve the detectability of QRPs and the credibility of science, conducted in the field of quantitative criminology by administering an anonymous survey, for example, noted no significant relationship between methodological training and either QRP or OSP use (Chin et al., 2023, p. 21).

5. See, for example, the plagiarism story of Christine Roth, analysed by Bailey (2019). The fact that she was only demoted, but kept her university job, despite the number of instances of significant plagiarism discovered, raises also the question of double standards. Or, as Bailey (2019), asks: 'Would a student at the university receive the same treatment if it were discovered they had plagiarized several works earlier in their student career?'

6. For example, according to one of the recent discoveries, only two pages (out of 56) of the university thesis by the prime minister of Luxembourg have been purportedly found not to be plagiarised (Henley, 2021). In Germany, a number of politicians have stepped down from the government when their academic credentials have been found questionable, in some cases leading also to revocation of doctoral titles (Olterman, 2021). In Slovenia, the former minister of education has stepped down after only five days in service when her master thesis was charged with plagiarism (A. Č. & Al. Ma., 2015).

7. This is not to say that plagiarism-detection software is not without its problems, as was most recently highlighted in the case of such software's checking for content that may be generated by AI – the advance of AI content-generating tools, such as ChatGPT, clearly posing a new set of integrity issues to be monitored.

8. For example, the Italian report for the GARCIA project noted that the picture of gender balance for the SSH disciplines, specifically humanities, shows that 'males are over-represented only among full professors, while females weight more than males in the distribution of the early stages positions' (Bozzon et al., 2015, p. 10). The She Figures report 2021 demonstrates that women represent around 55% of PhD graduates in the social sciences and around 54% in the arts and humanities across the European Union (EU) (European Commission, 2021, p. 36).

9. See the OECD (2022, p. 10) recommendations for ensuring integrity and security in the global research eco-system; one of which is precisely to 'develop clear guidelines, streamline procedures, and limit unnecessary bureaucracy'.

REFERENCES

A. Č., & Al. Ma. (2015, April 1). Markeževa odstopila. Cerar: Ta primer je še posebej nesrečen. *RTV SLO MMC*. Retrieved September 12, 2024, from https://www.rtvslo.si/slovenija/markezeva-odstopila-cerar-ta-primer-je-se-posebej-nesrecen/361857

Ahmed, S. (2021). *Complaint!* Duke University Press.

ALLEA. (2023). *The European code of conduct for research integrity*. All European Academies.

Antes, A. L., Brown, R. P., Murphy, S. T., Waples, E. P., Mumford, M. D., Connelly, S., & Devenport, L. D. (2007). Personality and ethical decision-making in research: the role of perceptions of self and others. *Journal of Empirical Research on Human Research Ethics*, *2*(4), 15–34.

Bailey, J. (2019). When professors plagiarize: Who watches the watchers? *Plagiarism Today*, October 1. Retrieved May 12, 2024, from https://www.plagiarismtoday.com/2019/10/01/when-professors-plagiarize/

Barber, B., Lally, J. J., Makarushka, J. L., & Sullivan, D. (1973). *Research on human subjects: Problems of social control in medical experimentation*. Russell Sage Foundation.

Bozzon, R., Murgia, A., & Poggio, B. (2015). Italy. In F. Dubois-Shaik & B. Fusulier (Eds.), *Academic careers and gender inequality: leaky pipeline and interrelated phenomena in seven European countries* (pp. 7–31). University of Trento. Retrieved May 25, 2024, from https://eige.europa.eu/sites/default/files/garcia_working_paper_5_academic_careers_gender_inequality.pdf

Chin, J. M., Pickett, J. T., Vazire, S., & Holcombe, A. O. (2023). Questionable research practices and Open Science in quantitative criminology. *Journal of Quantitative Criminology*, *39*, 21–51.

Dingwall, R. (1980). Ethics and ethnography. *Sociological Review*, *28*(4), 871–891.

Dolan, E. W. (2021). New study sheds light on why narcissists are so successful at attaining leadership positions. *PsyPost*, January 20. Retrieved May 12, 2024, from https://www.psypost.org/new-study-sheds-light-on-why-narcissists-are-so-successful-at-attaining-leadership-positions/

European Commission. (2021). *She Figures 2021: Gender in research and innovation statistics and indicators*. European Commission. Retrieved May 15, 2024, from https://op.europa.eu/en/web/eu-law-and-publications/publication-detail/-/publication/67d5a207-4da1-11ec-91ac-01aa75ed71a1

Fields, K. L., & Price, A. R. (1993). Problems in research integrity arising from misconceptions about the ownership of research. *Academic Medicine*, *68*(9 Suppl.), S60–S64. https://doi.org/10.1097/00001888-199309000-00036. PMID: 8373493. Retrieved May 15, 2024, from https://pubmed.ncbi.nlm.nih.gov/8373493/

Gopalakrishna, G., ter Riet, G., Vink, G., Stoop, I., Wicherts, J. M., & Bouter, L. M. (2022). Prevalence of questionable research practices, research misconduct and their potential explanatory factors: A survey among academic researchers in The Netherlands. *PLoS One*, *17*(2), e0263023. https://doi.org/10.1371/journal.pone.0263023

Henley, J. (2021). 'Only two pages' of Luxembourg PM's university thesis were not plagiarised. *The Guardian*, October 27. Retrieved 15 May, 2024, from https://www.theguardian.com/education/2021/oct/27/luxembourg-xavier-bettel-university-thesis-was-mostly-plagiarised

Henriksen, D. (2016). The rise in co-authorship in the social sciences (1980–2013). *Scientometrics*, *107*(2), 455–476. Retrieved August 15, 2024, from https://doi.org/10.1007/s11192-016-1849-x

Imperial. (n.d.). What is research integrity? *Imperial College London – Research office*. Retrieved May 15, 2024, from https://www.imperial.ac.uk/research-and-innovation/research-office/research-governance-and-integrity/research-integrity/what-is-research-integrity/

Kennedy, M.-R., Deans, Z., Ampollini, I., Breit, E., Bucchi, M., Seppel, K., Vie, K. J., & ter Meulen, R. (2023). "It is very difficult for us to separate ourselves from this system": Views of European researchers, research managers, administrators and governance advisors on structural and institutional influences on research integrity. *Journal of Academic Ethics*, *21*, 471–495. https://doi.org/10.1007/s10805-022-09469-x

Keystone-SDA. (2024). University of Zurich withdraws from international university ranking. *Swissinfo.ch*, March 13. Retrieved May 12, 2024, from https://www.swissinfo.ch/eng/education/university-of-zurich-quits-international-university-ranking/73693006

Khanyile, T. D., Duma, S., Fakude, L. P., Mbombo, N., Daniels, F., & Sabone, M. S. (2006). Research integrity and misconduct: a clarification of the concepts. *Curationis*, *29*(1), 40–45. https://doi.org/10.4102/curationis.v29i1.1042. PMID: 16817491. Retrieved May 12, 2024, from https://pubmed.ncbi.nlm.nih.gov/16817491/

League of European Research Universities. (2020). *Towards a research integrity culture at universities: from recommendations to implementation*. Retrieved April 30, 2024, from https://www.leru.org/files/Towards-a-Research-Integrity-Culture-at-Universities-full-paper.pdf

Lopez, S. H., Hodson, R., & Roscigno, V. J. (2009). Power, status, and abuse at work: General and sexual harassment compared. *The Sociological Quarterly*, *50*(1), 3–27.

Lynch, J., Glew, P., Salamonson, Y., & Ramjan, L. M. (2022). 'Integrity is integrity. IT doesn't matter the context': A qualitative exploratory study of academic integrity in an undergraduate nursing program. *Teaching and Learning in Nursing*, *17*, 465–470. https://doi.org/10.1016/j.teln.2022.06.013

Martin, P. Y. (2003). 'Said and done' versus 'saying and doing': Gendering practices, practicing gender at work. *Gender & Society*, *17*(3), 342–366. https://doi.org/10.1177/0891243203017003O

McLaughlin, H., Uggen, Ch., & Blackstone, A. (2012). Sexual harassment, workplace authority, and the paradox of power. *American Sociological Review*, *77*(4), 625–647. https://doi.org/10.1177/0003122412451728

Metcalfe, J., Wheat, K., Munafò, M., & Parry, J. (2020). *Research integrity: A landscape study*. The Careers Research and Advisory Centre Ltd.

Mody, C. C. M., Sibum, H. O., & Roberts, L.L. (2020). Integrating research integrity into the history of science. *History of Science*, *58*(4), 369–385. https://doi.org/10.1177/0073275320952257

Naezer, M., Van den Brink, M. C. I., & Benschop, M. (2019). *Harassment in Dutch academia: Exploring manifestations, facilitating factors, effects and solutions*. Landelijk Netwerk Vrouwelijke Hoogleraren.

OECD. (2022, June). *Integrity and security in the global research ecosystem*. OECD Science, Technology and Industry Policy Paper No. 130. Retrieved May 15, 2024, from https://www.oecd-ilibrary.org/docserver/1c416f43-en.pdf?expires=1718034627&id=id&accname=guest&checksum=0B7CFEE74A6E745DD9BB06D691AF24A5

OECD. (n.d.). *Best practices for ensuring scientific integrity and preventing misconduct*. Retrieved May 15, 2024, from https://web-archive.oecd.org/2012-06-15/129568-40188303.pdf

Olterman, P. (2021). German politicians suffer higher degree of embarrassment from plagiarism than from sex scandals. *The Guardian*, May 21. Retrieved May15, 2024, from https://www.theguardian.com/world/2021/may/22/german-politicians-suffer-higher-degree-of-embarrassment-from-plagiarism-than-from-sex-scandals

O'Reilly, C. A., & Pfeffer, J. (2021, April). Why are grandiose narcissists more effective at organizational politics? Means, motive, and opportunity. *Personality and Individual Differences*, *172*, 110557. Retrieved May 12, 2024, from https://www.sciencedirect.com/science/article/abs/pii/S0191886920307480

Robishaw, J. D., DeMets, D. L, Wood, S. K., Boiselle, P. M., & Hennekens, C. H. (2019). Establishing and maintaining research integrity at academic institutions: Challenges and opportunities. *The American Journal of Medicine*, *133*(3), E87–E90. https://doi.org/10.1016/j.amjmed.2019.08.036

Roth, J. A. (1966). Hired hand research. *The American Sociologist*, *1*(4), 190–196.

Sanjari, M., Bahramnezhad, F., Fomani, F. K., Shoghi, M., & Cheraghi, M. A. (2014). Ethical challenges of researchers in qualitative studies: the necessity to develop a specific guideline. *Journal of Medical Ethics and History of Medicine*, *7*, 14. PMID: 25512833; PMCID: PMC4263394. Retrieved May 12, 2024, from https://www.ncbi.nlm.nih.gov/pmc/articles/PMC4263394/

Sorbonne. (2023, December 8). *Sorbonne Université se désabonne du Web of Science, Sorbonne Université*. Retrieved May 12, 2024, from https://www.sorbonne-universite.fr/actualites/sorbonne-universite-se-desabonne-du-web-science

Sørensen, M. P., Ravn, T., Marušić, A., Reyes Elizondo, A., Kavouras, P., Tijdink, J. K., & Bendtsen, A.-K. (2021). Strengthening research integrity: which topic areas should organisations focus on? *Humanities & Social Science Communications*, *8*, Article No. 198. Retrieved August 15, 2024, from https://doi.org/10.1057/s41599-021-00874-y

Storr, L. (2004). Leading with integrity: a qualitative research study. *Journal of Health Organization and Management*. *18*(6), 415–434. Retrieved May 15, 2024, from https://pubmed.ncbi.nlm.nih.gov/15588012/

Taquette, S. R., & Borges da Matta Souza, L. M. (2022). Ethical dilemmas in qualitative research. A critical literature review. *International Journal of Qualitative Methods*, *21*, 1–15. Retrieved May 15, 2024, from https://journals.sagepub.com/doi/full/10.1177/16094069221078731

The Lancet. (2024). Safeguarding research integrity (Editorial). *The Lancet*, *403*(10428), 699.

Tijdink, J. K., Bouter, L. M., Veldkamp, C. L., van de Ven, P. M., Wicherts, J. M., & Smulders, Y. M. (2016). Personality traits are associated with research misbehavior in Dutch scientists: A cross-sectional study. *PLoS One*, *11*(9), e0163251. https://doi.org/10.1371/journal.pone.0163251

Trotman Reid, P., & Clayton, S. (1992). Racism and sexism at work. *Social Justice Research*, *5*(3), 249–268. https://doi.org/10.1007/BF01048666

UK Committee on Research Integrity. (2024). *Enablers and inhibitors of research integrity*. https://doi.org/10.5281/zenodo.13891202

Utrecht. (2023, September 29). *Why UU is missing in the THE ranking*. Utrecht University. Retrieved May 12, 2024, from https://www.uu.nl/en/news/why-uu-is-missing-in-the-the-ranking#:~:text=A%20conscious%20choice%3A,and%20disciplines%20in%20one%20number

Vaknin, S. (2008). Narcissists in positions of authority. *HealthyPlace*, November 10. Retrieved May 12, 2024, from https://www.healthyplace.com/personality-disorders/malignant-self-love/narcissists-in-positions-of-authority

Zhao, L., Li, Y., Feng, Y., Zhang, H., & Zhang, M. (2022). Research on the influencing factors of scientific researchers' integrity based on grounded theory. *Procedia Computer Science*, *214*, 1467–1475. https://doi.org/10.1016/j.procs.2022.11.332

CHAPTER 15

QUALITATIVE RESEARCH ETHICS: AN AGENDA FOR RESEARCHERS AND RESEARCH ORGANISATIONS

Helen Busby[a] and Mark Israel[b]

[a]*Independent Research Ethics Consultant, UK*
[b]*Australasian Human Research Ethics Consultancy Services, Australia*

ABSTRACT

New developments in methodologies, technologies, and evolving ways of conceptualising research relationships have added complexity to the existing ethical challenges faced by qualitative researchers. Although generalist rule-based ethics frameworks struggle to anticipate and respond to dynamic qualitative methodologies, reflections by researchers offer some important ways forward on these issues. We argue that qualitative researchers and research organisations should go beyond the project-based practice of research ethics review to: (1) reflect on ethical issues that qualitative researchers are encountering; (2) learn from the diversity of approaches to ethics appraisal and review; (3) embed ethics across curricula; (4) strengthen institutional resources for social research ethics; and (5) recognise that institution-wide measures to support research integrity are necessary to facilitate ethical research. While there has long been a focus on the responsibilities of individual researchers in this context, they also need a research ecosystem that will support ethical practice. We propose several ways organisations can reconfigure

Reframing Qualitative Research Ethics
Advances in Research Ethics and Integrity, Volume 12, 253–262

Published under exclusive licence by Emerald Publishing Limited
ISSN: 2398-6018/doi:10.1108/S2398-601820250000012015

structures and practices to better support ethics and integrity in diverse modes of qualitative research.

Keywords: Qualitative research ethics; ethical considerations in qualitative research; ethical research; Declaration of Helsinki; human research ethics; research organisations

INTRODUCTION

There have been unescapable tensions between qualitative research and systems for overseeing research ethics for some decades. Although we can point to a consensus on the need to reform research ethics in the social sciences to take account of the distinctive features of these approaches, changes have been slow in coming (Iphofen, 2017a) and have not always been progressive. New developments in methodologies, technologies, and evolving ways of conceptualising research relationships have added further complexity to this terrain. This is evident in the contributions to this volume exploring, for example, the nuances of applying principles of informed consent when researching online spaces and communities in Helena Webb's and Rhonda Shaw's chapters, in Bree Akesson and Karen Frensch's reflections on the use of GPS technologies in new contexts, and in Fride Klykken's account of her work in a 'technologically dense classroom'.

While the qualitative researchers who contributed to this volume are interested in exploring and mitigating the ethical concerns their methodologies give rise to, they found generalist rule-based ethics frameworks largely failed to do so and had proved unable to anticipate such issues. An additional concern, in common with researchers in other fields, is that outcomes of research ethics reviews seem unpredictable. In our view, the limitations associated with applying rule-based ethics frameworks to some of these qualitative methodologies pose a challenge for research ethics committees (RECs) in reaching decisions, namely, to find a way to balance predictability with responsiveness, a matter to which we return below. At the same time, as is clear from these accounts, researchers face challenges in finding the best way to put ethical principles into practice in complex situations. Here, isolation can pose as much of a problem for researchers as do rules: such challenges call above all for support and advice.

The ways forward generated in these chapters include the following agenda for qualitative researchers and for research organisations: (1) reflect on ethical issues to strengthen research; (2) learn from the diversity of approaches to ethics appraisal and review; (3) devolve and embed ethics in the curriculum; (4) strengthen institutional resources for social research ethics; and (5) recognise that institution-wide measures to support research integrity (RI) are necessary to facilitate ethical research.

REFLECT ON ETHICAL ISSUES AND PROBLEMS AS A RESOURCE FOR RESEARCH

Concerns deemed to be ethical issues may speak to wider questions. This is illustrated by Rhonda Shaw's chapter, in which exploring vloggers' 'understandings of "public" and "private" in relation to their intended audiences in online spaces' is seen to be important when thinking about the practices that will be appropriate for respecting their privacy. Drawing on Berlant's (2008) concept of 'intimate publics' (p. 5), Shaw's chapter explores how ethical issues raised by her research methodologies articulate with wider sociological work concerned with online narratives.

It can be productive to frame such dynamic issues as an area for research, rather than only as problems to be fixed for all times and places. To take one example, what term should be used for people who take part in research? Whether we call them 'research subjects' or 'participants' might appear to be a matter of convention or of changing fashions, yet underlying this are more substantial questions about how we understand people's agency within particular methodologies. Love and McDonnell (2024) have reflected on how, early in their careers, their proposed work with women who had had abortions and with psychiatric patients leaving hospitals was disapproved – and so disallowed – because their RECs focussed on the vulnerability of these groups rather than also acknowledging the moral agency of these individuals. Eventually, both went on to research in these fields and then to propose the development of 'a politics of presence in ethics [which] engages with vulnerability as a potentially positive field of force' (Love & McDonnell, 2024, pp. 4–5). This points to an important dimension to considering participants' potential vulnerability, an issue intensely debated in research ethics, underscoring as it does the importance of researchers' presence and commitment to their participants in this context.

In undertaking their analyses, qualitative researchers can inform thinking about ethics in other fields and so contribute to evolving understandings of what it means to be engaged in research in an ethical way. To continue with the example above, the question of terminology is of significance well beyond the field of qualitative research. Indeed, this is an instance where medical ethics can learn from social research ethics: while 'participants' has long been the term preferred by many social scientists, it was common to refer to 'human subjects' in clinical research. However, there has been a shift in understanding in the medical research community, and accordingly, the most recent revision of the Declaration of Helsinki has replaced the term 'subjects' with 'participants' throughout because it was considered more respectful of the rights, agency, and importance of those individuals (World Medical Association, 2024).[1] This misses the point; there are occasions when researchers deliberately seek not to offer agency to the researched – for example, those who perpetrate abusive or exploitative practices – and participant seems an odd choice of word, in those situations. A more sophisticated recognition of power relations suggests it would be appropriate to have a plurality of terms for people being researched, depending on the nature of their involvement, given a spectrum from passive to active roles.

LEARN FROM THE DIVERSITY OF APPROACHES TO ETHICS APPRAISAL AND REVIEW ACROSS DIFFERENT SYSTEMS

Although many publications about research ethics in the social sciences have focussed on problems encountered with RECs, this is a particular preoccupation of social scientists in selected, mostly Anglophone, countries in the Global North. At times, the debate takes a binary form – arguing in favour of, or against, abolishing RECs – yet there is sometimes, too, a quiet acknowledgement that these committees undertake an important role. As Michael Herzfeld (2023) has written: 'We do need some means of perpetually reminding ourselves that our actions affect our interlocutors, a concern not negated by horror stories about bureaucratic overreach. We need informed advice' (p. 3). Notwithstanding this, developing the view from anthropology, Herzfeld suggests in his chapter in this volume that 'static forms of bureaucratic oversight, well-intended though they may (in part) have been, do a disservice to the very concept of ethics. They not only posit a universal ethics; they posit an unchanging ethics'. Like Herzfeld, we argue research ethics regimes should be anchored in greater contextual specificity and historical awareness. One response to this position may be to say that some universal or generic ethics principles and standards can and should be agreed upon, especially given the growing number of multinational and interdisciplinary research endeavours. Certainly, it is important to have contributions to the development of ethical guidance and policy that go beyond disciplinary and national contexts. However, although we see more international exchange and a wider range of stakeholders invited to comment in consultations about such codes than in the past, these processes are rarely broadly inclusive. It remains an open debate whether some universal ethics approaches could be agreed upon if a sufficiently rigorous and inclusive process were to be put in place.

As we consider how ethics oversight can be reconfigured, there is much to learn from approaches taken beyond Anglophone institutional research ethics. Most countries in the Global South and many in the Global North do not require review of the ethics of social research. Although this can limit collective engagement with the ethical challenges of a particular context and discipline, some researchers working within such regimes have described how having the flexibility to improvise has generated good solutions to ethical and methodological problems. For instance, faced with methodological challenges in their work on the study of Muslims in Western Thrace (Greece) and Tamil immigration in France, Dequirez and Hersant (2013) have written about how they found it necessary to re-orientate their project, revisit the field, increase the number of field sites, organise access to some key informants informally, and undertake a more extended analysis of the local political context. Some of these strategies would have been impracticable if they had been bound by a predefined protocol as is typically required by RECs (Dequirez & Hersant, 2013). An alternative proposition would be to take a fine-tuned, nuanced approach to ethics review for social science research rooted in a range of closely related disciplines, as some universities in the Netherlands have done (Elfenbein & Hoffman, 2024). Institutions and jurisdictions that mandate RECs can learn from models such as these to explore a continuum of approaches for supporting ethical research.

Other approaches that could be adopted to allow for evolving methodologies are staged reviews that do not require projects to commit to particular responses in later stages, or more flexible and responsive forms of oversight such as the use of expert research ethics advisors or ethics advisory boards to support the development of ethical practice in context, an approach used by the European Union (EU) research agencies to provide additional support to and oversight of projects with complex ethical issues (European Commission, 2023).

DEVOLVE AND EMBED ETHICS IN THE CURRICULUM

Qualitative researchers are concerned that research ethics reviews often fail to allow the reflection needed to explore important issues that arise in their research and may not even help to foreshadow the multitude of small but ethically resonant decisions to be made upon entering the field. Among other things, these decisions relate to introducing oneself, seeking consent or, where appropriate, assent, thinking about how people's initial questions will be addressed, considering how the benefits and harms likely to flow from a research project are likely to be balanced and distributed, anticipating how research outputs can be made informative for those who took part, and considering how researchers can contribute to the participants or community that welcomes or hosts them.

Even as they struggle to facilitate reflection on such issues, RECs are increasingly charged with new tasks to be undertaken on behalf of the institutions they serve. In some European countries, one such addition is the funnelling of requirements for data management, data protection, and data archiving from the centre to individual investigators. Margaret Sleeboom-Faulkner argues in this volume that these developments in the United Kingdom have adversely affected research relying on ethnographic fieldwork to the point where the integrity of such research is under threat. While this is a well-reasoned critique of the way some university RECs in the United Kingdom interpret and implement legislation on data protection, other bodies, such as the UK Research Councils, lead policy on data archiving for funded research. Another way of looking at this situation is to see it as symptomatic of a tendency for organisations to freight these committees with responsibilities over and above reviewing research protocols, which may extend to aspects of research governance such as data protection, checking administrative and gatekeeper approvals, as well as scientific merit, researcher safety, protection of institutional reputation, and so on. This means RECs are perceived as 'moral bureaucracies' (Molina & Borgatti, 2021, p. 13), rather than as offering 'genuine' ethics advice. It may be necessary to de-couple many of the administrative, resource allocation, managerial and political tasks from the work of RECs, in order to allow the capacity for effective approaches to research ethics to flourish.

As the introduction to this volume argued, it is helpful to understand the history of RECs: originally, proposals for ethics review of clinical research were framed in terms of advice and guidance from peers (World Medical Association,

1975, p. 2). Today's RECs operate within complex organisations and systems, and it would be naïve to suggest a neat boundary can be drawn between research ethics advice and governance. Nevertheless, it will still be useful to maintain a distinction between research ethics review – an independent process of reflection concerned with acting in the best interests of those who will be researched – and research governance, concerned with regulatory compliance, standards of good practice, and corporate oversight (Iphofen, 2017b, p. 1). With this in mind, RECs should focus on supporting researchers with thinking about their responsibilities towards those being researched, rather than being distracted and perhaps subverted by questions of corporate interests and reputation. Research organisations, being learning institutions, need to think beyond committees for this process of reflection: if they are to develop cutting-edge approaches to research, researchers and reviewers need to keep pace and address the ethical issues posed by new methodologies, topics, collaborations, participants, and contexts.

Professional development opportunities should support a reflective approach to research ethics, yet ethics training can be counterproductive if an unduly didactic approach is taken (Allen & Israel, 2018). Indeed, the language of 'training' does not pay much respect to the quality of thought required to make ethical decisions. Many researchers and reviewers grudgingly turn up to institutionally mandated training expecting to be told the requirements for completing a form or the rules for passing the committee hurdle. Such sessions can be stultifying and dull and do little to prepare researchers to engage with new challenges that they encounter in their research or enable reviewers to build a community of ethical practice with stakeholders. Significant players in the research management ecology would do better to reimagine training as professional development and design opportunities for researchers and reviewers to build and practice their skills in ethical decision-making in authentic contexts. These opportunities should also be built into the curricula of research programmes so that ethics is embedded in research practice from the beginning of researchers' careers. Such opportunities should be constructed in terms of a shared endeavour rather than simply a 'dissemination' of policies, not least because many among the current cohort of researchers are already actively engaged with research ethics (Taylor & Patterson, 2010) and may be well ahead of the ethics bureaucracy in understanding the ethical challenges of new research contexts.

We now turn to the theme of wider measures for developing and strengthening institutional capacity for social research ethics.

DEVELOP AND STRENGTHEN INSTITUTIONAL CAPACITY FOR HANDLING SOCIAL RESEARCH ETHICS

We propose several preconditions for effective ethics review in this field: expertise, proportionality, predictability, principle-based decision-making, and appropriate resourcing. In combination, most of these are quite rare even when mandated by national policy.

First, we need better recognition of ethics review as a scholarly process that requires a deep understanding of what a research project is trying to do and reflection on how it might be achieved ethically. This requires a range of knowledge, skills, and experience to be brought into the decision-making process. No committee will have expertise in all methodologies, which means that ongoing dialogue and exchange of views between RECs and researchers are needed, with the aim of developing shared understandings (Mustajoki & Mustajoki, 2017). In general, we would argue RECs should be constituted at a level of granularity that allows for multiple perspectives, and so a multidisciplinary committee – with access to appropriate specialist expertise – is a good option, especially as larger projects increasingly require multidisciplinary responses. While a committee may seek additional external advice, it might also recruit a pool of researchers to draw on as members for particular kinds of research, rotating them to reflect the most significant projects that are being reviewed at a particular session. In addition, 'lay' representation is being reconceived as enabling research ethics review to draw on multiple community perspectives. Lloy Wylie et al.'s chapter describing their experience of developing research and health service partnerships with Indigenous people in Ontario speaks to the challenges of establishing and sustaining community partnerships that go beyond tokenist consultations. Such a broader engagement with stakeholder communities should include linguistically and culturally diverse communities and any vulnerable groups likely to be over-represented among research participants. A Community Stakeholder Reference Group comprising advocacy, community, cultural, and overarching interest groups may be an effective way of drawing on advice about distinctive ethical issues associated with researching in the region or the community.

Second, it will be necessary to differentiate between the kinds of reviews that are appropriate for various kinds of research. A proportional research ethics review matches the review process, timeframe, evidential burden, and monitoring, to the risks and ethical sensitivity of a proposed project. A central element of such oversight should be a risk assessment tool directing projects to review pathways where the level of scrutiny is proportionate to risk. Such a tool might distinguish between projects that are exempt from review; have been subjected to prior review; or require review by professional staff, a low-risk panel, the executive of the REC, or by the full committee.

Third, we face a situation in which outcomes for research ethics review of qualitative research are perceived to be unpredictable. If, historically, some RECs were like clubs – reflecting a framework of professional self-regulation (Wilson, 2014, p. 24)[2] – diversity and accountability are now expected: decision-making processes should be agreed, transparent to stakeholders both inside and outside the host institution, independent of capture whether by groups of researchers, management or special interests, and accountable with clear appeal and complaints processes.

However, predictability needs to be balanced with responsiveness, which brings us to our fourth point: moving towards principle-based decision-making can contribute to finding this balance. While some institutions have adopted rules or a set of precedents that advise what will (and what will not) be seen as acceptable, the use of rules risks ossification of what is allowable and may not be responsive to changes in practice and context. This is particularly awkward when rule-makers cannot change the rules, either because of a lack of resources or will at institutional level or because the rules have been embedded in legislation. Guidance based on principles should offer greater possibility of adapting to new situations. For example, an anticipatory model of review predicated on a positivist, hypothetico-deductive, approach to research may be poorly suited to many evolving approaches applied in social research such as those explored in this volume, as well as for participatory models which are increasingly used in diverse fields of research (Israel, 2015).

Finally, effective reviewing requires sufficient institutional capacity and resourcing. Research ethics review can occur against a backdrop of limited, overstretched, and sometimes even non-existent administrative support and inadequate institutional recognition of the work of reviewers. This can be compounded by the need to work around research management systems that are poorly configured for research ethics, poor access to expert advice, and a lack of funding both for professional development for researchers and reviewers and for guidance material relevant to the social sciences. Research institutions must therefore commit to resourcing research ethics at a level commensurate with the opportunities and risks associated with promoting ethical research and ensuring regulatory compliance. A balanced approach to research ethics would see investment in building the capacity of researchers and reviewers to make informed decisions. Although clinical research ethics has often received the lion's share of time and investment, support for social research ethics is imperative for qualitative research to flourish.

EMBRACE 'VIRTUE ETHICS FOR ORGANISATIONS'[3]

Ethical research is linked to the cultures of the institutions within which it is produced: the measures required to achieve RI go well beyond the remit of ethics reviews. As Nina Peršak argues, an agenda for tackling RI should include addressing workplace culture and negative impacts of hierarchies of power on practices of research production. In her chapter, Peršak indicates some specific ways this can be done, including inserting codes of conduct into professional contracts and providing confidential counselling and advice for researchers faced with difficult, inequitable, or unethical dynamics in their research. Despite the evident importance of these issues, it seems that a renewed focus on RI may currently be biased towards quantitative modes of research, according to a recent report by the UK Committee on Research Integrity (2024, p. 5), and the application of this agenda to qualitative modes of research should be explored in more depth.

This is consistent with the findings of Sørensen et al.'s study exploring what researchers and others working in research organisations think about RI: despite finding important differences in the perspectives between disciplines, they note the research environment was considered to be key by all the groups of researchers and stakeholders taking part in the study. The environment includes 'the norms and values of an institution, its handling of appointments, incentive structures, competition, diversity issues and so on' and in this context, the 'responsibilisation of RI is unevenly targeted at the individual researcher rather than linked to institutions [...]' (Sørensen et al., 2021, pp. 12–12). Similarly with research ethics, there has been a focus on *individual* responsibilities, with the cultivation of researcher virtues having a prominent place on this agenda. Still, it remains timely to continue to shift the emphasis to how organisations such as universities, ethics and governance secretariats, and funding bodies can reconfigure structures and practices to better support ethics in diverse modes of qualitative research.

NOTES

1. This reasoning was made clear by the World Medical Association during its Public Consultation on the Draft Revised Version of the Declaration of Helsinki, which was conducted online in 2024 but is no longer publicly accessible at the time of writing.
2. Characterising clinical RECs in Britain as being historically rooted in a framework of professional self-regulation, Wilson deploys Moran's concept of 'club regulation' (Moran, 2003, pp. 38–66; Wilson, 2014, p. 24).
3. We borrow this term from an editorial by Bernacchio et al. (2023).

ACKNOWLEDGEMENTS

We thank Ron Iphofen and Nathan Emmerich for their thoughtful comments on the first draft of this chapter.

REFERENCES

Allen, G., & Israel, M. (2018). Moving beyond regulatory compliance: Building institutional support for ethical reflection in research. In R. Iphofen & M. Tolich (Eds.), *The SAGE handbook of qualitative research ethics* (pp. 276–288). Sage Publications.

Berlant, L. (2008). *The female complaint: The unfinished business of sentimentality in American culture*. Duke University Press.

Bernacchio, C., Moore, G., Robson, A., & Marta, R. (2023). Editorial: MacIntyrean virtue ethics for organizations, work and employment: What more and what else? *Frontiers in Sociology*, *8* (Section: Work, Employment and Organizations). https://doi.org/10.3389/fsoc.2023.1145849

Dequirez, G., & Hersant, J. (2013). The virtues of improvisation: Ethnography without an ethics protocol. *Current Sociology*, *61*(5–6), 646–660. https://doi.org/10.1177/0011392113484454

Elfenbein, T. W., & Hoffman, A. S. (2024). Towards meaningful institutional change: Responsive bureaucracy and the governance of anthropological ethics. *Anthropology Today*, *40*(2), 4–7. https://doi.org/10.1111/1467-8322.12871

European Commission. (2023). *Ethics advisors and ethics advisory boards roles and function in EU-funded projects*. https://ec.europa.eu/info/funding-tenders/opportunities/docs/2021-2027/horizon/guidance/roles-and-functions-of-ethics-advisory-ethics-advisory-boards-in-ec-funded-projects_he_en.pdf

Herzfeld, M. (2023). Ethnographic responsibility: Can the bureaucratization of research ethics be ethical? *Anthropology Today*, *39*(3), 3–6. https://doi.org/10.1111/1467-8322.12811

Iphofen, R. (2017a). Achieving consensus in research ethics: An interim conclusion and some recommendations. In *Finding common ground: Consensus in research ethics across the social sciences* (*Advances in research ethics and integrity*, Vol. 1, pp. 211–225). Emerald Publishing. https://doi.org/10.1108/S2398-601820170000001017

Iphofen, R. (2017b). Governance and ethics: Maintaining the distinction. *TRUST Equitable Research Partnerships Newsletter*. https://trust-project.eu/wp-content/uploads/2017/07/3rd-eNewsletter-final-copy.pdf

Israel, M. (2015). *Research ethics and integrity for social scientists: Beyond regulatory compliance*. Sage Publications.

Love, G., & McDonnell, L. (2024). Presence as politics in qualitative research ethics: Feminist engagements with "risk" and vulnerability. *Qualitative Inquiry*, 1–13. https://doi.org/10.1177/10778004241256141

Molina, J., & Borgatti, S. (2021). Moral bureaucracies and social network research. *Social Networks*, *67*, 13–19. https://doi.org/10.1016/j.socnet.2019.11.001

Moran, M. (2003). *The British regulatory state: High modernism and hyper innovation*. Oxford University Press.

Mustajoki, M., & Mustajoki, A. (2017). *A new approach to research ethics using guided dialogue to strengthen research communities*. Routledge.

Sørensen, M. P., Ravn, T., Marušić, A., Elizondo, A. R., Kavouras, P., Tijdink, J. K., & Bendtsen, A.-K. (2021). Strengthening research integrity: Which topic areas should organisations focus on? *Humanities & Social Science Communications*, *8*, 13–19. https://doi.org/10.1057/s41599-021-00874-y

Taylor, J., & Patterson, M. (2010). Autonomy and compliance: How qualitative sociologists respond to institutional ethical oversight. *Qualitative Sociology*, *33*, 161–183. https://doi.org/10.1007/s11133-010-9148-y

UK Committee on Research Integrity. (2024). *Enablers and inhibitors of research integrity*. 10.5281/zenodo.13891202

Wilson, D. (2014). *The making of British bioethics*. Manchester University Press. https://www.ncbi.nlm.nih.gov/books/NBK248689/

World Medical Association. (1975). *Declaration of Helsinki – Recommendations guiding medical doctors in biomedical research involving human subjects*. https://www.wma.net/wp-content/uploads/2018/07/DoH-Oct1975.pdf

World Medical Association. (2024). *Declaration of Helsinki – Ethical principles for medical research involving human participants*. https://www.wma.net/policies-post/wma-declaration-of-helsinki/

INDEX

Printed and bound by CPI Group (UK) Ltd, Croydon, CR0 4YY
26/03/2026
14850677-0001